TREBLINKA
SURVIVOR

TREBLINKA
SURVIVOR

THE LIFE AND DEATH OF
HERSHL SPERLING

MARK S. SMITH

The
History
Press

For my family and the Sperling family.

Just as the water reflects one's face,
so does one's heart reflect other human hearts. – Proverbs.

First published 2010

Reprinted 2010

The History Press
The Mill, Brimscombe Port
Stroud, Gloucestershire, GL5 2QG
www.thehistorypress.co.uk

British Library Cataloguing in Publication Data.
A catalogue record for this book is available from the British Library.

ISBN 978 0 7524 5618 8

Typesetting and origination by The History Press
Printed in Great Britain

CONTENTS

ACKNOWLEDGEMENTS

The writing of this book was most painful to those closest to it. I am grateful to them for persevering with me in what was a difficult, at times lonely and often emotionally draining endeavour. Family and friends were always there to steady, guide and encourage me. I am in their debt.

The largest part of this debt of gratitude, however, belongs to Hershl Sperling's sons, Sam and Alan. I feared many times that I was probing too deep and reopening wounds that if not fully healed had at least fleshed over, so they might continue to live in this world. But I did probe and reopen their wounds, and they bled willingly, with honesty and courage. My gratitude to them carries with it the unease of knowing they were hurt by the memories they were asked to recall. On many levels, this book is borne through their suffering.

The contribution of Sam Sperling requires its own acknowledgement. His intelligence, gentle criticism and guidance – from the project's very conception to its conclusion – helped me immeasurably in making this work as honest a reflection as possible of Hershl Sperling. He was an inspiration at almost every stage of the book. It is to him I owe my greatest debt.

A writer also needs time; and I am indebted to the Scottish Arts Council, without whose financial support and belief in the project I would not have been able to take time out from the daily grind to sit at my desk each day and write. I also want to thank Ivor Tiefenbrun of Linn Products, who helped support the project. Leslie Gardner, my agent, stuck it out tenaciously, and I am grateful for her perseverance and belief in the book.

I want to thank Roy Petrie, my travelling companion in Treblinka and Warsaw, for the excellent maps he devised for this book, and also for his encouragement and for sharing the experience with me. I am grateful to Heather Valencia for her translations and Yiddish-language expertise.

I am indebted to my wife, Cath, and to my friend, Chris Pleasance, whose reading of the text in its umpteen stages helped me see my errors, inconsistencies and stupidities. Industrious study of the completed manuscript by Hana Sholaim and Ian McConnell located further errors and inconsistencies that even the most astute and diligent of readers would likely have accepted. The errors that remain in this work are mine alone.

To write this work, many books needed to be consulted. There were numerous sources, chief among them were Martin Gilbert's *The Holocaust: A History of the Jews during the Second World War*, *Jews in Poland* by Iwo Cyprian Pogonowski, *Revolt in Treblinka* by Samuel Willenberg, *Trap Within a Green Fence: Survival in Treblinka* by Richard Glazer, *If This is a Man* and *The Drowned and the Saved* by Primo Levi, *Extermination Camp Treblinka* by Witold Chrostowski, *Into that Darkness*, by Gitta Sereny, *Belzec, Sobibor, Treblinka: The Operation Reinhard Death Camps*, by Yitzhak Arad, *The Origins of the Final Solution: The Evolution of Nazi Jewish Policy* by Christopher R. Browning, *Memorial Candles: Children of the Holocaust* by Dina Wardi, *Dachau Liberated, The Official Report by the U.S. Seventh Army*, edited by Michael W. Perry, *After the Holocaust: Jewish Survivors in Germany After 1945* by Eva Kolinsky, and last but not least, *Treblinka* by H. Sperling.

PREFACE BY SAM SPERLING

When Mark first mentioned that he would like to write a book about my father I felt both happy and scared. Primarily, my fear concerned whether he would be able to remain faithful to my father's experience and produce a book that my father would have felt he could endorse, were he still here. These fears were allayed when Mark explained that he wanted to base the hub of the story around my father's testimony and that he would include the testimony in full within the book. My father's own account, his own words, would be included and I knew that he would be happy with that.

My next fear concerned whether I would be able to read the book. I have spent almost 50 years finding strategies to avoid the past, and the memory I have of my father's pain does not really subside as the years go by. Did I really want to focus on these? And then there were fears about how my brother would react. He is ten years older than I, and probably even more affected by the Holocaust's aftermath.

I found it surprisingly easy to read when Mark sent me the manuscript. I read it, I wept, then it was over. When a few days passed, I found myself wondering about the meaning of the book. As far as any experience has meaning, this struck me as a book that warns of man's condition. It is a story about prejudice and racism in general and a study of the potential beast within all of us, that could so easily consume us if we do not learn lessons from the past. Sadly, it seems these lessons have not been learned yet. Just as I play mind games that enable me to suspend the past and continue in the 'here and now', society does the same. I always remember my father having compassion but I rarely, or never, remember him showing such deep empathy openly as he did when he saw the film *The Killing Fields*. You see, it confirmed to him that it was not over. The herd could still be manipulated into acts of unspeakable evil, and if we could not learn from the Holocaust what would it take?

Anti-Semitism, the theme of this story, is only one manifestation of this evil. It is an old traditional form ingrained in many cultures, especially within Europe. It lives on in several forms, including within the right-wing fascist politics of hatred. Sadly, in today's Europe, it is increasingly thinly veiled as anti-Israeli sentiments within many supposedly left-wing organisations, too. I am not advocating that Europe suspend all criticism of Israel or that Palestinians should not have the right to as good an exis-tence as Israelis, but all too often I am found questioning the double standards and motivations of many of Israel's overly zealous critics.

In all too many cases it is the supposed 'intelligentsia' that are at the forefront of this group. Shamefully, they push a myth that says education defeats racism, as if to say they are immune because they have read a few books. They have missed the point. Anti-Semitism, and racism in general, is about what is in your heart, not your head. It is about being decent or not, it is non-discriminating of intellectual ability.

I hope and trust that readers of this book do not see this as an exclusively Jewish story; it is about all people and their right to a free life without any fear of the irrational mob that we are all capable of joining.

Sam Sperling

CHAPTER ONE

THE BRIDGE

On Tuesday morning, 26 September 1989, Hershl Sperling, a survivor of two Nazi death camps and at least five concentration camps, contemplated suicide. He was 62 years old. Strange, at least at first glance, that a man who had survived Auschwitz, Dachau, Treblinka and other hellish places – certainly in part through acts of hope and inner strength – would consider taking his own life. He was, after all, a survivor. He was also a widower, and the father of two adult sons who loved him. He was now in Scotland, far away from his old country and the source of his torment – places that today still conjure up terrifying images of fire and mountains of twisted corpses. Strange also to think that this quiet Polish Jew in the suburb of a faraway Scottish city, this man who had once lived around the corner from me and whose son was my best friend, had witnessed that fire with his own eyes and had dragged into it those twisted corpses. I see him now, sitting at his kitchen table in his house at 63 Castlehill Drive, Glasgow. He winks at me as I enter. I can tell he likes me. 'Boychik,' he says, watching me with his pale green eyes that are full of mischief and madness. 'How are you today?' There appeared no cause for survivor guilt or shame here. What did he have to feel guilty about? Hershl Sperling had been an innocent victim, not a perpetrator. Yet here he was at the precipice.

That Tuesday morning, there may have been something familiar about the day's beginning – some strange, lingering echo of that time, 47 years earlier, when his world changed forever. How normal the world was before the Nazis came – children playing, laughing, families working, living, cooking, struggling, loving each other without even knowing it, people simply being. Now thousands of skeletons, all those dead Jews he carried, reached out their bony hands to him – all those children. It is the murder of children that is the stuff of nightmares. In many ways, Hershl Sperling was crazy, and he knew it; but the world was crazier.

Dawn had come dim and dry. This was an Indian summer, at least for Glasgow's normally dreary climate. Hershl had slept the night inside the old Caledonian Rail Bridge over the River Clyde in Glasgow's city centre. His previous suicide attempts had been foiled by those who cared about him; this was not the first time he had disappeared to wander the streets of Glasgow, seeking out the company of down-and-outs. As he lay prostrate atop one of the iron girders, deep in the dim netherworld of criss-crossing metal supports and hidden platforms, there approached the haunting sound of clicking metal wheels on the track above him, shocking him out of an alcoholic stupor. The sound gathered pace until it shook the entire structure as it passed overhead and disappeared slowly into the silence of the morning. By 6.00am other trains had begun their deafening rattle across the bridge. Hershl dragged his thin body upright and moved like a phantom through the dark recesses of the bridge. He stepped around the unconscious, oblivious bodies of others who had sought a night's refuge here, and he climbed down on to the bank of the River Clyde.

Hershl had been one of the Treblinka *Sonderkommando* – a fifteen-year-old Jewish boy plucked from the mouth of death to become a slave of murderers. To Hershl, the entire world could be explained through Treblinka. The experience could never be forgotten and the wounds that had been gouged could never heal. He had witnessed crimes beyond belief, unimaginable in magnitude. He had also been one of the few who had revolted and escaped; he should have been proud of that. His very existence belied the assumption that all the Jews had gone to their deaths like sheep to the slaughter. Hershl and other escapees had torched the camp on the way out. He had wanted the factory of death to be obliterated. I remember how courage came easily to Hershl Sperling; but courage was not enough to keep him in this world. His final drama, on the streets of Glasgow, remains a testament to those who survived, but whose suffering did not end with liberation.

He wandered now in a haze of drugs and alcohol along the riverbank and through the city streets. Those who saw him likely mistook him for one of the many drunken homeless in this city. Traffic and crowds began to throng the streets. The odour of exhaust fumes from cars and trucks already permeated the air. Diesel and gasoline engines had been used by the Nazis to pump carbon monoxide into the Treblinka gas chambers. He could not forget that deathly stench.

★ ★ ★

That Hershl was alive on that Tuesday morning is in itself extraordinary. All except a minute fraction of those who entered Treblinka, let alone Auschwitz and Dachau, were consumed in its gas chambers and flames. Among the random sampling of human beings who were swept together in the Nazi round-ups and sentenced to death, they took a fifteen-year-old boy whom, it seems, could not be killed. Like all survivors, two prime factors kept Hershl alive – good health when he entered the camps and the improbable confluence of unlikely events. He could also be daring, cunning and fearless.

He was raised in a strictly orthodox Jewish home in an old Polish shtetl and had once believed in the innate justice of God and his fellow man. It has been said that when he was young, Hershl was kind, and that he laughed more than most, but what use was joy in the abject degradation of Treblinka, where beatings, cold, fatigue, humiliation and starvation had to be endured each day? It was Treblinka that stayed with him. He survived in part because of hope, inner strength and resourcefulness, but so many victims were just as strong and resourceful as he and had perished.

Many times I walked his probable routes through the city streets during those final days. I tried to imagine his psychological condition and the dreadful memories he carried. What would I have done in Hershl's place? Would I have survived? Statistically, the odds were massively against, but in the end it is too trite a question.

When I knew Hershl, he was still a kind man and he smiled often, although I also remember him howling in his sleep during afternoon naps. He spoke little of those terrible years – not because he had chosen to remain silent, but, as I came to understand, because he could not express all the horror he had seen nor the magnitude of the loss he felt. Later, when I asked his sons if they thought Hershl would want me to break his silence, one son replied that I was the only one who could. So now, long after the Glasgow rains and the Polish snows have washed away all the tears Hershl shed, I am writing his life. It is, in part, another warning. Hershl knew better than anyone that warnings must be repeated. In a decade from now, there may be no survivors left, and as the years advance the truth deniers and the glorifiers of the Nazis grow in strength. The number of Treblinka survivors alive today, as I write these words, can be counted on the fingers of one hand.

During the afternoon of that September Tuesday, a small article in the *Glasgow Evening Times* recorded the police search, which had been launched after Hershl's eldest son, Alan, reported his disappearance. During one of our many phone calls, Alan told me: 'My father had been absolutely furious in the past when we reported him missing. Police and ambulances had always found him and brought him back. He wanted to kill himself. But, I'm sorry, when a human being is in that state, never mind that he was my father, and he walks out of a house after taking a large handful of pills, gets into a car and drives off, you have to do something.'

The newspaper article noted that Hershl, or Henry as he was called in his adopted country, had been missing since Friday from his home in Newton Mearns, a suburb on the south side of Glasgow. He was described as five feet seven inches tall, with grey, receding hair and wearing a light brown windbreaker jacket and blue jogging trousers. The search, it said, was concentrated around Whitecraigs Golf Club – Jews unwelcome at the time – after Hershl's car was found in the club parking lot. This place likely served a dual purpose for Hershl: to confuse the search and to confront anti-Semites, even in death. His strategy worked well. Police asked local residents to check their outhouses, sheds and garages for any sign of him. Police and dogs also searched nearby Rouken Glen Park. There are many places in that park where a man could lose himself, or even lie undiscovered for days. But he was not there.

★ ★ ★

It was another warm day, exactly 47 years earlier, on 26 September 1942, when Hershl Sperling was packed on to the train that would take him to Treblinka. The Gestapo had discovered Hershl and his family hours earlier, hiding in a bunker in Częstochowa, the Polish city revered by Catholics as the home of the Black Madonna. Hershl spoke of the terrible thirst of the freight car, of the desperate souls crammed in like cattle, and the sweet odour of death that hovered over Treblinka as the train pulled towards its destination. 'Auschwitz was nothing,' he used to say. 'Auschwitz was a holiday camp.' How terrible was the hell of Treblinka if Auschwitz had been nothing to him?

In the sweltering heat of the boxcar, three days into the journey, the train slowed to a stop just outside the village of Malkinia, seven kilometres from murderous Treblinka. It was a beautiful autumn morning. Hershl pulled himself up amid the crush of bodies and looked through a grate laced with barbed wire. He saw Polish farm workers labouring in the fields beside the train. People called to them from other boxcars. Hershl had recalled: 'They shout one word at us, "Death".'

Recruitment into the *Sonderkommando* of Treblinka was conducted minutes before the doors of the gas chambers slammed shut. Perhaps the most ingeniously vicious crime at Treblinka was the formation of these death camp slave squads. Hershl's conscription was the unwilling price he paid for survival. These slaves were forced to operate the extermination process. They maintained order among new arrivals, cut women's hair, extracted gold teeth from the mouths of the dead, sorted the belongings of the murdered, removed the dead from the wagons and gas chambers and dragged them to the pits where their corpses were turned to ash. Yet the gift of life was intended only as a temporary reprieve, because they were also the keepers of the terrible truth. The SS was diligent in ensuring that the mass murder of European Jewry was kept secret. Their Jewish slaves knew everything and so were ultimately destined to share the fate of so many others.

Hershl's contemplation of suicide 47 years later begs yet another question: had he known then that his torment would outlive Treblinka itself, would he have tried so hard to live? Hershl had spoken of Treblinka's culture of death. In the barracks, death became a form of resistance. How could he forget the nights and the cries in the darkness of '*yetz*' the Yiddish for 'now'? One man, who could endure no more, climbed on to a wooden crate with a noose around his neck. Another man, in an act of friendship, kicked away the box from under his companion's feet. Death was everywhere – in the barracks, on the trains, on the ramp, in the camp courtyards, in the gas chambers, and in the fiery pits, the source of Hershl's nightmares, where the dead were dumped and burned.

Sometimes Hershl laid out old photographs of dead relatives on the kitchen table at his home in Glasgow for his sons to see. He spoke about his mother and father and his younger sister, but he never mentioned their names. Then he would begin to cry and leave the room. Did he feel that he did not deserve to be alive, in spite of what he had come through? There must have been guilt that he was alive in the place of others, and that he was not worthy. In the days before he climbed into the bridge, he had told one of his sons that his suffering now was 'worse than Treblinka'.

★ ★ ★

The police search was also conducted in the Scottish seaside towns of Ayr and Prestwick, where, the newspaper said, 'Mr. Sperling often visited'. This was true. In Ayr, he would walk along the pier and stare out to sea. The last time Hershl had disappeared, he was found in a hotel room in Ayr, drowsy from whisky and pills. He had also been found and returned by police after previous disappearances in nearby Prestwick. Once, years earlier in Germany, he had vanished for almost three weeks, but had come home of his own volition. Hershl was trying to foil the police as well as the inevitable search by his two sons. He did not want to be found.

The newspaper article's personal description made no mention of the blue-black number – 154356 – tattooed on Hershl's upper arm, a mute reminder of his year in Auschwitz. Hershl had been puzzled about the number, which had been imprinted unusually on his inner bicep, instead of the forearm where most Auschwitz prisoners had been tattooed. He always said there was something strange about the tattoo, not so much the number itself, but its position, and that other prisoners who had been similarly marked on the upper arm had also survived the camps. Perhaps the number's position had something to do with his contact with the infamous Nazi Angel of Death, Dr Josef Mengele, he had conjectured years earlier. Yet how could his survival and the number be connected when Mengele killed so many of his patients? Hershl said he had once looked into the eyes of Dr Mengele. Several times he recalled a prisoner who had returned castrated from a session with the Doctor.

Hershl would have been sixteen then, and in truth we will likely never know what Mengele did to him, or planned for him, if anything. Nor did Hershl really understand why he had lived through the camps. Over the years, he tried to find out about the unusual position of his tattoo, but he was unsuccessful. He had once met other similarly marked Auschwitz survivors in New York in the 1960s, but they had no answers either – they were equally confounded by their survival and the position of their tattoos.

Instead of the outhouses and sheds around Whitecraigs Golf Club, and instead of Ayr, Prestwick, or Rouken Glen Park, Hershl walked from the golf club parking lot, his mind already heavy with Valium and Amitriptyline. It was late afternoon. The traffic on Ayr Road, the main thoroughfare through Newton Mearns and Whitecraigs, was heavy as usual that day, and he walked the half-mile to Whitecraigs train station, where he purchased a ticket and boarded a commuter train to Glasgow's city centre.

Train journeys had long punctuated Hershl's existence. On his journey from the Częstochowa ghetto, in a stinking boxcar, he would have seen familiar station names rolling past – Radomsko, Piotrków, Koluszki. Hours earlier, he had witnessed savage attacks on his neighbours. People were dragged from the ghetto, beaten and shot. As a desperate escapee, a train had taken him away from a village some 40 km from Treblinka to Warsaw. He was one of the few Jews to see the Warsaw ghetto in ruins after the uprising. Another train had taken him from Warsaw to Auschwitz and from Auschwitz to Birkenau and, close to death, from the station at Gleiwitz to concentration camps at Sachsenhausen, Dachau, and Kaufering less than a year later. A train took him back to Polish soil after liberation, when life was hopeful again, only to encounter anti-Semitism of such fury among his former neighbours that he fled. While waiting for another train to carry him back to Germany, he met his future wife on a station platform in Czechoslovakia, and together they would take a train to the Hook of Holland, and later he would board a boat alone and another train that would take him to a new life in Scotland. Now he was on his final train journey.

HERSHL SPERLING'S LAST DAYS

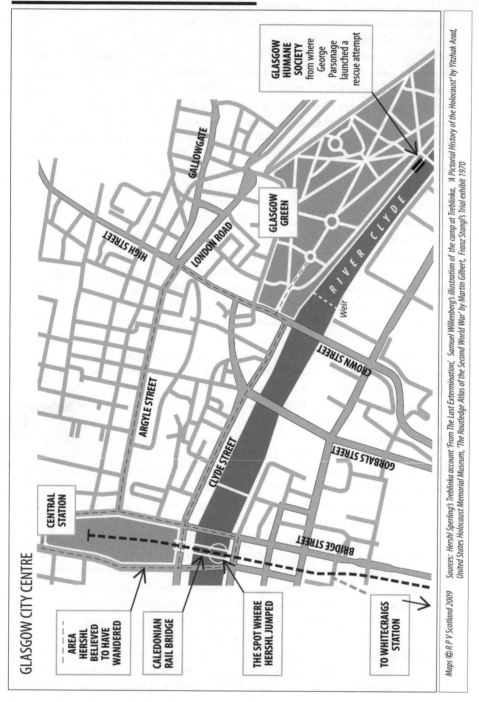

GLASGOW HUMANE SOCIETY
from where George Parsonage launched a rescue attempt

GLASGOW GREEN

GALLOWGATE

HIGH STREET

LONDON ROAD

RIVER CLYDE

Weir

CROWN STREET

ARGYLE STREET

CLYDE STREET

GORBALS STREET

CENTRAL STATION

GLASGOW CITY CENTRE

BRIDGE STREET

AREA HERSHL BELIEVED TO HAVE WANDERED

CALEDONIAN RAIL BRIDGE

THE SPOT WHERE HERSHL JUMPED

TO WHITECRAIGS STATION

Sources: Hershl Sperling's Treblinka account 'From The Last Extermination', Samuel Willenberg's illustration of the camp at Treblinka, 'A Pictorial History of the Holocaust' by Yitzhak Arad, United States Holocaust Memorial Museum, 'The Routledge Atlas of the Second World War' by Martin Gilbert, Franz Stangl's Trial exhibit 1970

Maps © R P V Scotland 2009

The locomotive pulled into Glasgow Central station. Did he recall the boxcar door sliding open at Treblinka, the blinding light, when the train finally arrived? Did he recall the truncheons and hear the savage cries of '*Raus*'? Most likely he exited Glasgow Central by its main entrance on to Gordon Street with the bulk of the crowd, and disappeared into the throng of shoppers and workers. Whether he first wandered the streets of Glasgow or if he went directly to the rail bridge, we do not know. For weeks now, his had become a world of death and phantoms. Certainly at some point he turned south and began to walk toward the river. He crossed the Broomielaw, the street running parallel to the northern bank of the Clyde, traversed one of the pedestrian bridges that span the river and then climbed into the iron rail bridge to spend the night. In limbo between life and death, he listened to the screams of trains as they passed above him.

Today you will find the same paved esplanade and railing. In spite of the attempts to regenerate the city's riverside areas with upmarket apartments, shiny office blocks and street clean-ups, this south bank of the river has remained dingy. As night falls, the vagrants descend. Hershl's final nights were spent among the city's drug addicts, alcoholics, homeless and the mentally ill.

Hershl's mental health had deteriorated sharply in recent months. In the weeks before, he seemed to slip gradually into the world of the *muselmänner*, a word used in the camps to denote the submerged, those human beings irreversibly beaten to the precipice of death. In the camps, *muselmänner* were those who had resigned themselves to death. The origin of the term remains unknown. One explanation is that these victims were so called because they often had bandages wrapped around their heads and took on the appearance of Muslims. Like Hershl, they no longer spoke. In Treblinka, Auschwitz and Dachau, Hershl had seen these emaciated walking corpses. Often *muselmänner* were clubbed mercilessly to death or they simply dropped from exhaustion. It is possible that Hershl's unfulfilled need to tell the world of the horror and his own loss had driven him in the end into the condition of a *muselman*.

In spite of the emptiness in his eyes, and the drugs and the whisky in his blood, Hershl's mind was far from empty. He had plotted to frustrate all attempts to find him, at least long enough for him to do what he had to do. He had come to this point with purpose. He had sought out the company of tramps in the past, and it is possible he knew when and where to come for shelter after dark, where his night-time, half-delirious and pained cries in Yiddish would not be disturbed, or even regarded as out of the ordinary. The day Hershl left home, sunset in Glasgow fell at 7.03pm. In northern Poland, at the site of Treblinka, it was at 7.24pm.

The time before the war was not so far away for Hershl Sperling, except his memories of happier times were painful – the life he had had with his mother and father, his red-haired sister, the town, his house, their animals – all gone now. Hershl had cried for his family, and all those others who were smoke. He had spoken of the shoes and the ashes, the terrible smell of burning bodies and the clothes and the yellow stars. In Treblinka, he had been forced to sort through the clothes of the dead. He was also assigned the job of opening the boxcars and, because of his ability to speak fluent German, Polish and Yiddish, to translate the orders of the SS men. After the victims disembarked, he cleaned the putrid wagons. He removed the bodies of those who had died en route and dragged them to the burning pits. He had spoken of these things as if he were the only one who knew of them, and the only one alive to care about them. There was a small lace-up boot – belonging perhaps to a child of five or six. There was a large man's shoe, a young woman's shoe with a high heel, a child's coat. What had become of those shoes and coats? He could never forget how the bodies had started to rot and stink beneath the earth in the mass graves nor how the Nazis had exhumed them, all the people who had owned those shoes and coats he had been forced to sort. He could not forget the corpses that were cremated on giant iron grills above the pits.

An article in a later edition of the *Glasgow Evening Times* updated the story. Police divers were called in as 'fears grew for the safety' of Hershl Sperling. It said police had already conducted extensive searches of Whitecraigs golf course without success, and that the search had been extended to nearby Rouken Glen Park and Deaconsbank Golf Club. The searches in Prestwick and Ayr were also being stepped up and police officers in the two towns had joined the hunt.

We do not know if he left the bridge the following day to wander through the city, or whether he remained. We know that he was there, probably lying across one of the girders, in the middle of the afternoon.

★ ★ ★

At 4.00pm, on Wednesday 27 September 1989, George Parsonage, the sole lifeboat officer of the Glasgow Humane Society, received a call from the city's police. A body had been observed floating in the shallow part of the river, just under the Caledonian Rail Bridge. Mr Parsonage rowed to the scene. 'I always row to these kinds of incidents,' said Mr Parsonage, who in four decades has dragged more than 2,000 bodies from the River Clyde, some 1,500 of them alive. I met him at his house on Glasgow Green in the summer of 2007. The river flowed fast over a weir a few yards in front of the house.

'A motor boat creates waves,' he said, 'and maybe, just maybe, there is a pocket of air in a jacket that can keep a person afloat and maybe alive.' Then his face darkened. 'I saw him lying face-down on the south side of the river, in about two or three feet of water as I rowed toward him. Men nearly always sink, unlike women. So, for a moment, I thought he might be alive. When I reached him, I turned him over, with his back to the boat, and pulled him on to the gunwales. I had to decide there and then whether to try to resuscitate him with mouth to mouth, but now I could see he was dead.' I asked him if he could tell how long he had been dead. 'I'd say maybe half an hour,' Mr Parsonage replied.

'I searched his pockets for identification. He was wearing a jacket, which I took off him. It was then I saw the number. I was utterly shocked. I realised that man in the water had been in Auschwitz. To think what he had been through was unimaginable.' He looked directly at me. I could see his eyes water. 'He had my respect. And what kind of society are we living in, when we let this happen to a man like this, who had been through what he had? I've never forgotten him.'

Mr Parsonage, who possesses an optimism that perhaps can only come with the kind of work he does, added: 'We cannot be sure it wasn't an accident. Personally, I don't believe in suicides. I have yet to encounter a suicide that didn't cry for help when he hit the water. Therefore, at the moment of death, it is no longer a suicide. It was clear the man had come off the bridge. But if he were lying on one of the girders, it would be easy to fall, either if he was sleeping or drunk. There is a big possibility he was sleeping and fell off the bridge.'

Indeed, Hershl had been drinking, and he was also taking large doses of Valium and Amitriptyline. He could swim – according to his sons he could swim well – but the intoxicants may have rendered him unconscious. I later put Mr Parsonage's theory to both Hershl's sons. His younger son, Sam, said: 'I don't think he had any intention of coming home again.' Alan agreed.

The following day, two brief paragraphs reported the conclusion of the police search for Hershl Sperling: 'The body of a missing Newton Mearns man was today recovered from the Clyde in Glasgow. Henry Sperling, 60 [he was in fact 62], had been missing since last Friday.'

In the end, the survival of Hershl Sperling was no survival at all. He wanted his mind to stop. The suffering that began 47 years earlier had continued for the rest of his life, forcing him each day to relive the punishment that the perpetrators had inflicted upon him.

But this was not the end. In 2005, I discovered Hershl had left behind him a hidden legacy that would reveal the truth about his survival and his death, a story that otherwise would surely have been lost. He had dared to put pen to paper in the months after his liberation, a raw truth in a written record of the things he – and all those who could no longer speak – had witnessed.

CHAPTER TWO

THE BOOK

The quest to understand Hershl Sperling's fate begins with the rediscovery of a secret and long-forgotten book. This was one of his most guarded and valued possessions. He kept it in a brown leather briefcase, which always remained in some out-of-the way cupboard, far from the reach of children or anyone else who might intrude into his world. In this book lay the terrible truth – not just about Hershl himself and what he had been forced to endure, but the truth about all people and what some of us are capable of. The American artist John Marin once wrote: 'Some men's singing time is when they are gashing themselves, some when they are gashing others.'

For more than 45 years Hershl kept the book beside him wherever he went, from country to country – and there were many such moves in his life – from home to home and place to place. In spite of the book's dreadful contents, it comforted him because it was evidence of what had truly occurred, and the truth was all Hershl had to live by. Its contents were as real as the voices of his tortured dreams. If he cried out while napping in the afternoon, his wife would run to his bedside and whisper comforting words in Yiddish. I remember the intensity of her voice as she pleaded with him to come back; he was always disoriented after these bouts. The book, with its pale green cover, the same colour as Hershl's eyes, held the secret of those night-mares. It was written in Yiddish in Hebrew script, and was published in Germany in 1947, some fifteen months after liberation. No-one inside or outside his family was permitted to look at it and few knew of its existence. Hershl's wife was among the few to know the book's contents. I was aware of Hershl's obsession with the contents of the briefcase, but only because my friend Sam had told me. I knew no more and I dared not ask.

We were a family of Americans in Scotland and we lived around the corner. Hershl liked Americans because they had liberated him in April 1945, as their armies swept through Germany toward Berlin in the final weeks of the war. Our shallow roots in Scotland were on my mother's side. My great grandmother had been a teenager en route from Riga to New York in the late nineteenth century when the steamer captain hoodwinked her, and a few hundred other Jews, into thinking she had arrived in America. The ship had in fact stopped at the Scottish port of Greenock. It was a common enough ruse among the captains of shipping companies that allowed them to take on more passengers. My great grandmother was a lone Jewish girl from a

Latvian farm, and she did not know New York from a piece of apple strudel. My Scottish-born mother, who had emigrated to the US in the 1950s, got homesick some seventeen years later and the family moved back.

Hershl and Yaja Sperling, both of them orphaned by the Holocaust, lived then in their house at 63 Castlehill Drive, Newton Mearns. I remember Yaja as a beautiful and stylish woman in her forties, always impeccably dressed, smiling and kind. Her hair was jet black and her eyes were a deep, dark blue. She worked as a manager at Skincraft, an upmarket leather and suede retailer in the centre of Glasgow. I remember thinking then that was an ironic name for a store for a Holocaust survivor to work in. Even then, I was vaguely aware of macabre atrocities in which the skin of murdered Jews had been fashioned into ornaments. The source of that, although I did not know it, was Ilse Koch, the wife of the commandant of the Buchenwald camp – Ilse is infamous for ordering the manufacture of furniture out of human skin and bones, including skin lampshades. The so-called 'Bitch of Buchenwald' committed suicide by hanging herself at Aichach women's prison in 1967. The Sperlings would not even purchase a throwaway plastic pen if it had been made in Germany.

Yaja Sperling was devoted to her family. She loved her husband profoundly and was enormously proud of her two children. Neighbours remarked that she and Hershl behaved like teenagers in love. They held hands and each evening after their meal they strolled through the neighbourhood arm-in-arm. I remember my father saying, almost every evening at around 7.00pm, as he looked out of the window: 'There go Yaja and Henry again.' In their house, when she would put down his lemon tea in a glass after dinner, I remember her smiling at him. It was an intimate moment. She never tired of caring for him. Yaja was Hershl's anchor, and I remember they loved each other with a painful tenderness and a secret passion.

She was born Yadwiga, or Jadwiga, Frischer. Jadwiga, a strange and jarring name to western ears, had been a popular name for centuries among Jewish girls in Poland ever since Jogaila, the Grand Duke of Lithuania, married the Polish Princess Jadwiga and was crowned King of Poland in 1385. She was one of at least seven children in a poor family from an unknown village near Warsaw, an obscure little community of religious Jews and Polish peasants. Her father, who had remarried after the death of her mother before the war, was a cobbler. Little else is known about her early life. She was ten months older than Hershl. When the Nazis came to her village, she began a tortuous journey through an unknown number of work camps. Almost six years later, she was liberated by the Russians and trekked westward over the Tyrol mountains, where she ate grass and drank snowmelt to stay alive. We do not know the names of the camps in which she was interred or what work she had been forced to perform in them. One of her brothers emigrated from Poland to Israel in the 1950s, but the remainder of her family, save another brother and one older sister, were murdered. She never spoke of those who had perished.

Her sons say Yaja lived in a world of fantasy, where there were no Nazis and no Holocaust. Unlike Hershl she did not dwell on the past, but rather willed herself to obliterate it from her mind and in this way she survived beyond liberation. Hershl could not forget and, perhaps, it was his suffering that helped her forget her own.

People said it was she who kept her husband in the world of the living. Just as there exists a hierarchy of suffering among survivors – some camps were worse than others – the same hierarchy prevailed in the Sperling household. Yaja had not lived through Treblinka; she told her sons, 'I didn't suffer like your father.' A photograph of her after the war shows her triumphantly holding a baby over her head outside the gates of an unknown forced-labour camp. If a single image had to be chosen to commemorate Yaja Sperling's sense of survival, it would be this. More than a celebration of life, it was a victory.

Not that the Holocaust had left her unaffected; the pair established a winking complicity. They took absurd risks together. On one occasion they stole a large mackerel from the buffet of the Danish Food Centre, a restaurant that had recently opened in Glasgow. When they were certain no one was watching Hershl stuffed the entire fish into Yaja's handbag. Food-obsession was something they shared with other survivors and their kitchen cupboards always contained enough canned food supplies to ensure the family's survival for at least three months. Sam said: 'They behaved as though they were preparing for a siege.' Food symbolised life and death for them. The theft of food was rampant in the camps, both among prisoners and guards. Guards stole prisoners' food and sometimes killed prisoners whom they suspected of stealing food. In the camps, where all else was stripped away, hidden food equalled a life prolonged. Hershl often stole small things from shops. Whether this was habitual or intentional thrill-seaking it is impossible to know.

To begin with, I regarded Hershl and Yaja just as Sam's slightly crazy parents. Before long, I had become a regular visitor to their house and at their kitchen table, a guest in their incongruous world of kosher food, Yiddish conversations and bouts of madness. Hershl had long-since abandoned his belief in God, for he had been a witness in places where God could not exist. Yet the Jewish motif of 'sanctifying God's name' – the willingness to sacrifice one's life in the cause of moral principles – ran like a thread through Hershl's being and must have made his Treblinka experience all the more painful. Yaja saw the beauty of God in everything.

As parents, they granted their children extraordinary freedoms. They rarely said no. I remember drinking beer for the first time at 14, sitting with Sam at his kitchen table, his mother washing dishes and watching us with a wry expression. Hershl once demanded a meeting with the headmaster of Sam's high school, a particularly dull and authoritarian man, and warned him never to lay a finger on his son. It was the 1970s, when Scottish school children were belted for misbehaviour, but the headmaster heeded Hershl's warning. A man who had looked Josef Mengele in the eye was not going to be intimidated by an over-zealous school master. I remember my mother saying, 'They have a right to be crazy.' I also remember Hershl yelling Yiddish joyously at his wife, who would laugh. He would then turn good-naturedly to torment and tease his children with crazy word games. Deep within him, there ran a natural love of language. I did not realize then, but it was a clue.

Besides his native Yiddish, Hershl spoke good Polish and German, as well as some Russian, and later English. He also spoke an archaic Hebrew, learned faithfully in synagogue class as a child. Language came easily to him, and it was a gift to which he owed his life. In Treblinka, only German speakers were selected for the *Sonderkommando*. Those who spoke further languages increased their chances of survival because they might become useful translators for the Nazis. In Auschwitz, Dachau and the other camps, those who did not understand the language of the masters were quickly brutalised and murdered, because they were useless. They could not understand the tirades of the SS or the kapos. Hershl's fluency in Polish – and many Jews there spoke only Yiddish and just a few words of Polish – had also been crucial and meant survival and opportunity in the aftermath of Treblinka. Yaja also spoke good Polish, and occasionally she and Hershl spoke it in the home – usually for the transmission of things they wanted to keep from Alan and Sam, who understood Yiddish and English very well. Both Sperling children inherited their father's language gift. I remember one evening sitting down with the Sperlings in their living room to watch *Call My Bluff*, the television game show in which contestants guessed the meaning of obscure words. Alan, a highly intelligent individual with an expert knowledge of Latin, deciphered every word, a rare feat. But Hershl would always correct him on the Slavic or Germanic pronunciations. And instead of congratulating Alan for his effort, Hershl instead would throw cushions at him and little hard-boiled sweets that were always heaped in a glass bowl on the coffee table, until the room was in chaos. Hershl often behaved more like a child than his children, perhaps because his own childhood had been lost.

There was also panic in their house; but I saw little of that. The outside world was perceived as threatening and frightening. The source of that fear was the memory of the Holocaust, and their behaviour was based on the belief that some future catastrophe might catch them unawares. Every minor incident became a crisis. Sam told me later: 'We lived as though the Gestapo were about to knock the door down.'

Sometimes crises were entirely invented. During one terrible bout of depression, Hershl became convinced Yaja was having a secret love affair. Alan told me: 'He was going through a very difficult period, and he accused her, over and over again. It was complete nonsense. She was utterly devoted to him. If she were being accused of robbing a bank, that would have been more probable.'

I remember another time I was sitting with the family in their living room. Hershl sipped his lemon tea, and we were watching a wildlife programme on television. A pack of hyenas squabbled over the remains of a carcass. 'So much like humans,' Hershl said, suddenly. 'We lived like that.' Sam asked him several times to tell him what it was like in the camps. He was desperate to know. 'We lived like animals,' Hershl said. That was all. Later, as if by way of explanation, Sam told me 'My father was in Treblinka.' The name meant nothing to me then, because I was hearing it for the first time.

Hershl Sperling had other names. In the shtetl of Klobuck, the little town in Poland where he was born, he was Hershl Szperling, the Polish rendition of Sperling, which is also the German word for sparrow. To his relatives and friends then, he was Hershle, the extra 'e' added as a Yiddish inflexion of endearment. But outside the shtetl, in Polish Klobuck, he was Henick, his Polish name. In Scotland he was Henry, except to his wife; at home, and to himself, he was Hershl.

Hershl kept many secrets about his past. His children could not understand whether he was protecting them or himself. The truth is probably that he was doing both. Yet, at the same time, he transmitted his suffering to them, his helplessness and his humiliation. On rare occasions, he would talk chillingly about the Treblinka burial pits, about how he had to go into them. Once, during a trip to Israel, he had watched Sam, then about eighteen, playing a game with his nine-year-old cousin. Sam recalled: 'He started to say that she reminded him of his sister, but then he became very upset. He started to cry and went inside. We still don't even know his sister's name.'

Yaja was the only one who could calm him, but she could not cure him. Psychiatrists could not help him either, nor could the anti-depressants or the other treatments they tried. They did not – could not – understand that 'Auschwitz was nothing'. They could not possibly understand that Treblinka was not a concentration camp, and as terrible as those places were, they were not death camps. In Treblinka, Hershl had been forced to participate in the systematic murder of at least 700,000 people. Doctors did not know about the pits of burning bodies or what suffering it was to toil among them. Alan said, 'He witnessed things that people are not intended to witness.' In Auschwitz, Hershl was beaten by murderous kapos and he spent weeks up to his chest in icy canal water, but it was Treblinka he relived each day. Throughout his life, Hershl insisted that 'the real horrors' of the Holocaust were not known – but he knew. Years later, doctors diagnosed mental illness but in fact he was profoundly traumatised.

Sam, desperate to understand, once asked his father if he had killed anyone – the worst crime his young mind could imagine – but Hershl said he had not. He later told Sam that after the war he had been driven by a terrible desire to take revenge on the Germans for what they had done. He wanted to murder indiscriminately, but he chose to take no action. He had preferred to remain as he was, even in his shattered state, than to become like those who had tormented him and had attempted to annihilate an entire people. In the end, Hershl Sperling was a moral man.

When Yaja became ill and died of cancer, Hershl's manic mood swings grew more pronounced and his disappearances grew more frequent and more prolonged. Studies of Holocaust survivors in Israel suggest that the loss of a spouse can reactivate Holocaust terror and increase the likelihood of suicide. Hershl and his wife had clung to each other in desperation and mutual dependence, and then she was gone.

A month or so before Hershl's suicide, he sat motionless in his living room chair. He had almost entirely given up food. His eyes were still and stared blankly forward. His head did not move. His body was limp. He reacted to nothing. Sam recalled that he had thrown accusations at him that day. 'I said things like "See what you're doing to us. You should never have had children. You should never have brought us into this world".' In a brief flash of recognition, he looked at his son and said, 'You're right.' Then he was gone. Those were the last words he spoke to Sam.

* * *

In April 2005, as the world's media commemorated the sixtieth anniversary of the liberation of Auschwitz, I was on the telephone to Sam, who was living in London. He had recently given up high-paid employment as a software consultant, and at 45 years old had taken up physics as part of a science degree. Like his father, he had long since given up on believing in God, but retained a fascination with creation and how the world worked at its most fundamental level. He described himself as an 'agnostic', because it was 'impossible to be sure one way or the other'. Hershl had been dead for almost eighteen years. He would have been 78 years old. Sam and I were talking about the Auschwitz commemoration, when he said: 'Well, you remember what my father always said. "Auschwitz was nothing".'

'I remember,' I said. There was a long pause. I could tell he was biting his bottom lip, as was his habit when something disturbed him. 'Did you know he wrote a book about Treblinka?'

'No,' I said, intrigued. 'Where is it? Have you seen it?'

Sam had seen the book only once. It was published just after the war, while Hershl was still in Germany, in a displaced persons camp in the American Zone, he said. He recalled that it had 'horrible pictures in it'. Hershl had become angry when he discovered his son had taken down the leather briefcase and had glimpsed the Hebrew script and the pictures in his book. 'He was trying to protect you,' I said.

'I know. He kept it in that leather briefcase, along with a strange South African seal,' Sam said. 'No one was ever allowed to look at it.' Later, Hershl told Sam he should read it when he was older. But he never did.

'Do you think he meant for you to look at it?' I asked.

Sam took a deep breath. 'I don't know. Maybe. My brother sent it to a Jewish library somewhere after he cleared out my father's house. Neither of us at that time really could bear to know what was in it. I'm not sure I could bear it now.'

'Do you know which library?'

'No, I don't.'

'Could you translate it if we found it?'

'My parents spoke to me in Yiddish and I answered in English. I can't speak it very well, never mind translate something.'

'Should I try to find it and get it translated?' I asked. There was another long pause, marking a conflict between curiosity and dread that was almost palpable. I sensed menace in his father's book, and perhaps he did too. I imagined Sam's hands trembling and I remembered, strangely, Hershl winking at me. I understood then the terrible hold Hitler's madness had on my friend, even though had been born fifteen years after the beast was slain. I also realised that if this was diluted, second-generation pain, Hershl's suffering must have been a thousand times worse.

'All right,' Sam replied.

So began the search for the book that would reveal Hershl's secret – the source of his nightmares, and also the source of suffering for Sam and Alan. I had no idea if it would help them, but both were eager for me to proceed. Nor did we have any idea what to expect. I also wondered how such a work could have been published in Germany after the war. Where did the publisher even find a Yiddish printing press in a country devastated by the Allied onslaught and for more than a decade stripped by Hitler of all things Jewish? Did the Nazis not smash Jewish printing presses all over Europe? And then there were the bigger questions. Why had he written it? What horrors would it tell? He was just nineteen years old when he put pen to paper to *schreibt* and *farchreibt*, the Yiddish exhortation to write and record.

Phone calls and emails followed. Within a few days, I discovered that the book had been sent by Sam's brother to the Wiener Library in London, one of the world's largest collections of material relating to the Holocaust, anti-Semitism and the rise and fall of Nazi Germany. A few days after my inquiry, an email arrived from librarian Howard Falksohn, who had tracked the book by locating the 'Thank you' note from the library to Sam's brother, dated 26 October 1989, one month after Hershl's death.

Falksohn wrote that the library had been grateful for the book, and that it had been catalogued in the Wiener's miscellaneous journals series. Its title was *Journal of the Jewish People During the Nazi Regime*. The book, in fact a journal, was Number Four in a series, and was published in March 1947, in Munich, by the Central Historical Commission of the Central Committee of the Liberated Jews in the American Zone. I immediately telephoned Sam. 'I found it,' I told him.

'*Mazel tov*,' he said, but I sensed trepidation in his voice. We agreed that I would come to London, that we would go to visit the Wiener Library together and photograph the book. Photocopies were not allowed because of its fragile condition.

Sam chain-smoked cigarettes. He was nervous. His father's pain had long been his pain. We walked toward the Underground near his home in north London, and he said: 'You remember Pigpen in the Charlie Brown comics, with that dust cloud always around him wherever he went? That's the way I felt for a long time, always dirty from the Holocaust, always tainted.'

We got off at Great Portland Street and walked five minutes to the library, hardly exchanging a word. Outside, about 11am on a Saturday morning, Sam puffed nervously on his cigarette, leaning for support on the Victorian railing that led to a grand black door of the old brick building.

'Are you going to be all right?' I asked.

'I don't know. I think so. Actually, I don't know what I'll do when I see the book. Maybe I'll do something crazy, like eat it.' We rang the buzzer. I stated our business into the intercom and we entered. Howard Falksohn was expecting us. He stood up to greet us from his desk, and shook our hands.

'So, the book,' he said, pulling it out of a brown Manila envelope. He handed it to me and I passed it to Sam.

'My God, that's it,' said Sam, running a hand over the faded green cover, its large Hebrew type drawing attention to itself. In roman type at the bottom, it read, 'Nr. 4' and the date '1947'. Sam bit his bottom lip.

'Can you read any of it, the Yiddish I mean?' I asked.

'Just a few words,' Sam said. He opened the book carefully at a random page and looked into the Yiddish text. I saw his hands trembling. 'Look, that word is '*krankeyt*' – sickness or illness – but, no, I couldn't translate this.'

He slowly flipped the book over. On the back, there was an English title: 'From the Last Extermination' and a sub-heading 'Journal for the History of the Jewish People During the Nazi Regime'. I ran my fingers over the cover, touching history, but also touching something terrible, the result of almost unspeakable evil.

Israel Kaplan, the book's editor, was listed. There were few other clues, at least to the untrained eye. On the inside back cover, a date, March 1947. A Munich print shop was named: R. Oldenbourg. We could make out the Yiddish words, *Tsentraler Historisher Komisiye*, and below that in English, 'Copyright by Central Historical Commission, Munchen, Mohlstrasse 12a. Edition: 8000 copies'. At the very bottom, a small line of print read, 'Published under DP-Publications License US-E-3 OMGB. Information Control Division.' There was information here that could be investigated.

A typed note, part of the library's cataloguing system, stated in Yiddish: *Fun Letzten Hurban,* the journal's title, and the dates '1946–1948 (discontinued)'. It noted this was book number four and had been published in March 1947. This was one volume in a series of eight publications but the library only had one. It also noted: 'Good condition. Important DP publication. Scarce.'

The library note heartened us. It was important that the book's value was recognised – but it was not what we expected. A table of contents ran below the title on the back cover page. It appeared to be a list of separate articles written by different individuals on various aspects of the Nazi regime, the murder of Jews and the annihilation of their communities – 'The Extermination of Jews in Eastern Galicia' By Dr Philip Friedmann; 'Polish Jewish Soldiers as War Prisoners (Memoirs)' by Mendel Lifschitz; 'Tchernowitz (Cernauti)' by Dr Jakob Ungar; 'In the Forests of White Russia (Eye-Witness Report)' a) 'Around Woloshin' by Mosche Mejerson, b) 'In the Braslav area' by Mosche Trejster, c) 'At Radun' by Lieb Lewin; 'My Experiences During the War (From the Series of Children's Reports)' by Daniel Burstin; 'Lullaby (Ghetto-song)'; 'Buna (Camp song)'; 'Nazi documents with comments; photographs of the Nazi period'. The name Buna chimed with me. It was the largest sub-camp of Auschwitz and the place where chemist and author Primo Levi had spent 11 months as a forced labourer. Levi's suicide in 1987, two years before Hershl's death, baffled some who knew his work. My scant research to-date had revealed that while suicides are rare amongst survivors, those who wrote of their experiences – and faced them – were more likely to kill themselves.

Two of the photographs drew immediate attention to themselves. One showed a Hassidic Jew on skis, a posed photograph to make the Jewish man in his long gabardine coat and sidelocks look foolish, confiscated by the Allies from a German after the war. No doubt this Jew had been murdered later. The second showed four men, hands on their heads, being taken away to be shot after being discovered in their concealed bunker in the town of Czortkow, in the western Ukraine, in 1943. Hershl had hidden in a bunker in Częstochowa. He had been caught up in the *Aktionen* or round-ups of late September 1942. There were 40,000–50,000 Jews crammed in the Częstochowa ghetto just before the first deportations to Treblinka from the city. It was baffling. What was Hershl's connection to this, and why was his name not listed among the authors?

'I don't understand,' said Sam, biting his bottom lip 'Perhaps he had simply contributed to someone else's story; but he always said he had written something about Treblinka.' He ran his eyes again down the table of contents. 'It's not here. What was he doing with this book? I don't know why it was so important.'

Falksohn confirmed this was definitely the only book that had been donated by the Sperling family. Why would he carry this book around for so long and protect it the way he did? Neither did Falksohn know much about the book, except that it was 'clearly an authentic piece of Holocaust testimony' that had been written during the chaos that had followed the end of the war, possibly to assist taking Nazi criminals to trial. Yet the fact that it was published in Munich was significant, because Hershl had been liberated in Dachau, half an hour's train journey from the city. I insisted to myself that this could not be a dead end. There must be a clue in the book itself and we had to get it translated to find it. Sam remarked that it was typical of his father that he should make even the discovery of his story an ordeal. He was like that; he enjoyed making others jump through hoops.

It must have been about a week later. I was back at home, sitting at my desk and searching through the internet for a local translator of Yiddish, no easy task in Scotland. I recalled the deep gentle green of Hershl's eyes, and the dark hair on the back of his hands. I suddenly remembered him remarking one day, completely out of the blue, that he had no idea why the Italians had joined the Axis during the war. 'They're short, dark and hairy, just like Jews,' he had said. The politics were unimportant to him. Now I saw him again, reclining on a deck chair in the late afternoon sun one summer long ago on his front lawn in Newton Mearns, his dark and tanned face, his chest, stomach and arms covered with hair. He was wearing only his underwear. People in Newton Mearns did not sunbathe on their front lawn, let alone in their underwear. The neighbours doubtless considered him strange, but he didn't care.

Out of the reverie, something occurred to me: Maybe we had the wrong volume. I put the name 'Sperling' into an internet search engine, together with 'From the Last Extermination' and up came the listing of a Jewish library in Montreal, in Canada. It listed the *Journal for the History of the Jewish People During the Nazi Regime*, volume Number Six − not the Number Four that Hershl had carried for years in his briefcase. Then below the Canadian library result, the site of an antiques bookseller in Jerusalem also listed the same book. I studied the description impatiently. The first chapter of the book, whose cover on the vendor's website looked identical to the book at the Wiener Library, was entitled 'Treblinka − Eye-Witness Report' by 'H. Sperling'. I had found it. I ordered the book immediately, confirming it was the book I wanted with the Jerusalem bookseller, a Rabbi Yaakov Shemaria − a title and name that persuaded me to part with $85.

Why had Hershl carried the wrong volume of a set around for so many years? Why was he so attached to it? It no longer mattered. Hershl's story would be with us in two to four weeks. In the meantime, I began researching.

★ ★ ★

Three weeks after the book arrived, the translation came by email, then a few days later in hard-copy form. I ran my fingers over the Hebrew letters of the original as I read aloud the English version. His was one account among ten others in the book, a mere 20 pages long. Yet it felt strange to read his words and to hear his voice again.

It was an account of terror and suffering, beginning with his discovery in the under-ground bunker in Częstochowa and ending after the war in a displaced person's camp – one of the so-called DP camps – near Munich. It makes no mention of his perished family in the aftermath of the bunker. Its tone reverberates with loss, but the writer is clearly also desperate to be heard and believed. If history is best represented by those who experienced it, this book was pure.

I reported to Sam. 'Do you want me to send you a copy of the translation?' I asked.

'I don't think I could bear to read it.' He paused again, before asking, 'But how is it?'

'It's very detailed and very sad. Most of it is terrifying. Incredible really, because it is so real.'

That was the way it would be for the next year. I would tell my friend about the things his father had written – I could even read sections aloud on the telephone – but he would not read it himself. It was the same for his brother, Alan, with whom I would also spend hours on the telephone. A similar system was applied to the story I was trying to write. I would describe events and discoveries to Sam and tell him about the journey I was taking, the one he was helping to guide. I would also tell him about the discoveries I made along the way, and together we pieced together the source of his father's pain, and perhaps even his own. I knew that I would have to go where Hershl's suffering began, and even to those places that pre-dated the pain. I would have to go to Poland, walk the streets he had walked. I needed to look into the faces of those who dwelt there.

CHAPTER THREE

POLAND

My plane touched down at Kraków's Belice airport on a crisp, sunny morning in early February 2007. A taxi took to me my hotel a little before noon. The hotel was fifteen minutes' walk from Rynek Glowny, Kraków's massive market square of giant flagstones and towering spires, but I had wanted to be close to Kazimierz. Kuzmir, as Hershl would have known it in Yiddish, is the city's old Jewish quarter. I asked the hotel receptionist for directions and wondered what she thought about Jews – here, in twenty-first century Poland, amid the former killing fields of the Nazis and this country's own infamous home-grown anti-Semitism. I wondered if the hatred persisted, even though only a handful of Jews were left. Had this country, brutalised by war and half a century of Communism, moved on? I had asked Sam to join me. His insights would have been important and incisive, but he said that setting foot anywhere in Poland would be too much for him to bear. For him, Poland was a graveyard, where rabid anti-Semites had aided and abetted the Nazis in the murder of three million Polish Jews, including members of his own family.

I travelled the same route through the medieval square for three days, veering southeast past the sombre façade of Grodzka Street and past the spires of the 1,000-year-old Wawel Cathedral, the most famous feature of Kraków's skyline. I knew that King Jogaila and Princess Jadwiga had lived and were buried at Wawel, and I thought of Yaja Sperling, who had shared her name. A few more blocks and I was in Kazimierz, where Poland's second-largest Jewish community had lived and flourished from the end of the thirteenth century until the Nazis came in 1939; the maze of narrow, crooked cobblestone streets, hidden market squares and low-slung, peeling buildings, many of which still bore the physical scars of the Second World War. This was exactly where I wanted to be before I ventured into the country's hinterland.

Kazimierz was once an independent town outside the walls of Kraków and was named after its fourteenth-century king, Casimir the Great, who granted the charter and set in law the right of Jews to establish their communities. This was not just a big town inhabited by Jews; it was a Jewish town and an integral part of Poland's Yiddish culture. At the same time, Casimir established the Kraków Academy, now called the Jagiellonian University, where medieval Polish intellectual life blossomed. At the end of the fourteenth century, a young astronomer called Niklas Koppernick – later latinised into Copernicus – studied there. Although the Jewish community in

Kraków had lived unperturbed beside its Christian neighbours under the protection of Casimir, relations had deteriorated by the reign of Jogaila and Jawiga in 1386 and pogroms occurred with increasing frequency. In later centuries, Polish kings allowed Kraków's Jewish community – always an essential part of the city's commercial and intellectual lifeblood – to build interior defensive walls and passed laws to ensure their places of business remained unmolested. By1939, Kazimierz had become one of Poland's major Jewish communities with 68,500 Jews, no less than a quarter of Kraków's population. Within four years of Nazi rule, all but a handful had perished in nearby Auschwitz, and a whole world was swept away.

As a child, Hershl visited the city many times, and I imagined him walking these streets as a young boy with his father, awe-struck by its clamour. I heard myself saying aloud as I walked, 'Enjoy, Hershl, drink it all up. It cannot last forever.' A couple of tourists turned to look at me as they passed. There are ghosts on every street here. Under Communism, Kazimierz was left in crumbling disrepair, and when I first visited in 1989, it was a haven for stray dogs and alcoholics. It would not have been wise to venture out after dark. Now, thanks in part to Steven Spielberg's 1993 film *Schindler's List*, which was set there, Kazimierz has become Kraków's bohemian quarter, and is drenched in a kind of bizarre, hip quasi-Jewishness. The place buzzed with cafes that bore Yiddish names, Jewish-style restaurants, Jewish art galleries. But where were the Jews? In Kazimierz's labyrinthine streets, it was impossible not to feel the weight of the absent culture. Original Yiddish inscriptions still front doorways, an old pharmacy and the ruined theatre. The sound of Kleizmer music poured out of a nearby café. While sitting in a café with the English word 'coffee' written in Hebrew script in the window, I scribbled in my notebook, 'All this Jewishness everywhere – except there are no Jews.' In 2007, there were fewer than 200 Jews living in Kraków.

On the second day, after another morning of wandering – I wanted to soak up as much of the old Jewish quarter as I could – I met a woman in her mid-twenties in the downstairs café of a bookstore in Kazimierz. I had exchanged a few emails with her before I arrived, and she agreed to meet with me on condition of anonymity in print. I'll call her Agnieszka. I told her I was writing about a man called Hershl Sperling, who came from Klobuck. She had heard of the little town but had never been there. It was two or three hours from Kraków, she said. I told her that Hershl had been one of the few survivors of Treblinka, that he was the father of a good friend, and that he had killed himself in Scotland many years later, still traumatised by the experience. I told her I wanted to know about the Jewish experience in Poland now, what was left of it, and if anti-Semitism still thrived here. Many Poles argue vehemently that they had no part in the Holocaust, that it was a German invention and that the death camps were established on Polish soil by the Nazis, not Poles. Yet could the Nazis have succeeded in their murderous enterprise without Polish anti-Semitism, fanned for generations by the Catholic Church, and the complicity and tacit approval of the local population? Nor did it end in 1945. Those Polish Jews who survived and returned, Hershl among them, encountered furious anti-Semitism. It is hardly surprising that almost as soon as they set foot in their old towns, most fled again. And instead of being honoured, those Poles who had sheltered Jews during the war – and there were many – begged to remain anonymous for fear that their neighbours would deride them as 'Jew lovers', and break into their homes to search for money the Jews must have left behind, or even kill them.

Agnieszka gulped the remains of her coffee and smiled, attentive to my words. She had looked moved when I told her about Hershl's suicide, but she snapped a hard gaze at me when I brought up Poland's infamous anti-Semitism.

'I don't want to be identified because my parents still don't want their neighbours to know they are Jewish, and I have to respect that,' she said. 'I can tell you that some of us come together on Friday nights at a synagogue here in Kazimierz and it's nice.' She looked across the room to reflect, and then, with a shrug, added: 'I didn't even know I was Jewish until a few years ago, although I always suspected we were not the same as everyone else, because we never went to church. But I do think that things are changing in Poland. The young people here don't live in the world of stereotypes anymore, the way the older generation did. There are people, many of them young like me, of very good will who want to preserve history. But you ask me if there is still anti-Semitism in Poland? Of course there is. I hear it all the time, mostly if I have to go to the small towns, although not so much in Kraków or Warsaw. But isn't there anti-Semitism everywhere? In Poland, they don't beat up Jews in the street or dese-crate Jewish graveyards and synagogues, at least not for more than 50 years, and I have read about those kinds of incidents taking place in France and Germany and Britain.'

'But, of course, there are so few Jews left to hate in Poland and perhaps that's why there are fewer incidents than elsewhere.'

'Maybe,' she said, smiling weakly. 'Actually, there are many Jews in Kraków, but they are all Holocaust tourists from America who come in summer, then go home after visiting Auschwitz.'

Agnieszka is part of a small but uncanny Judaic revival. Her grandparents had been hidden Jews during the Nazi occupation, and Agnieszka's parents themselves remained secret Jews afterwards, pretending to be Catholic. When she stood up to leave, she smiled again and reached to touch my arm. She said, 'It's difficult to know people who killed themselves, no? It's like you're always connected with death. That's sometimes how I feel here. There was once so much and now there is almost nothing.'

I sent her a couple of emails when I returned home and heard nothing back. Then, about two months later, an email arrived. 'I'm sorry I haven't replied to your emails for so long,' she wrote, 'but I had my master thesis exam, and also unfortunately my story is not so interesting. Good luck.' I disagreed, but clearly she did not want to reveal her Jewishness to the world. That email was the end of our communication.

The following morning, I sat in a café in an imposing old building that had until recently been a derelict, nineteenth-century Talmudic study house, but was now Kazimierz's Centre for Jewish Culture. It was Sunday morning, and I watched a group of elderly, genteel Polish women leave high mass at the Church of Corpus Christi and cross a market square that once bustled with Jews. The women flooded into this café, filled with Jewish symbols and artefacts, gossiping in Polish. It was a disconcerting sight. It suddenly became clear to me that just as stereotypes could not be applied to the Jews who once populated this nation, they are equally inapplicable to Poles. It was here I met the curator of the cultural centre, Joachim Russek, an extraordinary 56-year-old Polish Catholic, who has perhaps done more than anyone else to remind his country and that city of its Jewish heritage.

'I believe our recognition of the thousand years of Jewish history on Polish soil is intrinsically linked to the question of who we are in our new, post-Communist and democratic reality. I say to any democracy – show me how you treat your minorities,' he said. 'Here, we are striving to preserve the Jewish heritage in Kazimierz and to per-petuate the memory of the centuries-long presence of the Jews in Poland, living side by side with Poles. In doing so, we promote the values of a civil society.'

'But what about Polish anti-Semitism? And what about the future?' I asked him.

'Believe me, I know all about anti-Semitism in Polish culture. A few years ago when I was in America, I was introduced to a university professor, who told me his family had left Poland a generation earlier. I asked him if he spoke Polish, and he blurted out, in Polish, 'Beat the Jew'. I can't tell you how ashamed I felt. For centuries, Poland was the most tolerant country in Europe. That's why Jews came here in the first place. We need to return to the tolerance that is our heritage. Only then will we find our rightful place in Europe.'

Later that day, on Miodowa Street in the heart of Kazimierz, I ate in a restaurant that had been decked out to look like the home of a Jewish family, probably because it had been. There were brass candlesticks on the tables, and lace tablecloths. The people who once lived in this house were almost certainly murdered, and here I was eating *cholent*, a Jewish bean and meat stew, in their home, being served by the descendents of people who hated them and may even have been complicit in their murder. I scribbled in my notebook, 'Lame mea culpa meets gross commercialism'. I felt disgusted and left.

I met Joachim one last time that night, and I mentioned to him my thoughts about the Polish women in the café. Russek scratched his head, and said: 'What, you prefer they go to a Nazi café instead?' I laughed. He was right. But I was ready to leave Kraków. I went to bed early that night. My feet hurt from all the walking back and forth to Kazimierz. Besides, I had an early train to catch – the 7.44am to Częstochowa, from where I would make my way to Klobuck, Hershl's home town.

Some time during the early hours of the morning, I was awakened by a cacoph-ony of loud, aggressive cries in the street below my hotel room. I pulled aside the curtain and saw three young men in their 20s standing on a street corner opposite the hotel. They screamed into the night. Each of them had a skinhead haircut and a bottle of vodka, which they were gulping between cries.

The odd thing was that they were not screaming at each other or anyone in par-ticular. This behaviour obviously cemented camaraderie between them. They were aggressive screams, filled with menace, and I suspect if anyone had wandered past there would have been trouble. The loudest of them arched his body as he cried out, his green army jacket buttoned to the neck against this cold Polish winter night. He swayed on the street corner. Then he took a long drink from the bottle and smashed it through the windscreen of a parked car. He began kicking the car viciously. The other two joined in, screaming and kicking until they were spent, then they staggered off into the Kraków night. I remembered now that Hershl had spoken of how he had been chased habitually on his way to and from school by Polish thugs, and I imagined them to be thugs such as these.

★ ★ ★

The next morning, as the train pulled out of Kraków Glowny, the city's central railway station, the snow began to fall. Hershl must have travelled these tracks many times before the Nazis came. There remains something haunting about the sight of train tracks and boxcars anywhere in this country. In the carriage with me there was an old Polish woman in a fur coat with dyed red hair, and two backpackers wearing crucifixes. Częstochowa is the site of the Jasna Góra Monastery, a Polish Lourdes-like destination for Roman Catholic pilgrims. The city's claim to fame is that it is the home of the Black Madonna, an icon that, according to tradition, was painted by St Luke on a tabletop constructed by Jesus. Through the window I saw rutted fields of frozen snow, passing villages and people in leather coats and hats.

At around 11.30am the train pulled into Częstochowa Osobowy. I walked through the incongruously modern glass station to the line of taxis waiting outside. The city looked bleak and desolate, although perhaps it was just the snow and grey sky. I had the overwhelming sensation that I was in the hands of the enemy. I began to feel some of the dread I imagined Hershl must have felt. The driver took me to my hotel on Pilsudskiego Street, on the other side of the tracks. The receptionist did not speak English. My room was large, dusty and cold, smelling of cigarette smoke. A small television and an ashtray sat on a rickety table. The television did not work. I deposited my bag and went in search of the bus station to catch my connection to Klobuck, Hershl's town.

The snow was relentless and the wind icy. I made my way to the train station, hobbling through drifts with my aching feet, to ask for directions to the bus depot. No one spoke English. I was becoming exasperated and wandered into town, asking in vain for directions with the half a dozen Polish words in my vocabulary. I went into a pharmacy and found a man who knew a few words of English and he directed me to the bus station. I walked about ten yards before I looked at my watch and realised it was pointless. The bus for Klobuck was due to leave in less than five minutes. I would never make it. I stood for a moment, panicked and desperate. But then I gathered myself. Determined to get to Klobuck, I dragged myself back through the snow toward the station and approached the line of taxis. I asked four drivers if they spoke English and each of them said no. The fifth driver said, 'Yes, I speak English,' which turned out to be almost all he could say. But he showed me a Polish-English dictionary, which I knew would help. We negotiated a price, and I jumped in, relieved to be out of the snow and off my feet.

It turned out that Jerzy, my driver, spoke pidgin French because his grandfather had come from Lille in France to be a Polish coal miner. He said he considered himself Polish. He often touched an icon of the Madonna, which hung from his rear view mirror, usually when he went round a corner. He was about 60 and had also been a coal miner in his youth. I stated my business, and he nodded seriously. Shortly afterward, he took a right turn off the main road. We passed through the village of Krzepice and he pointed out a ruined brick building.

'Synagoga,' he said. I imagined the horrors that must have taken place. Jerzy seemed sympathetic, but he then said in English, 'Poland a Catholic country. Always. Poland only for Catholics.' Maybe this came across as more severe than intended, because of his poor English and my non-existent Polish, but it was a factual inaccuracy. In 1939, Polish Roman Catholics in fact made up 60 per cent of the country's population. Some ten per cent were Jews. Most of the rest were Protestants, ethnic Germans and Russian Orthodox groups.

I was a long way from the cosmopolitan streets of medieval Kraków. The taxi sped through the snow, deeper and deeper into the Polish hinterland.

CHAPTER FOUR

KLOBUCK

Pre-war Klobuck was like so many other little towns in Poland, with all the things a Polish town should have – a few thousand Jewish and gentile inhabitants, a synagogue, a poorhouse, a study house, a church and a Wednesday market. This was Hershl's town before the Nazis came. In those days it had just two major streets that intersected near the church. Across the market square stood the synagogue, from which spread the town's Jewish quarter, a shtetl of tumbledown houses and dirt roads. As I wandered the streets, I saw that war, progress and almost half a century of Communism had not greatly altered a beautiful little town that sat amid orchards, gardens and small lakes. The synagogue was gone, as were the Jews, but the core of the town was essentially the same. A traveller today with some knowledge of Klobuck's history might be surprised at how close the church and synagogue stood together. It also struck me that the Jews who once inhabited this place clearly did not conduct their affairs up back streets, but here, right in the middle of town. They were an integral and highly visible part of Klobuck's life. In 1939, when the Nazis marched in, there were around 1,600 Jews, more than a third of the population. They were a petty bourgeoisie of tradesmen and merchants. Most of the Poles were peasant farmers, but there was also a middle class, many of whom were fierce anti-Semites. Because Klobuck was a small town, Jews and Poles lived cheek by jowl, each a part of the other's landscape. All traces of that multicultural community have disappeared, save an overgrown Jewish cemetery that is now a cow pasture. Klobuck, like every other place in Poland, was brutalised.

Klobuck is located in the valley of Jura Krakówsko just across the Silesian frontier in what was once the far western edge of the Russian empire – although in character it has for more than two millennia been Polish. In Hershl's time, it was surrounded by forest. The town's name is derived from a local fifteenth-century heraldic symbol – a hat, or *klobuka* in old Polish – and alludes to the Klobuck family, its medieval rulers. Local legend has it that in the year 1135, when the foundations for the first house were dug, a hat was found. One legend claims that it was a Jewish hat, the yellow, cone-shaped, pointed type that was required to be worn by adult male Jews outside the ghetto in medieval western Europe and Muslim lands.

Jews, criss-crossing ancient Slavo-Turkic trade routes from the west, east and south, had inhabited what is now Poland since the days of the Roman Empire, and perhaps earlier. However, migration to Poland en masse is believed to have begun in the year

1095 when Pope Urban II launched the First Crusade with the stated aim of wresting the sacred city of Jerusalem from the Muslims. Jews, fleeing the murderous pogroms of opportunistic peasants and roving gangs of knights in Germany en route to the Holy Land, crossed into Silesia, which was then under the rule of the relatively tolerant Polish Piast dynasty. In the same decade, Jews from Slavic Bohemia and Moravia were driven north by Crusaders into Polish lands. Jews gradually moved deeper into Poland by trade routes at the invitation of local rulers, who were seeking goldsmiths, bankers and traders to bolster the economic development of their ducal states.

Over time, poor Jews followed rich Jews as the persecution elsewhere intensified. Word of Poland's tolerance spread quickly through the besieged Jewish communities, particularly after 1296 when Prince Henry IV of Wroclaw granted Jews legal protection and outlawed the common gentile practice of raising accusations that they killed Christian children for their blood to make Passover bread. For centuries, barely a decade passed without Jews in some western state being accused of this 'blood libel', and rooted in each anti-Semitic accusation – little different from so many incidents of anti-Semitism down through the ages – lay not differences in ideology or faith but human greed, spite and economic jealousies. German burghers, plotting to wipe out Jewish commercial competition, formed exclusively Christian trade guilds and often connived with the church to fan popular hatred against Europe's Jewish communities. Nazi anti-Semitism was rooted in a millennium of European religious hatred, whipped up in the name of Christianity. The Black Death in the fourteenth century – also blamed on Jews by the church and jealous burghers – brought about a new wave of migration to Poland, as did the terrors of subsequent crusades and the anti-Semitic preaching of Martin Luther, which in Hershl's time was given widespread publicity by the Nazis.

Although today Klobuck lies deep within Poland's modern borders, for centuries the town sat in a long-disputed frontier region that separated the Germanic and Slavic territories of northern-central Europe. During the Middle Ages, Jews called these western Slavic lands New Canaan, evoking a Biblical optimism. Poland's relative tolerance partly sprang from its limited involvement in the crusades. At the time of the First Crusade, Poland had been Catholic for less than 150 years, and it was difficult for the Papacy to drum up enough support. Also, the Polish rulers, unlike the Holy Roman Emperors, did not seek to have a finger in every pie. As long as the Jews paid their taxes, and the local dukes in turn paid their tributes to the Piastes, life continued in peace. Thus a Jewish 'nation' was left free to flourish in Poland.

The presence of Jews in Klobuck itself is also ancient. However, details of this early history are scant. The archives of the shtetl were burned by the Nazis, along with the town's synagogue. More Jews moved to Klobuck in the middle of the eighteenth century from nearby Dzialoszyn after fire destroyed their homes. Polish landlords held the Jews responsible for the blaze and demanded recompense, bankrupting the community. The earliest information available on Jewish life in Klobuck dates from 1808. In that year, the finance minister of the principality of Warsaw, a man named Lucztevski, issued the order that Jews must have their holy books stamped for a special tax. Lucztevski made each Jewish community responsible for the organisation of this payment and the Częstochowa community sent out a proclamation to all the outlying Jewish settlements under its jurisdiction regarding the new law. Klobuck was named among the settlements in the records.

It was hard to imagine this town before the Nazis came. I walked to the town hall, a Stalinesque concrete block across the main square from the church. A few weeks earlier I had written asking for information about the Jews who once lived here. Either they could not translate my request into Polish or chose to ignore it. Now inside, in a large, hospital-like reception area, I spoke to a middle-aged woman behind a counter.

'Do you speak English?' I asked.

'No,' she said, an exasperated look on her face.

'French?' I asked, hopefully. It would have been too much to ask that her grandparents were coal miners from Lille as well.

'A little English maybe,' she said at last. 'But slowly, please.'

'I am an American,' I told her. 'I'm writing a book about a man who came from Klobuck and I was hoping to get some information. Is there someone who can help me?'

'Ah, American,' she said, seeming momentarily impressed. Perhaps the woman thought I was Steven Spielberg. She paused and added: 'But I don't understand.'

'There must be someone in this building who speaks English,' I said, waving my hand around in a gesture that was meant to encompass the entire edifice.

'Wait, please,' she picked up the telephone, and within a few minutes a tall, thin man in a grey suit appeared. He shook my hand limply and introduced himself as the mayor's assistant. I will call him Pawel. I told him that I was an American, that I was writing a story about a man from Klobuck and that I was seeking information about him and his community. He nodded.

'Please, follow me.' Pawel walked with long strides, and I followed him through the maze of corridors, past personal offices and bigger areas that held what looked like old-fashioned typing pools, until we reached a room where three women sat at desks. Pawel introduced me in Polish and I shook their hands. 'Now,' said Pawel, 'tell me again what you are looking for please.'

I told him again that I was here seeking information about a man from Klobuck and Pawel translated my request into Polish. 'What was this man's name?' Pawel asked.

'Szperling,' I said. Pawel shook his head. I added: 'He was Jewish, and I'd like to know where he and all the other Jews lived. Can you show me where the shtetl was?' Pawel jerked back his head abruptly.

'There were never Jews here,' he insisted, shaking his head. I could see a look of distaste darken across his face. This was ridiculous, and I laughed out loud.

'Of course, there were Jews here,' I said. 'I'd like to see where the synagogue stood in Klobuck please.'

Pawel thought for a moment. 'Ah, *synagoga*,' he said at last. '*Zydzi*.' I understood him. *Zydzi*, one of my few words of Polish, meant 'Jewish'. '*Synagoga*, yes?' He began speaking to the three women in Polish, then turned to me and shrugged. 'I'm sorry,' he said, 'I can't help you. In Krzepice, yes, there is a synagogue there, but nothing here. Go to Krzepice. It's better.'

Just then, however, one of the women touched my arm. She spoke in halting English. 'Don't listen to them. There were many Jews here before. Look.' She pointed out the window across the square, to the right of the church. 'Over there,' she said, 'all those houses were built by Jews. Very old houses, more than 100 years old. And there, next to the church was their synagogue, where they prayed.'

I walked across the empty square to the place that had once been the shtetl of Klobuck. It was incredibly quiet. On the square, buildings that had once been Jewish homes were now shops. I saw a bookstore, a pharmacy and an art-supply shop. Behind them was the shtetl proper, and a narrow asphalt road winding down a hill. There was a lot of derelict land, where buildings had either collapsed or been torn down. In Hershl's time this was a tightly packed community. There had been a tearoom and a hairdresser and Hassidic cobblers who sewed *spatz* and repaired boots. There were grocery stores, hat makers, an ironmonger and countless tailors. A number of Jews also made a living by smuggling goods to and from Germany across the border, particularly tobacco, saccharin and silk. One Jewish entrepreneur was known for shooing his geese into the air just before the German frontier and gathering them up on the other side, where he could sell them for twice the amount without having to pay toll charges at the border. In Jewish textile shops, customers could find woollen fabric, white linen and the checked cloth worn by peasants. Now this was a muddy slope with a few ramshackle stone buildings arranged on the hillside. I followed paths to the left and right, feeling a terrible weight of sadness. I began to associate the life that had existed here with what I knew occurred later. All those Jews had one foot in the grave. Some buildings had bent roofs and cracked plaster scarred their walls. High, unkempt grass grew around them. A few were painted pink, blue and orange, like houses in a Chagall painting.

This is where Hershl came into the world on 10 March 1927, in the Szperling family home at 14 Staszysz. I knew that Hershl was the second of three children born to Icchak and Gitel Szperling, during the relative calm of the military dictatorship of Jozef Pilsudski. The eldest sibling died from a hole in his heart before the war. There was also a younger sister, whose name Hershl could not utter, but the little girl's flaming red hair lives on in the memory of the handful of Klobuck survivors. A testimony lodged with the Yad Vashem museum in Jerusalem in 1953 reveals the little girl's name was Frumet.

Together, the Szperling family operated a small livestock business in the summer, buying cattle from the countryside and selling it at various local markets. They also had a piece of land, acquired years earlier by Hershl's grandfather, for grazing cattle and horses. Icchak simultaneously ran a tailor's business and the family worked together repairing garments during the winter. They were not rich, but neither were they poor. In those days and in that place, they were considered well-off, at least compared with most of the other Jews in the town.

I followed another muddy pathway that bent to the left and back up the slope toward the town square. This little road had once been called Shul Street and it was where all the shtetl's religious institutions were found. There were ritual baths, Hebrew schools, and the little study-houses of the Hassidim. At the square, facing the church, an old stone wall joined a wooden fence, behind which was more empty ground. This was the site of the synagogue. Strange, I thought, that nothing had been built on the land. Perhaps the people of Klobuck were superstitious. An icy wind blew, and I bent down and looked through a gap between the planks on the fence. I imagined I saw a group of Jewish children, among them young Hershl, maybe seven or eight years old, running down the steps inside the synagogue. Hershl, trained for his Bar Mitzvah and a life of religious observance at the synagogue's school, knew that worshippers must enter the shul by descending a few steps to symbolically recall Psalm 1:30 – 'Out of the depths have I cried unto thee, O Lord.' How appropriate this quote was to Hershl's life. Hershl's community was deeply religious.

Hershl should have celebrated his Bar Mitzvah here, on this empty ground now covered with weeds and litter. More likely it was conducted secretly. On Passover, Klobuckers liked to say: 'It's not so much the seder, but the matzoh ball.' There was also communal mourning. Elie Erlich, a young man who had emigrated to Palestine a year earlier, joined the International Brigade during the Spanish Civil War and fell at the Battle of Estramadura on 16 February 1938, along with 100 other volunteers of the brigade's Jewish company, fighting against the rising tide of Fascism in Europe.

Yet Klobuck was an idyllic place for children. Little woods and meadows surrounded the town. Hershl ran in those meadows with the rest of the shtetl children to gather greenery for Shavuot. During the festival of Lag b'Omer, synagogue teachers brought their students here, where Hershl and the other children fought battles with wooden swords, one class against another. On summer evenings, the banks of the lake were crowded with young people. At the end of the summer, Jewish fish merchants rented the lake, let out the water and harvested the fish. It was here, too, that in the autumn, before the seven-day Succot festival, Hershl gathered willow-branches for the annual construction of the Sukkah, the Hebrew word meaning booth, reminiscent of the huts in which the ancient Israelites dwelt during their 40 years of wandering in the desert after the Exodus from Egypt.

Rebecca Bernstein, an old woman in Canada with whom I had been in contact before coming, told me during a telephone conversation a few weeks earlier how as a child she had lived next door to the Szperlings in one of two large buildings in the shtetl. She also remembered Gitel Szperling as a 'very tall and distinguished woman'; but she did not want to discuss Hershl. The Yizkor book of Klobuck records twenty Szperlings as household family heads in the town. Nearly all of them perished. Most of the Szperlings throughout the world today are the descendants of those who left Klobuck for Israel before the war. They had been part of the Hashomer Hatzair training kibbutz at Zarki, close to the city of Częstochowa, and attendance at the centre was a source of pride for many Jews in southern Poland. Surviving records list numerous Szperlings at Hashomer Hatzair, the purpose of which was to prepare Jewish youth for life in Israel. Emigration to Israel was the aspiration of almost every young Jewish man and woman in Klobuck, and Hershl was no exception. His plans to train at Zarki and make a pioneer's life in Israel were soon to be obliterated by the German onslaught.

Life for Klobuck's Jews changed drastically after Pilsudski's death in 1935. In the political battle to fill the power vacuum, a wave of anti-Jewish pogroms washed across the country, encouraged by Poland's new nationalist government amid an economic depression and the alarming events that were unfolding in Germany. Violent gangs called Endeks, supporters of the right-wing, pro-Catholic, anti-Semitic National Democrat Party, attacked Jews throughout Poland. Klobuck was not spared; abuse of Jewish children in schools became commonplace in the town. Polish high-school students, influenced by the Endeks, forced Jewish students to stand during Catholic religious lessons. The teachers, even those who were not anti-Semites, were often afraid to intervene. Years later, Hershl recalled the childhood terror and humiliation of attending the school in Klobuck. Bullies lay in wait for Jewish children with rocks in their hands. In the classroom, only Polish children were permitted to occupy the first rows of seats; the back was reserved for Jews.

Sundays were particularly violent, as were Catholic festivals. Endeks gathered outside the church on Jewish holidays and rampaged through the streets of the shtetl, shattering windows and stoning Jews. A passage in the Yizkor book tells of Klobuck's Endek leader, a lame man named Meyer, who was an employee at the Jewish-owned mill. The Jewish community ended up bribing him to leave the town, which he did, but he returned when the Nazis arrived and became a collaborator. Then, turning the screw tighter, the nationalists declared an economic boycott of Jewish goods. Pickets were stationed at Jewish shops and at traders' stalls on market days. The shtetl economy was in collapse and poverty was the norm.

My head began to spin; I realised I was hungry. It was already 4.00pm, and I had eaten almost nothing since breakfast. I walked across the square and into a restaurant, on what had been the Christian-Polish side of town. I sat down and ordered a pizza – all that was on the menu – and a beer. I was served by a teenage boy with good English. He told me how every summer the young people of the town would swim in a small, nearby river. It was the river where Hershl had learned to swim, and I thought about him floating face down in the River Clyde in faraway Scotland. The teenager told me his ambition was to travel in America. He said he wanted to meet people of different nationalities and different faiths, and I thought that there was hope for this town, this country. It also felt better to be off my feet, and my head began to clear with the first bite of warm food. But something was out of place in my mind, and I decided to call Rebecca Bernstein in Canada. It was morning in Winnipeg and she would surely be awake by now.

'Rebecca,' I said, 'I'm in Klobuck.'

'You're in Klobutsk?' she asked, using the Yiddish name for the town.

'Yes, I'm in Klobutsk.'

'You're crazy,' she said.

'Maybe,' I said. 'Rebecca, I need to know something about Hershl in Klobuck. I need to know what it was like to live next door to him when he was a child. I also need to know what happened here, and what happened to Hershl.'

I could hear her breathing and gathering herself to speak. At last, she said: 'I used to call him Hershele. It was a special name for the nicest and kindest little boy you could imagine. I was eleven and I think he was a year older. I really loved him you know, but there was another girl that lived across the street he liked better than me. But we were all friends, all the children from that corner of the shtetl, and we all used to swim together and play together. It was a wonderful time. Then the Germans came and everything changed.'

EUROPE 1939

By 1939, the map of Europe was already changing as a consequence of German opportunism and aggression. In 1936, Hitler moved troops unopposed into the demilitarized zone of the Rhineland, directly contravening the Treaty of Versailles. Neither France nor Britain took action against him. Although the Rhineland had been intended as a buffer zone between France and Germany, the French were clearly unwilling to fight for it. Emboldened, Hitler now turned his gaze east.

In 1938, the dictator annexed Austria, whose prime minister was soon assassinated. That same year, the Munich Conference gave Hitler Sudetenland, under the pretext of alleged privations suffered by ethnic Germans. The region now became the new protectorate of Bohemia-Moravia, and British Prime Minister Neville Chamberlain declared: "We have peace in our time." The remainder of Czechoslovakia, powerless to resist, fell to Germany on 21 September, 1938.

Less than one year later, on 1 September, 1939, Germany invaded Poland and the Second World War began.

'I'm sorry,' I said.

'It's not your fault,' she snapped. 'The Jews from Klobuck, those of us who survived, we all used to meet every year in Florida. Every year, I used to ask about Hershele, if he was here, what happened to him. We'd heard that he survived, but we didn't know where he was. Every year, I used to look for him, hoping that one time he would come, but he didn't.'

She asked if Hershl had grandchildren. I had to tell her Hershl's two sons were also haunted by the terror of the Holocaust. 'You never know, but I don't think there will be any grandchildren. I can't speak for them, but I don't think either of them want to bring children into a world where they will suffer like they did.'

'That's the real tragedy. I have a beautiful grandson, who is already 28. But Hershele was in Treblinka. That explains it. All those people went there to die and he had to watch it. My parents died in Treblinka, but I was taken to a work camp near Klobuck, and I survived. My parents ran away from the ghetto in Klobuck to Częstochowa, where we had relatives. But then the Częstochowa ghetto was liquidated. I haven't even got any pictures. I'm 80 now and I can't remember my mother's face anymore. But I do remember my little Hershele. He was such a wonderful little boy, always so kind. I could never forget him.'

★ ★ ★

In 1939, Klobuck lay just twelve miles from Germany. Hitler's rise to power, nourished by his racial ideology, focused at first on the country's deep sense of humiliation after its defeat in World War I and lingering resentment over the loss of the former German territories of Prussia and the city of Danzig. The Jews were blamed, in typically brutal language, for everything from the defeat in 1918 and the subsequent economic hardship, to rising inflation and even prostitution. Hitler demanded that the German people take up the 'harsh racial struggle' against the Jews. Germany could only become great again if the Jewish people were removed. But he did not just mean the Jews in Germany. His plans called for the annihilation of Jews everywhere. By attacking Poland, he could stake his claim to Prussia and at the same time launch a massive strike in a secondary war against the Jews in their largest community in Europe.

It began bizarrely, late in the evening of 31 August 1939, in the German border town of Gleiwitz, some 80 miles south of Klobuck. A small group of German operatives entered the town and, at gunpoint, seized control of the local radio station. They proceeded to broadcast in Polish a message urging the residents of Gleiwitz to rise up against Germany.

As part of the ruse, they brought along an ethnic German named Franciszek Honiok, who had been arrested the previous day as a Polish sympathiser, and murdered him with a lethal injection. Then they dumped his body outside the station and fired gunshots into it to make it look as though Honiok had been killed during an attempt to overrun the station. The idea was to make Germany look like a victim of Polish aggression. Honiok's was the first death of World War II.

GERMAN INVASION OF POLAND 1939

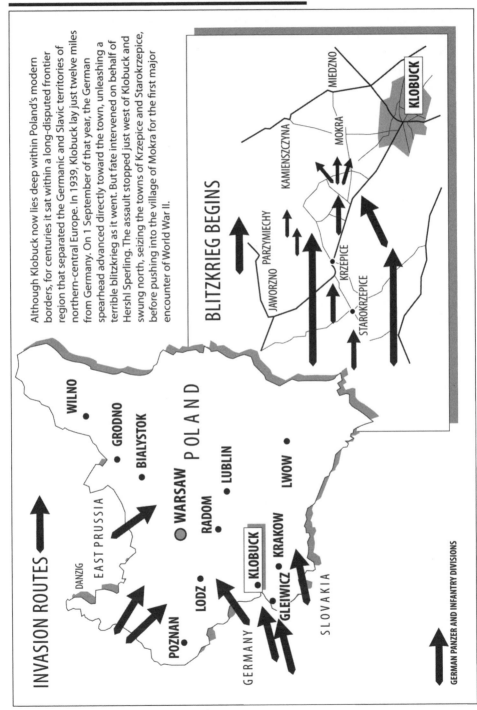

Although Klobuck now lies deep within Poland's modern borders, for centuries it sat within a long-disputed frontier region that separated the Germanic and Slavic territories of northern-central Europe. In 1939, Klobuck lay just twelve miles from Germany. On 1 September of that year, the German spearhead advanced directly toward the town, unleashing a terrible blitzkrieg as it went. But fate intervened on behalf of Hershl Sperling. The assault stopped just west of Klobuck and swung north, seizing the towns of Krzepice and Starokrzepice, before pushing into the village of Mokra for the first major encounter of World War II.

BLITZKRIEG BEGINS

KLOBUCK

MIEDZNO

MOKRA

KAMIENSZCZYNA

PARZYMIECHY

JAWORZNO

KRZEPICE

STAROKRZEPICE

INVASION ROUTES

WILNO

GRODNO

BIALYSTOK

WARSAW

P O L A N D

LUBLIN

RADOM

LWOW

DANZIG

EAST PRUSSIA

KLOBUCK

LODZ

KRAKOW

GLEIWICZ

POZNAN

GERMANY

SLOVAKIA

GERMAN PANZER AND INFANTRY DIVISIONS

The fact that he had been killed by lethal injection was ominous. The order for the Gleiwitz attack came from Reinhard Heydrich, head of the *Sicherheitsdienst*, or SD, the Reich's intelligence service. Heydrich had taken a special interest in the Nazi's euthanasia program. The headquarters were at Tiergartenstrasse 4, in Berlin, thus the codename T4. Under this initiative, some 80,000–100,000 Germans – physically and mentally disabled children and adults – were secretly killed by lethal injections or in gassing installations designed to look like showers. It was a vile foretaste of what was to come. Less than two years later, Heydrich would present the plans for the gassing of almost two million Jews in the death camps of Sobibor, Belzec and Treblinka. That murderous scheme was later named Operation Reinhard in Heydrich's honour. Hershl had called them 'Reinhard's camps'.

At exactly 4.00am the following day, the German battleship *Schleswig-Holstein* slipped its moorings in Danzig harbour and shelled a Polish transit base on Westerplatt. The war had begun. In the south, Klobuck found itself in the unfortunate strategic position of sitting directly in the path of the German Eighth and Tenth Armies and the Fourth Panzer Division. An hour later, these forces crossed into Polish territory.

News of the advance crackled by radio through the shtetl and the rest of Klobuck. The town went into a panic. Those Jews who had not yet heard about the German invasion were awakened by noisy crowds in the street. Icchak and Gitel Szperling had switched on their wireless early, as was their habit, and a sense of dread descended almost instantly. If they looked from their upstairs window, they saw a steady stream of citizens fleeing eastward out of the town. Against the advice of his wife, Icchak went out to make ready their horse and cart. Gitel woke Hershl and he in turn would have been instructed to wake Frumet. He was twelve and his sister was six. They dressed quickly and he helped her gather a few belongings. If Hershl looked from the window, he would have seen men from the Polish National Guard breaking into Jewish homes and shops, and looting them. It was not yet 8.00am, and some of the soldiers were already lying drunk in the gutter with their long French rifles at their sides. It was clear there would be little resistance to the Germans, at least in Klobuck. Icchak now returned. Their horse and wagon had already been stolen. They would have to flee on foot with the rest of the town. War had broken out, Icchak explained to his children, and because they lived close to the border, everyone in Klobuck would have to leave their homes.

The German spearhead advanced swiftly and directly toward Klobuck, unleashing a terrible blitzkrieg as it went. This was Hitler's new devastating style of warfare, based on speed, shock and ferocity. It began with the frightening wail of the Stuka dive bombers, fitted with sirens and whistles for additional terror, which struck at rail and road lines without respite, often in the middle of villages, towns and cities. They machine-gunned the fleeing population. Then, wave after wave of tanks and artillery fire pushed forward, pounding everything in their path.

Fate now intervened on behalf of Hershl Sperling, not for the last time. The assault force stopped just west of Klobuck and swung quickly north, seizing the towns of Krzepice and Starokrzepice, before pushing into the village of Mokra. Word came to the German command from the motorcycle reconnaissance squads of the Fourth

Panzer Division that Polish strongholds had been sighted near Mokra. And so began the Battle of Mokra, the first major encounter of World War II.

Every Jew in Klobuck, as well as hundreds of Poles, fled east, away from the battle. In the distance, they could see the Stukas dive-bombing Mokra, less than five miles away, and they could hear the wailing sirens and the anti-aircraft fire. As the Szperlings left town with the column of fleeing refugees, a Polish soldier with a torn jacket and a bloodied shoulder passed them on a motorcycle going back to Klobuck. Two Stukas flew above them and dove low, causing alarm among the escaping population, many of whom lay prostrate as the aircraft screamed overhead.

The ten-hour battle, which eventually dissolved into a series of disjointed skirmishes between a 15,000-strong Panzer division and a few Polish cavalry platoons in and around the burning, smoke-filled village of Mokra, ended after two Polish armoured trains arrived and attacked the tanks from behind. Through the confusion of the smoke, the Panzers several times fired on their own positions, instigating a retreat. This rare German defeat lives on today in the Polish national memory with much pride. However, Polish military tacticians decided, because of heavy casualties, to withdraw to a second line of defence. The main purpose of the resistance had been merely to buy time to allow the Polish reserve army to mobilise. Mokra had been defended in vain. The Wehrmacht now readied itself to crash through the defence armies of Lodz and Krakow, cross the Warta River and surround the Polish forces on the western frontier, thus clearing the road to Warsaw. That evening, German tanks pushed into Klobuck, which was now defenceless and almost empty.

Meanwhile, in a field, just ten miles east of their town, 3,000 people stopped exhausted after a full day of walking. Most of them had come from Klobuck, but others had joined the flight en route from nearby villages. There were old and young, Jews and Poles. Only the *Volksdeutsche*, the ethnic Germans who had been settled in Poland generations ago, and the old and infirm stayed behind. It was a Friday night and as twilight descended, the Jews said their Sabbath prayers, Icchak, Gitel, Hershl and Frumet Szperling among them. The Christians also prayed for God to have pity on their children and their town. Then they ate the food they had carried with them and went to sleep beneath the dark sky.

★ ★ ★

I found Jerzy, my taxi driver, in a dark underground bar on the opposite side of the square, as planned. He was sitting by the door with a small glass of beer before him, eyeing black-clad waitresses who squeezed between the tiny tables with trays of vodka shots and sandwiches. He waved as I entered. This was obviously the place where Klobuck's wastrels hung out.

'We go?' he asked. 'Częstochowa?'

Back in the taxi, I asked to look at Jerzy's map. I studied it and instructed him to drive north, even though Częstochowa lay to the south. I did not mention that it was obvious from the map that he had taken a great arching detour to arrive at Klobuck via Krzepice earlier in the day. I wasn't angry because it had clearly been made for my benefit and the ruined Krzepice synagogue was obviously a tourist site for visiting Jews. Now I wanted to return for a closer look. Jerzy held up his finger and then carefully wrote the extra charge on a small yellow notepad that was attached to his dashboard beneath the icon of the Madonna. I agreed, and in ten minutes we were back in Krzepice.

The ruined synagogue and a few old, stone-built homes lay a couple of miles beyond the town, close to the banks of the Listwarta River. It seemed a strange place to build what had obviously once been an ornate and elaborate construction, but I supposed the Jews of Krzepice must have lived here on the outskirts of town. The concrete had broken off to reveal the bare red brick, and four columns stood at the entranceway beneath a large semi-circular window and an ornate Star of David carved into a plaster tablet above the doorway. The round paving stones that led to the door must have once made a pretty courtyard in front of the building. The roof had long-since collapsed. It was a tragic sight.

'Please, wait,' said Jerzy, in French. 'I come back.' He walked over to the row of cottages beside the synagogue and moments later returned with an old man and his small yapping dog. 'We can go in now,' he added, introducing the man as Mr Ciesla and saying he was 90 years old. It seemed strange that we had to ask this old Polish man for permission to enter the synagogue. I regarded him with suspicion. We followed him into the ruins of the building. Mr Ciesla spoke in Polish and Jerzy translated into pidgin French. He told me that Jews had lived in Krzepice since the early seventeenth century and that this synagogue had been built some time in the early eighteenth century. His son had studied the town's history, he told us. The synagogue's floor was gone. Grass, weeds and earth covered the ground within the walls. I could see the enclave in the far wall where the ark of the Torah had once rested, and rows of arched window frames on either side of it. This had obviously been a magnificent structure before the Nazis came.

I asked Mr Ciesla if he knew what had happened here, and a look of sadness instantly fell across his face. It was hard to tell whether it was affected or genuine. His dog scrambled through the bushes and the tall grass.

'I was here when it happened,' he said. 'I've lived in that house next door all my life.' He spoke matter-of-factly. 'The Germans rounded up about 100 Jews when they first came here just after dawn in 1939, and forced them all inside the synagogue. Then they sprayed everyone with machine-guns.' He made the rat-tat-tat sound of machine-gun fire. He continued: 'Then they locked the door and set fire to the building. Everyone who was alive was screaming. Everyone was killed.' Then he shrugged, but I could see there was emotion in his eyes. He spoke to Jerzy in Polish.

'He wants to take us somewhere,' Jerzy translated. 'It's ok, we go.' We got into his taxi and drove along a dirt track at the side of a muddy field. We stopped at the edge of a small wood and got out, following Mr Ciesla. 'Come, come,' Jerzy said, beckoning me. We came to a clearing on the other side of the wood. There, amid the tall, unkempt grass and weeds, stood crooked grave stones, most of them broken and chipped. There were also cast-iron tombstones. The passage of time had rendered most of the Hebrew inscriptions indecipherable, but on one I could read – Yaakov, son of Yitzhak, and the date 5559, the year 1799. I could also see the carvings of candles used for women and the stars of David for men, and another with the motif of a broken branch, signifying a child. These were the lucky ones, I scribbled in my notebook. They had lived and died naturally in their own community, long before the Nazi onslaught.

We dropped Mr Ciesla and his dog back at the cottage. I called, 'Dziynkuja – thank you' to him from the car, and he waved his arm without turning back as he headed into his house. Jerzy gunned the engine and took off.

'Now Częstochowa?' he asked, clapping his hands together before touching his Madonna and placing them back on the steering wheel.

'First, back to Klobuck,' I said. 'I want to take the east road out of Klobuck. Then Częstochowa.' He nodded, rubbed his hands together and swung back to Hershl's village.

I took one last look at Klobuck as we drove around the market square and headed east. We passed through the villages of Lobodno and Ostrowy. It was unlikely that the mass of fleeing refugees would have made it beyond this point. Just past Ostrowy, I asked Jerzy to pull over. It would be twilight soon, and I got out the car and looked across the snow-speckled field. The sky was grey and heavy with broken clouds. It was winter, but I tried to imagine what it was like in this field on that late summer's morning in 1939. I knew what had happened here from what I had been told by Rebecca Bernstein and her cousin, Rubin Sztajer, the then thirteen-year-old son of the town's Mikvah keeper.

On Saturday morning, the refugees were still making preparations to continue their flight when a tank appeared behind them. Rubin, who now lives in Baltimore, wrote to me: 'I had never left home before, and I didn't know the difference between a Polish soldier and a German soldier. They told us we were liberated. We turned and marched home, but before we reached our village we were stopped, Jews and Christians alike. They immediately separated the Jews from the Christians, who were allowed to go home.'

The Jews were detained and spent another night in an open field. They waited in fear. Few slept. Germans guards surrounded them. Jews with beards and sidelocks bound their faces in cloth to hide their appearance, in the hope they would look as though they had a toothache. A rumour spread through the group that they were going to be shot. Others consoled themselves with the belief that they would be sent to a detention camp. Early the next morning, Sunday 3 September, Britain and France declared war on Germany, but it was of little consequence to the Jews of Klobuck, or anywhere else in Europe for that matter. A German officer addressed the Jewish refugees in the field. They were told they could return to their homes. On that same day, SS chief Heinrich Himmler gave the order for the army to kill anyone it deemed necessary in 'the combating of all anti-German elements in hostile country'.

The Jews were marched back toward Klobuck. It was now almost nightfall. They had walked for another full day. They were exhausted. I imagined Frumet crying, and Hershl picking her up. About three miles outside of town, the road divided near a small woodland. Hershl and his family, along with Rubin Sztajer, Rebecca Bernstein, and the majority of the Jews of the shtetl took the right fork to their homes. As they moved through the streets, they saw their homes had been looted and burned. No window was left unbroken.

Those who took the left fork – some 270 men, women and children – were driven towards the dark forest. There, they were given shovels and told to dig a large pit. They were then machine-gunned to death by troops into the mass grave. No Jew survived to recount precisely what happened in those woods. News of this bloody incident spread quickly through the shtetl.

The next morning, Monday 4 September, all Jews in Klobuck were ordered to gather in the courtyard outside the synagogue. Soldiers broke down doors. Some of the Jews were seen running from houses with their hands on their heads. Many were dragged out and beaten. Others were taken away, never to be seen again.

The Jews in the courtyard were commanded to go into the synagogue and bring out all the prayer books and Torahs. The Germans poured gasoline on the books and scrolls and torched them before the assembled shtetl inhabitants. Then the synagogue, the epicentre of Jewish life in Klobuck, was set ablaze, along with what remained of its holy books and the shtetl's historical records, some going back hundreds of years.

'You can't imagine what that was like,' Rubin told me, when I visited him months later. I saw anger and despair in his eyes as he remembered the incident.

This day also marked the beginning of oppression for the Jews in Klobuck. Rubin Sztajer recalled: 'We were told to come to the centre of town each day to read the new laws for Jews only. Not what we can do, but only what we cannot do.' All bicycles, radios, razors and cameras had to be handed over to the German authorities, as were all fur coats, gold, silver and jewellery. Every few days, new regulations were posted, insisting Jews relinquish everything from brass doorknobs, candlesticks and copper pans to lead and tin. If any of these items were discovered in the possession of Jews, the eldest member of the household was shot. Some were taken away to labour camps; others were put to work in the town itself, where they were forced to clear rubble, carry heavy loads, chop forests, and scrub toilets with prayer shawls. Some were harnessed to wagons and made to pull them like horses. All the while, they were mocked and beaten. Some elderly Jews in these work-groups had their beards ripped from their faces. Others were stripped and forced to work naked, while being prodded with bayonets. The object was not just to make these Jews work, but also to humiliate them, often in bizarre and perverse ways. A group who worked at the Klobuck mill were forced to conduct a mock Jewish funeral for a dead dog.

The war continued. The German Army thrust its way across the country, village by village, town by town and city by city, with the Polish Army in hasty retreat. By the third week in September, the Germans butted up against the western bank of the Vistula River, the land beyond which had already been occupied by Soviet troops as part of the Nazi-Soviet Non-Aggression Pact the previous month. Warsaw was now surrounded on three sides by Germans and faced the Soviets across the river. On the morning of 26 September General Von Brauchitich ordered the German Eighth Army to attack. The next day, at 2.00pm, Warsaw surrendered.

In the first 55 days of the German conquest of western and central Poland, more than 5,000 Jews were murdered. These were not soldiers or resistance fighters, but terrified families in their homes, the first Polish victims of Hitler's other war – his war against the Jews of Europe.

During the early autumn of 1940, Klobuck's Jews were instructed via posters in the market square to leave their homes and move into an area the Germans called the ghetto. European Jews had not lived in ghettos since medieval times. Rubin recalled: 'It was the biggest slum area they could find. Each family was assigned a so-called living quarters. We had no mode of transportation, not even a horse and cart, so we took whatever we could carry.'

However, the Szperlings decided that their chances of survival were greater outside Klobuck, which had now been annexed into Greater Germany. In the middle of the night, the Szperlings slipped away through the dark, silent streets, in spite of the 6.00pm curfew. They entered the woods at the outskirts of town and walked the ten miles until they reached the new border that crossed into the so-called General Government of Occupied Poland and on to the city of Częstochowa, where the number of Jews was far greater and, according to their reasoning, safer.

Like the Szperlings, Jerzy and I arrived in Częstochowa long after dark. I felt a terrible, heavy dread come over me, in the relative safety of a taxi in democratic, free Poland.

CHAPTER FIVE

CZĘSTOCHOWA

Hershl and his family arrived on the outskirts of Częstochowa – or Czenstochow in Yiddish – before dawn on one of the first days of October 1940. Hershl was thirteen years old. The Szperlings had not dared to travel on roads, especially during daylight, because German patrols and Polish anti-Semites were everywhere. Instead, they fled across the rutted fields and through woods under the cover of night. It was a desperate journey for a mother, father and two children to walk ten miles with murderers and informants at every turn. They were killing Jews everywhere. At times, the Szperlings took refuge in the barns of peasants, where they rested briefly and ate the food Gitel had prepared and carried with her. It was harvest time, and the fields and barns were piled high with hay in the moonlight. Little Frumet was often too exhausted to walk and the three took turns to carry her. In this way, they struggled on towards Częstochowa. The details of their arrival in the city are not known, but it is reasonable to assume that the Szperlings, like many others, had bribed a peasant to hide them in his hay wagon and to smuggle them into the city. Often, and in spite of the prohibition, limited assistance was offered at a price. A second transaction must also have occurred to smuggle them behind the walls of the ghetto, otherwise entry would have been impossible – because the gates were locked between dusk and dawn and the ghetto was guarded at all times.

On the eve of World War II, this former Russian frontier garrison was a sophisticated, industrial city and home to 30,000 Jews, one third of the entire population. There was a thriving Jewish culture here, with roots stretching back hundreds of years. In the mid-nineteenth century Częstochowa became a major industrial centre for steel fabrication, and the manufacture of textiles, toys and Catholic devotional articles connected to the Black Madonna and the Jasna Góra Monastery. Jews were at the centre of this economic boom, and by 1939 they owned around 80 per cent of the city's industry and commerce. The bulk of the remaining businesses – mainly the largest of the city's factories – were owned by French and Belgian industrialists, whose profits flowed out of Poland into western Europe. The broad, tree-lined boulevards and neo-classical buildings the traveller sees here today in Częstochowa are the result of generations of Jewish enterprise. Jews owned almost all of the city's small and medium-sized businesses. A large painting in the dining room of the shabby hotel in which I spent a night there depicted a Thursday market in 1919. It was a scene vibrant with the clamour of peasants, the well-to-do, Jewish factory workers and animals – goats, cows, horses and chickens – thronging amid a chaos of covered stalls and Jewish traders, many bearded and attired in the long black coats and wide-brimmed fur hats of the Hassidim. Close inspection revealed the market stalls of many of the traditional Jewish trades – tailor, furrier, cap-maker, shoemaker, butcher and baker. In the *Częstochowa Yidn* memorial book, written in the desolate years immediately after the end of the war, the reader can detect an extraordinary pride in being a Częstochower Jew, and a sense of being part of the great historical, national and cultural consciousness of Jewish people all over the world. But with the increasing Jewish participation in the city's economic life came increased anti-Semitism. I knew that in the same year illustrated in the painting, 1919, a pogrom causing many Jewish deaths had occurred in Częstochowa. It was an ominous, 20-year-old prelude.

This was a city the Szperlings knew well. Hershl and his family often drove their cattle and horses to the Thursday market there, along with hundreds of other Jewish traders from the surrounding villages. Sometimes Icchak came alone with the animals, or Hershl was brought along to help his father. At other times, Gitel and Frumet joined them, making use of the opportunity to visit relatives. Census records reveal that many Szperlings and Goldbergs, Gitel's maiden name, lived in Częstochowa at this time. The market was held each Thursday for good reason – so Jews, who made up the majority of the traders, could prepare for the Sabbath the following day. Icchak's customers were the horse traders and the kosher butchers who bought directly from him at the market, which had its own kosher slaughtering house. Gitel often purchased the family's Sabbath supplies there and returned laden in the late afternoon to Klobuck. Only when market days fell during Catholic festivals was caution required. Business boomed with the influx of pilgrims from every part of Poland, who had come to gaze upon the Black Madonna; but with them also came the fanatics who, encouraged by liberal quantities of vodka and the demonising sermons of priests, launched arbitrary attacks on Jews.

All the old rhythms of life were crushed by the German invader. Surviving Częstochower Rafael Mahler, writing in the Foreword of the *Częstochowa Yidn* memorial book, remarked, 'The disaster of the Częstochower Jews is as deep as the ocean … our book, *Częstochowa Yidn*, was not conceived as a headstone at the cemetery of Jewish Czenstochow, but as a Book of Life … The neighbourhood of Czenstochow that Jews built and inhabited is now either utterly ruined or settled by non-Jews.'

Thirteen months before the Szperlings arrived here, on 4 September 1939, as the massacre of innocents proceeded on the left fork outside Klobuck, another episode of violence and murder occurred just as dawn broke. Some 300 Jews were murdered in what became known as Bloody Monday. The murders were accompanied by countless beatings and the destruction and looting of thousands of homes. Groups of terrified residents, both Poles and Jews, were forced through the streets at rifle point. Some were herded into trucks. Numerous witnesses have testified to seeing victims savagely kicked, beaten with rifle butts and stabbed with bayonets. Others were forced to stand for hours in the burning sun at gunpoint with their hands in the air. Still others were lined against walls and fences and summarily executed. The testimonies of residents recall many were still half-dressed as they were forced into the streets. The sound of gunfire from different parts of the city grew louder as the number of round-ups increased.

Elsewhere in Częstochowa, Jews were marched to trenches that had been dug as air raid shelters, were shot and fell into the pits. In the Jewish quarter of the city, near the Jasna Góra Monastery, homes were set on fire with whole families still inside. When inhabitants jumped from the windows, they were shot. Photographs held at the United States Holocaust Memorial Museum in Washington DC, taken from a photo album belonging to a member of a Wehrmacht machine-gunners' unit, record such atrocities. One such photograph shows German soldiers standing guard on a street in Częstochowa. In front of them the bodies of Jewish men are lined up on the pavement. There is a smirk on the face of one of the soldiers. The purpose of the Nazi action that day was to terrorise, degrade and subjugate.

This was just the beginning. Over the next 72 hours, hundreds more Jews were brutalised and murdered. Witnesses have testified that many Poles watched approvingly and, as in Klobuck, often acted as spotters for German soldiers who picked off Jews with rifle shots as they fled through the streets. Accounts of *Judenjagd*, or 'Jew hunts', detail how Poles and *Volksdeutsche* pitched in to find stray Jews the Germans had missed. On 14 September the German administration issued Order Number Seven, which transferred all Jewish industrial and commercial enterprises into 'Aryan' hands. In December, it became compulsory for Jews to wear the yellow star on their clothing.

Then the kidnappings began. Over the next few weeks, more than 1,000 Jewish men between the ages of 18 and 25 were taken from the streets and sent to the Ciechanow forced-labour camp in the Lublin district to construct the 'Otto Line' of anti-tank ditches and artillery dugouts that would mark the German frontier with the Soviet Union. The conditions were brutal and the work gruelling. Only a handful of these young men survived. On 24 December yet another orgy of violence was unleashed. Instigated by the Germans, gangs of Częstochowan Poles, as well as collaborators from other areas, rampaged through the streets and set fire to the city's Great Synagogue and the New Synagogue, burning scrolls and an enormous library of Jewish books. The sight of the flames set off further mob violence. More Jews were beaten. More homes were looted and destroyed. The following month, a number of Jewish women and young girls were raped by SS guards in the city's New Market Place, in spite of Hitler's prohibition against 'racial defilement'.

The ghetto was established on 9 April 1940 by order of the city commissioner, *SS-Brigadeführer* Richard Wendler, in the eastern, old part of Częstochowa, and it was sealed off on 23 August. This was the place the Szperlings arrived at early that morning in October 1940. The world that Hershl observed on that first day in the ghetto was miserable, overcrowded and impoverished. A population of more than 30,000 souls had been squeezed into a squalid slum, barely fit for a population a quarter of that size.

They moved into a tiny apartment, probably with relatives, crammed in with several other families, on Wilsona Street, near the ghetto wall. I discovered their address in German ghetto records, where Icchak's profession was listed as a plumber, although this may signify that he was employed in the city's waterworks. There was little need within the confines of the ghetto walls for a tailor and livestock trader. They tried to maintain normality, in spite of the miserable conditions, and attempted to make ends meet. Schools were forbidden on penalty of death, although many parents organised classes for small groups of children to meet in different houses each week. This was their first resistance, the education of their children.

Clothing had to be constantly searched for lice, the carriers of typhus. There was rampant inflation on the black market in basic foodstuffs. Hershl watched, day-by-day, as the winter grew fiercer and conditions became more dire. The number of orphans and beggars increased by the week. Many Jews now wandered the ghetto with their feet bound in rags and their toes black with gangrene and frostbite. Soon, corpses lay neglected on every street. Dogs tugged at dismembered limbs, and crows pecked at the flesh of bodies not yet picked up by the special patrols of undertakers who toured the ghetto with their handcarts.

The impression this made on young Hershl's mind was lasting, yet so too was the courage he witnessed and the human dignity to which the deprived aspired. In spite of the daily struggle for survival, as well as the knowledge that any attempt at armed rebellion was futile and could only result in mass reprisals costing many Jewish lives, resistance groups organised clandestinely. We can be certain that Hershl witnessed many of these events – and that his courage in the months and years ahead remains beyond question.

The first act of rebellion in Częstochowa, however, was directed not against the Nazi masters, but against the *Judenrat*, the Gestapo-appointed Jewish Council of Elders, whose members were widely regarded by the people of the ghetto as puppets and collaborators. Their role was the enforcement of rules and regulations in the ghetto. Initially the *Judenrat* was welcomed because the kidnappings stopped and the Jews were given at least a modicum of self-government. But as time went on, the line between cooperation and collaboration blurred. In spite of the criticism that has been levelled at the *Judenrat*, it needs to be said that there were few alternatives available to these individuals. The Częstochowa *Judenrat* was regularly ordered to provide the Nazis with slave labour from the ghetto and tribute in the form of money and even foodstuffs from the starving population. Its members either obeyed or there would be murderous reprisals against the people of the ghetto.

Nonetheless, in December 1941, Hershl watched as more than 1,000 Jewish workers, his father likely among them, marched in anger after an impromptu meeting in the Maccabee auditorium to the offices of the *Judenrat*. These were the slave labourers from the Częstochowa waterworks, the railroads, and the forced-labour factories that supported the German war effort, all of this conducted under the lash of the Gestapo whip. They were tired and half-frozen from the biting cold. On their feet were wooden shoes. Paper-thin clothes covered their bodies. Their coats were torn rags. They had come to threaten a work stoppage and a hunger strike unless there was an increase to the bread rations and the minimum wage from 20 to 30 zlotys a week. There were also allegations that the *Judenrat* had skimmed food from the allocation and were distributing it at their own discretion. Members of the *Judenrat* now watched in alarm from a window on the second floor. In spite of the presence of the Jewish police force, the crowd tore off the entrance door and swept into the building.

At the door of Leon Kopinski, the *Judenrat's* president, one worker reportedly yelled: 'You want us to die from hunger. Give us the bread that we are owed for the work.' Then Kopinski's door was smashed. Kopinski relented fairly quickly. His leadership may have been self-serving and guilty of political cronyism, but he was no henchman. It was a small victory for the workers of the ghetto, but one that lifted morale enormously.

Six months later, the ghetto's population had increased to almost 50,000, after some 20,000 Jews from the surrounding area were forced in. This small, enclosed slum now heaved with the traumatised and the hungry. Food and water were scarce and sanitation became non-existent. Many Jews lived in mass lodgings known as 'death houses', because large numbers of the inhabitants died from disease and hunger. The establishment of these super ghettos was the brainchild of Reinhard Heydrich, and they were set up in every city as part of the plan to concentrate Jews near railway junctions for future deportation.

★ ★ ★

My hotel room in Częstochowa drew the cold and the damp of the night. This was possibly the shabbiest and most depressing place I had ever been. Somewhere beneath me, in the vast, high-ceilinged dining area, a two-man combo with a bass guitar and a cheap organ played a medley of monotonous tunes that vibrated continuously and irritatingly up through the floor. I couldn't wait to get out of there, but my train to Warsaw was not due to leave until 2.00pm the following day.

I decided I needed a hot shower, but instead stood freezing for a few moments beneath a rusty faucet-head that dribbled lukewarm water. The towel was the size of a dishrag and I dried myself hastily with a t-shirt before dressing quickly. I told myself this was nothing compared with what Hershl had gone through. But I was cold all the same, and I crawled into bed and pulled Hershl's pale green book out of the protective bubble-wrap in my backpack. I ran my fingers over the Hebrew characters and the title of his testament at the top of the first page. I deciphered the word 'Treblinka' out of the Hebrew at the top of the page, and something recoiled deep inside me. I suddenly felt terribly alone. The combo's bass guitar boomed upward and made the letters vibrate as I looked at them. I pulled the translation from my bag and began to re-read it.

Hershl's testimony began here, in the city of Częstochowa. There was no doubt about the historical veracity of his story. All the major events to which he referred and the people mentioned are confirmed by contemporary accounts and historical documentation. The central character of his story – himself – is neither rogue nor hero. He is simply an intelligent and bewildered young man, devastated by what he has witnessed and has been forced to endure, and also by the murder of his family. I could hear his voice clearly.

In September 1942, the deportation of the Jews of Czenstochow began … We had already sensed it coming for weeks. The town was surrounded by SS units. We were all woken from sleep before daybreak by the noise of wild shooting, vehicles, and people screaming and wailing.

I read that opening passage again and again, until I felt the terror in his words. I didn't want to be alone, so I telephoned Sam in London, but there was no reply. I pulled my notes from my backpack and looked back at what I had scribbled about Częstochowa and thought of our conversation the day after I had received the translation through the mail.

Sam said, 'I had no idea he had been in Częstochowa. Because he never spoke about it, we assumed he was taken straight from Klobuck to Treblinka.'

'He never mentioned Częstochowa at all?' I asked.

'Only that he had been there before the war – with his father, I think – and something about a monastery and the lunatics who came to pray at some Catholic icon there.' There was a pause. 'I'm trying to remember. I think his mother also had relatives in Częstochowa.'

'She did. I've found many Goldbergs in the old records of the city. There were a lot of Szperlings also.'

'Ah-ha,' said Sam.

'But I'm interested to know why he thought those people at Jasna Góra were lunatics? It's just a Catholic devotional site, where pilgrims come. There is a painting called the Black Madonna, supposedly made by Luke on a table top built by Jesus.'

'I guess he thought a lot of them were dangerous fanatics. A lot of them used to make trouble for the Jews during the Catholic holidays.'

'I see.'

'Have you found out anything else?'

'The ghetto made by the Germans was enormous in Częstochowa,' I told him. 'There were 45,000 people crammed into this little space, and the conditions were awful. There was a lot of starvation, and a lot of desperation and disease and death. There was resistance there, too, and a protest against the *Judenrat*. I think it's important to know these people weren't just victims. It's extraordinary to think of your father in the middle of all this, and he never even mentioned it.'

'There are a lot of things like that about my father.'

'Then there was the terror of the round-ups. Most of the people in the Częstochowa ghetto ended their lives in Treblinka gas chambers,' I told him. Sam groaned.

'He never mentioned that either.'

'He hid out in a bunker there until they found him,' I said, aware now that he was hearing this information for the first time. 'He even names the Nazi officer who led the round-up.'

'I had no idea,' he said, emotion beginning to strangle his words. 'He never said. It's odd, though, because when he spoke about the war and the camps, he often made out as if he were at the centre of things but we thought – well, we thought that was just the way he saw it because he was there. He said a lot of crazy things we didn't believe.'

'It looks like a lot of these crazy things were true,' I said.

'Yes, it does look that way.'

'You know, the more I learn about him and what he went through, it seems he really was at the centre of things. He experienced almost everything there was to experience as a Jew under Nazi rule, except death – although he certainly witnessed that. But he was there at the beginning, when the Wehrmacht first crossed into Poland. He saw the Stukas dive-bombing Polish positions during the Battle of Mokra. He lived through ghettos, round-ups, the death trains, an extermination camp, Auschwitz, the death marches to other concentration camps, and even liberation. I don't suppose there are many who did – or could – survive what he survived.'

Sam was silent for a moment. 'The important thing, though, is how that affected him.'

'I agree,' I said.

I got out of bed and looked from the window on to Pilsudskiego Street, where 65 years earlier tens of thousands of Jews were marched to the railway tracks and forced into the boxcars. Those who were old or did not move fast enough to satisfy the Germans' need for speed were murdered right there with bullets or were clubbed to death with rifle butts. Save a handful, the only Jews here today are ghosts, who are kept company, ironically, by the thousands of holy images seen everywhere of the most famous Jew of all. Jewish factories once produced these religious artifacts and souvenirs for the pilgrims of Częstochowa.

That night I dreamed I was on an old cobblestoned street. I assumed it was Poland. I was walking around dragging a very heavy package. Suddenly, Hershl was walking with me. I remember wondering what he felt about me and what I was doing. He was walking quickly, and I was having trouble keeping up with him because I was dragging this package. At last, we came to a pretty house with trees and a garden in front of it. It was the pink house I had seen in the Klobuck ghetto. At the side of the house, there were men digging a deep ditch, and as I drew closer I could see gravestones. One of them was mine. I woke suddenly, hardly able to catch my breath. I scribbled the dream in my notebook.

★ ★ ★

In June 1942, a Jewish fighting organisation, known as the ZOB (*Zydowska Organizacja Bojowa*), was established in the Częstochowa ghetto with the idea of mounting armed resistance against their Nazi oppressors. That same month, the *Judenrat* received an order to provide a precise plan of the ghetto with individual homes marked and named. Shortly afterwards, Jews were removed from a part of Kawia Street because there were pits to be dug for future victims. Homes located on Garibaldi Street were also emptied to make room for storehouses intended for plundered Jewish property.

The last stage in the preparations for genocide was played out the following month. The German authorities issued orders for a roll call, designated for 3.00pm, at which time all ghetto residents between the ages of fifteen and sixty were to assemble, including the *Judenrat* and Jewish police. Hershl was now fifteen, and so stayed behind with Frumet and watched the frenzied movement of people in the street below. They gathered and waited, surrounded by armed SS. Then they were sent home, unaware this was a dress rehearsal for liquidation. No-one believed the ghetto would be liquidated because everyone knew it was important to the war effort. The idea of extermination was unthinkable anyway – in spite of persistent rumours of mass murders in Lithuania and Latvia.

News of the killings at Chelmno, a pilot scheme extermination camp, also began to emerge. As early as January 1942, during the first weeks of its operation, two prisoners – Michael Podchlebnik and Yacov Griwanowski – escaped to the Warsaw ghetto and gave a detailed report to the Jewish underground there. News travelled frequently between Warsaw and Częstochowa. Their accounts were harrowing and desperate. Yet, still, it did not seem possible that so many men, women and children could be murdered. It was at this time that the name Treblinka began to enter the vocabulary of the ghetto. However, when in July and August 1942 a few Warsaw Jews escaped to Częstochowa and warned them about deportations to Treblinka, most of the inhabitants refused to believe it.

The Częstochowa ZOB, locally known as Fighting Group 66 because its leaders met at 66 Nadrzeczna Street, had enlisted around 300 fighters. They planned their first revolt on 22 September 1942. But the day before, on Yom Kippur, the holiest day of the Jewish calendar, the revolt was frustrated when a sudden *Aktion* barred access to the bunkers where their weapons had been hidden. During the night, SS and Ukrainian auxiliaries surrounded the ghetto and installed bright lamps on the streets. As soon as the lights were switched on, gunshots were fired. Panic broke out and the ghetto echoed with screams of '*Raus*' and '*Arbeitspass*'. Doors were smashed and Jews were dragged into the street. Hershl's testimony tells us that the sounds of wild shooting and people screaming filled the air. What lay ahead was twelve days of savage round-ups. Hershl tells us:

> On the day before the deportation, one loaf is distributed to each person for which they have to pay one zloty. This is a carefully worked out plan of the Germans. According to the number of zlotys, they will know the number of people and can estimate how many wagons they will need, and how many people should be loaded into each wagon.

SS Captain Paul Degenhardt, a Polish *Volksdeutche*, was the Gestapo official in charge of the operation. Degenhardt, who proclaimed himself the 'father of the Jews', was known to his fellow Nazis as the perfect organiser. It was said he had an ape-like face that provoked terror. In the early hours of the morning, Degenhardt summoned Leon Kopinski, the *Judenrat* president, and informed him an *Aktion* would soon begin and many ghetto inhabitants would be 'transported east' for agricultural work. In this first round-up, 7,000 Jews were to be deported.

As instructed by Degenhardt, Kopinski ordered the ghetto's 250 unarmed Jewish police units to muster at the metal factory at Krotka Street, where they were kept under guard, in spite of the fact that many had been the recipients of favoured treatment from the Germans as informants and aids. They were led by Shalom Gutman, the sadistic Jewish police commandant, who was despised for his collaboration and cruelty. Soon afterwards, at exactly 4.00am, several units of SS soldiers, Gestapo units and Ukrainian auxiliaries burst into the ghetto's illegal orphanage and the old people's home. All the residents were murdered.

Hershl looked from the window of his apartment into the brightly lit street, where he and his family were crammed in with a number of other families. He watched the SS and Ukrainians sweep through the ghetto. The order rang out that all residents from Kawia, Koszarowa, Krotka, Garibaldi, Warszawski and Wilsona streets were to assemble by 6.00am at the metal factory.

> We look out into the street and see SS men savagely bursting into people's houses and driving the occupants out into the street with blows from their rifle-butts.

The SS screamed in the street. Every Jew must possess a work permit or face the consequences. The Nazis and their auxiliaries rampaged through homes, smashing faces here and pulling triggers there. The panicked people were thus driven toward the metal factory. A few Jews, some of them from Fighting Group 66, attempted to challenge the round-up and were executed. By 6.00am the operation was proceeding as planned. A mass of people – women, men, children, the old and the young, the healthy and the sick, fathers, grandparents and pregnant mothers – gathered at the square on Krotka Street. They waited with uncertainty. Babies cried in their mothers' arms. The chanting of Hebrew prayers could be heard. Many held their *Arbeitspass* in outstretched hands, hopefully. They had all survived the misery and subjugation of the ghetto, and now they must endure this. The SS brandished automatic weapons, cudgels and whips to keep order.

The selection began. One by one, over a period of several hours, the Jews were driven across the heavily guarded square. Some of the police offered words of comfort to their fellow Jews about the work in the east, perpetuating a lie they believed themselves. Hershl witnessed the events that followed.

> We watch them arbitrarily dividing up people after a superficial glance at their work-permits. A very small minority is assigned to work, and the rest are transported away en masse. Some kind of premonition tells us that this is the route to death, and we decide to hide in the bunker, which we have already prepared.

We cannot know the precise location of Hershl's bunker. It almost certainly lay within the ghetto boundaries, because any attempt to escape over to the 'Aryan' side, with the city swarming as it was with SS and informants, would have been madness. In all likelihood they sought refuge in some concealed place within the darkness of one of the ghetto cellars. We do not know whether it was a cellar that had already been searched and marked or one that had been overlooked.

Outside, 7,000 people were force-marched towards the ghetto's exit to the sound of curses and whips. This mass of families, in many cases three and four generations clinging together, were already exhausted by the segregation, maltreatment, starvation and humiliation. Now they faced an unequal confrontation with more than 300 armed, well-fed men in uniform, many smirking and laughing, their weapons at the ready.

This first group of doomed Jews crossed Pilsudskiego Street at the border of the ghetto, conveniently located by the Nazis near the railway station, and near the hotel in which I spent the night. Apart from the occasional traveller like me, who still feels the heartbeat of the past, Jews rarely visit this city. Yet walking up Krotka Street to Wilsona, still one of the poorer parts of town with its derelict, grey buildings, I saw a collapsed brick wall running along what was in 1942 the edge of the Częstochowa ghetto. It was impossible not to feel the presence of a vanished people here. And it was impossible not to feel their terror.

They walked until they reached the Częstochowa-Kielce railway line. The sound of chanted Hebrew grew louder. A long train of 60 freight cars stood before them. Steam billowed from the undercarriages. Some were relieved at the sight, which they believed provided evidence that they really were being sent to the east for work. Most of the people halted at a ramp, as they were ordered. Some tried to resist or run. Terrible scenes of brutality and murder ensued. Just over an hour later, the doors to all the wagons were closed. The Jewish police units were spared on this day. The movement of the locomotive leaving the city drowned out the screaming and wailing, and the cries for help. The tracks ran directly to the most murderous place on earth – the gas chambers of Treblinka.

Behind them, numerous corpses lay in pools of blood. At Krotka Street, a few Jews were ordered, under the lash of whips, to gather the dead bodies and transport them on wheelbarrows to awaiting trucks. The bodies were then driven to Kawia Street and thrown into the large pit that had been dug earlier. It seemed the world had gone insane.

★ ★ ★

The air within Hershl's bunker was rank from the stench of human beings in close confinement for many days. We cannot know who these other people were, except that they were Jews from the ghetto, perhaps relatives – although we can be certain they existed in an atmosphere of constant fear, tension and terrible monotony. All conversation had to be conducted in whispers. Most of the time there was a deep silence, their sole method of defence, as they lay on their makeshift beds. There was probably no standing room. Their clothes and bedding crawled with lice.

> Some elderly Jews join us and we lie together, hidden in the bunker, cut off from the world. We discuss our dangerous situation. We do not dare to go out in daylight. At night, we creep out into the fields to find something to eat. There are cabbages, turnips and other vegetables. We bring them back and cook them on an electric stove. At night, when it is dark, we enter the houses of the deported Jews and search through the abandoned rooms.

It seems they refused to delude themselves with hope. I have no doubt that every sound, every footstep in the street would have made them hold their breath collectively. They could not escape. Where could they run? Even in the woods, Polish partisans killed

Jews. They may have imagined themselves aboard a sinking ship, as did one anonymous young Jewish woman hiding in an underground bunker during the final days of the Warsaw Ghetto Uprising. Her diary was found as recently as 2004. This young woman's final, desperate words read: 'We are living by the day, the hour, the moment.'

Meanwhile, the second assault of the Częstochowa *Aktion* was launched two days later, in the early hours of 24 September. Members of the Gestapo and the SS Death's Head squad swarmed through the ghetto, now combing Nadrzeczna, Garncarska, Targowa and Prosta streets, and drove the residents again toward the courtyard of the metal factory. The same treatment was meted out to those from the area around the old market in the south-east of the ghetto. At the factory courtyard, another selection took place. A further 7,000 were rounded up, and another 300 selected for work duty. More innocent blood ran in the street.

The following day, on the third day of the Jewish holiday of Succoth, German police cars crawled through the ghetto with megaphones and announced that all Jews sent earlier by train had arrived safely at their destination. They were told that the former ghetto inhabitants were now at labour camps in eastern Poland, and were working for the benefit of the Reich. They were told that food and warm clothing there were plentiful. At the same time, posters in Polish and German were nailed up outside the ghetto, warning that the penalty for hiding Jews was death – but for revealing Jewish hiding places, special rewards would be given. Later that day, the Gestapo came again with megaphones. They said all remaining Jews who assembled at the metal factory the following morning were to be given half a kilogram of bread, marmalade and a bowl of warm soup. The people were starving, and many complied. There was, of course, no bread or marmalade, and that morning another 7,000 Jews were marched to the railway tracks and loaded on to the train to Treblinka. More dead bodies were dumped into the pit at Kawia Street.

Eight days after the first deportation, Degenhardt instigated a fourth wave of round-ups. This time, the sweep was aimed at uncovering those Jews who had hidden themselves. Methodically, the Gestapo combed the streets of the ghetto, cellar by cellar. The Szperlings and their companions held tight. Their hiding place remained secure for most of the day. Then, near the end of the sweep, the Gestapo returned. Dogs barked ferociously. The doors of the bunker were suddenly flung open and light blasted in.

Our bunker is discovered almost at the end of the period of deportations. Whether we were betrayed by someone, or whether it is purely chance, we do not know. The commander of the deportations, Degenhardt, makes a personal appearance and commands us all to leave the bunker. We comply, because we know that if we were discovered during a second search, it will be certain death. We are taken to Przemyslowa Street, where the last deportees are just being taken away. Of the 7,000 Jews who are rounded up here, 300 men and ten women are assigned to a work-detail in Częstochowa. The remainder is forced into a large factory yard … They are destined for the furnace.

Hershl and his group were among those forced into the factory yard and destined for death.

Everyone has to take off their shoes, tie them together and hang them over their shoulders. Then begins, silent and barefoot, the march to annihilation. At the exit to the factory yard a box has been placed. Under threat of punishment by death, everybody has to throw all their valuables into it. Hardly anyone does it. As they marched on, however, their fear grows. They have second thoughts about it, and from all sides valuables, foreign currency and money are dropped by the wayside … The route of the death-march is littered with Jewish possessions.

They marched through the empty streets. Fresh corpses lay in pools of blood. Windows of abandoned ghetto apartments were smashed and curtains blew through them in the breeze. Dogs on leashes held by the SS barked and lurched at the marching Jews. They marched again to Pilsudskiego Street until they came to the Częstochowa-Kielce railway line. Now the planned mayhem was again enacted. Whips were cracked and people were beaten. To escape the violence, they climbed up on the ramp and into the freight cars. Hershl and his family were among them. We can only imagine the terror of the little red-haired girl who I imagine had clung to the side of her older brother, who in turn clung to his parents. The only alternative at that moment was death. They chose life as they were driven into the terrible crush of the freight car.

★ ★ ★

The following month, the day after the Jewish festival of Simchat Torah and a week after the death train containing Hershl and his family had left for Treblinka, a fifth round-up occurred in Częstochowa. Included in that selection were the Jewish police and their families. Most of the *Judenrat* were also deported. By the following day, some 35,000 Jews from the Częstochowa ghetto had been shipped to Treblinka for the Final Solution.

Early the following June, SS and Gestapo units swept through the tiny streets of the remaining so-called Small Ghetto with an even greater air of arrogance than usual. Degenhardt came in person to supervise the final phase of this important work. The business of liquidation and Jewish extermination in this city was almost complete. Vehicles screeched to a halt just beyond the old square and units armed with whips and guns began to spread into the streets.

No sooner had the first door been smashed in, and the first cries of 'Raus' heard, a shot rang out and a member of the SS lay dead in the street. Abruptly, a cheer went up and, although armed with just a few pistols and rifles and some home-made grenades, several dozen Jewish fighters began to open fire on the Gestapo from pre-arranged positions in bunkers. The resistance surprised them and, for the first time, Nazi blood flowed in the streets of Częstochowa. The Germans pulled back and, shortly afterwards, stormed the bunkers. The uprising was crushed with overwhelming force. Thousands more were sent to Treblinka that day. The remaining 4,000 Jews were transferred to two slave labour camps at the city's munitions factories. The Częstochowa ghetto was finally destroyed.

CHAPTER SIX

THE PLAN UNFOLDS

The demonic and impossible idea to murder every Jew in Europe sprang from the depths of Hitler's hatred. Yet the savage phenomenon we now know as the Holocaust – the systematic murder of six million Jews and some 250,000 Gypsies, as well as many political prisoners and homosexuals – could not have occurred without the venomous undercurrent of anti-Semitism and racial prejudice. The roots of this hatred had been embedded for centuries across Europe. We can only look back in horror at the ease with which all the petty spites and hatreds were harnessed and mobilised by demagogues and religious fanatics during the terrible years of the Third Reich. There were around eleven million Jews in Europe in 1939. The big problem for the Nazi planners was what to actually do with these people whom Hitler had doomed. In the beginning, they had no idea.

Hitler himself, it seems, had no specific plan either. It began with the broad notion of German racial imperialism and the creation of *Lebensraum*, or living space, in the east. The idea was to kill, deport, or enslave all the Slavic populations, whom they considered *untermenschen*, or sub-human, and to repopulate the lands with Germans. As the Wehrmacht swept across Poland, every foot soldier, lieutenant and commander was aware of the underlying determination to render the expanding German Reich *Judenrein*, or cleansed of Jews. All claims of ignorance are lies. Yet the chaotic terror unleashed by the Wehrmacht in Klobuck, Częstochowa and elsewhere throughout Poland during the first weeks of the war was not the implementation of systematic annihilation, for no such plan had as yet been devised. According to Nazi propaganda, all these people were less than human anyway, so it did not much matter how they were treated. In the absence of a specific plan, Hitler had only to express the depths of his hatred, and ambitious Nazis vied to outdo one another in brutality and, at the planning level, to produce proposals that would transform the Führer's vague ideological notions into realistic and murderous programmes.

Alfred Rosenberg, the Nazi Party's chief racial theorist in charge of building a so-called human racial ladder to justify Hitler's ideology, signalled early on that the Führer's wishes could not be realised at once, but rather via a series of practical steps. Rosenberg, at a conference in Berlin at the end of September 1939, indicated that all Jews – including those who had already been expelled from the Reich – were to be resettled in newly acquired Polish territories in the area 'behind Warsaw and around

Lublin', between the Vistula and the Bug rivers. Another strip of land between the German and Jewish settlement areas was designated as the 'primitive' Polish region. To achieve this enormous demographic shift, it was clear that first the Polish intelligentsia – considered to be teachers, clergy, nobles and anyone capable of resistance – would have to be 'rendered harmless', another Nazi euphemism that in reality meant either transport to concentration camps, or murder. The Jews, meanwhile, were to be concentrated in ghettos in the cities to 'have a better possibility of control and later of deportation', according to the minutes of a meeting between Reinhard Heydrich and his division heads in Berlin that same month.

The mass murder of Europe's Jews began in late June 1941 when four *Einsatzgruppen*, special SS killing squads under orders from Heydrich's Reich Security Office – the central organ of SS bureaucracy – advanced with the German Army into the USSR. Here, at locations such as the Rumboli forest near Riga, at Polnat near Vilna, Babi Yar at Kiev, and at numerous other sites in the occupied parts of the Soviet Union, more than one million Jewish victims were shot to fall into ravines and pits. The decision to organise and build death camps emerged from the gradual realisation that mass extermination could not be achieved with bullets alone. The vastness of the numbers involved created an undesired public spectacle, and there were also concerns about the psychological impact on the killers.

One eyewitness, Eric von dem Bach-Zelewski, the head of some 50,000 *Einsatzgruppen* and affiliate members – including SS troops, police and local auxiliaries on the eastern front – described what happened during Himmler's visit to Minsk during the killing of 100 Jews. As the firing started, Himmler became highly agitated. Then von dem Bach-Zelewski told him:

> *Reichsführer*, those were only a hundred. Look at the eyes of the men in this commando, how deeply shaken they are. Those men are finished for the rest of their lives. What kind of followers are we training here? Either neurotics or savages.

The green light for systematic annihilation can be traced back to 31 July 1941. On that day, in Berlin, Heydrich was handed Hermann Göring's infamous order:

> I hereby charge you to carry out preparations as regards organisational, financial, and material matters for a total solution of the Jewish question in all the territories of Europe under German occupation.

There had been deliberations for months over whether the extermination should be conducted before or after Germany's military victory. Then, some time in late December, according to separate diary entries by Goebbels and Himmler, the Führer gave the final go-ahead for the full-scale construction of what were to become the three Operation Reinhard extermination camps – Belzec, Sobibor and Treblinka.

The decision followed the completion of the experimental gassings in the remote Polish village of Chelmno. On 7 December 1942, 800 Jews from Kolo, about nine miles from Chelmno, were taken to a large house on an unused estate and held for the night. The next morning, the first 80 Jews were forced naked into a large van. This vehicle, they were told, would take them to a bathhouse. Some sensed the danger. Yet those who attempted to stop before the ramp were driven, some savagely beaten, into the van. When the van was full, the door was locked, the engine started, and carbon monoxide was pumped into the interior through a specially constructed pipe. Four or five minutes later, when the cries and struggles of the suffocating victims were heard no more, the van was driven to the Chelmno wood about two miles away, and the corpses were dumped. The van returned to the house ten or eleven times until all 800 Jews were gassed. After the Kolo murders, the Reich authorities went on to exterminate all the Jews from four other nearby towns, as well as several hundred gypsies. That month alone, some 20,000 people were exterminated at Chelmno. The 7 December round-up occurred on the same day that the Japanese attacked Pearl Harbor.

Hitler's decision to begin full-scale extermination was also likely to have been based on other factors. On 5 December the Wehrmacht was halted at the gates of Moscow by a massive Soviet counter-attack and the vicious Russian winter, the first significant reversal of German military fortunes. The Japanese attacked Pearl Harbor two days later and brought the US into the conflict, and Germany now had a world war on its hands. Hitler must have understood that a German victory was no longer a certainty – but still his plans for the annihilation of European Jewry were not to be jeopardised. The 'Jewish problem', it was reasoned, could also be solved more easily under the cover of war, regardless of the outcome.

Heydrich then set in motion the administrative and organisational coordination of the plan. This orchestration of mass murder occurred at the Wannsee Conference in Berlin on 20 January 1942. The conference had originally been planned for 2 January, but was delayed because of the Pearl Harbor attack. Heydrich told the conference the 'Final Solution' would include more than eleven million Jews. He stated bluntly: 'Europe would be combed of Jews from east to west.'

Josef Buhler, State Secretary of the General Government for occupied Poland, asked the conference that the Final Solution begin in occupied Poland because there was no transportation problem there, and most of the Jews in the ghettos were already too weak to be of use to the German war effort. The request was approved.

Adolf Eichmann, at his trial in Jerusalem in 1960, described Heydrich, his work done at the Conference:

> I remember that at the end of this Wannsee Conference, Heydrich, Muller and my humble self, settled down comfortably by the fireplace, and that then for the first time I saw Heydrich smoke a cigar or cigarette, and I was thinking: today Heydrich is smoking, something I have not seen before. And he drinks cognac – since I had not seen Heydrich take any alcoholic drink in years. After this Wannsee Conference we were sitting together peacefully, and not in order to talk shop, but in order to relax after the long hours of strain.

Within a matter of weeks, the plans for the three extermination camps – Sobibor, Belzec and Treblinka – took shape.

GERMAN CONCENTRATION AND DEATH CAMPS

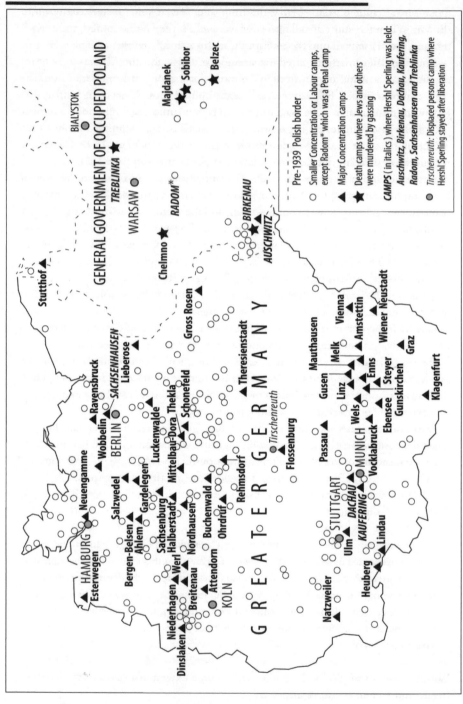

Legend:

- – – – Pre-1939 Polish border
- ○ Smaller Concentration or Labour camps, except Radom* which was a Penal camp
- ◀ Major Concentration camps
- ★ Death camps where Jews and others were murdered by gassing

CAMPS (in italics) where Hershl Sperling was held: *Auschwitz, Birkenau, Dachau, Kaufering, Radom, Sachsenhausen and Treblinka*

● *Tirschenreuth:* Displaced persons camp where Hershl Sperling stayed after liberation

GENERAL GOVERNMENT OF OCCUPIED POLAND

BIALYSTOK ●
TREBLINKA ★
WARSAW ●
RADOM* ○
Majdanek ★
Sobibor ★
Belzec ★
Chelmno ★
AUSCHWITZ ★
BIRKENAU

GREATER GERMANY

Stutthof ◀
Gross Rosen ◀
Theresienstadt ◀
Lieberose
SACHSENHAUSEN
Ravensbruck ◀
Wobbelin ◀
BERLIN ●
Luckenwalde
Mittelbau-Dora Thekla
Schonefeld ◀
Tirschenreuth ●
Flossenburg
Neuengamme ◀
HAMBURG ●
Esterwegen ◀
Salzwedel ◀
Gardelegen ◀
Sachsenburg ◀
Bergen-Belsen ◀
Ahlem ◀
Halberstadt ◀
Nordhausen ◀
Buchenwald ◀
Rehmsdorf ◀
Ohrdruf ○
Werl
Niederhagen ◀
Breitenau
Attendorn ◀
Dinslaken ◀
KOLN ●
Natzweiler ◀
STUTTGART ●
DACHAU
KAUFERING
Ulm ●
Lindau
Heuberg ◀
Passau ◀
MUNICH ●
Wels ◀
Vocklabruck ◀
Ebensee ◀
Gunskirchen
Mauthausen ◀
Gusen ◀
Linz ◀
Melk ◀
Enns ◀
Steyer ◀
Vienna
Amstettin ◀
Wiener Neustadt ◀
Graz ◀
Klagenfurt ◀

At the end of September 1941, Hitler had appointed Heydrich as acting *Reichsprotektor* of occupied Bohemia and Moravia. The radio reported on his inauguration at Prague Castle, where he returned after the fateful conference at Wannsee. But his reign was short-lived. On 27 May 1942, Heydrich was fatally wounded in Prague. Two British-trained Czech partisans, Jan Kubis and Josef Gabcik were parachuted into German-occupied Czechoslovakia with the aim of carrying out the assassination attempt on Heydrich in a plan that originated with the exiled president of Czechoslovakia, Edward Benes, in London. The General had been riding in his open car in the Prague suburb of Kobylisy at around 10.30am when Gabcik jumped in front of the vehicle. He drew a concealed British-made Sten sub-machine gun from his coat, but it failed to fire. Gabcik ran to the other side of the street and began firing with his pistol. At the same time, Kubis threw a grenade that exploded near the car, and the vehicle screeched to a halt. Heydrich did not appear to be seriously injured and tried to return fire, but his pistol was not loaded. His driver, a man named Klein, also tried to fire at the assailants, but in the confusion of the moment he accidentally pressed a button that released a cartridge. Gabcik attempted to escape through the streets, but was chased by the driver. Gabcik turned and fired wildly, and hit Klein in the leg. The two assassins went into hiding. Kubis escaped from the scene after stealing a woman's bicycle.

Although Himmler sent his best doctors, Heydrich reportedly died in extreme pain in a Prague hospital. He was 38. The cause of death was said to be septicaemia, which he had contracted from the bacteria in the horsehair and upholstery fragments in the car seat that had been driven into his body by the explosion.

The Nazi retaliation was savage, with the dual aim of revenge and warning against further armed resistance. On 10 June all males over the age of sixteen in the village of Lidice, 22 kilometres northwest of Prague, were massacred and the women were sent to concentration camps. The next day, the same retribution was meted out in the village of Lezaky, which was burned to the ground. The Nazis trumped up a connection between the assassination and the two villages. In all, around 5,000 lives were blotted out in retaliation for the death of this single monster.

Meanwhile, Kubis and Gabcik were hiding in the Church of St Cyril & Methodius in Resslova Street with five other members of the Czech resistance for several weeks after the attack until they were betrayed by a German spy amongst their number. The Nazis surrounded the church on 18 June. The partisans barricaded themselves in the crypt of the church and tried desperately to dig their way into the subterranean sewer network. The Germans pumped water and smoke into the crypt but the partisans refused to surrender. The Germans eventually broke through the barricade and Kubis, Gabcik and the other resistance fighters died in the gun battle that followed. The six-foot hole they dug in the darkness of the crypt remains today as an eerie memorial.

After Heydrich's death, the extermination camps of Treblinka, Sobibor and Belzec were completed and put to work on their demonic task. The project, which brought about the murder of something close to 1,700,000 Jews at these killing centres, was named Operation Reinhard in his honour.

Two months later, on 19 July 1942, Himmler met with Odilo Globocnik in Lublin, the Operation Reinhard commander, and Friedrich-Wilhelm Krueger, the SS and police chief for the entire General Government of Occupied Poland, to discuss the planned killing operations. Himmler now ordered that the 'resettlement' – another Nazi euphemism for deportation and murder – of all Jews in the General Government was to be completed by the end of 1942.

The savagery that was triggered in Częstochowa on 22 September – as witnessed and recorded by the teenage Hershl Szperling – marked Degenhardt's activation of *Aktion Reinhard*. Hershl's premonition that his march toward the tracks in Częstochowa had been 'the road to death' was correct.

CHAPTER SEVEN

TO THE GATES OF HELL

Hershl could not have known that the starvation, humiliation and brutality in the Częstochowa ghetto were merely a prelude to the fate that awaited that city's Jewish inhabitants. The train journey that followed marked yet another low in human degradation. The diabolical conditions in which the Jews of Europe were transported to their deaths served no practical function, but were instead the expression of senseless and abject cruelty, which most of the time was applied with astonishing zeal.

I travelled those same tracks in the relative comfort of a PKP Intercity train, part of the modern national railway of Poland, between Częstochowa and Warsaw on an icy day in February 2007. I tried to imagine Hershl riding these tracks, a fifteen-year-old boy and his family amid the crush of bodies. With 80–100 people in each boxcar, there was space to sit if everyone was packed tightly together, almost on top of one another. However, many instead pushed desperately toward the small air aperture. Their numbers included the old, the sick, the pregnant, nursing women and before long those who had gone mad from the journey. The chlorine sprinkled on the floor burned their eyes. If there were claustrophobics among them – as there must have been, because this was in many ways a random cross-section of humanity – their suffering is unimaginable.

Somewhere in the Polish hinterland, I pulled Hershl's pale green book from my backpack. The train was full and noisy. We stopped momentarily at a station. The platform was deserted, the town small, its name on the station sign to me unpronounceable. Five of the six people in my compartment began to doze. The sixth, a grandmotherly woman, watched me as I ritualistically ran my fingers across the dark blue Hebrew lettering of that terrifying title on the cover, '*Fun Letzten Hurban*' – From the Last Extermination. Then I began to read the translation.

The SS shove eighty to a hundred people into each of the wagons. The disinfectant, calcium chloride, is scattered liberally into every wagon. Each wagon receives three small loaves of bread and a little water. Then the doors are pushed shut, locked and sealed. Ukrainian and Lithuanian SS stand guard at the steps of each wagon. We are shut in like cattle, tightly crammed together. Only a tiny bit of air comes in through the one small wire-covered window, so that we can hardly breathe. The calcium chloride hardly helps to combat the unbearable smell, which gets worse all the time. Some women faint and others vomit.

They had been told they were being transported east for work. Few believed the story any more. It was still early morning and a beautiful autumn day was breaking. The train shuddered and began its slow, tortuous pull northward out of Częstochowa and across the bleak Polish landscape to Treblinka.

My train pushed into a wintry rural landscape. I saw brown rutted earth, speckled with snow. A solitary magpie wheeled and landed. Another unknown village off the rail line went by in the distance. It was impossible to imagine the intensity of the crush and confinement in that hot, airless container. Twenty minutes into the journey, I observed a fenced compound at the side of the track, and the shocking site of rusted old freight cars, some of them smashed and dented. Others were covered with graffiti. Who knows how old they were or for what purposes they had been used? In Hershl's time, those few who could see from the little grated window of the boxcar glimpsed golden fields of sun-dried grass. As the autumn sun warmed that beautiful day in 1942, the interior of the wagon became an oven. The smell was putrid because people had defecated in all four corners. Hershl wrote: 'The natural functions have to be performed in the wagon. It makes the situation more terrible.'

The train rolled on past flat fields. The passengers fought to reach the little window, jostling for air. Outside, a rusty track ran parallel. It was impossible to tell where they were. Suddenly, the train stopped. Then the sound of shouting; machine-guns and pistol shots was heard. The pandemonium in the wagon became the deathly silence of fear.

From my train I could see a collapsing wooden barn with holes in its rotten walls and roof. An old tree stood in the middle of a field, its limbs twisted and dead as though it had been struck by lightning; it may have been living when Hershl's train passed. By the end of the first day, all the water had been drunk. Hysteria broke out. Babies cried incessantly, their mouths wide open and desperately gasping for air. Other accounts recount how people gasped and groaned, their heads lolling and their bodies shuddering. Hershl wrote:

We are tormented by a dreadful thirst. We become utterly desperate and keep begging the SS guards to bring us some water. They refuse for a long time, but eventually they agree to give us some water, but only for money. We manage to collect a few thousand zlotys and give them to the guards. The SS take the money, but no water appears. Thus, in pain and torment, the journey drags on until we reach Warsaw.

Terrible as it was, this was not an extreme case. The transports from eastern Poland, where the Jews were considered to be even lesser merchandise than those from the west, sometimes contained as many as 220 persons per car. Often, no food or water was provided. The people were packed together so densely there was no place to sit or squat. Throughout the passage, Jews constantly tried to break out through the walls and ceiling of the train cars. Many succeeded, but were shot by soldiers guarding the train or were hunted down by police units. On some occasions, the guards used up all their ammunition shooting the fleeing Jews before the train reached its destination, and they had to resort to stones and bayonets to keep order. Sheep to the slaughter?

My ride to Warsaw took around three hours on worn-out, Communist-era rolling stock, and it was not an express train. Hershl's journey on these same tracks lasted around 24 hours, and it was still 80 kilometres short of Treblinka.

★ ★ ★

The requests for these so-called 'special trains', or *Sonderzuge* – the rolling stock of the sequestered Polish railway system – came from SS and Gestapo leaders in charge of the deportations in their districts. However, fulfilling those requests was the responsibility of *Generaldirektion der Ostbahn*, or Directorate of the Eastern Railroad, 'Gedob' for short. Its headquarters were in Kraków, and it had special responsibility for the scheduling of deportation trains for Operation Reinhard. However, for most of the deportations from the east, the number of trains requested or provided was not enough for the size of the transport. At the same time, many SS and Gestapo officers in charge of Jewish transports often overloaded the freight trains on purpose. There is ample evidence suggesting that many were so enthusiastic about their task of transporting Jews to the death camps in the minimum time and with maximum efficiency they disregarded the capacity guidelines, which were inhumane in the first place. At the same time, in a further perverse deception, some transports from western Europe and Bulgaria arrived at the camps in luxury carriages, for which the victims had to pay for their own tickets. The instructions were the same for all – bring warm clothes for work in the east, bring your money, furs and all the wealth and security you and your family have accumulated. The number of victims was chalked on the side of each carriage, be they passenger trains or boxcars.

According to Gedob's calculations, Hershl's journey to Treblinka should have lasted at most six hours. However, the train hit a snag on the outskirts of Warsaw. The planners of Operation Reinhard had designated that Jews deported for extermination from the Warsaw district were to be transported to both Treblinka and Sobibor; but between the end of July and early October, the Warsaw-Lublin-Sobibor line was under repair, so all the trains were directed to Treblinka. There was a bottleneck that clogged the railway system, already overloaded by the demands of the war on the eastern front. Moreover, Treblinka's refusal to process transports at night further extended the tortuous journey.

Hershl's train crawled through the outskirts of Warsaw some time the following evening, avoiding the central area of the Polish capital so as not to draw attention to itaself and its human cargo. Once it crossed the Vistula River and reached the north-eastern side of the city, it joined with the main Warsaw to Bialystok line. Later that night, the train pulled on to a siding a few miles shy of the village of Malkinia, seven kilometres from Treblinka, where it remained until morning.

The train was heavily guarded during the night by the SS as well as Ukrainian and Latvian watchman. The terror inside the boxes is impossible to imagine. The watchmen's purpose was not just to prevent escape, but also to guard against the robbery of Jewish valuables. At times, drunken Latvian guards proposed escape to their victims in exchange for money and valuables, and then shot them as they ran. On at least one occasion, a rogue SS unit hijacked a lightly guarded train en route from the town of Siedlce to Treblinka and killed the guards. They then entered each of the 60 wagons, machine-gunned the occupants and robbed the corpses. They also plundered the two wagons that contained valuables confiscated from the Jews before the train set off. The masters of Operation Reinhard were furious at the raid. This was an unlawful act of brigandry perpetrated by members of the SS. They had murdered Jews destined for their gas chambers and the booty rightfully belonged to the Reich.

Later the following day, Hershl's train passed slowly into deep woods. Once out of the shadows of the trees, it moved toward a clearing and came upon the village of Malkinia, a station on the main Warsaw-Bialystok railway line. It stopped again for a long time, perhaps several hours. It was the point at which the human cargo branched off the main line toward death. It was also the point at which the tracks from the major Jewish population centres of Warsaw, Bialystok, Siedlce and Lomza intersected. From the Nazi perspective, it was the perfect location for a secret extermination camp for Jews.

Somewhere between Malkinia and Treblinka comes a terrible warning. In the fields on either side of the track, Polish farm labourers worked among the hay. The train moved so slowly, those Jews crushed up against the grated windows of the wagons were able to call to them.

We just want to find out what our fate is going to be. They hardly lift their eyes from their work, and when they do, they just shout one word at us – 'Death'. We are seized by terror. We cannot believe it. Our minds simply will not take it in. Is there truly no escape for us? One of the Polish workers mentions burnings. Another shouts about shootings, and a third, gassings. Another tells of inhuman, unbelievable tortures. An unbearable state of tension mounts among us, which in some cases leads to outbreaks of hysteria.

The Polish farm workers slowly disappeared into the distance. No-one wanted to believe it. How could they send so many people to their deaths?

★ ★ ★

I had now crossed the rail bridge that spanned the Vistula River and looked over the city of Warsaw. I saw commuters push into tramcars with the sense of resignation that has survived the half-century of Communism. The dull architectural uniformity, the result of the city's almost complete rebuilding from the ruins after 1945, seemed complete. I recalled what Sam had said to me: 'What's important is how all this affected him.' He was right, of course. Yet in my research I discovered no study that attempted to understand the lasting trauma of those confined in these overcrowded wagons. Perhaps that is because the overwhelming majority of those who did not die en route were almost immediately put to death in the camps. And among the few survivors of these dreadful journeys, this pre-camp trauma was subsumed because worse followed. For Hershl, this journey, like Auschwitz, was minor compared with the hell of Treblinka. Hershl's train crawled across the Bug River, over a single-track wooden rail bridge where the river looped and bent, and on toward the village of Treblinka. Those at the grated window could see the landscape suddenly transformed from lush forests and fertile pasture into sandy and barren earth.

Treblinka village station was a station like so many others. But now the train pulled on to another sideline. Inside Hershl's wagon, after perhaps 36 dreadful hours, a new fear took over in the wake of the warnings from the peasants in the field. The foul air was filled with the cries of thousands of people. In the sweltering cars most of them called for water, but others called for a doctor. They had somehow retained their belief in humanity and charity and that perhaps even the Nazis would take pity on them and a doctor would come. Hershl writes: 'We don't have much time to think about all this. A special locomotive takes away 20 of the 60 wagons which made up our train. After five minutes, it comes back and takes another 20 wagons.' A woman beside him could no longer bear the anxiety and the ferocious heat and thirst. Hershl recalls her suffering. 'They're murdered already,' this unknown woman cried. 'They're dead, dead, dead. My God, why has this happened to us?'

Franciszek Zabecki, the Treblinka station master who was also a member of the Polish Underground, told Gitta Sereny for her book, *Into That Darkness*:

> There were guards sitting on the roofs of the cars, with their sleeves rolled up, holding guns. They looked as if they had killed; as if they had had their hands in blood and then washed before arriving. The train was very full, incredibly full, it seemed.

Hershl adds:

> An icy horror comes over me and I clench my fists helplessly. Now the last 20 wagons are being moved. I am in one of them. Slowly we roll on. One can clearly see that the forest here has recently been dug up. Full of trepidation, we roll towards a huge gate guarded by a large number of SS with machine-guns.

Hershl could see the curve of the track and the single sideline that ran through the camp gates. The forest was dark and heavy all around. The Jews had no idea where they were, or even if they were still in Poland. He could hear the escorts, SS men and Latvian, Lithuanian and Ukrainian volunteers, the so-called 'Hellhounds', being commanded to get off. Treblinka trains always stopped at the gate, where the escorts got off and the camp staff, usually SS camp personnel and Ukrainian auxiliaries, replaced them. No one from outside was permitted to enter the camp's grounds.

A Ukrainian auxiliary opened the gates. For just a moment, Hershl saw what looked like a station house. The spur was very short, and the engine waited for the cars to be unloaded of their human cargo on the other side of the gate, outside the camp.

> The gate opens and the locomotive shunts all the wagons into the camp. It remains outside. The gate closes behind us. The wagons roll slowly towards the big ramp. Round about it stands an SS unit, ready to receive us with hand-grenades, rubber truncheons

and loaded guns. Now the doors of the wagons are flung open. Half-fainting, we are driven out on to the ramp. We can hardly stand up, and we desperately gulp deep breaths of the fresh air. There is terrible wailing, screaming and weeping. Children are searching for their parents, weak and sick people are begging for help, desperate women are tearing out their own hair.

Immediately, the Ukrainians began hitting them with their rifles and clubs. They shot those who did not disembark quickly enough, mostly the elderly, the sick, and those who had fainted. Scores of Jews met their end in the freight cars or on the Treblinka extermination camp platform. The smell of death hung in the air. The living did not know for sure what awaited them; but they could smell it.

CHAPTER EIGHT

GHOSTS OF TREBLINKA

Against the advice of well-meaning staff in the Czarny Kot Hotel in Warsaw, I drove a hired car some 60 miles through a mid-February snow blizzard to reach Treblinka. This was Hershl's personal hell and the place where I most needed my friend Sam to be with me; but he was beyond persuasion. He groaned when I first asked him, and later flatly refused when I persisted.

'It's not like I couldn't go if I wanted,' Sam said. 'I mean, if I couldn't go, that would be different. Then I would want to go. But the fact that I can go, well, why should I?'

His abstruse logic made me smile. It reminded me of Hershl. But I sensed that the idea of spending even a few minutes in Poland, let alone Treblinka, was abhorrent to him. It was understandable and, in the end, another friend agreed to meet me in Warsaw and make the journey to the camp. I wasn't sure that I could face the place alone, knowing what I did and what had occurred there.

It was a journey I had calculated would take no more than two hours, but we crept for four hours along a busy, snow-packed highway behind long columns of heavy trucks travelling the main trade route between Warsaw and the Baltic states. My friend, an artist named Roy, was 62 at the time, Hershl's age when he had taken his own life. I could see concern on his face as we proceeded through a snowstorm and the driving conditions grew steadily worse. The farther from Warsaw we travelled, the heavier the snow fell and the more the gloom descended. In 1942, when Hershl and his family went through this wild region on the death train, the woods whispered with partisans and escaped Russian prisoners of war. They blew up bridges and roads to hamper German military operations, but no attempts were ever made to disrupt the murderous deportations to Treblinka.

After the turn-off for Malkinia, the landscape suddenly became flat and completely white, as though the terrain were a large piece of bleached cloth that had been stretched and ironed. White flakes of snow swept across the car's windshield. As far as the eye could see lay an empty land. There was not a fence in sight. I was out of season for Hershl's journey, his deportation train had passed through here in the autumn. Now there was only a frozen plain as bleak as the Siberian tundra. The Nazis had often used the weather as a weapon against their victims, both heat and cold, to inflict suffering and punishment. Hershl had lived through a terrible Treblinka winter.

We entered the village of Malkinia at last, the railway crossroads where the Warsaw-Bialystok-Vilna track branches off to Treblinka. I knew from Hershl's account that the camp was not far. A few elderly peasants trundled through snowy streets lined with wooden houses, some with bundles of sticks on their backs, and I wondered if it was them, or maybe their fathers, who had called out 'death' to the doomed passengers, or who had come to the gates of Treblinka to barter goods with the Nazis and Ukrainians. How much Jewish gold – perhaps just a man's pocket watch or a wife's beloved bracelet – had found its way into the possession of these peasant families in exchange for Zubrowka, the potent bison grass vodka so coveted by the Ukrainians, or meat, or bread? Perhaps these people were among those who had dug the thousands of holes on the site of the former camp in 1945, despoiling the ground into a pockmarked lunar-like landscape in their search for gold fillings and money amid the bones and ashes. Rumours had been rife among the local population after the war that some of the murdered Jews had been buried in their clothes, in which valuables were hidden.

It was difficult to fight the rising hatred I suddenly felt for these peasants. My own sense of justice wanted to reject such feelings, because it dishonours those Poles who found ways to resist the Nazi tyranny and assist the persecuted – but to my mind the courageous were too few, and Poland's guilt is that of a nation that could have saved the lives of hundreds of thousands of people, in spite of the Germans, but did not. The peasants who made their way through the snowy streets of Malkinia that day were in all probability innocent, even if not among the courageous, but without a doubt the inhabitants here still harboured the guilty among their number. In a kind of bewilderment brought on by the overwhelming gloom in this village, Roy and I asked one another simultaneously: how could people continue to live on this blighted spot?

There were no signposts to the camp. Only the dedicated make the journey. We followed a road through Malkinia that according to our map should have taken us straight to the site, but instead carried us into a snowy, unpopulated wasteland in the opposite direction. The visibility was appalling, but the white road was as straight as an arrow. Great drifts, maybe three or four feet high, lay unbroken near the half-hidden road. After about five miles, a large four-wheel drive police vehicle came up behind and followed us closely for a short distance. I pulled over and, with map in hand, got out to ask two policemen wearing Russian-style fur hats how far to Treblinka. They were friendly enough and directed us back the way we came with the instruction to turn right at the railway line to Siedlce.

The road carried us to the Bug River, which until the German invasion of Russia in June 1941, marked the border between the Nazi-occupied General Government of Poland and the zone occupied by the Soviet Union. We crossed a wooden Communist-era railway bridge, over which extended a tilting single track. Trains that rumbled over the former German bridge that had previously spanned this river could be heard from the camp. The road grew progressively narrower, and was distinguishable from the fields only by the lines of telephone poles along the sides. There was a railway embankment with no tracks. Four parallel tracks once ran along this route to death, but had since been removed. Slave labourers from an existing penal camp at Treblinka, tormented by twenty SS guards and 100 Ukrainian auxiliaries, had been used to drain the marshes near the river and strengthen the embankment into a long, raised bed in preparation for the extermination centre and the transportations that would come. At the village of Treblinka, where there was a small train station in the 1940s, I asked an old man in front of a wooden shack if we were on the right road to the site of the former camp. He told us, expressionlessly, that the '*muzeum*' was just one kilometre distant.

Through the hamlet of Poniatowa, the forest suddenly became denser. It was like nowhere I had ever been before. The outside world seemed a million miles away. There was a signpost and I drove along a narrow road thick with snow and heavy overhanging trees to an empty parking area near a dilapidated visitors' centre. An outside light went on as I stopped the car, and we got out, calf-deep in snow. The caretaker and his family lived above the half-empty museum. It was bitterly cold and an icy wind blew. There were a million ghosts here.

It was already late afternoon and the light was fading rapidly. Perhaps only half an hour of daylight remained. The mile-or-so walk toward the site followed the route of a rail line, which had not survived. The path beside the rail route had once been paved by the Nazis with Jewish gravestones and those had also been removed. Some of the gravestones were on display in the visitors' centre. About a quarter of a mile before the camp, concrete railroad ties had been laid as part of the monument to this factory of death. Nothing remains of the original camp. I stood upon the first railroad tie and, driven by an impulse I could not comprehend, began walking them in long strides, one after the other, block by block, toward the camp, advancing at the pace that Hershl's slow-moving train probably inched along the track half a century earlier, further extending the agony of those being carried to their death. Roy did the same, but not a word was spoken between us.

I became impatient and defiant. I jumped off one of the concrete blocks into the snow and, in spite of the deep drifts, strode toward the symbolic stone gates of Treblinka, where a separate concrete track spurred sharply on to a sidetrack and into the camp toward the platform ramp. It was the act of a free man, and I felt, absurdly, I was doing it on behalf of all those whose existences had been blotted out here. The symbolic concrete track continued toward the separate and little-known Treblinka penal camp set up at a local gravel quarry a mile and a half away and which had been in operation before the extermination centre was constructed. It had provided its own, separate catalogue of horrors for its inmates and the 10,000 Poles who were murdered there. Now I climbed up to the reconstructed platform, marking the place where the Jews had disembarked. The air was still and silent.

As soon as the Jews descended from the cattle wagons, groups of SS and Ukrainian auxiliaries charged at them with shouts and swinging truncheons. It first seemed as though the train had stopped at the edge of a dense pine forest. Everyone moved towards a dark wall of trees. But it was another Nazi ruse. The Germans had made a fence from the trees; barbed wire had been intertwined between the branches. Hershl recalls: 'The SS herded the rest of the men and women down from the ramp with their truncheons and drove them through a gate leading to a large square.' Some of the SS cracked whips; others held barking dogs on leashes. Children and adults screamed in terror. Noses and mouths were bloodied by punches and kicks, bones were broken with clubs, and faces were lacerated by whips. To avoid further blows, the victims ran.

A telephone conversation with Hershl's elder son, Alan, came back to me. He said, 'My father used to say that sometimes, in Treblinka, it was like being there, and not being there. I know that makes no sense.' It made sense to me now. Groups of silent Jewish slave workers wearing strange, colourful attire and blue bands at their wrists climbed into the wagons and pulled out the bodies of those who had died en route. The slave Jews did not speak. Fear dictated their every move. They passed like ghosts, like dead men walking.

Amid the mayhem and the terror, the suffering mass of Częstochowa Jews was herded group by group toward a wide gate in the fence, where a Ukrainian stood guard, his machine-gun trained on the crowd. They were driven into a square. '*Tempo schnell*,' the guards screamed. What was this place?

Moments later, Hershl heard one of the Jewish slave workers mutter the 'terrible truth' about Treblinka under his breath. They were not being transported to the east for agricultural work after all. They had all come to this barren, desolate place in the middle of nowhere to be exterminated.

★ ★ ★

I walked up the cobblestone path from an area that had been deceptively called Station Square, where Hershl and the rest of the Jews that late September day in 1942 were driven from the platform toward the equally cynically named Deportation Square. Trainloads of 5,000–7,000 people at a time arrived daily. At this point, the men and women were separated and forced to undress. I walked up the slight slope, trembling with cold, next to a number of large standing stones on which were inscribed the names of countries whose Jews – some 800,000 souls, probably more – were brought to this remote spot and murdered.

The camp was intended originally to expedite the extermination of Jews within the General Government of Occupied Poland. But, in time, Jews from Greece, Czechoslovakia, Belgium, France, Germany, Austria, Yugoslavia and the Soviet Union were also brought for extermination. The path I walked led to the giant stone monument where the gas chambers had once stood. A stone engraving at the base of the monument read 'Never Again' in six languages.

The shortness of the distance from the train platform to the death chambers was in itself shocking. How quickly and efficiently these people were processed and killed. Behind the monument lay the symbolic grates, which in 1943 had been rails placed on supports of reinforced concrete in giant pits, where the bodies of the gassed were burned. All around was the symbolic graveyard. It was not an actual graveyard, because there are no bodies beneath this earth, only dust.

Roy and I walked in the sea of 17,000 memorial stones, large and small, jagged and rounded, hunched and still, each of them representing a Polish–Jewish community that had been blotted out in this place. Roy snapped photographs blindly against the falling snow. Over and over again, I repeated the words of the Kaddish, the Jewish prayer for the dead. I could not stop the words on my lips.

There was no wind. Ours were the only footprints for miles. I wanted to find the stone marking the 40,000 Jews from Częstochowa, but it was too dark to search. The community of Klobuck, with just 1,600 Jews, was too small to have a stone of its own, but was symbolically represented among those thousands of stones with no name. I kept trying to imagine Hershl here, his desperation and his suffering, but also his hope and his determination to live. This was where he had learned to survive, improbably and against all the odds, but 47 years later those lessons had betrayed him.

Some impulse drew me toward the darkness of the forest to the south of the camp. It was where many of the prisoners, including Hershl, had run during the escape. Most were killed before they reached the woods, but others made it. It was so quiet and, in spite of the snow, I no longer felt the cold. I was numb. Before I realised it, I was deep in the woods. Illogical as it was, I wanted to call to them and tell them that it was all right now, that it was safe to come out. I pulled myself out of my reverie and headed back toward the memorial stones. Before I had come, I had imagined that somehow this ground was hallowed and sacred, if only because of the number of dead beneath the muffled earth. But I now knew there was nothing sacred about it; it was just the site of a mass murder. It was cursed ground, and like Hershl I clenched my fists in anger and frustration, but also in utter disbelief at the human horror and sheer senselessness of it all.

CHAPTER NINE

TREBLINKA IN HISTORY

Roy and I returned to the Czarny Kot late that night, our nerves frayed, but the hotel's ever-helpful staff rustled us up some creamy borscht, (Polish beetroot soup), fish cakes and salad. They also brought us vodka and, sitting by ourselves in the hotel's big dining room, we drank copiously with our food and for several hours afterwards.

'I think we were very lucky,' said Roy.

'You mean lucky to be alive, after that drive through the blizzard?' I asked, trying to ignore the terrible gloom that had followed us from Treblinka.

'No, I mean we were lucky to have been there in that fading light and in that silence and that solitude, with the snow falling the way it was,' Roy said. 'I think that no matter how many times you return there, you'd never repeat that experience. It was special, a one-off.' He gulped down another vodka quickly and sat silently for a moment. Then he asked me, 'How do you feel?'

'Terrible,' I confessed. 'And angry. But I guess I also feel my emotions are worthless, that they're cheap and easy, compared with the real horror that people went through there.'

I collapsed into my hotel bed that night, tormented by dreams I could not remember on waking. In my notepad the next day, I wrote simply, 'Miserable night'.

Later that morning I said goodbye to Roy, whose flight departed just after noon. I spent the rest of the day wandering the slushy streets of Warsaw, hungover and hazy, trying to figure out how Hershl could have survived that terrible place and yet end up killing himself years later. I stayed close to the Old City, the heart of the Polish capital, which has been so meticulously and perfectly rebuilt that it has been awarded a Unesco World Heritage designation. Critics complain it is a mere Disney version of the city's pre-war self.

I wandered from bar to bar, sipping coffees and beers, and rereading the handful of the few Treblinka histories I kept in my backpack and in which I had immersed myself over the past few months. I had called Sam often over that period, perhaps two or three times a week, and relayed to him each new fact about his father's hellish experience in Treblinka as I discovered it. I took meticulous notes of our conversations and re-read those also.

The body of authoritative and reliable works about Treblinka, and that includes two books by survivors and a few testimonies, can be counted on two hands. I had no doubt that Hershl's memoir, long-forgotten and referred to in no scholarly work on the subject, added significantly to the history of what occurred there. Yet Sam often responded in a muted fashion to the information. I began to feel guilty about what I was putting him through. I knew Hershl's pain was also Sam's pain, and that of his elder brother, Alan. Hitler's hatred had not ended with those who had been touched directly by its evil, but had continued to torture those of a generation after his death.

Within a few years of Hershl's suicide, both his sons would attempt their own suicides – and, thankfully, they would fail. One son took an overdose after watching a news report about a Kosovo massacre in 1999. 'I thought, what's the bloody point,' Alan recalled painfully, months later. 'The human race is stupid.' The other son, my friend Sam, felt that his own suffering simply needed to end. The last thing I wanted to do with their father's story was hurt them more by bringing back the horror of the death camps, and brow-beat them with it. One day, I asked Sam outright if these terrible details were too upsetting for him.

'Should I stop?' I asked him. 'Should I stop telling you about all this stuff? Should I stop everything? Should I stop writing this terrible story?' I could feel tension in the silence.

'It's all right,' he said, at last. 'It's difficult sometimes. But if I ever want you to stop, I'll just say I need a break and you can call back later. If it hurts too much, I wouldn't do it. I think it's important my father's story is told. It's another piece of the Holocaust puzzle. My father always said the worst parts of the Holocaust were not known, and I think that's true. The world wants to hear about Auschwitz orchestras and the diary of Anne Frank. No one wants to know the details of how she suffered and died in Bergen-Belsen. It's not uplifting enough. It's too much for them – too much reality, too much truth. I think you should tell my father's story as it was. People should know what really happened in Treblinka. Whether it will do any good, I don't know. But at least it's true. We don't need any more fairy tales.'

I was also plagued by self-doubt. Why me? Why was I doing this, and for whom? Hershl had been dead for almost eighteen years. Sitting in that quaint, stone-built bar in the Old Town of Warsaw and looking again through the Treblinka histories, I suddenly realised what I was doing here – I was trying to save my friend's life.

The revelation shocked me at first. It seemed naïve and even embarrassing, but it was true. I was trying to prevent my friend – and his brother – from attempting suicide again. Somehow, I hoped that by filling in the blanks in their father's story – and there were many of them – it would make their burden lighter, and help them go on.

The bare facts about Treblinka are available in a few specific histories, and they are corroborated by eyewitness accounts. The book containing Hershl's story even includes a map of the camp, presumably taken from a drawing by his own hand. To be sure, Treblinka was not a concentration camp, or a slave labour camp. Neither was it one of the feared torture centres that had been built for the enemies of the Reich, nor a transit camp, as the Nazis attempted to convince their victims and as Holocaust deniers have continued to claim. Those who survived, as well as the perpetrators, have left us a historical record in testimonies and personal interviews that tell us precisely what Treblinka was. Treblinka was an extermination camp and it was established for one purpose only – the murder of Jews on a massive and efficient industrial scale.

The order for construction of the camp came from a mid-ranking Nazi called Odilo Globocnik, the Himmler-appointed head of Operation Reinhard, at the beginning of April 1942, when Belzec and Sobibor were already functioning. Its grounds were designated to stand within a concealed area of fourteen acres of sandy, infertile ground in the middle of a pine forest, about a mile from an already-existing Treblinka penal camp. The design was based on the blueprint for Sobibor. The maze of linking rail lines in the vicinity made it particularly convenient, and the surrounding heavy forest was deemed perfect for keeping operations secret. Prisoners from the penal camp were exploited as construction workers, as were many Jews from nearby villages, none of whom survived.

Murders occurred there even before the gas chambers were erected. Jan Sulkowski, a Polish prisoner from the penal camp, who worked as a bricklayer during the construction, recalled: 'The Germans killed Jews either by beating them or shooting them. I also witnessed cases where SS men … during the felling of forests, forced Jews to stand beneath trees which were about to fall down.' Franciszek Zabecki, the Treblinka village station master, said Teodor Von Eurpen, the SS commander in charge of the construction project, even took pot shots at Jews for his own sadistic pleasure, 'as if they were partridges'.

A road was built through the forest and a telephone line was connected from the camp to Treblinka village and to Malkinia. A double barbed-wire fence was raised around the 600- by 400-metre perimeter. High watchtowers were positioned at the corners and also intermittently. It was then partitioned into three zones – housing, arrival and extermination. The latter was kept totally separate and hidden from view by branches intertwined with barbed wire; it was a camp within a camp. This area also contained three gas chambers, disguised as shower rooms. As in Sobibor and Belzec, a 'tube' – cynically called by the SS the *Himmelstrasse*, or the 'Street to Heaven' – led from the undressing barracks to the extermination zone. Also based on the plans for the two other camps, a Lazarett – a sham infirmary – was constructed. In spite of the Red Cross flag posted outside its door, it contained not doctors and medicines, but an execution pit and a fire, where the old, sick and the troublesome were led and into which they fell when shot or were pushed.

For key personnel positions at the camp, Globocnik called upon members of the Third Reich's secret T4 euthanasia programme. These functionaries had had little to do since August 1941, when the programme was halted, and Globocnik decided to make use of their special knowledge. He appointed Christian Wirth, the former director of a dozen euthanasia institutes and a fanatical anti-Semite, as the inspector of all three Operation Reinhard camps. Wirth was a brutal psychopath, nicknamed by his fellow Nazis 'Christian the terrible'. The Ukrainian auxiliaries called him Stuka. Dr Irmfried Eberl, another T4 functionary, was the first commander of Treblinka.

The gassings began on 23 July 1942, with the arrival of a transport of Jews from the Warsaw ghetto. Amongst one of the transports two weeks later was Janusz Korczak, the Polish-Jewish children's author, who in spite of offers of sanctuary accompanied 196 children from his orphanage in Warsaw to their death in the gas chambers of Treblinka Death by asphyxiation was achieved in about half an hour, and the victims arrived in their thousands. However, under a system devised by Wirth, a few

Jews were selected from each transport to make up a special task force – a Jewish *Sonderkommando* – to carry out the manual and most grotesque aspects of the extermination process. These Jews pulled the corpses from the gas chambers, buried and burned bodies, extracted gold from the mouths of the dead, sorted through clothing and cleaned the trains. The *Sonderkommando* lived a brief existence. They were selected for their youth and strength, but were kept alive for only a few days, two or three weeks at best. This human material was granted a little more life in exchange for work, and when their usefulness had been expended they were murdered. From the point of view of the camp's SS masters, the Jewish *Sonderkommando* were also the keepers of all the terrifying secrets of this extermination factory, so they could not be allowed to remain alive. Their ranks, which varied between 600 and 1,200, depending on the number of arrivals expected, were perpetually reduced by a routine of daily executions, and then replenished from new transports.

Although some 245,000 Jews were deported and murdered during Eberl's reign, his tenure did not go well. August Hingst, an SS sergeant who served at the camp at that time, testified that 'Dr Eberl's ambition was to reach the highest possible numbers and exceed all the other camps.' He added: 'So many transports arrived that the disembarkation and gassing of the people could no longer be handled.' Eberl's incompetent command was also a concern. As more transports arrived each day from Warsaw, Bialystok and Lublin, mountains of corpses and victims' belongings were piled all over the camp. Globocnik was also furious over reports of corruption. Large sums of money and valuables disappeared into the pockets of camp staff, and Eberl channelled money into the coffers of his former T4 commanders in Berlin.

During the final week of August, Globocnik and Wirth travelled to Treblinka to investigate. He dismissed Eberl immediately upon arrival. His replacement was Franz Stangl, another former T4 operative, who was transferred from Sobibor. Stangl immediately got to work transforming Treblinka into the world's most efficient killing factory. Kurt Franz, a sadistic psychopath who had also served with the T4 program, was appointed Stangl's deputy. It was Stangl and Franz who exercised total control over the camp during Hershl's ten-and-a-half months there.

★ ★ ★

I left Poland a couple of days later, my head swimming with deathly images. I could see the dead clearly and I had a sense of the suffering of those who had miraculously survived and what they had to carry with them. I could also see the faces of the perpetrators. The day after I got home, I called Sam to tell him about the trip. I told him I had been in Klobuck and that I had seen a pink house in a part of the town that had once been the shtetl, and perhaps that had been where the Szperlings had lived. I also said I had seen the little river that Rebecca Bernstein had spoken of, where Hershl had learned to swim and where the rest of Klobuck's youth had once amused themselves on hot summer days. I told him also I had been to Treblinka and how it had affected me.

'I'm sorry,' Sam said. 'This must be getting to you.'

'I dream about it,' I said. 'Several times a week.'

'You're maybe feeling just a little bit of what my father felt,' he said. But I wasn't sure that was true. I was beginning to understand that so few could possibly feel what Hershl felt, because so few had suffered the particular hell of Treblinka and survived.

'When I left Treblinka, I was angry,' I said. 'But I felt my emotions were worthless and cheap and easy, compared with the real horror of what people went through there.'

'That's just part of the disease of the place,' he said. 'That's just what my father felt when he thought about his family and what they went through there.'

'Sam, I think I've found a clue,' I told him.

'Go on,' he said, interested. 'A clue to what?'

'To why he survived, or at least part of the why, maybe the beginning of the why – bizarrely it has nothing at all to do with him.'

'My father always said he survived for two reasons – the first was his friend, Samuel Rajzman, who was a kind of surrogate father to him, and the second was luck.'

The odds against survival in Treblinka were enormous. The intention was that every Jew who arrived was to be exterminated, so in theory the chances of emerging alive were zero, barring a miracle or an accident. In the tragic reality, around 60 Jewish men and two Jewish women survived out of the 800,000-plus victims processed for murder. Assuming you were not immediately driven into a gas chamber, asphyxiated and then burned, as was the fate of the overwhelming majority, you were still likely to be beaten to death, shot, hanged, or torn to pieces by Kurt Franz's ferocious dog. You could also drop from exhaustion, starvation, disease, or even suicide. Yet of all the incredible and unforeseeable events that occurred in that miserable place, one episode, which took place less than three weeks before Hershl's arrival, expanded his chances of survival beyond zero to, at best, 14,000 to one.

It happened on 11 September 1942, the eve of the Jewish New Year. SS Sergeant Max Bialas was in charge of the inspection of the Jewish *Sonderkommando* in Treblinka's Roll Call Square that day. He arrived with Kurt Franz, whom the prisoners called '*Lalke*', the Polish word for a doll, because of his deceptively handsome appearance.

Before them was the desperate assembled mass of slave workers. Some had been selected for the *Sonderkommando* that very day from a transport of Jews from the Warsaw ghetto. Surrounded by Ukrainian auxiliaries with whips and guns, they were bruised and blood-ied. Their first hours in Treblinka had been marked by a rain of blows, whiplashes, punches and kicks. Some of the Jews were so traumatised after the day's gruesome proceedings that their spirits were already broken and they were ready for death. Approximately 45,000 Jews from the Warsaw Ghetto had been transported to Treblinka and gassed between 3–11 September, and these included the ones who had been selected to assist the killers. Many faces were nothing more than bloody masses. These 'marked' Jews were always the first to be noticed and the first to be taken to the Lazarett, where they were shot and fell into the burning pit, or to be fed into the gas chambers at the next available opportunity. This bat-tered group now stood at stony attention in a parody of a military parade.

Among them was one Meir Berliner, an Argentinian citizen, who had been visiting his parents in Warsaw when war broke out. His family had accompanied him from South America, and they had all become trapped in the Polish capital. He had arrived at Treblinka on a transport a few days earlier with his pregnant wife, five children, and parents, all of whom were separated from him on arrival and were murdered in the gas chambers. Berliner, who was selected for the *Sonderkommando*, had been in Treblinka long enough to learn the terrible truth.

Bialas walked among them, inspecting the ranks and occasionally pulling out new victims for the Lazarett. He ordered those who had arrived that day to step out of the ranks and line up on the side. However, it was not clear who was to be liquidated – the new arrivals or those who had arrived earlier. Testimonies of witnesses recall that the tension was agony in that moment. No-one moved. The Ukrainian guards began beating the Jews mercilessly with their whips and cudgels. Suddenly, Berliner broke free from the ranks and charged at Bialas. Witnesses saw the silver flash of a knife in his fist, and Berliner thrust the blade directly into the SS sergeant's back. Bialas collapsed in the courtyard. Survivor Abraham Krzepicki, one of those who witnessed the event, recalled: 'SS men came … They looked petrified … Berliner did not even try to escape. He stood quite composed, with a strange, mild smile on his face.'

SS Sergeant August Wilhelm Miete ran at Berliner with a shovel in his hand, and swung it into his face. Berliner fell, and Miete proceeded to hack him to death where he lay. Several Ukrainians also rushed forward and began beating Berliner. Other Ukrainians picked up shovels and lurched into the ranks, swinging their implements murderously. At the same time, guards began firing wildly from the watchtowers into the crowd. The prisoners ran in all directions to escape the gunfire. Dozens were killed and wounded. Franz screamed for the shooting to stop in an attempt to regain control. He ordered the Jews to reform in their ranks, and he had the fatally wounded Bialas taken away.

The Jews, shocked by the attack, gathered back into the line up, surrounded by nervous and heavily armed SS and Ukrainians. Franz ordered the Jewish Camp Elder, an engineer from Warsaw named Alfred Galewski, to stand in front of the roll call, and then beat him bloody with his whip. Then ten prisoners were pulled from the ranks at random and shot. A short time later, Bialas died en route to the military hospital in Ostrow.

The Germans were also shocked at this first act of violent resistance in the camp. It became clear that these Jews were not as harmless as they had thought, and that in despair they could be extremely dangerous. The following day, another 150 Jews were selected and shot into the pit in the Lazarett in a further act of revenge. The rest of the Jewish *Sonderkommando* was deprived of food and water for the next three days. While Berliner's solitary act of resistance did nothing to halt the grinding of the death machine, the *Sonderkommando* had won a modicum of respect though it also underlined the futility of solitary acts of rebellion. Yet, at the same time, the episode provided a glimmer of hope by proving that human dignity, or resistance at least, still existed here.

More importantly, the incident brought about lasting changes to the way the *Sonderkommando* were organised – a change that gave Hershl and others a chance for survival, or at least a temporary reprieve. While most of the thousands of Jews transported to the camp each day knew nothing of their fate until they were in the gas chambers, Stangl now realised something important: those who learned that they had come here to die – but were being kept alive for just a few days to work –

posed a serious threat to the efficiency of the killing process. This was especially so if they discovered what had already happened to their families. He concluded that with nothing to lose, members of the *Sonderkommando* were capable of desperate acts. So Stangl did what any good Nazi might have done in the circumstances – he introduced false hope, and ordered the establishment of a 'permanent' slave group. This order put a stop to the constant selections and replacement of workers. When Hershl arrived three weeks later, this permanent group of slaves was still being amassed.

Meanwhile, Wirth came personally from Lublin to inform the Jews of this new regime. Tanhum Greenberg, a Treblinka prisoner whose testimony is held at the Yad Vashem museum in Jerusalem, recalled the announcement. 'You Jews should work hard,' Wirth told them:

> Whoever works shall have everything. He shall get good food and drink. Workers will get medical treatment … You Jews should remember that Germany is strong. Five cities shall be built for Jews. There they will work and live well, and no-one will be taken away. Treblinka will be one of those cities where Jews will live. There will be no more selections.

In this 'city' of Jews, there now existed for the first time the possibility of survival. However, the price for those that remained alive would be enormous.

CHAPTER TEN

THE SELECTION

Hershl Sperling arrived in hell some time in late September or early October 1942. A reconstruction of his terrible first day in Treblinka is possible because Hershl described it himself in considerable detail in his book. But he does not tell it all. Perhaps he could not tell it all. Notably, the most painful aspects of his personal suffering and grief are omitted from his words. For this, I turned to Sam and, later, Alan, who had lived in the presence of that suffering for many years, and who retain a profound sense of their father's agony, but little concrete detail. Taken together, a sharp and disturbing picture emerges. Our conversations were not cathartic for them, because I offered no solution or solace. Nonetheless, they provided important clues to the impact of Treblinka and what had been going on in Hershl's traumatised psyche.

During one of these long conversations, Sam told me, 'My father could tell me about the piles of bodies, but he couldn't tell me the name of his mother or his sister. I have a sense he was always a fifteen-year-old boy who had lost his family. There was a very big void. He would always be a child whose parents had been murdered.'

I turned to Hershl's words once more. But it might have been easier to understand the man who had written them by standing on my head and reading the characters upside down. It occurred to me that he had devoted almost two-thirds of the first half of his Treblinka account to the events of his first day there, but made no mention of those things that terrorised him the most – the loss of his family, his culture, his people.

Sam said, 'It's a bit like this mystery of why he carried around a book that wasn't his all these years. He wanted to have something that was connected to what had happened, but the real thing was too much. In our dining room, in our house in Glasgow, there was an old black and white family photograph taken around 1907 or 1908. It showed my father's mother when she was maybe seven or eight years old. The photograph was always there, but he hardly ever went into that room. It's the same thing. He wanted to have these things close, but not so close that it made him remember and suffer.'

'Strange, I think, that he makes no mention of his family in his testimony.'

'The omissions were intentional,' Sam said. 'I don't have any doubt about that.'

* * *

That first day, the air was filled with the sound of weeping, choking, of children crying. The people were driven from Treblinka's Station Square through the guarded gate and into the 'Reception Square'. There was fear and confusion everywhere. The SS did everything in their power to disguise their greatest weakness – their small numbers – with wildly brutal and cruel behaviour. Guards screamed orders. Dogs on leashes barked and lunged ferociously. Whips cracked. Truncheons and rifle butts smashed into faces. At the same time, the SS still attempted to perpetuate the deception that this was a transit site, and that the Jews were being ushered towards showers. Few believed this anymore – although, somewhere in their hearts, there flickered the twin sparks of hope that both were true, that just maybe they were really going to be sent to the east for work. But the pungent, nauseating odour of decomposing corpses wafted across the camp. Hershl writes:

> On the right stands a large open barracks, the women's barracks. On the left stands another high, open barracks for the men. We are dying of thirst and scream for a drink of water. But we are not given it, even though there is a well in the middle of the yard, as if to spite us ... A command rings out: women to the right, men to the left. There are indescribable, heart-breaking farewell scenes, but the SS drive the people apart. The terrified children cling to their mothers.

This laceration of family ties debilitated the victims further, after the trauma of their train journey. However, for the Nazis, the division of the sexes had one primary purpose – the women must be separated and sent to the 'hairdressers' to have their hair shorn. Yet it also served to eliminate the possibility of triggering the protective instinct among fathers and older brothers, who might resist at the sight of their wives and sisters being driven into the gas chambers. At the same time, the men were dissuaded from rebelling for fear that it might endanger the lives of their loved ones.

Hershl does not mention that one of those agonising scenes was his own. I imagine the family clinging desperately to one another. I hear the cries of little, red-haired, nine-year-old Frumet piercing the chaos around them.

Sam and I had many telephone conversations, during which I attempted to jog his memory for anything Hershl might have said to him about Treblinka. On one occasion, he told me an astonishing story. I knew Hershl had spoken very little to his sons about Treblinka, if only because Sam has the most extraordinary power of recall that I have ever known, and he most certainly would have remembered such things. Often, Sam delved deep into his memory to recall incidents and even conversations that had occurred years earlier and that sometimes took a few moments. However, he answered quickly this time, when I brought up the subject of Hershl's arrival and selection at the camp. It was a story, he said, his father had sworn was true.

As Sam spoke, I immediately saw Hershl in the dust of Reception Square, just before father and son were separated from mother and daughter. I imagined the mayhem around them, and the noise and the terror. I also saw Gitel, fighting back her tears and her desperation. She gripped Hershl by the shoulders and stared into his face; one hand caressed his cheek.

Sam said, 'According to what my father told me, they were walking in a line and his mother stopped to explain to him what was happening to them. She said they were being chosen to live or die, and that he alone would survive to tell their story, and that one day he would leave Europe and escape to Scotland.'

'It was like a prophecy, almost Biblical, given the annihilation and suffering that was going on all around them.'

'That was how it was told to us, like a prophecy. My father told us about this more than once, a few times.'

'It's also amazing that he even knew where Scotland was, this fifteen-year-old boy from a shtetl in Klobuck.'

'His mother had relatives – the Goldbergs – who had moved to Scotland in the 1930s,' Sam said. 'In Scotland, they called themselves Gilbert.'

I would later meet the offspring of one of these relatives. But now, so clearly, I imagined the truncheon that came down hard on Hershl's head. I saw him fall in the dust, momentarily blinded. When he got up, his mother and sister were no longer there. Hershl writes: 'At last, the people have been divided into two groups.' The SS guards screamed at them: '*Alles herunter*' – 'everything down'. Across the square, the men could see women standing in front of the wooden barracks, spilling out from the crammed interior. Terrified families called to one another across the square. Hershl stood with his father. I imagine them clasping one another's hand. 'Savage SS let fly with their rubber truncheons and force the people to undress. Some more slowly, some more quickly, with greater or lesser degrees of embarrassment, the men and the women undress and lay their clothes aside.'

Amid all this chaos, one Jewish slave worker in colourful attire – this one with a red armband – made his way through the confused crowd. He was muttering indecipherable words and handing out pieces of thread, with which people were supposed to tie their shoes together. Had this man gone mad? Now other strange, muttering characters began to move among them. They were also dressed in odd clothing – silk shirts, pyjama bottoms, colourful chiffon scarves and caps – each of them wore a different type of cap. One of them, at last, spoke directly to Hershl.

> We are told the terrible truth. From this camp, no-one comes out alive. There can be no question of escape. We have come to our death. But we simply cannot believe it. The human being is too attached to life, even if the truth of these predictions should be confirmed a thousand times.

In Reception Square, all the naked women were driven into the barracks.

> They do their best to cover their breasts with their arms. At the entrance to the barracks, a shearing-squad awaits them. With one cut, all the women's hair is hacked off and immediately packed into waiting sacks. Then the women are assembled in groups and, with their hands above their heads, they are led through a back door into the death-camp.

Whips cracked again as the naked men were forced to pack all the clothing – male and female alike – and pile them in an area for disinfection.

Everyone has to carry a heavy load and go at a running pace through another gate into a second huge square surrounded by long, single-storey barracks. The clothing is laid down by the barracks. Then everyone has to get into line, their hands above their heads, and at a marching pace, to the rhythm of the beating rubber truncheons, we return to the main square.

Near the door of the men's barracks, a cashier set up his operation. The deception continued. All gold, money, foreign currency and jewellery must be deposited in return for a receipt. The men formed a line amid whiplashes from the Ukrainian auxiliaries. Regulations required that everyone bathe before continuing their journey, they announced. They were marched to Roll Call Square, where a new order rang out. Hershl writes:

> The men are made to run many times round the square until they are completely exhausted. This is so when they are marched to their death they will be so tired that they will not be able to offer any resistance.

Hershl and his father were assailed with whips and truncheons, and cut with bayonets, as they ran, naked, with their hands in the air, deprived of human dignity. '*Schnell, schnell,*' the guards screamed. Some of the guards laughed at the sight of these Jews on the brink of collapse. Others called out insults. Some of the Jews were old men. Others were ill. Still others, like Hershl, were adolescent boys. The weakest among them grew breathless, staggering as they fell in the dirt. None had consumed food or water for at least two days. Those who went down either picked themselves up beneath a rain of blows or were dragged to the Lazarett and shot into the pit. Hershl watched in disbelief as the cruelty unfolded. Indeed, a tone of disbelief and shock runs through his entire account of Treblinka. It was the start of an education for him. He was beginning to understand that every aspect of human endeavour in Treblinka carried with it the possibility of death. The run had a secondary purpose for the SS. The idea was to make certain the men were fully distracted and properly cowed during the roughly thirty minutes it took to stuff every woman and child into the gas chambers and murder them, from the closing of the door to the moment the first corpses were dragged out the other side. Efficiency was everything.

Now the men were marched back to a narrow dirt strip between the two sets of wooden huts, so-called Deportation Square. There were no choices. There was no question of resistance. With their receipts in their hands, this doomed procession of naked men was herded toward a gate in the fence. Fierce dogs snapped at their naked bodies to be sure no one dallied. An SS man called out: 'Faster, faster, the water is getting cold.' They fled through the gate to escape the terror behind them.

Then an extraordinary thing happened. An SS man – one of no more than 20 possible individuals – grabbed Hershl by the arm and yanked him to the side. 'At the very door, 30 men are pulled out. I am one of them.'

We cannot know what thoughts went through his mind as his father was driven through the gate toward death. The SS man spoke to him in German.

'You understand me?'

Instinctively, perhaps with his mother's prophecy spinning around in his head, he answered, 'Ja.'

'Good. Go get into your clothes. Special work.' The German's tone was almost friendly. 'Chatty,' recalled Richard Glazar, another Treblinka survivor, who experienced a similar selection less than a week later.

A Jewish prisoner, the head of the work group, wearing a blue band on his sleeve, appeared and divided the 30 young men into six groups of five. He led one group across the square to a storeroom piled high with clothes. Hershl was among this group. This foreman's name was Samuel Rajzman.

Hershl was instructed to tie the clothes in bundles and wrap them in sheets. Rajzman urged the workers to work quickly. Hershl writes: 'We have been chosen to form the work-squads in the camp. For the meantime, we are safe.' The annihilation of 7,000 people – the entire transport of Jews, save 30 souls, who had set off that late September day from Częstochowa – was complete.

★ ★ ★

No member of the Jewish *Sonderkommando* survived Treblinka without friendship. Every survivor was helped by someone else – even though in many cases in the end that 'someone else' did not survive. Samuel Rajzman, who was already 40 years old by the time he was deported to the death camp, was Hershl's 'someone else', and almost immediately became a kind of surrogate father to Hershl. This is not to suggest that Hershl did not possess an inner strength that helped him survive – but in the grotesque hell of Treblinka, that was not enough.

Rajzman, who would become the only Treblinka survivor to testify at the Nuremberg trials, arrived at the camp on a transport from Warsaw on 21 September 1942, a week or so before Hershl. He was born in the Polish town of Wegrow in 1902. Before the war, he lived with his wife and young daughter in Warsaw, where he had been an accountant and translator with an import-export business. Years later, even long after Rajzman's death, Hershl spoke of him with an extraordinary admiration.

In February 1947, Rajzman told the 69th sitting of the Nuremberg trials:

> I was already quite undressed, and had to pass through this *Himmelstrasse* to the gas chambers. Some eight thousand Jews had arrived with my transport from Warsaw. At the last minute before we moved toward the street, an engineer, Galewski, an old friend of mine, whom I had known in Warsaw for many years, caught sight of me. He was the overseer of workers among the Jews. He told me that I should turn back from the street. And as they needed an interpreter for Hebrew, French, Russian, Polish, and German, he managed to obtain permission to liberate me.

So it emerged that while Rajzman helped and protected Hershl, as far as was possible in a place like Treblinka, Rajzman himself was helped and protected by his friend Galewski, the camp elder. In turn, Galewski was most likely protected to a degree by

Franz Stangl, the omnipotent commander of Treblinka. Galewski, the tall, aristocratic professional from Warsaw, spoke impeccable German and his leadership qualities would have been difficult to replace, given Stangl's desire for Treblinka to run smoothly.

Like Rajzman, Hershl also possessed considerable language skills. He spoke good Polish, Hebrew, Yiddish, German as well as some Russian and a smattering of other Slavic languages. Apart from the obvious benefit of understanding German – especially the words spoken to him at the door of the *Himmelstrasse* – he may have been kept alive for a purpose unknown even to Hershl himself. Treblinka's initial purpose, as part of Operation Reinhard, was the extermination of Jews who lived within the General Government of Nazi-occupied Poland. However, plans had also been drawn up for Jews to be brought there from Holland, France, Greece, Yugoslavia, Germany, the Soviet Union, and perhaps Great Britain. From the perspective of the camp masters, languages would become crucial for getting foreign Jews off the trains and into the gas chambers.

Nonetheless, it was Rajzman who took Hershl under his wing in those first few hours, and confirmed to him that everything that had been rumoured was true. This was an efficient, top of the line death factory, operated by Jews and specifically designed for the mass murder of Jews. He had descended into a brutal and vicious underworld, where his people were slaughtered each day in enormous numbers and the Nazis grew rich on murder and plunder. In this place, Jews were stuffed naked into gas chambers and suffocated, and the world did not care. Hershl's mother, father and little sister, like Rajzman's own family, were already dead. He must accept this; and somehow he must hold on to his life.

Hershl's testimony tells us that he was immediately assigned to a work group called the *Lumpenkommando*. His job was to sort the mountains of clothes left by the victims. As Hershl worked, Rajzman began teaching him how to survive. It was Rajzman, Hershl said later, who had taught him the crucial 'how to look, but not look' at the SS. From the clothes of the dead, Rajzman also provided Hershl that day with his first cap, the most essential item a Jew could possess in Treblinka. In this perverse world, possession of a cap was a matter of life and death. Without one, a prisoner stood out and was thus marked to die in the daily ritual of murder. Treblinka survivor Samuel Willenberg wrote eloquently about the lethal cap games played by the SS and Ukrainian guards at the camp. Willenberg writes of his first day at the camp in his book, *Revolt in Treblinka*:

> When SS men come by, stand at attention, whip off your cap and report, '*Ich melde gehorsam*' – 'I report in submission.' I noticed that no prisoner from kommandant to rank-and-file ever parted with his cap.

Hershl learned the fundamentals quickly. If he had not learned quickly he would not have survived long. Hershl also learned that each cap infringement equalled punishment, and could mean a beating or even immediate death. Caps had to be removed whenever an SS man passed and when the block commander reported the headcount at roll call each day. The guards would shout '*Muetzen ab*' – 'hats off' repeatedly during the line-ups and over the course of the day. The Germans also insisted that during line-ups all caps were removed with the right hand only and with the synchronised motion of all prisoners together. Moreover, when removed, all caps had to slap the thigh to emit a specific type of thud. If the sound produced was not just as the Germans desired, it would have to be repeated, sometimes for hours, and always with brutal consequences. Only Galewski was exempt from this bizarre ritual. Instead, even more peculiarly, Galewski had to press his cap tightly to his left shoulder when in the presence of the SS. He also had to hold up his whip in a certain way. The Germans had issued him this whip as a mark of his authority – but, according to witnesses, he never used it.

That first night, Rajzman showed Hershl where to sleep, how to arrange the pile of multicoloured rags into a bed and he told him how best to avoid blows to the face – because to be 'marked' meant being noticed by the SS and therefore murdered shortly afterwards. Prisoners in Treblinka were permitted to take what they needed in terms of food and clothing from the belongings of the murdered, but the Ukrainians often prevented this. Nor were heads shaved here, except among the women in the moments before death, and there were no striped pyjama-style uniforms, as in concentration camps and work camps. The *Sonderkommando* slaves of Treblinka had but one purpose: to assist with the genocide of their own people. Then they themselves would be killed when their usefulness had expired. It did not matter whether they had hair on their heads or not.

Hershl barely moved during his first night in the Treblinka barracks, atop his bed of rags, as though the realisation had now struck him that the important thing in this extermination camp was not to be noticed. In his sorrow and loss, did he already understand that if he were to stand out in this place he would almost certainly be killed? I remembered him sitting in a maroon easy chair in his home in Glasgow. The television was on, but he was not watching it. He sat so still and quiet, as if deep in a trance. As I sat sipping a beer in old Warsaw, I wondered if he thought then that he would not be killed if he did not move.

Some time that first evening before the 'lights-out' command at 9.00pm, word came from a prisoner who had been asked to pass on a message to a fifteen-year-old new arrival named Hershl Szperling. His father had been recognised, probably by one of the Częstochowa Jews pulled from the transports in the preceding weeks, in the moments before he was driven into the gas chamber. Now, in this twilight world of suffering, the prisoner entered the barracks.

'Your father is dead,' the prisoner said. 'He asked that you say Kaddish for him.'

This message was, in turn, passed on by Hershl to his children. I thought about it for a long time after Sam told me the story. They were a religious family, so of course Hershl would say Kaddish for his dead father. It seemed a peculiar last request, because he was stating the obvious. Then it occurred to me that what he was really saying was 'Remember me.'

But there was no time to grieve. All Hershl's strength was now focused on survival.

CHAPTER ELEVEN

BETWEEN LIFE AND DEATH

It is late November and a typical Treblinka day begins. A persistent drizzle falls in the early-morning darkness. Hershl has been in the camp for almost two months. He lies half-awake as usual in a part of the camp called the ghetto – a fenced-in section comprising a large, wooden horseshoe-shaped barracks, a few workshops and the *Appelplatz,* or Roll Call Square, just north of Reception Square, where the human transports are unloaded from the trains. We cannot know precisely what Hershl – this fifteen-year-old boy – feels about all he experiences here, but we know it will traumatise him for the rest of his life. The psychological wounds gouged by Treblinka are deeper than anything else the Nazis could ever force him to endure.

The lingering smell of death hangs in the air like a poisonous cloud. For weeks on end, wagonloads of victims have been arriving in enormous numbers – sometimes two and three trains each day. The November air is cold and damp. This is where Hershl's most horrific nightmares begin, scenes he will return to again and again. Terrible and violent images from this place will mutilate his sleep for the rest of his life. Bizarrely, he is probably clothed in silk, the night-time attire of choice in Treblinka, because it is said that lice find it more difficult to grip the smooth fabric. The silk is pilfered from the belongings of the dead. Yet, each morning, the prisoners' clothing is covered with blood spots. Infected bites turn into angry pustules, and boils cover their bodies.

Now a screaming Ukrainian auxiliary guard, one of around 150 recruited by the SS, throws open the barracks door and rushes at the prisoners with his whip. It is a morning ritual. This Ukrainian is probably around twenty years old and most likely a former prisoner of war from the Soviet Army. Cruelty can be discerned in his eyes. Copious supplies of vodka exacerbate his brutality. Like all his compatriots in Treblinka, he is despised by the Jews and the SS alike. He does not care. Not in his wildest dreams can he have imagined himself knee-deep in so much free food, vodka, money and women – and all for simply killing and beating Jews. As he enters, most of the prisoners jump to their feet, terrified.

The prisoners' tin bowls clatter loudly. Tired and miserable, they rush into the *Appelplatz* and at the same time try to avoid blows and whiplashes from the Ukrainians and the kapos – prisoners who have been appointed to positions of authority by the Germans. The urination and excrement buckets are taken at a run to be emptied. In

Treblinka, everything is done on the run. During this morning's turmoil, a voice rings out in an exchange between two prisoners: '*Henick, prosze ciebie*' – 'I beg you, get up, you've got to get hold of yourself.'

I am back at my desk in Scotland, trying to understand Hershl in Treblinka, when I find these words. I discover them buried in the memoir of another Treblinka survivor, Richard Glazar, who recalls one winter's early morning in the same barracks, at the same time Hershl is there. I am struck by the possibility that this remembered slice of life might be an exchange between Hershl – Heniek in Polish – and a pleading, fatherly Samuel Rajzman. The words are an entreaty from one comrade to another. It strikes me also that the appeal comes in Polish, but the response is in Yiddish, before it is 'swallowed up by other voices', Glazer writes. I immediately call my friend Sam.

'It seems to fit,' I say. 'Rajzman, of course, would have spoken and understood Yiddish as part of his culture, but Polish was the language of sophisticated, multicultural Warsaw, where Rajzman had spent much of his life. It seems appropriate that he should make his plea in Polish but that the response should come in Yiddish, Hershl's mother tongue.'

'It's within the realms of possibility,' Sam says. 'Rajzman was the closest thing he had to a father.' After a long moment, he adds, 'It's strange and upsetting to imagine him there. But we'll never know for sure if this is him.'

Rajzman died in 1979, and Glazar, a Czech Jew who, like Hershl, was also pulled from the door of the *Himmelstrasse* for his language skills, committed suicide in 1997. However, if it really is Hershl, this moment must mark his turning point, the threshold across which he pushes. All his instincts are honed on one thing – survival. This is Hershl's coming of age in the kingdom of death.

I ask Sam one more question on this day – it is a recurring question that always produces the same answer – 'What do you think he felt during his time in Treblinka?'

'Mostly, he was frightened, I think,' he says.

The Ukrainian auxiliary has now completed his morning routine of bullying and a meagre breakfast of lukewarm ersatz coffee and stale bread is consumed by the prisoners before roll call at 6.00am. The prisoners are divided into work groups and as this November day breaks, another nightmare begins. They toil for twelve hours a day, with a half-hour break at noon. It is long and hard physical labour, and emotionally tormenting. Not only does Hershl witness daily mass murder, but also its aftermath.

Between early September and mid-December 1942, the camp's peak period of activity, more than 400,000 Jews are annihilated. At the same time, the number of Treblinka's Jewish *Sonderkommando* swells to around 1,200. Many in the *Sonderkommando* are former residents of the Częstochowa ghetto because, as it happens, this new, semi-permanent group of slave workers is still in the process of being established when more than 35,000 Częstochowa Jews are dumped in the camp. This blind, random bit of luck increases Hershl's chances of survival, statistically. Had he arrived from the city of Radomsko a few days later, for example, he would have been sent directly to the gas chambers. Among those selected from the Częstochowa transport, aside from the young and relatively strong, like Hershl, are carpenters and architects to design, construct and repair camp buildings, dentists to extract gold teeth from the dead, saddle makers to produce the fearsome Treblinka whips, tailors to sew suits and uniforms for the SS, cobblers to make boots, physicians to tend the Nazis' ailments, bakers for fresh bread, goldsmiths to value and sort the gold and precious stones after the victims were murdered and young boys – known as *putzer*, from the Yiddish and German verb 'to polish' – to work as personal servants and shoe shiners. A few women, mostly the young and attractive plucked from the death trains, are also included in the permanent *Sonderkommando* to do laundry and work in the kitchens.

To the crack of whips, Hershl and the rest of the *Lumpenkommando* run to the sorting yard. What lies before them is a familiar sight – towering, multi-coloured mountains of clothing and other plundered belongings in parallel rows, tens of metres long. Jewish slaves run between the mountains, climb upon them and toil like devils. There are separate piles for shirts, underwear, vests, towels, shoes, glasses and suitcases. Each suitcase bears the name of its murdered owner painted on the lid. They contain shaving brushes, fountain pens, tablecloths, gloves, family photographs, medical syringes, keys, tradesmen's tools, children's toys and every other conceivable item considered essential for life in the east. Long human chains soon carry bundles between the sorting yard and the storeroom. I see Hershl among them in the chain, running, working, looking but not looking, trying not to be noticed, trying to survive. The enforced rapid movement is accompanied by thunderous shouts, beatings and murders by the SS and work group leaders. Jewish kapos lash their whips to demonstrate their enthusiasm to their German masters. The speed at which the prisoners are compelled to work is part of the brutality. Hershl writes:

> Every garment was minutely examined to see whether any valuables were sewn into or hidden in it. From each garment the Star of David had to be removed as carefully as possible, so that no-one could see it had belonged to a Jew. Each tin of shoe-polish, each pocket-torch or belt is prised or cut open to find anything of value that might be there. Watches and gold are put in separate piles. The following things are also put in separate piles – diamonds, rings, gold roubles, gold dollars and so on … When each bundle is tied up, the Jewish sorter has to put a piece of paper with his name on it in the bundle, so that it would immediately be known which individual to punish for the smallest breach of the regulations.

This peak period of extermination is also the most dangerous and fearful for the *Sonderkommando*. The SS vie with each other. They often kill members of each other's work groups in acts of spite and petty revenge. At the same time, sadistic SS officers tour the camp seeking victims. Murders are arbitrary, random and whimsical.

> In the camp, which in any case was so full of terrible cruelty, there were individual SS men who were famous for particular specialities.

The Jews have codenames for the cruellest of the SS – the 'three pillars of Treblinka' – which they use to warn one another when the deadliest SS are approaching. Hershl identifies Sergeant August Miete as one of them. Hershl refers to him as '*Mütter*' – the names of the SS are only ever heard, and never seen written down. Miete's domain is the Lazarett, the execution pit and fire disguised as a field hospital, where the sick and the troublesome are led. Miete carries out most of the killings in this sham hospital personally. The Jews know him as the Angel of Death.

Another 'pillar' is Kurt Küttner, known as 'Kiewe', who beats and murders prisoners regularly. He is also feared for his network of informants. Kurt Franz, the deputy camp commander under Stangl, is the final 'pillar' and another psychopathic sadist. The prisoners perhaps fear him more than the others, particularly if he is with his dog, Barry, who has been trained to attack victims' genitals.

Hershl's every movement in Treblinka, the most mundane function, is a stark choice between life and death. Hundreds of offences are punishable by death or beatings. Death is imposed for carrying a piece of bread, or a coin, or a wedding ring. Death is also meted out for not working to a commanders' satisfaction. Prisoners are killed most often by a gunshot in the mouth. Victims are forced after beatings to open their eyes and stare into the gun barrel. Many Jews are bludgeoned to death with their shovels. Hershl writes:

> *Untersturmführer* Kurt Franz … used to pick out people from the work-brigades every day, and under various pretexts – working too slowly, giving hostile glances and so on – he would order them to strip naked and then beat them to death with his riding whip … One man was killed because he was so cold that he lay down on a heap of clothes and covered himself with a torn fur: for that crime he was torn to pieces by the dog Barry, which was specially kept for such things. The man's overseer, who had not reported him, was killed on the spot by Franz with one blow to the face … I only once met an SS man in Treblinka who was unwilling to participate in the inhuman deeds. The first day he was there he found everything so incredible that he took a Jew from a work-squad aside and asked him to tell him the absolute truth. 'Impossible, impossible!' he kept on murmuring, shaking his head as he spoke. From that day, he was never seen again.

I would like to find this SS man, and even if he is no longer alive, I would like to identify him – but I fear it is no longer possible. I want to know why he was repelled by the horror of Treblinka and others accepted it and even thrived on it.

★ ★ ★

On this typical Treblinka morning comes the clamour of a locomotive pushing wagons toward the platform. It is a transport of Polish Jews. Documents of the German railway authorities, discovered after the war, reveal that between 3–7 November 14,000 people from the Konskie region in central Poland were deported to Treblinka. A long, piercing whistle heralds their arrival, followed by the terrible but familiar sound of wailing. What is Hershl doing amidst all of this? He is in the sorting yard, watching, silent, tormented, angry. His people are being murdered before his eyes. He tries, but he cannot become inured to it. Yet he learns quickly how to adapt. He imagines escape and revenge. He remembers the murder of his family and the tears of his little, red-haired sister, whose name he could never utter again. Sometimes he weeps to himself at night. Unlike other men, he does not disremember all the monstrous information to preserve his sanity. He takes in everything. He remains human with the help of his friend Rajzman. Their nightly talks and their quasi-familial bond renew and nourish him.

Upon the tracks at Reception Square each wagon contains piles of dead, who lie on the excrement that has been left after the long journey. The bodies of those who have died en route must be stripped and dragged individually into the burning pit in the Lazarett. In the months to come, this will be Hershl's work too.

> This squad has to cleanse the wagons of their dead bodies, filth and excrement as quickly as possible … The squad works with brooms. Each pair of workers has to clean out one wagon in ten minutes.

Meanwhile, men, stripped of clothing and dignity, many clutching suitcases in trembling hands, are herded through the undressing area. The temperatures are near zero. The men are whipped and punched. Most know they are being driven toward death.

Across the yard, women are forced to strip themselves and their children. Some weep desperately as they stand in line in the icy air, their children pressed to their breasts. The wailing of the women and children is unbearable. The guards lash at the naked bodies, demanding silence, order. Instructions are screamed at them. The Germans are expert at control via mass hysteria. The victims' brief stay in Treblinka is filled with carefully orchestrated violence and they have no time to think. Two-and-a-half years later, as Hershl is writing his testimony, he will recall naked women and children as they are driven through the *Himmelstrasse* toward the barbers, on to their deaths in the gas chambers. He recalls also those who are not strong enough to make it to the *Himmelstrasse*. These victims are instead shot into the burning pit. 'The red squad, men with a red-cross symbol … carry the old, the sick and children up to the age of six, or those who have lost their parents, on stretchers or in their arms from the ramp to the Lazarett.' The flaming ditch of burning bodies is surely the pit of Hershl's nightmares – all the burning children. 'Our life is a constant round of fear and pain … Death is constantly before our eyes.'

Members of the *Lumpenkommando*, Hershl most likely among them, are directed to the women's barracks to collect the discarded clothes. The garments are gruesomely warm from the heat of the victims' bodies. In the yard, other prisoners push baby carriages back and forth between the bundles and the storerooms, transporting bottles, containers and other small objects. The children and the mothers who once used these carriages are already murdered – perhaps just moments earlier. 'They arrived and were dead within two hours,' Stangl tells interviewer Gitta Sereny in 1971.

Meanwhile, all birth certificates, education diplomas, letters, as well as photographs must be taken to the Lazarett and burned in the pit. Every trace of those who are murdered must be blotted out. This is now Hershl's task.

> The collection and sorting of pictures is … strictly controlled. For the crime of taking a picture to keep, a Jew was punished by death. Mass shootings took place simply because one of the Jews had hidden on his person a picture of his wife or his near relatives.

TREBLINKA DEATH CAMP

100 *metres*

1   Main gate
2   SS relaxation area
3   SS barracks
4   Arms storeroom
5   Petroleum tank
6   Camp Commandant's office and living quarters
7   Living quarters for female auxiliary workers
8   Zoo
9   *GoldJuden* where Jewish prisoners had to sort out gold taken from prisoners
10 Vegetable garden
11 Waste disposal
12 The Ghetto: Jewish prisoners' living and working quarters
13 Assembly Square

14 Platform where the human cargo arrived
15 Reception Square and undressing barracks
16 'Himmelstrasse': camouflaged passage through which prisoners were chased to the gas chambers
17 Ten new gas chambers
18 Three original gas chambers
19 Cremation area
20 Mass grave: originally victims were buried, later they were cremated and their ashes buried
21 High sand bar to restrict view
22 Mass grave
23 Barracks for *Sonderkommando* prisoners working in death camp

24 Sorting yard for victims' clothes and valuables
25 Lazarett (field hospital), an execution site disguised as a hospital
26 Building where victims' possessions were sorted

■ *Watchtower*

▬ ▬ ▬ *Anti-tank defences*

--------------- *Railway*

▬▬▬▬ *Camouflaged barbed wire*

– – ▬ – – *Barbed wire*

▬▬▬ *Internal road*   *Tree screen*

There is no respite. Weeks later, trains from western Europe begin to arrive. One such transport, Hershl tells us, consists of either 'German or Czech Jews', and it requires a different strategy. Instead of the controlled hysteria and violence, they are 'received with all kinds of tricks and pretences which masked the true situation'.

The Germans go to extraordinary lengths to deceive these Jews, perhaps because they are better educated and it is feared they will more quickly grasp the monstrous reality of Treblinka and resist. In his testimony, Hershl identifies SS sergeant Josef Hirtreiter – known as 'Sepp' to both the Jews and the Germans – for his particular cruelty.

> These people were not beaten on arrival and even the commands were given in a polite and friendly fashion. One woman who has brought a lot of suitcases with her and does not want to go into the Lazarett, is given assurances that her luggage will be sent on after her. She, however, won't hear of it. All her life, she says, she has worked for the things she has brought with her and she isn't going to entrust them to anyone else. *Unterscharführer* Sepp finally loses patience with her and cannot resist using his whip. Then she leaves her suitcases and goes weeping and wailing to the Lazarett with the man from the red brigade … *Unterscharführer* Sepp… had the habit of choosing small children from the newly arrived transports, and skilfully splitting their little heads with a spade.

The mass exterminations in Treblinka take place in a section called the upper camp, the Totenlager, or Camp II. This is the murderous heart of Treblinka, isolated from the main camp by camouflage fencing. Stangl has recently installed ten new gas chambers, replacing the original three, increasing the killing capacity from 600 to 3,800 at a time. The height of the new rooms is some two feet lower than previously. The change in dimension is deemed necessary because incidents have occurred where children have not been asphyxiated as the gas rose to the ceiling. Showerheads and pipes criss-cross above the prisoners. The new design maintains the illusion of a shower room. An ante-room contains the engine – appropriated from an abandoned Soviet tank – that pumps the poisonous carbon monoxide through pipes into the chambers. Hershl writes:

> It was strictly forbidden to cross from one camp to the other. In the early period, the food carriers used to come to us from Camp II and bring us all the minutest details of the cruel deeds that were being perpetrated there. When we heard about them, we choked and our heads whirled feverishly. It often took hours before we could start working again. The tears running down our faces did not alleviate our helpless rage and our searing pain.

The work of the death camp *Sonderkommando* in the Totenlager – whose ranks vary between 150 and 350, depending on the number of transports – is gruelling, both physically and emotionally. Recruitment for the extermination area takes place in the lower camp – never directly from the transports and often as punishment. Those sent to the extermination area never return.

TREBLINKA KILLING AREA

The time taken to process the human transports in Treblinka varied according to the number of victims. The following estimates are based on testimonies of surviving Jewish Sonderkommando and some of the perpetrators. Camp commander Franz Stangl said: 'A transport of 30 freight cars with 3,000 people was liquidated in three hours. When the work lasted for about 14 hours, 12,000 to 15,000 people were annihilated.' Later, the Germans improved efficiency and reduced the duration of the killing process to one and a half hours for 3,000 victims.

GAS CHAMBERS: 25-30 minutes

The gassings began on 23 July 1942. By the time Hershl arrived in September, there were 10 gas chambers in Treblinka, each with capacity for 1,000-1,200 victims. It took roughly 30 minutes to murder them with carbon monoxide, from the closing of the doors to the moment the first corpses were dragged out the other side.

HIMMELSTRASSE: 20-50 minutes

The Himmelstrasse, also called the Tube, was some 100 metres long. This is where the women were met by the "barbers". An SS 'bademeister' called: 'Quickly, the water is getting cold.' But the people were not herded passively like sheep to the slaughter. They were beaten into the gas chambers in their final struggle to resist death.

RECEPTION SQUARE: 20-50 minutes

Men and women were separated and ordered to undress to screams of 'Alles herunter' – 'everything down'. Children remained with the women. The men were ordered to run around the square. Women and children were driven first into the so-called Himmelstrasse, or Road to Heaven, toward death.

STATION SQUARE AND ARRIVAL: 20-50 minutes

Twenty wagons at a time were shunted into Treblinka's Station Square. Here, between 1,600 and 3,000 victims were pulled from the wagons and driven brutally through a gate into 'Reception Square'.

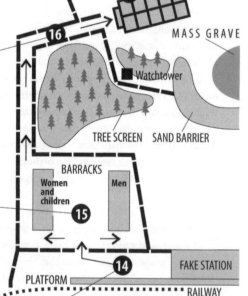

The food-carriers describe to us how the path to the death camp goes through a garden. Just before you come to the death-shower there is a hut, where everyone is instructed once again to relinquish money and gold. This is always accompanied by the threat of punishment by death. The greed of the Nazis is such that they won't let even the smallest item of any value slip through their hands.

Now the victims are beaten viciously as they are driven from the undressing barracks in Camp I and through *Himmelstrasse*. The people run naked with their hands in the air. High green walls of pine branches and barbed wire rise up two-and-a-half metres at the sides. An SS man, the *bademeister*, calls: 'Quickly, the water is getting cold.' The *Himmelstrasse* bends sharply to the right, so no one entering the tube can see what is occurring at the exit. These people are not herded passively like sheep to their slaughter, as is the perception of many. They are beaten, kicked, punched, and hacked into the gas chambers in their final struggle to resist death.

At the shower room of death, which is adorned only by a Star of David, the victims are received with bayonets. They are driven into the shower rooms, prodded with these bayonets. Whereas the men go into the showers in a fairly restrained fashion, terrible scenes take place among the women. Showing no mercy, the only way the SS can think of to quieten the women is with their rifle-butts or bayonets.

It is here that two Ukrainian guards meet the victims. One of them is Ivan Demaniuk, nicknamed 'Ivan the Terrible'; the other is his fellow executioner Nikolaj Marchenko. It is a series of trials in the late 1980s in the US and Jerusalem of a man accused of being Ivan the Terrible that will later bring Treblinka to the world's attention. With a long sword, Demaniuk amputates hands, slices bodies, cuts off women's breasts. Specially trained dogs are also at the doors, and they bite chunks from victims' flesh, driving them toward the apparent safety of the shower room. Demaniuk is peculiarly sadistic towards the women. Many witnesses have testified to his cruelty. Hershl will never forget him.

Inside the gas chambers, the walls are covered with white tiles. There is no light once the doors are closed. People desperately struggle against death. None live to tell of the experience.

When all the wretched victims have been forced into the showers, the doors are hermetically sealed. After a few seconds, horrifying screams are heard through the walls. These screams go up to heaven, demanding revenge. The screaming becomes weaker and weaker, finally dying away. At last everything is silent. Then the doors are opened, and the corpses are thrown into huge mass graves, which hold about sixty thousand to seventy thousand people.

Sometime in the middle of November the Germans begin to burn the bodies.

They would dig out a deep trench, and throw in a few old trunks, boxes, wood and things like that. All that is set alight, and a layer of corpses is thrown on to it, then more branches, and more corpses, and so on.

One witness, Jankiel Wiernik, a member of the totenlager's *Sonderkommando*, tells grotesquely of how the bellies of dead women who had been pregnant, 'would burst open. The foetus would be exposed and could be seen burning inside the mother's womb.' I asked myself in my notepad, 'How can any man survive Treblinka intact?' I scribbled beneath that question, 'Impossible.'

★ ★ ★

At 6.00pm whistles blow from every direction, signalling the end of the work day in the lower camp. But the terror and the murder are not yet over. Evening is the most dangerous time for the prisoners, because the punishments are always doled out during the late roll call. Infringements might include possession of food or money, or not working quickly enough or with appropriate zeal. Those deemed guilty are given between 25 and 50 lashes with a special strap made in the camp by the Jewish saddle makers. The victims are placed on a specially designed bench with their bare buttocks exposed. They must count the number of whiplashes aloud, and if there is an error the ordeal is repeated. The sadist Kurt Franz is the camp's whipping expert and also the designer of the special bench. He conducts the roll-call punishments with a pleasure that has been recorded by numerous witnesses.

> I can still see before me the punishment that was meted out to a nineteen-year-old boy who had forgotten to remove the Star of David from one garment. He is shot dead on the *Appellplatz* before the eyes of the assembled work-squads. He is forced to look directly into the gun-barrel. For making a movement of his head when the final command is given, he gets two brutal blows to the face. A few seconds later he falls to the ground, his head shattered, and is quickly removed.

Roll call often lasts several hours. After attendance is taken and the punishments are carried out, Küttner or Kurt Franz conduct what they like to call 'sports'. Prisoners are made to run in circles and on command they must drop to the ground and then jump to their feet, all while SS and Ukrainians lash with their whips. This ordeal proceeds until the weakest of the Jewish *Sonderkommando* has collapsed. They are then taken by Miete, the Angel of Death, to the Lazarett, and murdered. Any prisoner who has been bloodied or marked belongs to Miete.

The Germans' entertainment continues.

> In the evening, when we are dead tired, we have to sing various songs to the accompaniment of an orchestra. First the Treblinka March, then a Polish song which tells of a mother who sells her child in order not to die of hunger.

Late at night, those who still believe in God pray. Witnesses will recall how each night, Zev Kurland, the Lazarett kapo, recites the Kaddish, the Jewish prayer for the dead, for those he has seen murdered that day. Others find comfort in writing. Some write and also read aloud their poetry. Others pen descriptions of the horror they witness. Kurland, whose task is to help the victims undress in the Lazarett, is known to have recorded his tragic experiences and often reads them aloud to other prisoners. None of these works have been discovered. Other prisoners select themselves, hanging themselves in the middle of the night. Hershl writes: 'We often envied those who had it all behind them.'

CHAPTER TWELVE

THE SPITE

It was early spring in Scotland. I was at my desk trying desperately to imagine Hershl in Treblinka, when I came upon some bizarre facts about the camp. I looked out of my window and the rain came down in grey sheets. I began thinking how strange Scotland must have seemed to Hershl, but I ended up realising that everywhere – and everything – must have been strange, because Treblinka had infected him, so it didn't much matter where he was. I called Sam to tell him what I had discovered.

'You wouldn't believe some of this stuff,' I said. 'I can hardly believe it myself, and I'm sitting here reading it as a historical record.'

'Go on,' said Sam, exhaling smoke from another cigarette.

'Well,' I began. 'I know it's hard to imagine anything crazier than murdering a million people. But while all that was going on, there were other crazy things happening. I mean, if we think of Nazi Europe as an evil kingdom, then Treblinka was a separate little principality of evil – connected but autonomous. It was part of Nazi Europe but it was also its own universe.'

'What do you mean?'

'Aside from the big fact that Treblinka was a killing centre, there were other things about the place that were simply insane,' I said.

'Go on, then, tell me.'

'Well, for example, in no other place did off-duty killers relax, bizarrely, at their own zoo in the middle of the camp. There is something terribly shocking about these men, given all their murderous brutality and the suffering they caused, being off-duty there, relaxing. The SS men could look at captive foxes and exotic birds, and they had a beer garden with tables and sunshades. But at the same time, just yards away, thousands of victims were driven with whips into the gas chambers. It's such an ugly paradox.'

'I see what you're saying.'

I could not stop myself. 'The stench of the gas and all that rotting flesh must have been overwhelming.' I heard Sam groan to himself when I spoke of the rotting flesh, but continued, 'I suppose they were accustomed to it. That's strange in itself, don't you think? Where does this kind of madness fit in the scheme of human behaviour? I admit, I don't understand. Is it power, boredom, escapism? What is it?' Sam thought for a long time in the pregnant silence.

'I think it was a way for the Nazis to fool themselves. It was the same thing with their camp orchestras. They could tell themselves they weren't really so inhuman if they still had high culture and zoos and beer gardens.'

'You think it was a way for them to deal with their own barbarism?' I asked.

'That's exactly it,' said Sam.

I knew that the ten-man Treblinka orchestra had a dual purpose. They performed in the evenings for the SS's entertainment and during the late roll call while the *Sonderkommando* were being punished. During the day, the musicians played beside the gas chambers in an attempt to drown out the screams of those being asphyxiated.

I opened a copy of Gitta Sereny's *Into That Darkness*, which was based on her interviews with Treblinka commander Franz Stangl, and I read to Sam what he had said about the zoo. Sereny quoted him: 'We had any number of marvellous birds there, and benches and flowers. An expert from Vienna designed it for us. Of course, we were able to have experts for anything.'

'All of the experts were Jews, the vast majority of whom were later murdered. Stangl, oddly, also expressed the view that the camp "became really beautiful", with its flowerbeds and colourful paint schemes,' I said. 'Here was the man who controlled the most efficient killing machine in history, and he speaks about flowerbeds and experts – most of whom he ended up murdering – from Vienna.'

'Ah-ha,' said Sam, quickly. 'Vienna, you see, the place of high culture, experts. The fact they ended up murdering these experts is like the story of Jesus. They murder the Jew and then praise him. It's the story of Christianity in Europe. This supposed high culture was used to distract their minds from the raw animals that lay at their core. I despise their high culture, and my father did, too.'

'I'm not sure that it's the culture that is to blame,' I said. 'Isn't it just a question of perspective? Music didn't murder anyone. It was the Nazis who murdered people.'

'No,' he said. There was now anger in his tone. 'I still distrust Europeans bleating about culture. They pick and choose at will – they want us to associate Mozart and fine cuisine with their tradition and yet they still cannot face the more essential aspects of their culture – the two-thousand-year-old pathological hatred of Jews, based on a supposed love of one Jew and a vitriolic revulsion of the rest of us. This is still the way in Europe when it comes to feelings about Israel – the Israel-hating left-wing offspring of right-wing European Jew-haters. Most of them are so infected that they don't even understand. Thousands of years will pass and they will never get it.'

I knew that he was right. It wasn't just the zoo. I understood this now. There was something pathological at play here. In Treblinka, SS men jogged through nature trails and swam in the Bug River, while a giant excavator dug pits for corpses pulled from the death chambers. Later, the excavator was used to exhume the corpses. A gruesome photograph held in the United States Holocaust Memorial Museum in Washington DC shows the mangled bodies of Jews hanging from the digger's claws. Yet at the same time, just yards away, off-duty Nazis laughed and sipped beer in a zoo.

However, this pathological denial of the terrible, grotesque reality of mass murder did not end with the zoo and the beer garden. By the spring of 1943, flowers and plant pots had been placed outside the Ukrainian barracks – by then called the Max Bialas Barracks. The new guardhouse at the northwest corner of camp was constructed to look like a Tyrolean chalet. A fake but quaint-looking railway station was built by the offloading ramp where the victims disembarked. It was in fact the old storehouse for the belongings of those who had been murdered. A painted clock with numerals permanently reading six o'clock adorned its facade. Hershl tells us, in a tone of utter incredulity, about a fake ticket window, bogus timetables, signposts and arrows indicating 'toilet' and train connections 'To Warsaw', 'To Wolkowice' and 'To Bialystok'. All of it was designed to deceive Treblinka's victims and make the job of cramming them into the gas chambers that much easier.

At the end of the *Himmelstrasse* stood an entrance with columns, constructed to look like an ancient classical temple. Five steps decorated with baskets of flowers led to a doorway, covered with a large curtain stolen from a synagogue, masking the gruesome reality of the place. Above the portal, a Star of David was mockingly engraved and the Hebrew words inscribed: 'Through this gate only the righteous pass.' In the margin of the Treblinka history book, in which I again re-read this information, I scribbled the inadequate word, 'Spite'.

Spite, I suspected, also played its part in the relationship of the SS with each other. Greed and robbery perhaps made them feel they were something other than murderers and barbarians. Yet, economic plunder was always part of the plan at Treblinka.

> When each order for clothes comes in, the carefully sorted and packed stolen clothes are sent away. Usually a whole transport will depart with one article. There goes, for instance, a transport consisting entirely of suits, another consisting entirely of women's silk dresses, a third of shoes, and so forth. Gold is loaded on to lorries and taken away separately.

A letter from Globocnik to Himmler in 1944 reported the value of goods and cash taken from those killed in Treblinka, Belzec and Sobibor – the three Operation Reinhard camps – at around $75 million (worth $1.2 billion in 2009). But not all that was plundered ended up in designated Reich accounts.

Treblinka was the centre of an enormous black market. The Ukrainian guards, SS, and the local population all reaped rich rewards from the murder of Jews. The economics of supply and demand ran riot. Ukrainian guards pilfered food and sold it at hyperinflated prices to prisoners, who themselves maintained illicit hoards of currency, gold and diamonds – in spite of certain death if discovered. Among the testimonies from SS men and prisoners regarding the trade between the Ukrainians and the local population, there are stories of prisoners paying the equivalent of hundreds of US dollars for packages containing bread, sausage and vodka. At the same time, the price of material goods deflated because of the enormous supply. Men's watches sold for pennies. Farmers were seen with dozens of them in egg baskets, offering them for sale on market days in the local villages. Expensive fur coats were a common sight among village women. Some black marketeers arrived in the forests surrounding Treblinka with truckloads of vodka and bread to exchange for valuables they would then sell for hundreds of times their purchase price in Warsaw.

Between 3 September 1942 and mid-February 1943, some 438,600 men, women and children were brought from the General Government of Occupied Poland and a further 110,000 from the Bialystok district in the north-east were deported and then killed. A single person from one transport of 5,000 Jews might be selected for work; maybe two or three from another. In October 1942, some 6,800 Jews from the town of Zarki, the home of the kibbutz training camp, not far from Częstochowa, were deported to Treblinka. Population records reveal numerous Szperlings in the town and at the kibbutz-training village, who had intended to make their home in Israel. Many had come from Klobuck. Hershl watched them driven naked to their deaths. He, too, had intended to prepare for kibbutz life at Zarki when he was old enough. 'New transports arrive at Treblinka all the time. Sometimes there is a break of a few days. But on average ten thousand people per day are murdered in Treblinka.'

The possessions of those people ended up in the sorting yard, piled into mountains, and in the sorting barracks, organised for shipment, where the SS and Ukrainians dipped into piles of ladies' underwear, men's coats, and babies' clothing, like customers at a vast outdoor market, to pull out something for their wives, friends or children.

> The SS units become enormously rich. As compensation for the gruesome work in the camp, they are granted four weeks' leave and always travel dressed in civilian clothes. Each time, they take with them about ten suitcases. They take the best and most expensive clothes and the most beautiful gold and diamond jewellery for their families.

Sometimes, the clothing sorters were instructed to keep a look-out for a nice fur coat, and a pack of cigarettes was thrown down in payment. Deals were struck that very quickly became choices between life and death. At other times, depending on the SS officer, requests for certain items of clothing came simply as a command. Workers sometimes slashed fur coats as they were sorted, flawing the garment in a small act of resistance.

At the same time, just as bizarrely, the prisoners were able to dress and eat like barons. Many of them ate better in Treblinka than in two years in the ghetto. Each transport of victims brought with it hundreds of food packages containing meat, potatoes, bread, jam, butter, and jars of protein-rich egg barley, all undoubtedly prepared by a concerned wife or mother. Good-quality clothes and sturdy boots were also plentiful. The many Jews who believed they were being 'sent for agricultural work in the east' came prepared.

CHAPTER THIRTEEN

CONSPIRACY

One night in December 1942, Hershl witnessed a terrible struggle between the SS and a transport from Kiellbasin concentration camp near the town of Grodno in Belarus. Some 2,000 Jews arrived during the evening. That was unusual in itself, because Stangl had insisted that trains come only in daylight hours. Nonetheless, Hershl was among the 'Blues' of the *Lumpenkommando* who had been sent to unbolt the wagons. The people inside had no idea where they were, and many began asking questions as soon as the doors opened. The very mention of Treblinka was enough; rumours had reached Grodno. When the Jews disembarked, they were met with the usual orders and blows. Once in the square, they were ordered to undress and then proceed to the showers. Some obeyed and had already begun their run on the *Himmelstrasse* toward the gas chambers. However, shouts now rang out in the darkness: 'Don't obey the Germans! Don't undress!'

Spontaneous resistance erupted. Scores of people from the transport suddenly grabbed sticks, pulled out knives and attacked the guards. Some of them even fought with their fists and teeth, while others 'had brought with them some revolvers and hand-grenades', Hershl writes. Explosions and gunfire rang through the camp. The rebels attempted to escape. They ran, but the barbed-wire fence blocked their exit. The Germans and Ukrainians opened fire. In a matter of moments, the square was littered with the dead. Some were captured alive. They were later tortured. Hershl: 'The punishment for the rebels was very severe … [Kurt] Franz deliberately kept them alive in order to beat and torture them until death released them.' The rest of the Kiellbasin transport had by now been driven into the gas chambers, where they were murdered, many of them still fully clothed.

These events served to remind the Jewish *Sonderkommando* that escape was impossible and that physical resistance was futile. Although superior in numbers, the Jews would have to overcome a trained and well-equipped force of Ukrainians and SS units. Against pistols, machine-guns, rifles and grenades, the prisoners with a tiny number of exceptions had only blunt knives, spades, hammers and sticks. A number of failed breakouts that month blackened the mood of the prisoners further. Seven members of the Blue group had attempted to flee, but they were caught and taken by Franz to the Lazarett. In the extermination area, later in December, an informer thwarted the escape plan of 24 Jews. All the participants were seized and killed.

In yet another attempt, late on New Year's Eve 1942, seven prisoners in the exter-mination area tried to flee through a tunnel they had dug beneath their barracks. Five of them succeeded in getting out of the camp but a Ukrainian guard spotted them from a watchtower and opened fire once they reached the other side of the fence. Two of the group remained in the barracks because there was no time to get through the tunnel. In the bad luck that often accompanies desperate escape attempts, the fleeing prisoners fell victim to a fresh snowfall that night. The German and Ukrainian pursuers followed the tracks into a neighbouring village, where they caught the escapees trying to rent a wagon from local peasants. One of the prisoners managed to get to Warsaw, where he later joined the ghetto uprising in April 1943. The remainder were cornered. In an act of desperation or courage, or both, one prisoner was shot as he tried to attack a German. The other three were returned to the camp, where they were tortured and hanged in front of the assembled prisoners.

> For trying to run away, people were hung up by the feet on a high pole until they breathed their last in terrible agony. Once, two Jews were hung up like this. As they hung there, they kept screaming at us: 'Run, run, all of you. In the end, death awaits you, too. Don't be fooled because you've got enough to eat today. Tomorrow you'll share our fate.'

In addition to the severe penalties for those who were caught attempting to escape, punishment was meted out to the other prisoners as a matter of policy in acts of brutal retribution. For every prisoner who escaped, ten were executed. Hershl tells us that only once did a group of Jews 'leave the camp alive'. But then he adds, bitterly 'The Front had demanded women. So 110 of the most beautiful Jewish girls, accom-panied by a Jewish doctor, were sent off.'

Security in the camp was also strengthened at this time. More barbed wire fencing was added around the perimeter and additional watchtowers were built. At night, the prisoners were locked in their barracks, and the so-called ghetto was cordoned off and locked. Another deterrent was the simple fact that the escapees had nowhere to run. By the end of October 1942, most of the ghettos in Polish cities had already been liquidated. Few prisoners had non-Jewish contacts they could trust and who might shelter them.

★ ★ ★

Everything changed during the first few months of 1943. A bitter Polish winter descended. The prisoners' spirits darkened further. A few transports arrived from Bialystok and Warsaw, but the level of camp activity decreased dramatically to about two transports a week. The task of annihilating the Jews of Poland was almost com-plete, save a few shrunken ghettos and labour camps that were associated with the German war effort. Nonetheless, the brutality continued.

> Reporting sick is not possible either; you are only admitted to the hospital with a fever of over 40 degrees, and anyone who is ill for more than six days was shot. In general,

death by shooting became a daily occurrence. The Jews who had been shot were replaced by new workers from the latest transports.

In Sorting Square, the mountains of belongings that had been a feature of Treblinka since the beginning had disappeared. Everything had long since been packed on to trains and sent to Germany or the Russian Front. With fewer transports, food supplies dwindled. The SS and Ukrainians took all the food that had been brought with the victims for themselves. Prisoners caught with a piece of bread were executed. They began to starve on the meagre rations supplied by the camp.

> The food is never adequate and all the time we have to work out methods of stealing little bits of food such as bread, potatoes and so on from the newly arrived transports. We steal, even though we know that we run the risk of suffering a terrible death.

The prisoners, who during the day now lacked full employment, sat in their barracks. Hershl writes: 'Our situation becomes more dreadful every day. Day and night, we think about ways of avoiding our terrible fate.'

A conspiracy developed among the German-appointed Jewish leaders of the prisoners. The SS always chose individuals they felt were like them to be the camp's block leaders, kapos and foremen. They chose men like so-called 'camp elder' Galewski, who as mentioned earlier spoke perfect German and had an air of authority, culture and intelligence about him. Stangl's primary concern was that the massacre ran smoothly. He needed men such as Galewski to stabilise the workforce and permitted them a degree of authority over their own people. Ironically, the roots of the camp's destruction lay in that strategy. These Jewish camp leaders included Dr Ilya Chorazycki, a 57-year-old former captain in the Polish Army and also a physician, Lazarett kapo Zev Kurland, Zelo Bloch from Czechoslovakia, the foreman of the workers in Sorting Square, the agronomist Israel Sadowitz, and Samuel Rajzman, the interpreter and accountant from Warsaw. Where Razjman went, Hershl followed. They formed a Treblinka underground, the aim of which was to acquire weapons and organise a rebellion. They called themselves simply 'the Organising Committee'.

While a few prisoners in the early days made it out – particularly during the disorder and confusion of the first couple of months – it was now evident that individual or small-group escapes were no longer viable. The Organising Committee concluded that the only possibility of survival for the Jewish *Sonderkommando* was through large-scale organisation aimed at overpowering the guards, taking control of the camp and enacting a mass escape. With proper planning and organisation, they believed, the prisoners could stage an effective revolt and flee into the forest. No more single escapes and no more ten executed for each escapee. They would all get out or all die, they decided. If even just one prisoner escaped to bear witness, it would be worth it.

Camaraderie and trust also began to grow among the rank-and-file prisoners. In spite of the informants among the Jews – and there were several – the inhuman conditions they shared, the sense of their own loss and injustice and the growing suspicion that the work of Treblinka was coming to end, signalling that they would all be murdered as witnesses to the horror, bound the prisoners together.

The first plan, concocted during the long winter, was to overpower the SS one by one as they came to the tailors' shop each evening to listen to the orchestra. They would then take their weapons. One of the prisoners would put on a German uniform and call over the Ukrainian guards, who would also be killed. But just as their hopes began to rise, disaster struck.

As February gave way to March, an epidemic of typhus spread among the prisoners, transmitted rapidly by lice thriving in the unsanitary conditions, in the prisoners' clothes and on their bodies. The physical complications that followed were pneumonia, diarrhoea and delirium. Plans for rebellion ground to a halt.

The sick bay was now filled with feverish, vomiting patients. Witnesses tell of bearded, forlorn faces with half-open mouths, staring with empty eyes as their bodies lay tormented and covered with red, bleeding sores. They laid in unimaginable filth. At the same time, *muselmänner*, prisoners who moved like zombies, filled the camp in increasing numbers. Those who were deemed hopeless were handed over to Miete to be shot and dumped into the flames of the Lazarett. Hershl listened to the gunshots.

The physical appearance of the workers also changed at this time. The Germans were terrified of typhus and they ordered each prisoner to shave his head and body clean as a defence against the lice. Sick prisoners dragged themselves to work and feigned good health for fear they would never return from the sick bay. They were easily discovered during Kurt Franz's enforced sports session, and they too were taken by Miete to the Lazarett.

The leaner, more active men seemed to recover more quickly from the illness than those who were heavier set. Hershl, physically always lean and in Treblinka more boy than man, makes no mention of whether he contracted the disease, but he does describe how the sick were treated.

> In order to prevent the spread of the epidemic, the sick people were separated from the others, stripped naked and only allowed to wrap themselves in a blanket. They were driven outdoors and chased up the high, piled-up mounds of earth by the death-chambers. There the SS opened fire on them, and the bodies rolled down into the fires, which were already burning in the ditches below. Shortly after this, barbed wire fences were erected between the two camps. This work was carried out by the work-squads of both camps. Once again we had the opportunity to pour out our woes to each other, and to lament our terrible fate.

As spring advanced, the camp became infested with flies that fed on the decomposing corpses that had not yet been incinerated. Typhus gave way to dysentery. Küttner now noticed an 'exaggerated' use of the toilets by prisoners, and introduced another bizarre feature into camp life – the *Scheissmeister*, or shit master. For their amusement, the SS made him wear a rabbinical outfit, an eight-cornered cantors' hat and carry a whip. They also put an alarm clock around his neck with which to check the prisoners' toilet time. Two minutes was the maximum. It was an especially cruel restriction for those suffering from the unrelenting diarrhoea symptomatic of dysentery.

'Spite,' Sam said again when I told him about the shit master.

By February, the transports ceased and famine gnawed at the prisoners' bodies and minds. It was during this 'quiet' period that the workers were given alternative employment. The large clock face was put up at the fake station, the Tyrolean chalet was constructed as a guardhouse, flowers were planted and the buildings were painted in a wild mixture of unnatural colours.

Then, one day in March, a terrible and tragic miracle occurred. Kurt Franz appeared before them at the evening roll call to announce enthusiastically that new transports would begin arriving the following day. Survivor Richard Glazer recalled: 'We didn't say anything, we just looked at one another and each of us thought: "Tomorrow no more hunger".' He later remarked that he had relived that moment each day of his life, and every day he 'died a little more'. For many, it struck them for the first time that their survival depended on the continuation of the annihilation process.

The new transports consisted of Jews from Salonika, which had been annexed by Bulgaria. The previous month, the Bulgarian government bowed to Nazi pressure and agreed that 14,000 would be delivered for 'transport to the east'. These people were the descendants of Spanish Jews who in 1492 had fled the Spanish Inquisition. They were wealthy and the deception perpetrated on their journey to Treblinka was absolute.

> The SS take even more care over the transports of Bulgarian Jews. They arrive in nicely appointed passenger coaches. Their trains have coaches with wine, bread, fruit and other foods. The SS make a real banquet of these delicacies, and the Bulgarian Jews go with carefree minds to their death. They are given soap and bath-towels. Whistling to themselves and waving their towels they go merrily to the death-camp.

All but three selected for labour were gassed. According to Glazer, 'The trainloads from the Balkans brought us to a horrible realisation: we were the Treblinka factory workers and our lives depended on the whole manufacturing process, that is the slaughtering process at Treblinka.'

The Germans, however, were unhappy. While the amount of supplies brought by these transports was enormous, there was little money and valuables – unlike the Polish transports, whose victims had gold sewn in their clothing. The Germans did not know, or at least they could not prove, the money, gold and jewellery from the victims had already been snatched and buried by the Jewish Underground – probably by Chorazycki, who was gathering funds to buy weapons from the Ukrainians.

★ ★ ★

During their work tasks a few prisoners managed to steal glances at newspapers that contained reports about German military losses. A few weeks earlier the Germans had capitulated at Stalingrad, their Sixth Army destroyed, marking the beginning of Hitler's long retreat from the east. The news grew steadily worse, and the reports exacerbated fears that with the end of the Third Reich, the prisoners – witnesses to the most terrible crime imaginable – would be annihilated.

At the beginning of March, Heinrich Himmler, Hitler's second in command, visited Treblinka and ordered that all the bodies that had been buried in mass graves before mid-November be dug up and burned. He was concerned with hiding the crimes, now that the tide of the war was turning. There were also German newspaper reports in early 1943 about the discovery of mass graves in the Katyn Forest, where Soviet military authorities had buried the bodies of 8,000 murdered Poles. The Nazis had exploited the Katyn discovery as anti-Soviet propaganda, and the last thing Himmler needed was physical evidence of German mass murder. There may also have been an order to begin winding down Treblinka's operations at this time, although the available evidence is unclear. More than 800,000 Jews had already been exterminated in its gas chambers by the second half of February, and there was little further need for the killing centres of Operation Reinhard. Auschwitz-Birkenau had by now increased its murderous capability with more ovens and gas chambers, and was well equipped to handle Europe's remaining Jews.

Within days of his visit, the gruesome task of opening the pits that had been dug behind the gas chambers and cremating the remains of several hundred thousand decomposing bodies began. This was to be the main task of Treblinka for the rest of its existence. Hershl writes:

> Between Camp I and Camp II, three massive excavators work day and night, piling up huge mountains of earth between the two camps. Day and night, the bright glow of the burning bodies rises up to the sky. It is visible for miles. When the wind blows in the direction of our camp, it brings such a terrible smell that we can't manage to do any work. Only when the wind changes direction can we start doing our normal work again.

Witnesses have said that from a distance it looked like a volcanic eruption boiling up through the earth's surface, spreading flames and lava.

> When the corpses, which are already decomposing, are dug up, a considerable amount of money and valuables is found in the stomachs and guts of the victims. This proves that even when looking death in the face, the Jews still believed in life. Later, communication between the work-squads from the two camps was forbidden. Even during the handover of shoes or clothes by the squads of Camp II, our people were only allowed to go up to the border between the camps. There, the workers from the death camp hand over fearfully stinking, blood-soaked clothing.

The more troublesome victims had probably been shoved into the gas chambers fully clothed, perhaps the result of tragic acts of resistance that we can never know.

The business of burning the corpses required more slaves in the extermination area, and additional prisoners were transferred from the lower camp, where the workload had been drastically reduced. Only one trainload of victims arrived per week. These people were gassed and their bodies were cremated along with those that had been dug up from the pits.

The smell of blood, the dreadful stench of the decomposing and burnt corpses wafts death itself over the workers of the death-brigade. No one can stomach this work for more than a few weeks. Even the SS units are changed every two weeks, and sent on immediate leave. Even the murderers themselves cannot bear this diabolical bestiality.

Talk of escape now reached fever pitch, although among the core planning group, everything remained secret. Then one evening, Küttner burst into the barracks and sent two members of the Organising Committee, Zelo Bloch and another man called Adesh, to the extermination camp. It is unclear whether the pair had been informed upon, or whether Küttner, a former jailer, smelled a conspiracy in the air. It was a blow to the plans for escape.

Chorazycki had now accrued enough money to purchase a small arsenal – but his efforts had not come to fruition. On several occasions, the Ukrainians took the money, but produced no weapons. Then something unusual occurred. Almost every account from Treblinka survivors and perpetrators alike refers to what followed as a key event in the camp's history.

One warm spring day, as the prisoners from the sorting area returned to the ghetto for their midday break, four Ukrainians were seen carrying what first appeared to be a bloody bundle from the SS barracks. Before the prisoners reached the pile of tin bowls, Chorazycki's name was suddenly on everyone's lips.

In the camp there was a Jewish doctor, Chorazycki, who used to treat the SS. Once *Unterscharführer* Franz came to be examined by him. He suddenly noticed the doctor's bulging wallet, and asked the doctor about the contents. The doctor answered him by grabbing a surgical knife and plunging it into Franz's body. The latter ran around the yard, and the doctor pursued him with the knife. Instantly, Ukrainians appeared from every side and threw themselves on the doctor. He managed, however, to swallow poison. Straight away all the doctors in the camp were alerted. They did their best to keep Dr Chorazycki alive by pumping out his stomach. When that didn't help, Franz took revenge with his riding whip and beat the dying doctor until he was completely dead.

Another important member of the committee was gone. Nonetheless, the incident did not end with Chorazycki's death. The Germans suspected the Gold Jews of being the source of the doctor's cash, and conducted an investigation. The Jews were assembled near the Lazarett and ordered to strip. Bizarrely, each man was ordered to leap-frog naked into the Lazarett and stand before the burning pit, where Franz interrogated them with pistols pressed to the napes of their necks. It is a mark of the prisoners' solidarity that none confessed. All were freed. It seems the greedy SS still required their services. Hershl writes: 'The next day a search is made of the belongings of the Jewish kapo and a sack of gold is found among his things. He is shot dead on the spot.'

This kapo was almost certainly Benjamin Rakowski, who had been planning an independent escape with fifteen men. He was arrested and murdered by Miete after sums of money and gold were discovered hidden in the walls of the barracks.

One night in the middle of April, as the stench of burning corpses fouled the air with ever greater intensity, Hershl and Samuel Razjman slipped into the tailors' shop and under the pretext of a card game, joined another meeting of the Organising Committee. Card games were outlawed in camp, and if discovered the penalty was 25 lashes, but they took the risk. That night, a daring plan was concocted to smuggle weapons out of the arms depot. It was decided that if the break-in were successful, a revolt would be initiated as soon as they had the weapons in their hands. Under this plan, they would kill the guards and free every prisoner. They would also burn Treblinka to the ground.

The following day, the wind changed direction and the stench of burning bodies was carried full force into the lower camp. A number of survivors mention this in their testimonies. Some of the prisoners vomited. However, around noon, Edek, one of the young *putzer*, ran to the door of the munitions depot, and stuffed metal shavings into the lock. Later, when the SS could not open the door of the arms store, a locksmith predictably was summoned. He tried the lock, and explained to the SS that it would have to be removed to the workshop in the ghetto and repaired. It was all part of the plan. While Ukrainians stood watch, the entire door was removed from its hinges and taken to the ghetto, where the lock was cleaned. The scene was stage-managed to perfection. In the workshop, under the watchful eyes of the SS, an imprint of the key was taken.

One obvious problem with the plan was that the storeroom stood beside the German barracks, so the weapons had to be removed during the day, while the SS were making their rounds. This fact also determined the timing of the prospective rebellion. The following day, Edek and three other young *putzer* stole undetected into the arms depot and removed two boxes of hand grenades. They hid them under a heap of garbage in a wheelbarrow. If caught, the reprisal would have been brutal for all the prisoners. Nonetheless, they brought the grenades to the shoemakers' workshop in the ghetto, where several members of the Organising Committee were waiting, ready to instigate the revolt over the next few hours. However, when the boxes were opened, those with military experience quickly saw that the grenades had no detonators. The *putzer* had not known the difference. Grenades without detonators were useless. Word was passed to the rest of the committee that the uprising had to be halted. Now they had to return the grenades to the storeroom. No survivor testimony exists to provide details of how this was achieved. However, the *putzer* succeeded in returning the grenades to the armoury unnoticed and the episode was never discovered. Yet it remained another bitter blow.

★ ★ ★

During May, small transports again began to trickle into Treblinka from Warsaw. By all accounts, they were an awful sight. These were the survivors of the courageous Warsaw ghetto uprising, beaten and bedraggled. After the uprising was crushed and the ghetto reduced to rubble, the survivors were thrown into the rail cars – many of them bayoneted, starving and suffocated. They carried little or no baggage. Witnesses described these as the most miserable transports that had ever arrived in Treblinka, more dead than alive. There was nothing for the *Lumpenkommando* to sort in the yard and they brought no food with which to feed the workers. Many of the Jews on the transports were so tired and beaten they had not even the strength to carry themselves to the gas chambers and were taken instead to the Lazarett on stretchers. But, at the same time, word was passed from the victims to the prisoners about the heroism that had occurred in the Polish capital. They were told how 750 Jewish fighters fought to protect the remaining ghetto inhabitants against the heavily armed and well-trained Germans for nearly a month, until the resistance was finally crushed. They had fought desperately because they knew what awaited them. Of the more than 56,000 Jews captured, about 7,000 were shot, and the remainder deported to the death camps. Some 7,000 were transported to Treblinka.

As if one were needed, there now came a sign. One of the last transports to arrive included several members of the Warsaw Ghetto Underground. Determined to die with dignity, they had smuggled grenades and pistols beneath their clothing. When this transport was brought into Reception Square and ordered to remove their clothing, one of them pulled out a grenade and threw it into the middle of the yard. According to the testimonies, the grenade killed a Ukrainian guard and wounded one SS man, as well as three Jews from the Red Group. A number of the Jews who had arrived on the same transport were also injured.

Nonetheless, around 200 men and a few women were pulled from the transport to replace some of those who had died in the typhus epidemic. The detail of what had occurred in Warsaw acted as a spur to many, bolstering the prisoners' resolve to rebel and escape.

★ ★ ★

Spring gave way to a scorching Polish summer and the workload of Treblinka's Jewish *Sonderkommando* dwindled. A suffocating heat settled over the camp. A strange limbo descended upon this death factory with no-one to exterminate. The Ukrainians were bored and a few deserted. Melted black tar dripped from the rooftops of the barracks. A hot, stifling wind blew sand around the camp and carried the stench of death everywhere. The excavators still worked late into the night and the slaves in the extermination area continued their gruesome task of burning the corpses.

The idea of a summer in Treblinka without transports inspired the Germans to use their Jewish slaves for further construction work. Perhaps Stangl hoped to persuade his masters of the continued usefulness of the camp. Roads were resurfaced, the ground was levelled and spread with gravel, and rolls of barbed-wire were placed between the two perimeter fences as anti-tank traps. The cultivated area outside the camp was enlarged. A carved wooden globe with a compass now hung above the main gate, with the SS insignia cut in it. The Tyrolean guardhouse was decorated with new carvings. Elsewhere, asphalt was laid on pathways that were edged with multi-coloured stones. At every corner stood a new signpost, each decorated with carvings. Under the words, 'To The Ghetto', the image of a bent, hook-nosed Jew carrying a bundle on his back was wrought. Another sign read 'Karl Seidel Strasse', named after the oldest member of the Treblinka SS.

I imagined Hershl now, labouring with cracked lips, his eyes aching and his head pounding with delirium, sweat pouring down his face, his chest and his spine bent. It must have seemed to Hershl there were no other Jews left in the world. He and this pathetic group of prisoners had watched their people murdered, transport by transport. Then, one day in the middle of all the construction work, the whistle of an approaching train was heard and then the screeching of metal wheels on the track outside the camp. At first there was speculation that the Wehrmacht had crossed the English Channel and it was the English, Scottish and Irish Jews who were coming to be exterminated. How Hershl's heart must have sunk as this misinformation circulated. However, these were not British Jews. Little by little, in a series of small transports over the next week or so, groups of wasted individuals came – first in threadbare prisoners' jackets, then in civilians' rags. They were prisoners from a penal camp. Then came the Gypsies. Hershl writes: 'The Gypsies are not brought in wagons but in small groups on horses and carts. They are not sent to the death camp, but are brought to the Lazarett, where they are shot and burned.'

It seemed the suffering would never end. Between these latest meagre shipments of human transports, and amid the SS boredom and human suffering, the sadist Franz now decided to introduce a boxing programme. Prisoners were forced to punch one another as part of so-called training sessions. A ring was set up in the *Appelplatz*, and matches were held on Saturday afternoons after recitals from the camp orchestra. Around the ring, chairs were positioned for the SS. Prisoners were made to watch and applaud. Franz forced barbers, tailors, rabbis and 'shit masters' into the ring to beat each other amid jeers and cries. Sometimes he went into the ring himself but the prisoners were not allowed to punch back.

It was during these bouts that Wolowanczyk, a twenty-year-old Jewish tough from the Warsaw underworld makes his first appearance in the testimonies of survivors. One afternoon, Franz pulled Wolowanczyk into the ring, but Wolowanczyk was able to avoid the punches. Witnesses recorded that Franz grew angry and grabbed him by the lapel. He was ordered to remain still, but when Franz swung, Wolowanczyk threw himself to the ground. Franz missed, lost his footing and fell. The deputy commander of Treblinka then pelted him with stones and bricks, and kicked and beat him mercilessly. Hershl watched this apparent murder in horror. However, when the beating was over, Wolowanczyk 'gave himself a shake and walked off', according to one witness. The Jewish Underground soon enlisted Wolowanczyk for special tasks.

★ ★ ★

News seeped in from the extermination area into the lower camp, relaying the information that the task of burning the excavated corpses was almost complete. In the continued absence of transports, that meant the work of Treblinka would soon end. The number of prisoners in the lower camp was also dwindling. Some had been transferred to the body-burning corps, others had been murdered in the Lazarett and others still had simply died from disease or exhaustion. One day, a message came from the extermination area stating that if a time was not fixed for the rebellion, the prisoners in the death camp would act alone. Galewski knew that if a rebellion broke out independently in the extermination area, all the prisoners in the lower camp would be killed. It was time to act. The Organising Committee, with Hershl present, met again for cards that night in the car body shop. Hershl writes:

> A while ago, we buried money and valuables, knowing that without financial means we cannot even think about running away. We have also managed to procure a few weapons. Now we have to organise the attempt.

So confident were the SS that the Jews in the death camp would shortly be eliminated without difficulty, they held a party to mark the approaching fulfilment of Himmler's orders. They fired salvos into the air beside the excavators and held a banquet. Many prisoners concluded that these would be their last days on earth.

On the night of either Friday 30 July 1943 or Saturday 31 July, it was agreed the uprising would take place on the afternoon of Monday 2 August. It was also determined that with proper planning, all the SS could be overcome separately, quietly and at the same time. The leaders assumed correctly that within a very short time, German security forces would be called in to pursue the escapees, and their chance of avoiding capture was far greater at night. Thus, zero hour was fixed at 4.30pm. Sunday afternoons were reserved for Franz's boxing bouts, so Monday was the first available opportunity. Moreover, the passage of Polish prisoners from the Treblinka penal camp, who returned from work at Malkinia at 4.45pm, was taken into account. The idea was to stop the train, free the prisoners and persuade them to join the uprising.

According to the plan, the weapons would be acquired on Monday afternoon. A key to the armoury was already in their possession. The *putzer* would remove the weapons and distribute them among the fighting groups, and this time they would collect the detonators. Weapons would also be acquired from the Ukrainian guardhouse. The SS men would be eliminated as quickly as possible. The prisoners would then take control of the camp and set it ablaze before abandoning it. The Ukrainians at the guard posts and watchtowers would have to be killed, but the rest would be captured alive and held in their barracks until the time came for them to flee. The Jews hoped that once the SS were killed, the Ukrainians would submit. The rate of desertion among the Ukrainians was high already, increasing in direct proportion to the number of German military defeats on the eastern front. Many were fearful that they would be executed once the camp was closed.

Hershl described the events of the eve of the rebellion.

> A fourteen-year-old Jewish boy steals into the Ukrainian guardroom at night and removes weapons, bullets and several machine-guns. The arms are divided out, and the day on which the revolt will be launched is decided upon. As far as I remember it was a day at the end of the summer 1943.

There was little sleep that night. Most of the prisoners had already packed small sacks of belongings and valuables for their escape. 'At four in the morning, we fear that our plan is in danger of collapsing … There is enormous tension among the Jews.'

Galewski made the rounds of the camp, attempting to calm the prisoners. A fatigue settled in, masking the electric tension. At last, everything was ready. I imagine dread rising from the pit of Hershl's stomach. I imagine him looking around at the rest of the *Sonderkommando*, his eyes wide open in the dark, his heart pounding. This was all that remained of the hundreds of thousands of Jews who had come to this place.

CHAPTER FOURTEEN

UPRISING AND ESCAPE

Dawn came bright and dry on Monday 2 August 1943. Hershl had barely closed his eyes; none of them had done so that night. Only a few of the prisoners knew the exact date and time of the uprising. The precise details of the plan to revolt not only changed often, but were kept secret from most prisoners, for fear that they could be revealed to the SS under torture. Yet, as the day wore on, there was palpable excitement in the air that would soon become difficult to mask. Hershl was among the few who knew everything. His testimony reveals that even though he was not among the leaders, he was nonetheless a part of the secret planning and a participant in one of the most courageous escapes of World War II. He told his sons that he had never taken another human life, and from that we can infer that he was not among the few who were armed. The vast majority of prisoners had never fired a weapon. This was a revolt that would be undertaken by people who were already beaten and bullied almost to the point of death and who had no contact– or hope of assistance – from the world outside. That Hershl survived this revolt beyond the camp's confines is miraculous, but it is also in no small measure owing to those who died so that he might live.

For the SS, this was a day like any other. A Ukrainian flung open the doors of the barracks. A few felt the lashes from his whip. Then came the predictable roll call. The Germans and the Ukrainians barked their orders as usual. That day, there was not a whisper of wind in the air. The trees around the camp stood motionless. The heat was already beginning to build. A cloud of smoke rose from the burning bodies in the extermination area and the nauseating stench of death hovered overhead as usual. The SS may have noticed that the prisoners formed ranks quicker than usual that morning – but if they did, they thought nothing of it. The prisoners looked utterly innocuous, like an army of depleted beggars, their clothes torn and filthy with dirt and sweat. The Underground knew that this would be their last day in Treblinka, and for many it would be their last day on earth. Yet, by the same token, they also knew that an uprising was their only chance of survival. The only hope that remained was to obliterate this death factory and tell the world.

The precise details of what occurred that day vary considerably in the memories of survivors and in the accounts that were laid down. Yet there is broad agreement among them – as well as with the SS perpetrators who have spoken – on the events of this extraordinary day. The details differ for two main reasons. Firstly, the fallibility of memory in the aftermath of such an explosive event and after so long under the brutal conditions of Treblinka must be taken into account. Secondly, the normal routine of this day at a certain point degenerated very quickly into chaos and each prisoner – from his own desperate perspective – looked into the madness and saw something unique.

The sun climbed as the morning progressed. In the workshops, prisoners sharpened knives and axes with a particular zeal. In the storeroom, Jews prepared Molotov cocktails. The work brigades plastered fake smiles on their faces as they greeted the murderers; others were beside themselves and could barely work at all. Foremen begged them to appear busy. At various positions in the camp, other Jews stood wringing their hands together. One of the SS curiously observed two of the *putzer* boys saying goodbye to one another, as another prisoner stood beside them weeping. Galewski fobbed him off with a story about the boys' mental state.

Meanwhile, Yankel Wiernik, the head of the carpentry squad in the extermination area who would later deliver the first account of Treblinka, persuaded the SS official in charge that he needed some building materials from the storeroom in the lower camp. The Organising Committee now got word to him that zero hour had been set for 4.30pm. Later that morning, Galewski visited the extermination area himself. Stanislaw Kon, who was part of the corpse-carrying squad, recalled: 'Galewski informs us that today we will finish our work earlier because Scharführer Reuter is going to Malkinia to bathe in the River Bug. He tells us discreetly how we are also preparing for another "bath" today.' Kon had arrived in Treblinka on 1 October with his young wife and his mother-in-law, both of whom went straight to the gas chambers.

In the lower camp, the plan called for the *putzer* boys to start removing the weapons from the munitions storeroom at 2.00pm. However, by the time of the noon roll call, it had become clear to Galewski that the prisoners' excitement could be concealed no longer and he reorganised the work teams for the forthcoming battle. Such reorganisations were not uncommon and raised no suspicion. Hershl was assigned to work in one of the ghetto workshops with Rajzman. Meanwhile, Galewski strengthened the potato team and the vegetable garden workers with members of the Underground. The vegetable garden was near the weapons storeroom, and the *putzer* were ordered to begin removing the arms immediately.

Now, at the last, a stroke of luck. Hershl writes: 'On that day, the terrible *Oberscharführer* Franz and forty Ukrainians are due to leave the camp to bathe.' However, it was discovered that SS guard Müller had been on duty the previous night and had stayed behind to rest in the barracks, next to the weapons storeroom. The *putzer* reported his presence to the agronomist Sadowitz, the committee member who was in charge of the vegetable garden and to whom Galewski had assigned the key role of supervising the removal of weapons. Sadowitz resorted to tricking Müller, whose presence threatened the plan. The agronomist feigned a problem with the potato workers and told Müller that he was needed there.

After Müller left the barracks with Sadowitz, the *putzer* got to work in the storeroom. A horse and cart stopped in front of the munitions depot under the pretext of a garbage pick-up. One *putzer* removed a bar from the back window of the storeroom,

House of the Wannsee Conference. The Wannsee Conference was a meeting of senior officials of the Nazi regime, held in the Berlin suburb of Wannsee on 20 January 1942. The purpose of the conference was to inform senior Nazis and senior Governmental administrators of plans for the 'final solution to the Jewish question'.

Above left: Reinhard Heydrich, the man who chaired the Wannsee Conference and presented the plan for the deportation and annihilation of Europe's Jews. After his assassination in Prague on 27 May 1942 the code name for the secret building of the death camps Belzec, Sobibor and Treblinka was made 'Operation Reinhard' in his honour.

Above right: Jews prepare to board a train to an unknown destination. During mid-1942 a whole series of resettlement 'actions' were being conducted across occupied Poland. The majority of Jews were sent to Belzec, Sobibor and Treblinka. (HITM ARCHIVE)

Deportation of Jews from the General Government of Poland in the late winter of 1942, or early 1943. (HITM)

Above: A Jewish man waits to board a train for an unknown destination in the East. Having been told that they were to be re-settled, many Jews brought all the valuables they could carry. (HITM)

Left: The remains of the Klobuck shtetl where Hershl spent his childhood. (Author)

The ruined synagogue at Krepice, about four kilometres from Klobuck. In 1939, more than 100 Jews were forced into the building and killed with machine-guns. (Author)

Above left: Częstochowa – The New Synagogue at the heart of the town (destroyed 25 December 1939).

Above right: Częstochowa Ghetto – Rynek Warszawski Square, where Jews were assembled for forced labour and deportation (circa 1944). Hershl and his family spent months in the ghetto before their deportation to Treblinka.

Częstochowa Ghetto – A German soldier and two Jewish men who are clearing snow on a street.

Above left: Dr Irmfried Eberl, the first commandant of Treblinka. Approximately 245,000 Jews were deported and murdered during his reign. He was replaced by Franz Stangl following accusations of corruption and inefficiency. (H.E.A.R.T. Holocaust Education and Archive Research Team)

Above centre: Franz Stangl, the second commandant of Treblinka, former commandant of another Operation Reinhard death camp, Sobibor, and former superintendent of the T-4 Euthanasia Program. (H.E.A.R.T.)

Above right: Kurt Franz, second in command at Treblinka under Franz Stangl. He was nicknamed *Lalke* ('doll') by the prisoners because of his deceptively handsome face, and was feared for his relentless sadism. (H.E.A.R.T.)

Barry, the St Bernard dog, probably taken by his owner *SS-Oberscharführer* Kurt Franz. Barry was trained to attack Jews on the order 'Man, get that dog'. (H.E.A.R.T.)

SS-men on the buckets of the excavator (left). These photographs were probably taken in the first half of 1943. At least two types of excavators were used in Treblinka, bucket and cable excavators. It was later realised that the bucket excavator was not very effective for digging burial pits.

The Treblinka excavator was brought over from Treblinka I and used to help bury the dead and dig corpse pits. The photograph (right) was taken by Kurt Franz, found in his Treblinka album *Schöne Zeiten* ('Pleasant Times', or 'Happy Days'). (H.E.A.R.T.)

Above left: The Treblinka station sign, now held at the Yad Vashem complex.

Above right: The camp zoo constructed near the Ukrainian barracks on the orders of Stangl in the early summer of 1943. Here the SS spent their leisure time sitting on wooden benches and tables relaxing and looking at the animals. (ARC)

German soldiers round up Jewish men on Strazcka street in Częstochowa some time between 3 and 8 September 1939. (United States Holocaust Memorial Museum, courtesy of B. Ashley Grimes II)

Above left: Treblinka today – The large granite memorial stone, designed to resemble a Jewish tombstone. It was built between 1959 and 1963 and is located approximately on the spot where the gas chambers stood.

Above right: Treblinka today – A view of some of the 17,000 stones in the symbolic cemetery. Each stone represents a Jewish community wiped out at the camp.

Auschwitz – The infamous gates with the words *Arbeit Macht Frei*. Hershl arrived there on 2 October 1943 and was assigned the number 154356.

Above left: Auschwitz – ovens in the crematorium.

Above right: Auschwitz – Dr Josef Mengele, the Angel of Death. Hershl spent time in Mengele's barracks.

Sachsenhausen – Hershl arrived there on 26 October 1944, and was assigned the number 110572.

Dachau – aerial view of the camp where Hershl was imprisoned from 17 November 1944 until the camp's liberation by the US Army.

Dachau – gates at the main entrance, 1945.

Dachau – prisoners celebrate liberation.

Above: Hershl just a few months after liberation in Germany.

Left: Hershl and Yaja Sperling's wedding picture, taken in Tirschenreuth, Germany, in 1947.

Hershl and Yaja Sperling's wedding party.

Above: Hershl in Scotland in the 1950s.

Right: Hershl with his son Alan in the early 1950s.

Above: The Caledonian Rail Bridge.

Left: Hershl Sperling in the months after liberation. He is only eighteen years of age but already has the air of an older man.

FROM THE LAST EXTERMINATION

JOURNAL FOR THE HISTORY OF THE JEWISH PEOPLE DURING THE NAZI REGIME

Editor: ISRAEL KAPLAN

CONTENTS

The front and back cover of *From the Last Extermination*.

Konzentrationslager DACHAU Art der Haft: Jd. Pole Gef.-Nr.: 127871

1002

Name und Vorname: SZPERLING HEMEK
geb.: 10.3.1927 zu: Ktobuck
Wohnort: _____ " , Staszyca 14
Beruf: Schlosser Rel.: Isr.
Staatsangehörigkeit: POLEN Stand: Led.
Name der Eltern: Irek, Gitla Goldberg Rasse: Isr.
Wohnort: W.o.
Name der Ehefrau: _____ Rasse: _____
Wohnort: _____
Kinder: _____ Alleiniger Ernährer der Familie oder der Eltern: _____
Vorbildung: _____
Militärdienstzeit: _____ von — bis _____
Kriegsdienstzeit: _____ von — bis _____
Grösse: 165 Nase: m. Haare: d.bl. Gestalt: s.
Mund: h. Bart: _____ Gesicht: ov. Ohren: anl.
Sprache: d.p. Augen: gr. Zähne: 3f.
Ansteckende Krankheit oder Gebrechen: _____
Besondere Kennzeichen: _____
Rentenempfänger: _____
Verhaftet am: 9.8.1942 wo: Koluszki
1. Mal eingeliefert: 17.11.1944 2. Mal eingeliefert: _____
Einweisende Dienststelle: KL Sachsenhausen
Grund: _____
Parteizugehörigkeit: _____ von — bis _____
Welche Funktionen: _____
Mitglied v. Unterorganisationen: _____
Kriminelle Vorstrafen: _____

Politische Vorstrafen: _____

Ich bin darauf hingewiesen worden, dass meine Bestrafung wegen intellektueller Urkundenfälschung erfolgt, wenn sich die obigen Angaben als falsch erweisen sollten.

v. u. u. Der Lagerkommandant

Szperling H.

KL/62/8.44 200.000

Nazi document marking Hershl's arrival in *Konzentrationslager* Dachau – where he was given another number, 127871, with the word '*Jude*' above it. The document also draws attention to his 'attached' earlobe, which in the pseudoscience of Nazi racial theory was regarded as a Jewish trait.

Lfd.Nr.	Zu.Nr.	Häftl. Nr.	Zu- und Vorname	Geb.Daten	Einstand	1944 von	bis	
65		154 334	Mroxik Boleslaw	30. 5. 13	b.a.w.			gest. 14.2.44
66		154 356	Szperling Heinrich	10. 3. 27	"			gest. 15.2.44
67		156161	Grzeszczyk Apoloniuś	18. 5. 02	"			
68		156164	Gubarew Dymitr	11. 5. 87	"			
69		156 328	Mikulowski Tadeusz	28. 10. 84	"			
70		156 529	Wusiaty Edward	28. 6. 11	"			
			14. Februar 1944					BV 522
071		26382	Large Alexander	9.12. 19	b.a.w.			entl. 12.4.44
072		64385	Schubert Theodor	11. 1. 19	b.a.w.			verl. 4 Au I
			16. Februar 1944					BV 545
2073		113643	Beyerlein Christian	22. 9. 08	laut Strafvord. vom 18.2.44 6 Monate	18. 2.	18.8.	entl. 5.44
2074		137579	Stasiuk Tichon	12. 2. 07	b.a.w.			
2075		R-11221	Alexandrow Alexander	18. 11. 12	b.a.w.			
			18 Februar 1944					
2076		33485	Stern Elias	1. 10. 09	3 Monate	18. 2.	18.5.	vollstr. 18.5.44
2077		39371	Telleis Heinz	15. 6. 16	b.a.w.	18. 2.		
2078		58568	Sklarek Piotr	4. 6. 24	3 Monate	18. 2.	18.5.	
2079		84000	Dobry Chaim	5. 8. 19	3 Monate	18. 2.	18.5.	vollstr. 18.5.44
2080		108983	Ernst Friedrich	14. 5. 20	3 Monate	18. 2.	18.5.	entl. 12.4.44 BV 522
2081		111705	Dobborczyk Isaak	10. 1. 18	6 Monate	18. 2.	18.8.	entl. 18.5.44
2082		135895	Mandelbaum Moses	28. 7. 17	3 Monate	18. 2.	18.5.	vollstr. 18.5.44
2083		137579	Stasiuk Tichon	12. 2. 07	b.a.w.	18. 2.		verl. 4 H au
2084		164680	Jewestihniejew Iwan	13. 1. 23	3 Monate	18. 2.	18.5.	vollstr. 18.5.44
2085		165722	Witoschkin Pawel	29. 6. 10	3 Monate	18. 2.	18.5.	gest. 11.5.44
2086		Z- 480	Dottner Weis, Karl	5. 5.14	4 Monate	18. 2.	18.6.	entl. 2.6.44 BV 572
2087		111820	Ofter Chil	- 6. 8. 12	6 Monate	18. 2.	18.8.	entl. 18.5.44

Hershl's name on Birkenau's *strafkompanie* register. The length of his detention suggests that he had probably committed the worst possible crime in Auschwitz – attempted escape.

Konzentrationslager AUSCHWITZ Art der Haft: Sch. J. Der Nr. ~~110576~~ *110572*

Name und Vorname: **Szperling**, Henryk-Israel.

geb.: 10.3.27 zu: Kłobucko kr. Blachstadt *Distr.*

Wohnort: Tschenstochau. Warschauerstr. 43 *Radom*

Beruf: Arbeiter Rel.: mos.

Staatsangehörigkeit: ehem. Polen Stand: led.

Name der Eltern: Jacg u. Silla geb. Kolberg Rasse: Jud

Wohnort: unbek.

Name der Ehefrau: - Rasse:

Wohnort: keine Auskunft.

Kinder: — Alleiniger Ernährer der Familie oder der Eltern:

Vorbildung: 6 kl. poln. Volkssch.

Militärdienstzeit: — von — bis

Kriegsdienstzeit: von — bis

Grösse: 170 Nase: geradl. Haare: d. braun Gestalt: schlank

Mund: li. u. Lippe Bart: keinen Gesicht: oval Ohren: o. art.

Sprache: poln. dtsch. Augen: braun Zähne: 2 fehlen

Ansteckende Krankheit oder Gebrechen: keine

Besondere Kennzeichen: keine

Rentenempfänger: nein

Verhaftet am: 9.8.43 wo: Tschenstochau

1. Mal eingeliefert: 2. 10. 4 2. Mal eingeliefert:

Einweisende Dienststelle: Kdr.d.Sipo u.d.SD.in RADOM

Grund:

Parteizugehörigkeit: keine von — bis

Welche Funktionen: keine

Mitglied v. Unterorganisationen: nein

Kriminelle Vorstrafen: ang. keine

Politische Vorstrafen: ang. keine

I.T.S. FOTO No. 1561 au

Ich bin darauf hingewiesen worden, dass meine Bestrafung wegen intellektueller Urkundenfälschung erfolgt, wenn sich die obigen Angaben als falsch erweisen sollten.

v. g. u. **Der Lagerkommandant**

Szperling Henryk

KL 500.000 10. 5. 1. 4

Copy in conformity with the ITS archives

Hershl's registration document from Auschwitz, which followed him to Sachsenhausen, where his old number was crossed out and replaced with 110572.

and began emptying its contents – two boxes of hand grenades and 37 pistols and rifles – about 80 pieces in total. They did not forget the grenade detonators this time. The weapons, wrapped in sackcloth, were passed through the window and hidden in the cart beneath the garbage. However, Müller returned and they did not manage to remove everything.

The cart was taken to the SS garage, where mechanic Rudek Lubrenitski, another Underground member, took charge of the distribution. The weapons were loaded on to a wheelbarrow and delivered to the other Underground members at their workplaces. The grenades were distributed among the potato workers. Marian Platkiewicz, one of only two women believed to have survived Treblinka, wrote:

> Like everyday, we were working at a pile of potatoes. Then a handcart pushed by two men from the construction group passed by. Swiftly, they handed over to us some grenades and detonators. We put them into the buckets we used for the potatoes.

At each delivery, Lubrenitski demanded a password; when he said 'death' the response was 'life'. Bottles of gasoline that were to be used as Molotov cocktails were now also distributed among the Underground members.

At the same time, a young man named Bendin, whose day-to-day job was to disinfect the buildings and clothing in the camp, filled his spray canister with gasoline. He went about the camp spraying the barracks, workshops, storerooms and huts. The guards smelled nothing except the burning bodies in the extermination area. Messengers ran to and fro to different parts of the camp.

At around 2.00pm, word passed around the camp that no more Jews would be murdered in Treblinka. Shortly after that, Galewski received a message that preparations were complete in the lower camp. A message was sent out for the prisoners to continue as normal until 4.30pm, when the signal of a single shot would ring out and the revolt would begin.

In the extermination area, the few weapons that had been procured from the Ukrainians were now dug up from the barracks floor and cleaned. The workers carried out their ghastly tasks with great speed and energy, purposefully pulling more bodies from the last pit than could possibly be cremated in one morning. By noon, when their working day concluded in the heat of summer, mountains of freshly dug, decomposing bodies lay piled near the grates. The foreman of the 30-man corpse-burning work group – probably Adesh, who had previously been transferred to the upper camp with Zialo Bloch – volunteered himself and his team to work into the afternoon to complete the task. Adesh now negotiated with the SS man in charge – a guard named Karl Petzinger – for double bread rations for his men in return for the extra work, in order to avoid arousing suspicion. Petzinger agreed.

In the afternoon, when the rest of the prisoners had been locked in the barracks, a group of 30 hand-picked men reappeared at the grates in the searing afternoon heat with the tools of their hellish occupation – pitchforks, shovels and axes. At the same time, Bloch, now the kapo of the extermination area, joined the water-carrying brigade, which was allowed out of the barracks each afternoon for a trip to the well.

Bloch increased the squad number from three to five men. They worked particularly slowly on the afternoon of 2 August 1943, to ensure they were not locked in the barracks when zero hour came upon them.

In the lower camp, tension mounted among the Jews. They laboured and wiped the sweat from their faces. The Ukrainians in the watchtowers sat sunning themselves. Suchomel, the German sergeant, was on a break and was observed pedalling past the ghetto on a bicycle. Soon after he passed, just before 3.30pm, an unexpected incident occurred.

Küttner, the feared commander of the lower camp, made a sudden and unexpected appearance in the ghetto. What was observed next was shocking – a conversation between Küttner and Kuba, the barracks kapo and a feared informer. The pair entered the barracks for a private conversation and suspicion arose that Kuba had sensed a rebellion was imminent and had passed on what little he knew to Küttner. The information was dispatched quickly to Galewski, along with a request for an armed man to be sent to kill Küttner. Galewski sent them Wolowanczyk, the twenty-year-old thug from the Warsaw underworld.

As Küttner was leaving the barracks he came upon two prisoners who should have been elsewhere during working hours. Küttner searched them and found their pockets stuffed with money and gold. Some versions have Küttner taking the two men behind the barracks and beating them mercilessly. Other versions tell of more prisoners being arrested. According to Hershl's account:

> *Oberscharführer* Kittner [sic] has arrested twenty Jews whom he found in possession of gold. Finding Jews with gold or valuables was a sign for the SS that people were planning to escape and therefore had to supply themselves with valuables so that they could live illegally. In such a case the SS would instantly carry out a search of the other Jews in the camp. It is not long before we see the SS taking these twenty Jews off to the Lazarett in order to kill them.

Just as Wolowanczyk slipped into one of the workshops, Küttner was marching his prisoners through the ghetto gate toward the Lazarett. Rajzman, who was present in the workshop as Wolowanczyk entered, wrote in his testimony: 'One of us went to the window and shot at Kiewe with a pistol. Kiewe died on the spot.'

Küttner, in fact, did not die that day, although he may have appeared dead. He lay bleeding and wounded at the gates of the ghetto. It was Wolowanczyk's pistol shot that triggered the Treblinka rebellion.

★ ★ ★

The single shot rang out into an abrupt silence. The entire camp stood as if petrified for an interminable few seconds. The prisoners in the work groups stopped what they were doing, as did the SS and Ukrainians. The Underground combat units outside the ghetto were confused, because the rebellion was not supposed to begin for another 45 minutes. Kurland and Galewski were in Sorting Square, too distant to dispatch centralised orders to other units, thus rendering any chance of a coordinated attack impossible. Now a short exchange of fire between Suchomel and armed prisoners rang out. Rajzman recalled: 'Franz Suchomel appeared on his bicycle. He was also shot, but inaccurately, and he responded with fire.' Now, in the absence of orders, several groups decided to initiate attacks by themselves. Hershl writes: 'After a short discussion we decide to launch the revolt this very minute.'

Prisoners rushed out of the workshops and ran through the gateway of the ghetto, past the bakery and on to Kurt Seidel Strasse. Hershl was among them. I imagine him with a Molotov cocktail in his hand. A few of the prisoners were armed with rifles; others carried axes, shovels and garden rakes. A grenade appeared on the asphalt. It bounced and rolled toward the SS barracks, which earlier that day had been sprayed with gasoline. The grenade stopped and then exploded. The barracks burst into flames and the first 'Hurrah' went up.

Flames shot into the burning sky. A second grenade was thrown, then a third, which exploded on the asphalt of Kurt Seidel Strasse. The hurrahs grew louder and rose over the camp. The sound of gunshots grew louder. The Ukrainians in the watchtower, after recovering from their initial surprise, began firing at the Jews, who were swarming through the camp. Many of them were mowed down there and then: 'The signal to fight is given and the Ukrainian SS open heavy fire on the Jews. But the Jews remain firm. They throw hand grenades and position their machine-guns.'

On the ground, most of the Ukrainian guards ran for cover as the prisoners rioted through the camp; some Ukrainians fell. The insurgents began operations against their pre-determined targets. Other prisoners opened fire at the Ukrainian guards in the watchtowers, although with little success. Lebrenitiski and Stenda Lichtblau, a fellow Underground member, set fire to several gasoline drums; the blaze spread to nearby buildings. The air shook with explosions. Black clouds of smoke filled the sky. Prisoners were running in every direction.

Now the potato workers, armed with grenades and rifles, moved toward their predetermined target – the SS headquarters, which were to be set ablaze. This was a crucial part of Galewski's original plan. Several grenades were thrown, which exploded, but caused no casualties. Hershl writes: 'A hand grenade is thrown at *Oberscharführer* Franz.'

This is a curious error, which contradicts his own earlier statement that Franz and 40 others had gone swimming – unless he is referring to Franz Stangl, the camp commander, although the rank would then be incorrect. He might also be referring to Franz Suchomel, who was indeed an *Oberscharführer*, or sergeant.

Stangl, during his interview with Sereny, recalled the advance of the potato workers.

> Looking out of my window, I could see some Jews on the other side of the inner fence. They must have jumped down from the roof of the SS billets and they were shooting. I … took my pistol and ran out. By that time the guards had begun to shoot, but there were already fires all over the camp.

The largest blaze of the Treblinka uprising, however, was yet to be ignited. All the accounts of survivor-witnesses and the concurring SS accounts tell of this giant explosion. Lubraniecki and Lichtblau, both with grenades and rifles in their hands, had been ordered to take out the camp garage and the gasoline pump at the far eastern end of Kurt Seidel Strasse. Here, they discovered an armed vehicle with a mounted machine-gun parked beside the pump. Lichtblau drove and Lubraniecki fired at the Ukrainians in the watchtower and on the ground. The vehicle's loud rumble and the wrenching sound of its gun turret turning and the rapid fire of its bullets rose above the chaos.

At some point, they turned back toward the gasoline pump and were hit by gun-fire. Nonetheless, they managed to launch an assault on the pump and gasoline store, which went up in a thunderous explosion, shaking the entire camp. A pillar of fire burst into the sky. The flames spread to the SS barracks and the bakery, engulfing everything. The heat was infernal, as though a lid had been lifted from hell itself. Lubraniecki and Lichtblau died in that moment. Hershl writes:

> All the telephone lines are cut; the vehicles are disabled, so that they can't be driven; whatever petrol we can obtain is poured out and lit; the death-camp Treblinka begins to burn. Pillars of fire ascend to the sky. The SS shoot back chaotically into the fire.

Eyewitness Samuel Willenberg, in his *Revolt in Treblinka,* writes:

> The Germans' huts burned in a devil's dance. The dry pine branches we had inserted in the fence burned as well, giving the fence the appearance of a giant dragon with tails of fire. Treblinka had become one massive blaze.

Franciszek Zabecki, who was about four kilometres away, recalls:

> Observing from the railway station in Treblinka on a hot Monday 2 August 1943, at 15:45 we saw huge wreaths of smoke mixed with tongues of fire in the skies over the death camp. It was different smoke from that which we saw every day, that smoke of martyrdom. At the same time, the sound of shots and detonations grew nearer. We began to realise a revolt had broken out in the camp, that the camp had been set on fire by the Jews and that fighting was going on there.

The insurgents now fired furiously at the Germans and Ukrainians, who attacked from all sides and were shooting at the Jews through the flames. Several Ukrainians were wounded and their weapons were taken from them. At some point, an exchange of gunfire between prisoners and SS men brought down Seidel, one of only four SS men who were to die that day.

Just after the first shots and the explosions of grenades, Zialo Bloch signalled the beginning of the rebellion in the death camp. He and the others in the water-car-rying team attacked their two Ukrainian guards with an axe and killed them, taking their rifles. They then threw the guards into the well. Bloch sent one of the carriers running to the barracks to call out the secret words: 'Revolution in Berlin'.

At the same moment, near the watchtower at the far corner of the Totenlager, sur-vivor Berek Rozjman played his part:

I was assigned to get rid of one of the Ukrainian guards in the watchtower near where I worked. The man on duty in the watchtower that day was called Mira. He was sitting in the tower dressed only in his shorts getting the sun. When he heard the first shots from the lower camp and realised there was trouble, he jumped down in his shorts. I ran up to him and said, 'Mira, the Russians are coming.' I took his gun away from him and he didn't move to stop me. 'You run,' I said, 'but I must have your gun.' He ran.

The prisoners near the Totenlager barracks, armed with pitchforks and shovels, charged out of the barracks and broke through the compound gate, where they killed another Ukrainian guard and took possession of his weapon. Other prisoners broke into the guard room and removed more weapons. The prisoners at the cremation site attacked and killed their Ukrainian guard also. Bloch and others were seen firing at the watchtowers.

Within a matter of minutes, the Jews had taken complete control of the death camp area. The gas chambers were set alight, as were several wooden buildings which housed the Totenlager women's barracks, the kitchen, the kapos' quarters and men's barracks. A desperate bid to escape ensued. Some of the prisoners headed for the southern fence of the camp, near the burning barracks, and cut through the barbed wire with axes. Elsewhere along the perimeter fence, prisoners threw blankets over the wire, and boards and boxes up against it, and began to flee. On their way toward the second fence, they had to cross the anti-tank rolls. Many were caught in the barbed wire and shot by Ukrainians from the towers. Witnesses have recalled how Bloch and Adesh ran from one group of prisoners to another among the flames, rousing everyone to fight and escape.

In the lower camp, some 300 prisoners were trapped in the ghetto when the flames spread from the bakery on Kurt Seidel Strasse to the roof of the ghetto kitchen and to the prisoners' barracks, blocking the gate and the prisoners' exit. Hershl and Rajzman, as well as several armed members of the Underground, were among this panicked group. As the flames spread over the wooden huts, the Jews surged into the courtyard. A score was settled amid the chaos. Witnesses have recalled how prisoners murdered Kuba, the notorious informant, near the ghetto workshops, as the flames climbed high into the sweltering afternoon.

A large crowd now gathered at the carpenters' and locksmith's workshops, whose windows backed on to the eastern edge of the ghetto fence. The prisoners used axes and hacksaws to break the iron bars on the window and now grappled through the opening. The first ones through the windows used pliers and axes to cut through the fence. They all fled toward the Totenlager. The fence of the *Himmelstrasse* was broken down and en masse they flooded into the extermination area. This terrible route, through which had passed so many innocents, now served as an escape channel. Now another score was settled. Paulinka, or Perla, the women's kapo and a notorious informant, had betrayed at least six Jews to Küttner and was herself feared for her cruelty. The SS later found her with her head shattered on the *Himmelstrasse*.

Meanwhile, the battle raged on between the insurgents and the guards. The Underground's idea – heroic from the start – was to pin down the SS and Ukrainian guards and allow the prisoners to escape. They were determined now – in spite of their failure to take control of the lower camp – that at least some of the prisoners would escape. Rajzman wrote: 'They dreamed of setting fire to the whole camp and exterminating at least the cruellest engines at the price of their own lives.'

In the general confusion, the camp's telephone line to the outside world was not cut. Nor did they manage to completely destroy the gas chambers, the only structures in the camp made of brick, and they did not eliminate the threat from all the watchtowers. The insurgents continued their assault on the Ukrainians in the watchtowers and at the SS at various positions, but their ammunition and grenades began to run out. Prisoner Rudolph Masarek, a 29-year-old from Prague, who had accompanied his wife to Theresienstadt and on to Treblinka, was seen lying on top of a roof, taking shots at the SS. He was heard calling: 'This is for my wife and my child who never saw the world!' His pregnant wife had been taken to the gas chambers on arrival some ten months earlier, but he was left alive to work. Those prisoners who were armed were last to make for the fences. Most were hit and died where they fell. Masarek did not survive the revolt.

Eyewitness Glazar, in his *Trap Within a Green Fence* writes: 'He died, deliberately, for us.' Bloch and Adesh, and many of the other armed rebels, continued firing to cover the escapees. However, they too ran out of bullets and fell where they were shot.

Those running from the lower camp now joined the prisoners fleeing in the extermination area. Others fled through the Sorting Square southward, some with pitchforks and shovels in their hands. Bullets whizzed around them and over their heads. Hershl writes: 'The thousand or so Jews in the camp break through the fence … A frenzied activity begins.'

The prisoners scrambled wildly over the fence, many climbing over the bodies of their fellow Jews who had already fallen, now so deep that a bridge had been made over the perimeter fence complex. Dozens of prisoners jumped through the flames and into gaps in the fence. Many of them got caught up in the barbed entanglements of anti-tank rolls between the two fences and were shot by the Ukrainians. Others were killed on the second fence. At some point in the chaos, Hershl and Rajzman were separated. Miraculously, neither was hit. Survivor Rachel Auerbach wrote that she saw Galewski killing himself with poison after being surrounded, still covering the escapees by drawing the guards' fire. Hershl writes: 'On the other side of the fence a path leads into the woods. Heavy fire from the Ukrainians accompanies the escapees. Some are hit, but the great majority reach the woods in safety.'

By 6.00pm, about two hours after the uprising began, 400 of around 800 prisoners had been killed in the fighting, and almost 300 were killed trying to escape into the nearby forest. Around 100 got away. A few prisoners, those who were too weak or fearful, stayed behind in the camp.

SS guard Suchomel, in an interview years later, recalled:

A few days before the revolt, I advised Masarek and Glazar to break out, but I said they should do it in small groups. And they said they couldn't do that, because if they did there would be terrible reprisals. That's really something if you come to think of it. And they say the Jews aren't courageous. I tell you I got to know the most extraordinary Jews.

BREAK OUT FROM TREBLINKA

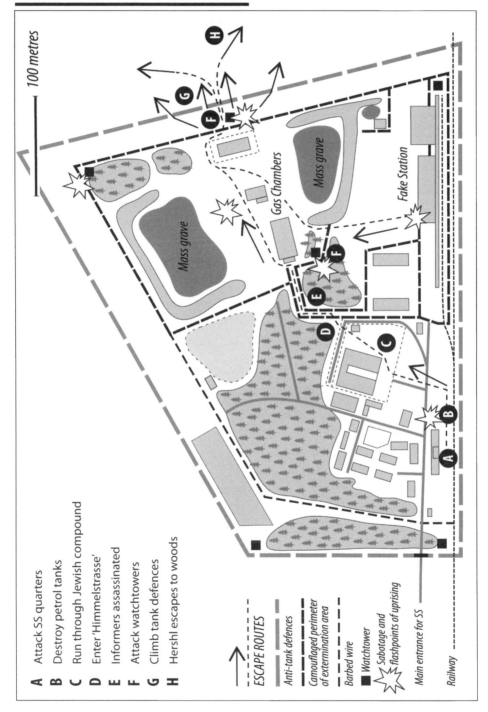

100 metres

A Attack SS quarters
B Destroy petrol tanks
C Run through Jewish compound
D Enter 'Himmelstrasse'
E Informers assassinated
F Attack watchtowers
G Climb tank defences
H Hershl escapes to woods

ESCAPE ROUTES

--- Anti-tank defences

--- Camouflaged perimeter of extermination area

--- Barbed wire

■ Watchtower

✦ Sabotage and flashpoints of uprising

— Main entrance for SS

--- Railway

Mass grave

Mass grave

Gas Chambers

Fake Station

Now the prisoners fled for their lives across the fields toward the woods. Hershl was one of a group of four who found themselves together. The machine-gun fire from the guard towers was relentless. Bloodied bodies fell all around them. Hershl writes: 'A mad pursuit begins. The Jews divide themselves into very small groups. I am with three other people. Now there is just one command: "Forward, forward!"'

Behind them, Treblinka burned.

CHAPTER FIFTEEN

THE FOREST

One night at my home in Scotland I awoke breathless from a terrible dream. I was in an enormous, muddy pit filled to the brim with corpses. They were mangled and twisted in all manner of unnatural positions, and they lay piled upon one another for as far as I could see in every direction. Eyes and mouths were frozen wide in terror. I was desperate to free myself but the bodies were extraordinarily heavy and I could not extricate myself. I felt trapped and started to panic, struggling desperately to free myself. Suddenly, a hand touched my shoulder and I awoke. It was my wife's hand; I had been making noises in my sleep and woken her.

'You were whimpering,' she said. 'You couldn't seem to catch your breath. Are you okay?'

'Shit,' I said, wiping the sweat from my face and neck. 'I'm going to get up for a while. I don't think I can get back to sleep right now.'

I shuffled to the bathroom and then went to check if my children were still breathing. It had been one of those dreams. I stood for a long time watching them. I realised that Hershl was just a couple of years older than my daughter during his time in Treblinka. What would become of my child, if her mother, father and younger brother were suddenly ripped away and murdered? It was unthinkable, and I hesitated to scribble these things into my notebook later that night, as I sat at the kitchen table with a large Scotch beside me. There are children like this everywhere today, I thought – in places like Darfur, Rwanda, the Balkans and Iraq – and there have been children like this through the ages. What would become of my little girl if she were beaten and bullied to work in Treblinka with the smell of death in her nostrils and the procession of the doomed constantly before her eyes? I could not bear the thoughts any longer, but then I realised that Hershl could not bear them either.

I began to see the child he had been in the late afternoon of 2 August 1943, running from the burning death camp with a group of three other Jews, their backs against the dipping sun. They ran toward the east across a meadow in a frenzy of elation and then plunged into the darkness of the woods. Hershl carried a small sack containing diamonds and gold US dollars. Other groups of fugitives, some with clubs and axes in their hands, ran beside and in front of them. Fear and excitement drove them deeper into the forest's depths. The pace was exhausting. They leapt over bushes and through dense thickets. They waded waist-deep through ponds and stumbled through water-logged marshland and swamps. They must get as far away from Treblinka as possible.

The next day, I turned again to Hershl's pale green book. As elsewhere in his account, the description of the desperate escape into the forest, although eventful and rich in detail, omitted those things that had traumatised him the most. I called Sam in the hope that Hershl might have uttered some clue and that he might remember it. Sam paused before answering my question. I sensed this was a difficult subject, because it required him to remember his father's suffering yet again. Finally, he said:

'Something terrible happened in the forest.'

'I knew it,' I said. 'I'm beginning to sense in your father's writing when he purpose-fully leaves things out. Do you know what it was that happened there?'

'There were some things my father could speak about, but he could not speak about the forest. I remember the horror on his face when he tried. That same look of horror – and it was real terror – came to him when he tried to speak about the pits and the bodies at Treblinka. He also had that same look whenever Mengele was mentioned.'

'There are those gaps again,' I said.

He thought for a long moment. 'My father mentioned the forest only once that I can remember.'

'Maybe if you can think about what triggered it, that might help,' I suggested.

'I remember when I was living on a kibbutz in Israel and my father came to visit for a few weeks,' Sam said. 'It was Yom Ha'atzmaut, Israeli Independence Day, and he wanted to stay and be part of that. I also remember he was speaking Hebrew, and I was surprised at how well he could speak it. I was a little embarrassed actually, because the way he spoke was with this funny Yiddish accent, the same way all the old people on the kibbutz used to speak.'

'We know he had this gift for languages. It kept him alive.'

'I have a cousin in Israel, who was then about six or seven. We were in Tel Aviv and my father was taking her out to buy her things, and at one point I think she started to remind him of his sister who had died in Treblinka.'

'So what did he do?'

'Well, he became very upset. I guess that brought things back, because afterwards, that night, he started remembering and speaking about things. It was then he men-tioned the forest, and he had that look of horror on his face.'

'What happened in the forest?'

He took a deep breath. 'I need to think some more about this.'

'Sam, I think I might have found out something about how he managed to avoid getting captured in the forest.'

'Tell me.'

'Well, it's to do with Samuel Rajzman,' I said.

'Go on.'

'Rajzman came from the village of Wegrow,' I told him. 'I don't know why I hadn't done it before, but I decided to look up Wegrow on a map of Poland. I discovered, to my surprise, it was less than twenty miles from Treblinka. That means he probably knew the area extremely well, and I suspect he passed that information on to Hershl. It's speculation, of course, but it would make sense.'

'We can be absolutely certain that wherever he went in those woods, he was guided by instructions from Rajzman,' Sam said. 'There was something about getting to neutral Switzerland, where they intended to meet up and wait for the end of the war.'

'That seems a long way to go, although the choices of where they could safely wait out the war were limited. They would have to get through, let me see …' I quickly pulled up an internet map of Europe. 'Possibly four countries, all of them under Nazi sway, and one of them would probably be Germany itself – unless they planned to go through Austria, which was just as dangerous as Germany in those days. The truth is that there weren't many places they could go. But then again, I suppose if Rajzman gave him this kind of information, he would try to use it.'

'My father said again and again how Rajzman had saved his life. He was almost like a deity to him. Look, my father was a crazy character who argued with everyone, but he never argued with Rajzman. I think they had a calming effect on each other. I know Rajzman lost his wife and child in Treblinka. My father also lost his family. They were a surrogate father and son who found each other.'

'I suspect that just after the breakout, while almost everyone else headed north and east towards Belarus and the front, Hershl headed south, in the direction of Wegrow,' I suggested. 'Rajzman also seems to have taken this route to the south, and he managed to hide in the forest for much of the rest of the war – although, to my knowledge, he didn't make it to Switzerland.'

★ ★ ★

The escapees' chances of success that day were impeded by the Küttner incident, which triggered the premature start of the uprising. This provided the SS with more daylight to hunt down the fugitives. However, their flight, as it was, was at the same time aided by two significant factors. The first was the fact that Franz Stangl, the camp commandant, had been entertaining a visitor in his quarters and they had been drinking heavily since before noon. Former Treblinka guard Franz Suchomel said:

> By the time the revolt started in the afternoon, Stangl and his friend were both drunk as lords, and didn't know which end was up. I remember seeing him stand there, just stand and look at the burning buildings.

This delayed the start of the pursuit. Although the Treblinka telephone lines were still open, Stangl did not alert the authorities in Malkinia until after the camp's gasoline store had exploded. They also benefited from the fact that so many guards were swimming and sunning themselves at the Bug River that day. Stangl's adjunct, Kurt Franz, contrary to what has been claimed, was not at the Bug River, at least according to Suchomel: 'Franz was not in Treblinka that day – that was true enough – but neither was he swimming, though perhaps Stangl thought he was. In fact, he was with his tart in Ostrow.'

After Stangl raised the alarm, all garrisons from Malkinia to Siedlce were mobilised. The Malkinia fire department was also contacted to help quell the flames that were devouring the camp. Indeed, almost all the Germans in Malkinia rushed to the aid of the Treblinka authorities – the gendarmerie, the Gestapo and the railroad guards. They arrived with rifles and pistols, in cars and on a special train. A force of hundreds of men took up the pursuit of the Jews. Ukrainians combed the fields and woods on horseback with tracker dogs. The Polish police were also called in to assist the operation.

Before long, the woods echoed with the sound of galloping horses, barking dogs, gunfire and screaming. Most of the Jews continued east and north, where, if they made it that far, they would eventually have to cross the Bug River. The idea was to keep moving until they reached the front line, where they could cross into Russian territory. Minsk, the capital of Belarus had been retaken on 3 July. Ten days later, the Red Army reached the pre-war Polish border. The Belarusian forests also crawled with partisans and underground resistance fighters. However, few made it that far; most of those who went north and east were caught and murdered within the first 24 hours.

Hershl and his group went south and then west, most likely guided by instructions from Rajzman. They ran for perhaps three hours without stopping. By sundown, all the roads in the area were blocked, and dozens of houses, barns, buildings and rail cars were searched. In railway stations and villages, posters were nailed up alerting the local population to the escape of 'fifty Jewish bandits'. Poles were warned not to hide them, because it was said they carried typhus. The posters also noted the Jews could be spotted easily by their shaved heads. A number of Poles joined the hunt; a few helped Jews with directions. Fewer still hid them. There were also cases of Poles who hid Jews then denounced them. Still other Poles joined posses. However, most did nothing and remained in their homes for fear of German violence.

Night fell. In the darkness of the forest, Hershl's group stopped for the first time.

'We manage to get twelve kilometres away from Treblinka.'

It was high summer and the forest buzzed with insects, which landed on their sweat-dripping faces and sucked their blood. The sweat on their bodies cooled in the night air and they trembled. Hershl was sixteen and the ashes of his mother, father and Frumet, whose beautiful red hair he knew had been shorn in those terrifying moments before her death, were behind him. The distant sound of barking dogs now began to cut through the darkness. Then came the sound of shouting – German from one direction and Ukrainian from another.

Sam called back the following day. 'I've been thinking about the forest, and I've remembered some things,' he said.

'Okay,' I said, flicking open my notebook.

'My father told me once that he had spent a long time hiding in a tree. He told me a lot of crazy things, which at the time I thought were just plain crazy. But that night in Israel, he was saying something about another prisoner that was on the ground that he could see while he was hiding in this tree. I don't know whether this prisoner was one of the people my father escaped with or whether he was another prisoner who had come into the forest. He was wounded in some way, and he knew my father was in the tree because he was begging him to come down and kill him before the Germans arrived. I got the impression this went on for a long time, this begging and pleading. I don't know whether my father couldn't kill him or if he was just too frightened to come down from the tree.'

'That would have been utterly terrifying,' I said.

'It was something that haunted him,' Sam said. 'There was a memory of watching this man die slowly, right in front of him. And there was the guilt either about not helping him or not killing him. I don't whether he was eventually killed by the SS or whether he died right there, below my father.'

While the posters mentioned only 50 fugitives, around 300 prisoners made it into the forest. However, less than half of them survived until the following morning. Most were captured and murdered in the forest by the pursuing forces, and local peasants murdered others for reward money. Yet the remaining 100 or so escapees, Hershl amongst them, managed to avoid the extensive dragnet.

During that first night, Hershl climbed down from the tree and rejoined the rest of the group. Perhaps they too were up trees. They continued their desperate march through the night under the protective cover of the dense woods. They were covered with dried blood, scratches and mud. The next day they hid and slept, and at nightfall continued their flight.

> At night fear drives us on. By day we do not dare to move for fear of being seen. We hide in inaccessible places. We wonder whether we still have any chance of staying alive, or whether it would not be easier to take our own lives. One of us talks of hanging himself. But in the end the will to live is stronger.

By the third night, the ache in their bellies became unbearable.

> We are beginning to be tormented by hunger. Being the best Polish speaker, I creep into the nearby village to get something to eat.

By now, the group must have been somewhere near Rajzman's village of Wegrow.

> Slowly, hesitatingly, indecisively, with a pounding heart, I come out of the wood and approach a peasant house standing on its own. It is about thirty kilometres from Treblinka. Raising my eyes to heaven and praying, I step onto the threshold of the house.

The risk was enormous, given the rewards on offer for information about the Jews and the rumours that many of them were carrying large quantities of valuables, which was certainly true in Hershl's case. Yet they were desperate. The fate of Hershl and his group were now in the hands of the inhabitants of this house.

> One glance at the woman tells me that she realises what I am. 'You must have escaped from Treblinka,' she exclaims. The state I am in, my clothes, and above all the expression of desperation on my face have all given me away. I am prepared for the worst.

However, chance worked in his favour on this occasion. He had stumbled upon the home of an apparently decent family. Yet it must surely have been strange for Hershl, after eleven months in a death camp, to be standing inside a house.

> The woman reassures me, saying that I must not be afraid, that she will help me as much as she can. She can't hide me, however. The SS are snooping around and searching all the villages in the area. She is not prepared to expose herself and all her family to mortal danger. She gives me bread and milk, and tells me to come back at eleven o'clock at night. At the appointed hour, all three of us are in her house. This time her husband and daughter are also there. We discuss the situation and decide that the best thing would be to go to a particular place and jump on to the roof of the moving train. At that particular point, the train moves with a speed of ten kilometres per hour at most. We have no other way out and we agree to try this.
>
> They give us a substantial supper and bread and eggs for our journey. As an expression of our gratitude, we leave them twenty gold dollars.

At some point on their southward journey, the group turned west or south-west, and eventually they hit the main Bialystok to Warsaw railway line.

> Under cover of darkness we set out on our way. We come to the agreed place, but we decide not to jump on to the roof of the moving train after all, because we might fall through into the train itself. Instead, we carry on by foot until we reach Rembertow.

It would have taken them several days travelling through the woods to reach the village of Rembertow, avoiding security police and their tracker dogs, also the Ukrainians and Poles who continued to pursue the Jews long after the Germans had given up.

★ ★ ★

Behind them, in Treblinka, a massive clean-up operation was under way. The work was supervised by Stangl, who was worried that the escape would be blamed on him. The prisoners who had remained behind, along with about 100 Polish prisoners from the Treblinka penal facility, were used to put the camp back in order. The barracks that had been burned down during the uprising were cleared away and not reconstructed.

Under the directives of Operation Reinhard, 25,000 Jews still in the ghetto of the old industrial city of Bialystok, near today's Polish-Belarusian border, had to be exterminated. About two weeks after Hershl arrived in Rembertow, a transport of 78 freight cars containing 7,600 Jews arrived at Treblinka on 18 and 19 August. These were the last transports to arrive at the camp. All of them were gassed and their bodies burned. Between 22 August and 21 September, single wagons loaded with the sorted belongings of the final murdered victims were sent from Treblinka to Lublin, capital of the General Government of Occupied Poland for distribution. In a matter of weeks, Stangl and a number of others from Operation Reinhard, including the fanatical anti-Semite Christian Wirth, were transferred to Trieste for anti-partisan combat on the Italian front.

The posting was intended as a death sentence. Not only had the Jewish survivors of Operation Reinhard been witness to its terrible truth, but so had its commanders.

Two further Bialystok transports continued on to extermination centres at Majdanek and Auschwitz. The last remaining transport from the city, which was made up entirely of children, crossed the Polish landscape towards Theresienstadt, in annexed Czechoslovakia. These children were used as part of a Nazi bargaining tool under a plan orchestrated by Himmler in early 1945. It resulted in the release of 1,200 Dutch and Swiss Jewish children to Switzerland after $1.25 million was placed by Jewish organisations into Nazi-controlled Swiss bank accounts. The remainder, which included 400 Bialystok ghetto orphans, were sent to the gas chambers at Auschwitz.

After Stangl left for the Italian front, the sadist Kurt Franz was appointed Treblinka's third and final commander. Franz's task was to dismantle the camp and remove all traces of its existence.

★ ★ ★

Rembertow, now an eastern suburb of Warsaw, was in 1943 an independent town of 20,000 people on the edge of a wild area of open swamps, meadows, peat bogs and dense forest. Hershl emerged from the woods some time during the first week of August. Earlier that year, the Germans began disconnecting the electricity and the smell of the substitute carbide lamps permeated the town. It heaved with the destitute. Rows of miserable, dilapidated wooden buildings housing poverty-stricken families, dosshouses, and shady businesses stood along Ulica Żołnierska, the town main's street. Nearby stood a German garrison, where Ukrainians, Latvians, Belarusians and Lithuanians who had been captured or had deserted from the Red Army were being trained. Żołnierska Street thronged with the desperate, many of them drunk on vodka, on their final spree before being sent to the Russian front. Such circumstances fuelled an enormous black market in goods and false identification papers. Hershl and his group walked these streets, attempting to melt into the crowd. Fortunately, their dreadful appearance was not out of place: 'We have decided to go on from there by train, but we haven't any Polish money. We sell a diamond ring worth twenty thousand zlotys to a peasant, getting only five hundred zlotys for it.' Rembertow station thrummed with people. Trains came and went. Passengers charged the trains as they stopped, as if they were launching an attack. He writes: 'Quaking with fear we buy our tickets.'

★ ★ ★

Samuel Rajzman also fled east then south from Treblinka, but he did not emerge from the woods as quickly as Hershl. He escaped through the camp's fencing complex into the forest with a group that included one of the camp's few Jewish girls, the girlfriend of survivor Joseph Siedlecki. Even in the tragic reality of Treblinka, intimate relationships developed between a few a male prisoners and young Jewish women in the camp. Siedlecki, perhaps also acting on Rajzman's guidance, like Hershl, chose to flee south and he later met up in the forest with Rajzman and his group. However, in the heat of a pursuit, they were separated again, and Siedlecki's girlfriend – the name of this young woman is not known – ended up staying with Rajzman's group.

Siedlecki, a former Polish Army soldier whose wife was gassed on arrival at Treblinka, ended up in Warsaw, where he managed to acquire papers and spent the rest of the war passing as a gentile Pole working with a construction firm attached to the German army. Siedlecki, who later emigrated to America and became a maitre d' at Grossinger's Hotel in upstate New York, where Hershl years later visited him, told interviewer Gitta Sereny in 1971: 'No, I don't know what happened to her.' However, Rajzman and his group stayed in the forest. One day after returning from a village where he had gone to get food for his group, Rajzman found them all dead on the forest floor. Among them was Siedlecki's girlfriend, killed by Polish partisans, who discovered the Jews in their hiding place and were doubtless aware that they were in possession of diamonds, gold and other valuables.

Rajzman's wandered through the forest alone, eking out the food he brought for his group, too fearful to return to a village and wary of every noise in the forest. Years later, Rajzman told Hershl – who in turned passed the story on to his sons – how in desperation one evening he approached a lit farmhouse on the outskirts of a village. The farmer looked at him and took him into his home. He then fed him and told him he could remain hidden at the farm. We do not know for how long.

One Sunday afternoon, most likely the first Sunday after the escape of the previous Monday afternoon, the farmer returned from church and told Rajzman that the priest there had given a sermon about Treblinka's escaped Jews. He told the congregants that it was their duty as Poles and Catholics not to harbour any of the 'Christ-killers' in their homes. Rajzman asked him what he was going to do and the farmer responded by telling him, as related to Hershl's son Sam, that 'it was not a priest he had heard in his church, but the devil himself' and he agreed to hide Rajzman. We do not know where he was hidden or how long Rajzman stayed at the farm, amidst the random searches by the Germans, Ukrainians and Polish posses, however, it was long enough for him and the farmer to develop a close relationship. After the war, Rajzman kept in contact with the farmer and sent him and his family gifts each year until Rajzman's death in 1979.

Rajzman stayed hidden in the forest for a full year. He does not reappear until 1944, where he is seated at the centre of a photograph of twelve survivors, most likely taken somewhere behind the lines of the advancing Red Army. By January 1944, the Soviet forces had already thrust into what had been pre-1939 Polish territory. The photograph is captioned 'Reunion of Treblinka survivors' and lists the names of those photographed from left to right, many of them in leather jackets and boots, the attire of partisans.

★ ★ ★

Hershl does not reveal what occurred on that train journey between Rembertow and Warsaw. I imagine him, a sixteen-year-old boy with his Treblinka cap pulled down over his face and covering his shaven head. Miraculously, he arrived in Warsaw safely. He then parted company with the three who had escaped with him.

HERSHL'S ESCAPE ROUTE

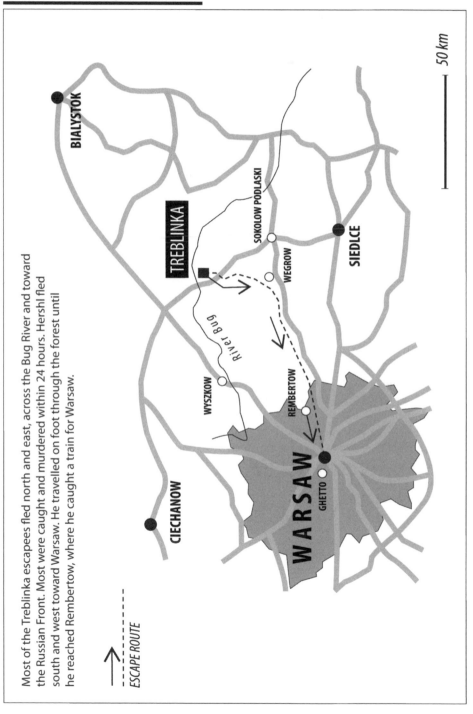

Most of the Treblinka escapees fled north and east, across the Bug River and toward the Russian Front. Most were caught and murdered within 24 hours. Hershl fled south and west toward Warsaw. He travelled on foot through the forest until he reached Rembertow, where he caught a train for Warsaw.

- - - → ESCAPE ROUTE

The Warsaw he entered was a city entirely under German control. The overwhelming majority of the 300,000 Jews who had once lived there were already ash in the Treblinka sand. Meanwhile, most Warsaw Poles had been reduced to poverty. Records reveal that Warsaw residents received the lowest food rations anywhere in German-occupied Europe and correspondingly the city became an enormous centre for illegal commerce.

We do not know how long Hershl remained in Warsaw, but probably only a few days. The Warsaw ghetto was now empty and in ruins. We can only imagine Hershl's reaction as he peered over the broken ghetto walls into the desolate shells of silent, burned-out buildings.

SS documentation I obtained from the International Tracing Service, which manages a vast repository of wartime and post-war records in the small German resort town of Bad Arolsen, reveals that Hershl had tasted freedom for just seven days before being apprehended in or near the town of Koluszki in central Poland. The address he provided at his capture was Warschawska 43, Częstochowa, a main thoroughfare in the city, part of which ran across the small ghetto. It is unclear whether this location was a former address, a destination or even an address invented on the spur of the moment to disguise the fact that he was on the run.

Sam told me, 'He was captured on a train. My father said there were two Germans – I presume they were SS, or maybe soldiers – who saw him from the other end of the carriage, and they started shouting, '*Jude, Jude*', you know, 'Jew, Jew'. I think my father tried to run away, but they caught him. He said one wanted to let him go. I think he said something like, 'He's young. We should just leave him.' But the other one said they had to turn him in. So they arrested him. From there, as far as I know, they took him straight to Auschwitz. But he never said any more about it than that.'

Hershl's written account is also unhelpful. Between the inconclusive utterance that '[we] manage to get to Warsaw safely', which marks the end of his account, and a paragraph-long epilogue, in which he names some of the Treblinka survivors he met in a displaced persons camps two years later, there is yet another void in Hershl's story.

I had no desire to return to Poland, and I did not want to visit any more death camps. I had had enough. Sam was right – for Jews, Poland was a graveyard. But where did the Angel of Death Dr Josef Mengele, the mysterious position of Hershl's tattoo, Auschwitz itself and all that occurred afterwards fit into Hershl's final tragic act? There was more to discover. I knew I would have to return.

CHAPTER SIXTEEN

AUSCHWITZ

Just before I left for my third trip to Poland, I confirmed an appointment with Dr Franciszek Piper, the chief historian at Auschwitz, and I mailed off some further requests to the International Tracing Service in Bad Arolsen and the records department at the United States Holocaust Memorial Museum. I wanted to know what there was of Hershl in history. I wanted to see his name in black and white in historical documents. Placing him objectively at specific points in history corroborated and confirmed his suffering.

I travelled with my wife on a westbound train from Kraków to Oswicim one early sunny morning in mid-September 2007. Oswicim is the town the Germans renamed Auschwitz in the wake of the 1939 invasion. In the carriage were a few Polish commuters and three sets of visitors – Japanese, American and British – each of them holding Auschwitz travel guides. Less than fifteen minutes into the journey, I saw a swastika scratched on a signpost hanging above the platform of Kraków–Lobzow station. I checked my guidebook and read that the town of Oswicim had been founded 700 years earlier and that its name in Polish meant 'a place to be made holy'. Auschwitz held as many as 20,000 prisoners at one time and it murdered more than two million in its gas chambers and through starvation, forced labour, lack of disease control, executions, and medical experiments. It has become the symbol of Nazi evil. Yet those words Hershl had uttered kept returning to me: 'Auschwitz was nothing. Auschwitz was a walk in the park.'

As the train sped west, bales of hay stood in fields that bordered lush forests. It was between summer and autumn – the season in which Hershl had travelled to Treblinka – and the leaves were just beginning to turn. The commuters disembarked at Kraków Business Park, a modern complex of concrete and glass, created as part of a regional economic initiative in 1997. How strange it must be each day to travel the tracks that had once been the route to death. I saw more anti-Semitic graffiti – a Star of David hanging from a gallows. Meadows gave way to dense forest and green hills rose gently in the north. Just past Krzeszowice station, lines of rusting boxcars stood motionless in rows on half-a-dozen parallel tracks. On the platform at the station at Trzebinia, once the site of a large Auschwitz sub-camp, a burly, moustachioed man wearing a black leather skip-cap and jacket walked the platform with a cigarette dangling from his mouth and his hands in his pockets, but he did not get on the train.

At Oswicim, a nondescript industrial town, a local bus took us to the camp. We walked through the main gate, infamously bearing the words '*Arbeit Macht Frei*'. The complex was a circus of visitors and guides touring the camp and its museum of terrifying exhibits. I thought it odd how the presence of these tourists did not detract from the horror of the place. But I didn't want to see any more atrocities. I already knew what murderous carnage and tortures had been perpetrated here. I had come in 1989, during the months after Hershl had taken his life, and I walked along the deserted pathways between crumbling brick buildings and studied the photographs of prisoners' faces in its then-small museum. I remember the mounds of glasses and hair. I also remember the hotel receptionist in Kraków telling me there was 'nothing to see in Auschwitz'. It was a different place these days. Now I walked directly through the throng of school parties and tourists to my appointment with Dr Piper in his office at Block 24. The building had once served as the Auschwitz brothel, staffed by women who had been selected for the purpose soon after they emerged from the trains.

Dr Piper was a gentle, sad-eyed Pole with a scholarly grey beard and glasses. He had worked as a historian here for more than 40 years. I told him I was conducting research for a book that I was writing about a man named Hershl Sperling, who had been among those who had escaped during the Treblinka uprising, and that he had ended up in Auschwitz some time in late 1943. He was later moved to Dachau before the Russians arrived, I told him.

Dr Piper nodded, and smiled politely, but I saw suspicion in his eyes. I discovered later that Holocaust deniers had edited film interviews with him in an effort to support perverse historical interpretations.

'Fact or fiction?' he asked, matter-of-factly. I told him that Hershl had killed himself in 1989, and that he was my friend's father. Dr Piper's suspicion gave way to a look that was both emotional and disturbed. He raised one eyebrow. 'This is not a typical story,' he said. I could sense his interest pique. I smiled, pleased at this small acknowledgement. 'Is there a memoir?' Dr Piper asked, hopefully.

'In part,' I said. 'He left a testimony, a kind of eyewitness account, that was published in a journal in 1947, but it more or less stops after the escape from Treblinka. Auschwitz is not mentioned. I know he was here, because he said so and, of course, he had a number tattooed on his arm. I have the number here.' I flicked open my notebook. 'I was hoping you might be able to tell me when he came and what kind of work he did. Is there a record of him here?'

Dr Piper did not speak as he rose from his seat and went to a computer on his desk, on which stood mountains of papers and books. I told him Hershl's number, or at least the number that Sam had given me – 154356 – and that it had been placed high up on the inside of his arm. I was also curious about the tattoo's position, but at this stage, I did not even know if the six-digit number that Sam had reeled off to me before I left – seared on his brain since childhood, but not seen for at least eighteen years – was correct. I waited.

Dr Piper said suddenly. 'I've got him. Heniek Szperling, number 154356. Born 10 March 1927.' It was an extraordinary moment. Here was Hershl, my friend's father, on the database of the Auschwitz-Birkenau Memorial and Museum. He was now real in history, and there could be no denials.

Dr Piper remained at the computer for a few minutes longer, apparently searching for information. I looked out of the window into the courtyard toward a brick wall. 'My own cousin was hanged on the gallows, just below that window,' he said, and smiled politely. At last, he came out from behind his desk and sat down again in the chair in front of us.

'Well, I have some information,' he said. 'Your Mr Szperling arrived at Auschwitz on 2 October 1943, from a penal camp at Radom. He came with 869 prisoners on that day, and 194 of them were women. The numbers started at 153522 and ran to 154391.'

This was new information. I later learned that conditions were brutal in the prison camp at Radom, a town in central Poland, not too distant from where he was arrested in Koluszki. It all made sense. Earlier that year, some 1,600 Jews from the Radom camp were rounded up in the so-called 'Palestine Aktion' in which they were told they were going to Israel. They were instead sent to Treblinka. Hershl had probably cleaned the boxcars in which these Radom Jews had come and dragged their dead to the pit at the Treblinka Lazarett. From the date of his arrest on 9 August 1943 to his arrival at Auschwitz, I now knew that he had spent something like seven weeks at the prison camp.

'No one had any idea he was at Radom, at least not to my knowledge,' I said. 'They seemed to have held him for a long time there. Obviously, they didn't know he escaped from Treblinka.' Dr Piper nodded intently.

'The interesting thing about this particular transport is that it did not undergo a selection,' he said.

'What does that mean?'

'This was a transport of Polish prisoners – political prisoners and so-called intellectuals – and Mr Szperling was among them. It is quite clear the Germans did not know he was Jewish. This was unusual, because the Germans were very suspicious. I mean to say they were extremely suspicious. All they needed to do was to check for circumcision.' He took a deep breath, then added, 'I can also tell you this was one of the biggest Polish transports, and when they arrived at Auschwitz, they all stayed together.'

'Are you absolutely sure?' I asked, now scribbling madly in my notebook. I thought again of how Hershl's language skills and his daring had kept him alive. Hershl would have used the Yiddish word, *chutzpah*, for his own behaviour in those days. He had been arrested as a Jew on the train in Koluszki, but had somehow managed to become a Pole by the time he entered Auschwitz. I said, 'This is extraordinary, quite a thing to pull off.'

'It is very unusual, and, yes, I am certain. There is a 'P' next to his name and number,' Dr Piper said. 'Polish, not Jew.'

'Does it say what he did here, his work?'

'I'm sorry. When the Germans evacuated Auschwitz on 18 January 1945, they destroyed 90 per cent of the prisoner records. Ten per cent have remained. Before you leave, you should check with Auschwitz archives. There may be more information there.'

'I see.' Dr Piper's eyes seemed to radiate sadness.

'There is something else,' he said.

'What?'

'On 10 February 1944, Heniek Szperling, prisoner number 154356, was sent to the *strafkompanie*, that is to say the Birkenau penal commando.'

'Do we know how long his sentence was, and what offence he committed?' I asked. Dr Piper shook his head.

'Most likely he tried to escape, but it's also possible he was either engaged in the resistance movement or else in black market activities. These were the three reasons prisoners were most often sent to the *strafkompanie*.' He now leaned forward in his chair and stared at me. 'Let me tell you, this was the worst punishment in Auschwitz. The prisoners died from executions, punishments or exhaustion. Many prisoners in that commando were murdered by kapos. That was where they assigned all the cruellest kapos.'

Hershl, of course, had experience of all three potential infringements. I have no difficulty imagining him engaged in all of them – trying to escape, organised resistance and also black marketeering.

* * *

About a week later, I called Sam and told him what I had learned. I was struck now more than ever by Hershl's contention that 'Auschwitz was nothing'. It seemed a sacrilegious comment, given the suffering and death that had occurred there.

'At one level, I think, even in a place like Auschwitz, he was still glad to be away from Treblinka,' Sam said. 'At another level, it's about the hierarchy of suffering, which exists even though I suppose a lot of people don't want to admit it. But survivors are aware of it. Some people suffered more than others. There was even a hierarchy of suffering in our house. My mother used to always say, "I didn't go through what your father did" – and she lost both her parents and spent years in a labour camp.'

I told Sam about the harsh conditions of the *strafkompanie* and that Dr Piper had described it as the 'worst punishment in Auschwitz'. Records revealed that Hershl was sent to the penal commando in Birkenau on 10 February 1943, and on that day 41 others from the Polish contingent with whom he had arrived joined him. Alas, the length of his sentence is unknown because of incomplete records.

The prisoners were isolated in the notorious BII section of Birkenau. The workload was murderous. What remains of the Book of the Penal Company reveals that some of Hershl's fellow Poles died within days of arrival. Food was distributed at the whim of the block leader. Punishments were severe. Often the unit worked up to their waists in water to maintain the Königsgraben canal, the main drainage ditch that ran through the camp. They worked in winter without socks, in Dutch clogs, and clad in ticking. There was no toilet, only a bucket – although Hershl was used to that after Treblinka. His barrack held 36 wooden bunk beds, and inmates were squeezed in five or six across a wooden plank. As many as 500 prisoners could be lodged in a single barrack.

'Still,' said Sam, 'compared with Treblinka, Auschwitz was nothing. Treblinka was the big thing for my father. Everything went back to Treblinka. The rest didn't really seem to matter. Do you remember *Colditz*, that programme about the prisoner of war camp in Germany? My father refused to watch it. He called it a holiday camp. Remember the prisoners used to sit around in deck chairs? Auschwitz was nothing and Colditz was a holiday camp, he insisted.'

'You know, I went to the Auschwitz archives department to see if they had any more information, and I ended up filling out forms about your father. It turned out they didn't even know that he'd survived the war.'

'So now they've updated the records?'

'Now they know everything I know. Beforehand, they didn't even know he was Jewish or that he was from Klobuck or that he'd moved to Scotland.'

'That's good. Now the Holocaust record is a little more complete.' Sam's voice trailed off and a long silence hung.

'Are you okay?' I asked, after a moment.

'I'm remembering something.'

He was remembering an odd remark Hershl had made one evening years earlier. It must have been January 1977. The Sperling family had just finished their meal. Yaja had finished in the kitchen and was sitting next to Hershl on the sofa. Alan, who was then 26, and Sam, who was nearly sixteen, almost the age of Hershl in Auschwitz, were sitting in the two easy chairs facing the television. Like much of the rest of the British public that night, they were awaiting the start of the new epic mini-drama called *Roots*, the story of an American family tracing its ancestry back to Kunte Kinte, the Mandinka tribesman in the Gambia who was captured by slave traders and brought to Virginia and sold.

Yaja used to slip out of the room and Hershl would call after her in Yiddish. A few moments later she brought him his glass of lemon tea, which he sipped while he watched the television. As the drama unfolded during the first two-hour episode, Kunte Kinte was forced to wear leg irons attached to an iron ball and chain to prevent him from escaping.

Sam said, 'My father turned to me and said suddenly, "I had to wear shackles like that in Auschwitz." He said a lot of crazy things, which no one believed. I remember he also said something about the Germans not knowing he was Jewish, which seemed really crazy to me because we're talking about Auschwitz.'

'More crazy things turning out to be true,' I said.

'He liked Kunte Kinte. I think he related to him, the way he kept trying to escape and just wanted to be free.'

★ ★ ★

My wife and I were too late for the hourly bus that ran between Auschwitz Main Camp and Birkenau, the site of the gas chambers and the ovens, so we ended up taking a taxi and the driver charged us a small fortune. Birkenau was the site of the notorious Block BII, where the penal commando spent its nights and mornings, conducting its mindless drills, roll-calls and daily executions.

During the four-minute taxi ride – we would have walked had we known the way – my wife said 'What an awful job Dr Piper has. I can't imagine having to work everyday in that place and analyse SS documents about death and murder and punishment.'

I agreed, but before I could answer, Birkenau loomed up before our eyes. We walked along the remains of the single track, which cut through the archway in the dark brick of the main guard tower – the so-called 'hole in the world' – and into the camp. The vastness of the place was overwhelming, driving home the scale of the Nazis' extermination plans. Hershl had not arrived here on a train, but probably in a truck with the 43 other Polish prisoners who were sent to the *strafkompanie* that day. Again, we did not bother with the museum. I had come here to look at BIId, the barracks where Hershl had been confined, and to try to get a sense of what he must have felt. We consulted the rectangles on the Birkenau plan, and moved through the enormous camp. While some of the buildings had been reconstructed, Hershl's barracks was a ruined pile of bricks. It was surrounded by barbed wire and we couldn't get in. The outline of the building was barely visible; the roof was gone and its walls were rubble. All the same, I imagined a sad young man here, free of Treblinka, but still suffering. I imagined I could feel his presence and see him standing amid the ruins, head bowed and motionless.

In spite of being isolated from the rest of the prisoners, the *strafkompanie* was housed next to the Auschwitz *Sonderkommando*, the men who dragged the bodies from the gas chambers, burned the corpses in the crematoria and cleaned the wagons. Terrible memories must have surfaced as he watched those Jews return from their tasks each day. Sometimes through the barbed wire he would have seen the trains unloading their victims on the ramp, and the procession of death that followed. That ramp was where Dr Josef Mengele stood each day and, with a movement of his hand, sent those 'unfit for work' to the left, signifying death in the gas chambers, and to the right those he deemed healthy. Guards marched up and down the ramp calling '*zwillinge, zwillinge*,' – 'twins, twins'. Escape was almost impossible. Electrically charged barbed-wire fences surrounded the killing centre.

A few days later, Sam told me, 'My father spoke about the people who ran to touch the fences to die on purpose.' Then he asked, 'Did they tell you anything about his tattoo and how he got from the *strafkompanie* into Mengele's group?'

Hershl's Auschwitz tattoo – the bluish-black number 154356 – was, as previously mentioned, placed atypically on his upper inside left arm. Altogether 404,222 numbers were issued. Of these, 270,726 went to men and 133,496 went to women. Everyone, including children – excluding those selected for extermination – received a number as soon as they arrived. To Hershl, the significance of his tattoo was enormous. He believed it had aided his survival, possibly by marking him for one of Mengele's experimentation programmes, for which in the end he was not selected. In the 1960s Hershl had met other former Auschwitz prisoners in New York, who were also tattooed this way, and they, too, were convinced that the positioning had saved their lives.

Sam said, 'It was neater than the other Auschwitz tattoos I've seen, and the lettering was bigger and bolder, and its position was different.'

'Dr Piper thinks that some of the Radom prisoners were probably tattooed the same way,' I told him. 'And that it probably had nothing to do with Mengele.'

Dr Piper had brought in a Mengele scholar when I was there, a dark-haired, serious woman with glasses, who refused to smile and spoke only Polish. She said she was unaware of Mengele-specific tattoos. Then I asked Dr Piper if he had ever seen a tattoo like Hershl's before, and he said probably no more than 100 out of the thousands that he had studied. He also said – and now I looked in my notebook and read Dr Piper's quote directly to Sam – 'There is no explanation and there is no mention of Mengele near his name. There are not enough records and there is no information about the way the tattoos were made. But I have been here 43 years, and I exclude nothing.'

'It doesn't make sense,' said Sam. 'If my father had been tattooed with all the prisoners from Radom, and at the same time as them, presumably he would have known that. He wouldn't have spent such a long time trying to find out if it meant something significant.'

'That's true,' I said. 'What do you think about it?'

'It's not a mystical thing; he believed the tattoo had a practical purpose. I think there is no doubt it had something to do with earmarking him for Mengele's experiments. But the information to prove that has simply not been found.'

'You know, Sam, Mengele didn't conduct any of his experiments on Poles at Auschwitz – to my knowledge, it was only Jews and Gypsies.'

'I see what you're saying. At some point, they must have discovered he was Jewish.'

'Exactly.'

'Well, they certainly knew that he was Jewish in Dachau, because my father said there were German women calling him names like 'Jewish pig', while he was doing slave labour on the roads in the town.'

Given the time that he spent in Auschwitz, it seems likely this discovery came during his time in the *strafkompanie*. The dangers of such a discovery anywhere in the camp, let alone while serving in the feared penal commando, cannot be overstated. If he had been found out after an attempted escape, or any other of the major offences, he would have been executed immediately. It is safe to assume that he was sent to Birkenau penal commando as an offending gentile, and that from his arrival at Auschwitz on 2 October 1943 until his internment on 10 February 1944 in the *strafkompanie*, and probably for several months thereafter, Hershl successfully passed himself off as a Christian Pole. Conditions for a Pole in the penal commando may not have been any better than those for Jews at Auschwitz, but at least there were no selections, and it was always an improvement over Treblinka.

'My father was always an extremely convincing actor,' said Sam. 'He could carry out a bluff and give nothing away. One time, he even flew from Israel to Britain on someone else's ticket. He had been able to convince the security people he was another person. And you know what Israeli security is like. Another time, one of those times when he'd disappeared and the police found him in Ayr, he managed to convince the hotel manager and the police that he was Swedish.'

So Hershl committed an infraction during his time in the *strafkompanie*. It occurred to me that perhaps he had tried to run away again. Under typical procedure, he would have been stripped for whipping in the execution yard of Block BIId, and perhaps it was at this point he was revealed as a circumcised Jew. He was lucky not to be murdered on the spot. As an alternative, he may have been sent into a selection and from there was pulled for Mengele's 'special work detail'. If Hershl and Sam were right, then Hershl had already been marked out and was pulled from the *strafkom-panie* specifically for Mengele's experiments. A third possibility is that he served his sentence in the penal commando and his Jewishness was discovered some time later.

Nonetheless, it is possible to estimate the date of Hershl's arrival in Mengele's barracks. During the summer of 1944, Mengele's sterilisation program sought out relatively healthy young men and women in their late teens and early twenties. The initiative aimed to develop a cheap and efficient method of mass sterilisation that could provide another weapon against Germany's enemies. They experimented with all manner of techniques, including massive dosages of X-ray and surgical castration. Sam's father was among those 'perfect' specimens.

Mengele, always eager for a new specimen for his research programme, had looked directly into his eyes. Yet by then Hershl would have been skilled in the technique of 'looking but not looking', which had been taught to him by his surrogate father, Samuel Rajzman in Treblinka. He was inspected but never chosen. Mengele's victims were spared from beatings, forced labour and random selections in order to maintain their good health. Here was luck contributing to the survival of Hershl Sperling.

The subjects selected for Mengele's experiments were housed in three special barracks. The doctor reserved one barrack for his twin subjects, which also held dwarfs, the physically disabled and other so-called 'exotic specimens'. This barrack was known as 'the zoo'. The Angel of Death holds a special, nightmarish place in Holocaust history. He was driven by a desire to advance his career through notoriety in scientific publications, and he believed he had found his great opportunity in Auschwitz. He attempted to change eye colour by injecting chemicals into children's eyes and conducting amputations and other brutal surgeries without anaesthetic. There was another barrack for pregnant woman and yet another for his castration victims. The majority of prisoners who had any connection with Mengele died.

'Do we have any idea how or why he escaped from Mengele's experimentation?' I asked. 'Did he ever hint at anything?'

'Nothing, except the tattoo. My father said Mengele had inspected him several times, and made him look this way and that way. It wasn't just once, but he was never chosen.' He let the silence hang for a moment. Then he added, 'My father told me once there was someone he knew in this barracks, and that guards had come in the middle of the night to take him. My father said when he returned one of his testicles had been removed. He was in agony, because they had done the operation without anaesthetic. That was the kind of thing they did. This wasn't just a one-off encounter. This was a man my father knew very well in Auschwitz. He survived and my father kept in contact with him. Before I was born, when Alan was a child, they visited him in Israel. This was a real person who had had his testicle cut off.'

I called Alan to ask what he remembered about this visit in the 1950s. Like Sam, his brother possessed acute powers of recall.

'I have a very clear memory of that day,' Alan told me over the telephone. 'It was a hot, stifling room in Tel Aviv and we met a man who was a little older than my father. I was maybe seven or eight. I remember my father and him were having a conversation in Yiddish. They were speaking as if I wasn't there. Then I heard them talking about these terrible things. I don't remember the exact words, but I knew what they were talking about. English and Yiddish were the same to me then. I never spoke about it with him later. When you grow up in a house with a Holocaust survivor – and in our case it was both our parents – you learned from a very early age that you didn't ask about anything that was discussed. You just absorbed it and then it messes you up.'

★ ★ ★

A week after I returned from Poland, I went through a terrible period of hardly sleeping for a couple of months. I spent my nights immersed in thick volumes of Holocaust study. My mind was in turmoil. I argued with my wife and my children. My days were spent writing long tracts of mediocre accounts of human atrocities, which I later eliminated with angry strokes of red pen.

Over a period of three nights, I watched all nine hours of Claude Lanzmann's *Shoah* documentary, absorbing barbarity after barbarity. Another night, sitting at the kitchen table with my notebook and a tall glass of Scotch in my hand, I traced my gloom back to Poland. I had not wanted to return and I was sickened by it. The source wasn't even Auschwitz or Treblinka, I realised, but Poland itself and the hatred that had made the German killing centres possible.

Running parallel to this was a crisis with my daughter and her secondary school. I had been blissfully unaware of it, until one Friday evening she and I went to the store for some ice cream. I parked in the little lot around the corner, gave her money and she ran in. A couple of minutes later, she ran back to the car, a panicked look on her face.

'Where's the ice cream?' I asked.

She could hardly catch her breath and her face was red. A group of teenagers had harassed her at the entrance to the store, and some were shouting at her, 'Jew, Jew, Jew.'

I was furious. I got out of the car. 'Come with me,' I said.

We went round the corner toward the shop and when the teenagers saw my daughter coming back with her father, they took off. But they stopped a little farther up the street and I walked toward them. I pointed at their faces and I threatened them. Then they smirked and denied they had done anything wrong.

'Consider yourselves warned,' I said, and we walked in to get the ice cream.

'Did you know them?' I asked my daughter.

'They're from school,' she said. We didn't go directly home, but drove around the streets a little bit, talking. It gradually emerged that as the only Jewish kid in a school of about 1,000 pupils, she had become the brunt of daily anti-Semitic taunts. What Jewish child in Europe has not suffered this humiliation? She was probably the only Jew the children had ever come across, and still, here it was. Where did this ugliness come from, in this little town in Scotland? Was it learned from their parents, who had learned it from *their* parents?

My wife and I complained to the school and we were told: 'It's not really racism. They're just picking on her. It would be the same if she were fat or wore glasses. They're just looking for something to pick on.' Perhaps that kind of low-level tolerance of anti-Semitism is at fault, a kind of thin end of the wedge. The Scottish government at the time was running a 'No Place for Racism' poster campaign around the country. Although it was clear recognition of a problem, it seemed it did not apply to Jews. The school's response either implied that a little bit of racism was acceptable or that they recognised the problem, but had neither the will nor the inclination to confront it.

My daughter was angry when she found out we had complained to the school. I told her, 'You've got to deal with these kind of things head-on, or else it just won't stop, believe me.'

'I wish I'd never told anybody I was Jewish,' she said.

'You should be proud of what you are,' I told her. I pulled her into a hug. I could see how upset she was and how these daily taunts were grinding her down. 'You shouldn't have to hide,' I said. 'Look, what do you want to do about it?'

'Nothing,' she said. 'I'll just keep dealing with it in my way. I don't want to make it worse.'

'Believe me, it will get worse, especially if you don't deal with it right away. I think you should report it, and if you don't want to do that, I'll report it for you and I want the names of individuals.'

She sighed as if I were being impossible. 'It won't help. It'll just make things worse for me.' The discussion was going round in circles and I was becoming frustrated. 'Okay,' I said, 'let's agree that if it gets worse or continues, either you or I – or both of us – will go up to the school to confront this. There are laws against racism, you know. You shouldn't have to go through this. No-one should.'

'It doesn't matter,' she said, stubbornly.

'Do we have an agreement?' I persisted.

She pouted, the way teenage girls like to, and she eventually agreed. I hugged her again, but I knew she was right. That night I sat on my back step and thought how easy it was to hate the Jews, and no number of Holocausts past or future would ever change that fact. Jews were different from everyone else, and they were a minority. The point was that we weren't really different, they just thought that we were. I understood the roots of anti-Semitism perfectly, the Christ-killer teachings of the Catholic Church and the economic jealousies – but there was something deeper. I scribbled thoughts into my notebook about modern-day tribalism and the natural defence mechanism of the primitive herd mentality. Things that are different threaten us and must therefore be annihilated. Was that really all that human beings were?

I remembered Hershl and his fascination with wildlife documentaries. He had understood man's animalistic ways perhaps better than anyone else, and that our pre-cious civilisation was nothing more than a thin veneer. Was that the truth he couldn't live with in the end? He had seen things that no human being should ever see.

Sam told me on the telephone one night, 'If there were only twenty Jews left in Europe, they would still want to kill them. Europe is a primitive backwater for Jews. It cannot change its essence.' Like a battle between good and evil, as long as anti-Semitism and all forms of racial hatred persisted, stories such as Hershl's would have to be written.

The next morning, Nazi documentation from the International Tracing Service in Bad Arolsen arrived by email. There would be more revelations now.

CHAPTER SEVENTEEN

GERMANY

I waited until after lunch before calling Sam to discuss the collection of documents from Bad Arolsen. He had told me previously he didn't think he could handle 'that kind of thing' during the morning and, besides, Sam was a late riser. The International Tracing Service had sent these particular papers directly to Sam, after I had applied for him – because they would only release the information to a relative of Hershl. When they arrived, Sam scanned them and emailed them to me – but he had not studied them very closely. In all the Nazi documentation that has survived, Hershl's name appears just five times. When I called, I sensed Sam's reluctance to look at the documents with me, but in the end he relented. I was grateful, but again I felt guilty for asking him to look.

The collection included two concentration camp documents – one from Auschwitz and the other from Dachau. Both bore the name 'Szperling' and three different numbers in the spiralled handwriting of some unknown, low-level Nazi functionaries.

'It really annoyed me that they gave him more than one number,' Sam said.

'I know,' I replied. 'It's part of the inhumanity.'

On one of the documents, bearing the words '*Konzentrationslager Auschwitz*' across the top, one administrator had crossed out Hershl's number, 154356, and replaced it with 110572. This was bewildering until the document bearing the words '*Konzentrationslager Dachau*' – which had given him yet another number, 127871 with the word '*Jude*' above it – revealed he had come from Sachsenhausen, the principal Nazi camp in the Berlin region, and that 110572 must have been his number there.

'I had absolutely no idea he was in Sachsenhausen,' said Sam. 'He didn't mention it even once, just Dachau after Auschwitz. That was all he said.'

The Auschwitz document, which was undated, related to Hershl's transfer to Sachsenhausen. A document from the International Tracing Service revealed that his Sachsenhausen number was issued on 26 October 1944. A further document confirmed that he was liberated in Dachau itself, as Sam already knew, although he had been shipped first to one of the eleven Kaufering sub-camps. Precisely which Kaufering camp he was in was not specified. However, the bare bones of the clinical documents belied the death marches, the cramped freight trains, and the torments of each new camp he entered, each one with its own number and its own brand of inhumanity.

'He never spoke about Kaufering either.'

'That makes, let me see –' I counted through all the camps – Treblinka, Radom, Auschwitz, Birkenau, Sachsenhausen, Kaufering and Dachau – 'seven' I said. 'That must be some kind of record.'

From the late spring of 1944 onwards, the Germans were fighting a defensive war on all fronts. The Allies had advanced northward through Italy. In the west, they had crossed the English Channel to Normandy on D-Day. The bombing of German industrial sites and key military positions continued without respite. To the east, the Soviet westward advance was unstoppable. Hitler's dream of a 1,000-year Reich and a Jew-free Europe populated by German settlers and their slave *untermenschen* was now in tatters.

The more Germany's defeat became inevitable, the more Hitler's hatred of the Jews increased. According to the Führer, the Allied bombing of German cities was the work of the Jews. Beginning in the late spring of 1944, Auschwitz conducted the swift and frenzied annihilation of 400,000 Hungarian Jews. Hershl must have watched in dismay as those trains arrived, the chaos that followed as the wagon doors were flung open, and all the tears, the wailing, the selections and the tragic processions to the gas chambers. Hershl's *strafkompanie* barracks at Birkenau's BIId looked directly onto the so-called 'ramp' where these trains stopped – all of it sickeningly familiar to him.

At the same time, the Germans were pulling back to the fatherland. By July 1944, Soviet troops had reached the border of Poland and, in the process, had stumbled upon Majdanek concentration and extermination camp nearly intact, in spite of Nazi attempts to destroy the evidence. As the Red Army offensive pushed farther west during the second half of 1944, the SS administration began evacuating Auschwitz. In spite of Hitler's anger, necessity dictated that the last stage of the Final Solution be delayed and the Führer finally conceded the need for Jewish slaves on German soil to support the war effort. Over the next six months, thousands of prisoners were transported to camps in Germany.

The documents from Bad Arolsen reveal Hershl was still in Birkenau's *strafkompanie* on 10 August 1944, when the list of detainees notes that one of the prisoners was released. It is the last date in the incomplete documentation. The length of Hershl's detention suggests that he had probably committed the worst possible crime in Auschwitz – attempted escape. However, it also meant that he had probably managed to hide the fact that he was Jewish for at least a year and a day, before he ended up as a potential specimen for Mengele. The list of *strafkompanie* detainees is particularly moving because it notes the names of some of those who had arrived with him in the Polish contingent from Radom and also the dates of their deaths, some just days after their transfer to the penal commando. The list reveals the names, dates of birth and the abbreviation '*Gest*' for the German '*gestorben*', or deceased. Hershl appears to have been the youngest prisoner in the *strafkompanie* by at least ten years. Many of those listed as '*Gest*' were in their late fifties when they succumbed to the harsh conditions of the penal commando. Next to Hershl's name was placed the abbreviation 'B.A.W.', signifying 'for the present' and meaning that he was currently serving his time in the *strafkompanie* and 'for the present' he was alive.

On 7 October 1944, several hundred *Sonderkommando* prisoners assigned to Crematorium IV at Auschwitz-Birkenau rebelled after learning they were going to be killed. During the uprising, the prisoners killed three guards and blew up a crematorium and an adjacent gas chamber. They used explosives smuggled into the camp by Jewish women who had been assigned to forced labour in a nearby armaments factory. The Germans crushed the revolt, and killed almost all of the prisoners involved. The women who had smuggled the explosives into the camp were hanged in January 1945, an event that Hershl was not around to witness. According to Sam his father never mentioned the revolt at Birkenau.

We can never be certain, of course, what Hershl was thinking. But I suspect he would have considered the revolt courageous yet foolhardy. His system for survival – taught to him by experts and through his own experience at Treblinka, and perfected at Radom, Auschwitz and in the Birkenau *strafkompanie* – was to be invisible, and when possible to use daring, cunning and intelligence. Isolated acts of bravery were futile against the Nazis.

Sam said, 'He was always able to act normally in abnormal situations. He never did anything hastily. He was always capable of being inconspicuous. That was something he knew from Treblinka, but I suppose it was partly instinctive as well.'

'The less you move and draw attention to yourself, the greater your chances of survival,' I said.

'That's exactly it.'

Some days before 26 October 1944, Hershl and the rest of the transport were sent through Birkenau's 'hole in the world' for the last time, and they were marched north to Gleiwitz, the town on the former Polish-German border where the war had been triggered on 31 August 1939, now Gliwice. The prisoners, most of them skeletal, were not told where they were going. Many wondered if they were being taken to a field to be shot. Instead, they were marched 30 miles in a tight column of bodies, five abreast. SS guards shot anyone who fell behind or could not continue. More than 3,000 prisoners perished on the road to Gleiwitz over the next few months. Upon arrival, they were crammed into boxcars and transported directly to Sachsenhausen concentration camp.

'Maybe this is how he escaped Mengele, by somehow getting himself into a transport that was leaving Auschwitz,' I said to Sam. 'When you're in Mengele's barracks, I don't suppose it matters where you're going, as long as it's out.'

'It's possible. You know what a convincing actor he was. He'd already fooled the Germans and the Poles by pretending to be one of them.'

'The great irony of this,' I said, 'is that most of your father's time in Auschwitz was spent pretending to be a Polish political prisoner – and as bad as it was, conditions were still better than they had been for the Jews. For a start, there were no selections. Then he spent two or three months in the barracks of Dr Mengele – and as terrifying as that was, he would have been fed reasonably well and was secluded from the selections and daily violence. By the time he was marching to Gleiwitz, he must have been in relatively good shape.' I added, 'You know, he also missed the worst of these death marches, which took place in the freezing winter. And that was lucky.'

The train rolled slowly westward through innumerable days and nights deep into the hinterland of the Reich. It was Hershl's third sealed wagon in as many years. The train arrived at its destination and the prisoners, dressed in their grey and blue striped concentration camp fatigues from Auschwitz, fell out of the box car half-dead, the light suddenly assailing them. SS guards stood waiting on the platform.

The documentation reveals Hershl spent less than a month at Sachsenhausen, a concentration camp that had primarily held so-called political opponents and Russian prisoners of war, but was now rapidly filling up with Jews. A year earlier, it had been the centre of a massive counterfeit operation, in which more than one billion pounds worth of fake £5, £10, £20 and £50 notes were manufactured by Jewish forced labourers and injected into circulation in an effort to wreak havoc on the British economy. Six months after Hershl's arrival it was also the starting point for one of the most gruelling death marches. More than 30,000 starving prisoners were marched northward away from the Allied and Russian advance. All, save a handful, were shot or dropped from exhaustion. But Hershl was long gone by then.

In mid-November 1944, he was shipped to Dachau, where upon arrival he was lined up with the other arriving prisoners, counted and dipped in a tub of disinfectant. The date of his arrival is noted as 17 November. The prisoners were then given a shower and issued clean uniforms that had been disinfected with Zyklon-B. Following this, they were kept in quarantine for two weeks in an effort to prevent the spread of disease, a precaution that had been introduced in the wake of a typhus epidemic the previous year.

Dachau was not an extermination centre like Treblinka. Nonetheless, the dual aim of Dachau was the use of manpower and the dehumanisation of its workers through a regime of savagery. Located on the grounds of an abandoned gunpowder factory near the medieval town from which it took its name, about ten miles north-west of Munich, it was the first concentration camp. It began its brutal operations within weeks of the Nazi takeover in 1933. Guards began murdering inmates from the very first days of the camp's existence. The total number of dead may never be known. Soviet prisoners of war were summarily executed by the thousand, and civilians were arrested and sent to the camp by the Gestapo for *Sonderbehandlung*, or 'Special Treatment', another Nazi euphemism for murder. Camp records reveal there were 28,838 Jews brought from Auschwitz to Dachau between 18 June 1944 and 9 March 1945, Hershl amongst them.

In the early days of Dachau, before World War II, living conditions were relatively good, at least as a prison. However, the camp deteriorated as the war progressed, and by the time Hershl arrived, it was already overcrowded and disease-ridden. After the two-week quarantine, prisoners were assigned to work in one of Dachau's 123 sub-camps.

Hershl was transferred to one of the eleven Kaufering camps, where – as the fury of the Allied bombing raids on German military installations increased – prisoners were used to lay roads and dig out massive semi-underground chambers for the construction of German warplanes. Bomb-proof production of the Messerschmitt fighter jet, the Me 262, was the goal. Conditions were brutal. Each prisoner had his tin cup and spoon tied to a string belt. Without these items, they would not receive their meagre rations at the end of the day. Witnesses have noted that prisoners dropped and died with extraordinary speed. Todt, the private German civil and military engineering company in charge of the operation, proved itself to be just as brutal as the SS in their maltreatment of prisoners.

The Kaufering camps, all between 40 and 50 miles south-west of the main Dachau camp, were located near the town of Landsberg, where Hitler had written *Mein Kampf* during his imprisonment after the Beer Hall Putsch in 1923. The first Kaufering camp had been set up in June 1944, but by the end of September workers were so weak that many of them were transported back to Auschwitz for gassing.

'My father told me the Germans used him for road building work,' Sam said. 'He told me that they harnessed him like a horse or ox, and made him pull things. German women in the town used to laugh and mock him and throw stones at him while he worked. That was something he sometimes spoke about, presumably because it wasn't as painful for him as Treblinka. He spoke about Dachau and Auschwitz as if they were some kind of strange adventures. But Treblinka was a different story. He always said it was Treblinka that had done the damage.'

Conditions at the Kaufering camps, all of them created solely to house the Reich's slave labourers, were awful. The guards reeked of alcohol and the prisoners reeked of urine, sweat, and terror. Inmates were bullied as they laboured twelve to fourteen hours a day with little food or water and were routinely beaten. In the ten months before liberation in April 1945, more than 14,000 prisoners were either murdered, died of malnutrition or dropped from exhaustion. They slept in semi-underground wooden huts with dug-out earthen floors. After the liberation of Auschwitz by Soviet forces in January 1945, the the *muselmänner* were locked in their huts, which were then set ablaze. The ones that managed to get out were shot.

★ ★ ★

Closer scrutiny of the concentration camp documents revealed some startling details about Hershl, but far more about the oddities of Nazi form-filling requirements. The Auschwitz and Dachau papers state at the top that he was arrested under '*Schutzhaft*'. Translated from the German as 'protective custody', this was a term commandeered by the Nazis and used as a euphemism for the paralegal round-up of political opponents and Jews. The Auschwitz paper notes that Hershl had received six years of elementary schooling, which took his education to the summer of 1939, a couple of months before the Nazis arrived in Klobuck, when Hershl had been twelve years old. The same document states his occupation as 'worker', but mistakenly identifies his mother's maiden name as 'Kolberg' instead of Goldberg, and gives Hershl the middle name of Israel, which he did not possess. Also somewhat bizarrely, his occupation on the Dachau document is stated as '*schlosser*', the German for locksmith.

When I first saw this reference to '*schlosser*' I grew somewhat excited because the locksmiths had played an extremely important role in the Treblinka uprising when they copied the key to the armoury, and thus allowed the insurgents access to weapons. I asked Sam if Hershl had ever demonstrated any knowledge of the mechanics of locks.

Sam laughed and said, 'He wasn't a locksmith. I can tell you he knew absolutely nothing about locks. He was useless at fixing anything. I remember he couldn't even screw on a toilet-roll holder in the bathroom.'

Most peculiar were the descriptive physical details listed about Hershl on his 'personal sheets'. The Nazis considered such information extremely important in their identification of Jews. The shape of his nose, which in Auschwitz was thought to be 'straight', was said to be 'normal' in Dachau. Oddly, my recollection is that Hershl's nose was slightly hooked, something I would have thought the Nazis might have latched on to. However, perhaps it simply was not hooked enough for them to characterise it as a stereotypical Jewish nose. His mouth, it was said, was distinguished by a hanging lower lip in Auschwitz. But in Dachau, his lip was considered normal. I would concur with the Dachau description, because I recall nothing distinguishing about his bottom lip. It certainly did not hang. However, in both camps, his earlobe was regarded as 'attached', which in the pseudoscience of Nazi racial theory was regarded as a particularly Jewish trait. The noting of these characteristics was in part an attempt to associate Jews with images of the devil in medieval Christian folklore, all of which reappeared in Nazi propaganda – the huge, hooked nose, thick lips, bleary eyes and fat fingers. The issue of the earlobes was a Nazi twisting of the genetic terms dominant and recessive, which to them meant superior and inferior. All good Germans were handsome, blond, courageous, proud, with small noses, thin lips and, apparently, hanging ear lobes.

Hershl had two teeth missing on leaving Auschwitz one document reveals, but he had apparently lost another by the time he got to Dachau, a month or so later. His height was noted as 170 centimetres in Auschwitz, but he had lost five centimetres on arrival at Dachau.

'All these discrepancies,' said Sam, in a tone of mockery, 'don't really display Teutonic efficiency. It's odd actually.'

'It's almost like the Auschwitz guy was in a hurry and he just made a cursory inspection and filled in some stereotypes, but the guy in Dachau took a slightly closer look,' I said. 'It also seems a little weird to me that they required his signature on these concentration camp forms, as if there was some kind of pretence going on that he had agreed to be there.' I then asked Sam, 'I take it that is his signature.' Sam looked at the signatures at the bottom of the two documents. His voice seemed to tighten and I realised the sight of them had upset him.

'Yes, that's definitely his signature,' he said, after a moment. The other documents that arrived included a copy of his *schreibstubenkarte*, or registration card from Dachau. It was dated 17 November 1944, the day he arrived at the camp. His new number and the word 'Dachau' on the card was typed – but next to it, in a handwritten pencil scribble, was the word 'Kaufering'.

A few days later, I called Alan to tell him what I had discovered. He said, 'I had no idea he was in Dachau, let alone any of the other camps. I thought he was in Treblinka and then liberated in Auschwitz, I knew he was liberated by the Americans, but to tell you the truth, until I was about seventeen I didn't even know that Auschwitz was in Poland and that it had been liberated by the Russians. I thought Auschwitz was in Germany. It just shows you how little this kind of thing was discussed in our house.'

★ ★ ★

By the beginning of April 1945, the Allies had tightened their stranglehold on the heartland of the Reich and American and British bombers now flew virtually unchallenged across German skies. Hitler moved his headquarters from his Chancellery building in Berlin to a deep underground network of bunkers that lay just behind it. Poland had fallen and the Red Army pushed through Prussia and Hungary. On 2 April, Soviet and Bulgarian forces captured Nagykaniza, the centre of the all-important Hungarian oil industry. Germany lost the ability to power its tanks and aircraft. In the west, American and British forces surrounded the economically vital Ruhr pocket, whose industrial towns had been devastated. The Allied armies continued to push deeper into the Reich's fast dwindling territory. Germany was now not only starved of fuel, but also essential medical supplies. Hitler refused to surrender, and to the end he was determined his enemies would not survive. Nonetheless, his concentration camps were in a state of chaos. On 11 April, the Gestapo headquarters contacted the administration at Buchenwald concentration camp, informing them that they were sending explosives to blow up the complex and its inmates. But the authorities there had already fled and the inmates were operating the camp. They sent a return message telling the Gestapo that Buchenwald had already been blown up. A few hours later, American troops arrived. One of those liberated that day was Elie Weisel, the Nobel Prize winning author.

Meanwhile, transports from the evacuated camps in Germany arrived continually at Dachau, resulting in a dramatic deterioration of conditions. The front was in a constant state of retreat. From the beginning of 1945 until liberation, some 15,000 people died in Dachau. After days of travel, the prisoners arrived weak and exhausted, often near death. There was little food or water for them on their arrival in a camp already overcrowded and lacking basic sanitation. Typhus was rife and prisoners died in ever increasing numbers.

On 12 April, the day of President Roosevelt's death, General George Patton's US Third Army crossed the Kyll River on the Western Front and advanced into the heart of the Reich, a spearhead that had been launched ten months earlier from the beaches of Normandy. The following day, the Russians took Vienna. Hitler issued a proclamation to the speedily retreating German troops on the Eastern Front. He promised: 'A mighty artillery is waiting to greet the enemy.' But the German Army was beaten and Allied bombers cut off the lines of retreat. This mighty artillery that Hitler had warned of would be just a few small battle groups of Hitler Youth with anti-tanks guns. In spite of Germany's increasing hopelessness, armed units were still employed in moving and killing Jews. A handwritten note, now held in Bad Arolsen and dated 14 April 1945, bears the signature of Gestapo chief Heinrich Himmler. The note reads: 'A handover is out of the question … No prisoner must be allowed to fall into the hands of the enemy alive.' That same day, the Ruhr pocket was crushed by the US First and Ninth Armies, and a British air raid on Potsdam killed 7,000 people. French forces overran Stuttgart and, in Italy, Polish forces entered Bologna. In Berlin, the Red Army had reached the city's southern and eastern suburbs and the city's defences were pierced.

On 18 April, Allied bombers carried out a final and massive air attack on Berlin, already piled with debris and blackened. The following day, as Hitler celebrated his fifty-sixth birthday with a party 50 feet below the ground in his bunker, Berlin shook with the sound of Soviet artillery. Hitler was now the Reichsführer in name only. To those who saw him, he was an old man, stooped, skin greyish, his face deathly pale. He shuffled when he walked, his left leg stiff from the explosion of the assassination attempt the previous July. Faithful Himmler, who had been one of the guests at the party, in an attempt to secure his own future once the war was over, made contact with the Red Cross in Sweden and tried to strike a deal with the Allies by sending 7,000 women prisoners from Ravensbruck concentration camp to Scandinavia. That same day, 20 Jewish children and 20 Russian prisoners of war who been taken from Auschwitz to Neuengamme concentration camp near Hamburg for medical experiments were hanged.

On 22 April, Hitler ordered an all-out counter attack against the Russians in the suburbs of Berlin. The attack was to be led by SS General Felix Steiner. Later that day, Hitler held a military conference in the tiny bunker conference room and was told of the catastrophic state of affairs. The Russian and US armies would shortly link up at the River Elbe. In the south, the Americans were continuing their rapid advance on Munich, and the Americans and the British had taken up positions in the north. To the east, the Oder Front had collapsed. During the meeting, news also arrived that Russian troops had broken through the defences to the north of Berlin. Hitler then asked what had happened to Steiner's counter-offensive. He was given disastrous news. Steiner had been unable to muster enough of an army and the attack was never launched. Steiner had also disappeared, clearly having decided this counter-attack was nothing more than a fantasy. The fall of Berlin was inevitable. On hearing the news, Hitler flew into a rage – a widely reported and infamous outburst – lashing out against the Jews. He told those assembled that the war was lost and that he would shoot himself when the end came.

As the US 42nd and 45th Infantry progressed toward Munich, some time between 24 and 27 April 1945, an estimated 12,000 prisoners from the eleven Kaufering camps – those who could still stand, Hershl among them – were mustered and marched toward Dachau. Around 2,400 prisoners were packed into trains and mistakenly attacked by Allies from the air. Meanwhile, those that were incapable of travel were locked in huts and burned.

The following day, members of the Twelfth Armored Division came upon the first Kaufering camp. They had been through 511 days of combat but what these battle-hardened soldiers saw at Kaufering was worse than anything they had witnessed on the battlefield. I found video footage of their experience in a short film made by the Abilene Christian University in Texas. It was devastating, showing the piles of twisted, emaciated bodies that littered the camp and in ditches, desperate expressions on the faces of the dead, interspersed with the traumatised recollections of the liberating soldiers. One of them, Carold Bland, said, 'We drove in. There was a few of the Jewish prisoners, some almost crawling … I never believed a human being could look like that and still be alive.' Another former solder, Brad Dressier, said:

This one guy collapsed. The rest of us were so busy crying and throwing up. It was pitiful. This was at the end of combat, and we hadn't seen ... I mean the pits were bad enough, with the bodies and the quick lime, and some of the bodies were still alive. But when we got to the ovens, that destroyed us completely.

This was what Hershl had left behind on the march toward Dachau. When the Bad Arolsen records first became publicly available in 2007, the Associated Press was given access to the files on condition that the victims were not identified. I discovered their report during my research. The documents examined included a sixteen-point questionnaire the Allies had given mayors and witnesses in several German towns in the days after the war – a unique picture emerges of a weakened SS brutally driving thousands of dying prisoners for days along the roads on no more than pieces of stale bread. In those questionnaires, most of the population claimed to have seen nothing. However, one German woman wrote:

On the next corner a prisoner was being kicked. One guard was particularly cruel. I would recognise him immediately. He was tall, slim, a real SS type. He had a brutal look on his face.

An SS officer on a motorcycle threatened to kill his own men if any prisoner received food or drink from the townspeople, she said. Sam recalled, 'My father told me he was rummaging through garbage for food.'

At some point during the march, Hershl did what he had always tried to do – he broke away from the group and escaped. Whether he hid or ran, was shot at or even pursued, we do not know. He was certainly starving, desperate and as close to death as he had ever been in his life.

'He told me that he broke into a house and held up the people inside,' Sam said. 'He didn't just go in and ask for help. He actually forced his way into the house. He was armed with some kind of weapon, maybe a stick or a knife. I don't know whether the people in this house were sympathetic to him or hostile, but he went into the kitchen and began gorging himself with food. Then he collapsed unconscious.'

The documents sent to Sam and me from Bad Arolsen stated that Hershl had been 'transferred to the Concentration Camp Dachau/commando Kaufering' and that he was 'freed as a prisoner of the Concentration Camp Dachau by the American Army'. In fact, in the end and teetering on the edge of death, Hershl had freed himself.

Dachau was liberated on 29 April 1945. A few days later, he woke up in an American field hospital in the camp, where he was informed that he had been liberated. There is no possibility now of finding out how he had arrived there. He was malnourished, exhausted and had contracted typhus.

The following day, the 1,000 -year Reich ended with Hitler's suicide, a single pistol shot to the head. As Soviet shells rained down on the Chancellery, Hitler's body and that of his mistress, Eva Braun, were carried from the bunker to the courtyard. Their bodies were doused in gasoline by those who still remained faithful, and set alight. He left this world still blaming the Jews.

I imagine Hershl rising slowly from his hospital bed and moving to the door. Outside, bodies are still piled around the camp. American soldiers stride confidently about the grounds. Around them, the sick and demented move as if through a fog. A few weeks earlier, Hershl had turned eighteen. It was a new and terrifying world, and certainly not the one he had known before the Nazis came.

CHAPTER EIGHTEEN

RESTLESS AND HOPEFUL

Hershl found himself in Dachau in the aftermath of liberation in a strange limbo between the trauma that lay behind him and the uncertainty that stretched ahead. This was the post-war chaos of Europe. Physically, he also lay between life and death. He was pencil-thin and ill. Beyond the doors of the army field hospital, there extended a reminder of the mass carnage that had occurred. A gruesome exhibition of corpses remained. An inspection team noted on 6 May 1945 that around 1,500 bodies were still strewn about the camp. The US Army, caught between the need to improve conditions and the determination to expose to the world the crimes of the Nazis, wanted to create a public record of the atrocities they had found. Within days of liberation, Dachau teemed with political observers, journalists and film crews. One of those was Hollywood director George Stevens, whose footage of the liberation and the immediate aftermath was soon played on newsreels in American and British cinemas. Hershl witnessed these scenes first-hand from the hospital door. It struck me now how almost every aspect of the Holocaust had touched him – from the panzers that ploughed toward Klobuck on the first day of the invasion, through the ghettos, death trains, the tortures and extermina-tions of Treblinka, Auschwitz, Mengele, concentration camps in Germany and liberation at Dachau. I wondered how anyone could ever hope to recover from so much horror.

In my search for clues, I scoured my notebooks, which were piled high on my desk and stuffed with scribbled pieces of paper I had slotted between the pages. I was con-vinced the answer to Hershl's survival and his death lay in the memories and thoughts of his sons, because his suffering had been transmitted unconsciously to them over many years. I found one notebook, dated 23 March 2007, a time when I was just start-ing to write Hershl's story. The notes were scribbled in a small, brightly lit Arab cafe on Finchley Road in London, where I had gone to eat with Sam, at about 7.00pm.

'I eat here quite a lot,' Sam said, smiling amiably. 'The food's good.' He joked with the Moroccan waiter as we sat down on plastic chairs at a Formica table. I ordered some kind of couscous, and Sam ordered fish and chips.

'Fish and chips in an Arabic café?' I asked.

'They make good Western food, too. Sometimes I have couscous or a kebab.'

We got down to the business of his father's liberation. I began by telling him some of the things I had discovered in books about Dachau – about how it had been the Nazi's first concentration camp, and that from its beginnings in 1933 had been intended for political prisoners, the majority of whom were not Jews. Its prisoners included the children of Franz Ferdinand, the Archduke of Austria, whose assassination at Sarajevo in 1914 sparked World War I. It was toward the end of 1944, I told him, that Dachau really began to fill up with Jews, when they were emptying the camps in the east as the Russians advanced westwards. On liberation, about a third of the 32,000 prisoners were Jewish. Now the waiter returned and asked what we wanted to drink. I ordered a beer, and Sam ordered coffee.

'I haven't drunk alcohol in years,' Sam said. 'It just makes my headaches worse.'

Again, I tried to jog his memory about anything Hershl might have said to him about that time. The drinks came. Sam was silent for almost half a minute. At last he said, 'There wasn't much about the period just after the camps. I do remember that my father told me that when he was in the hospital, there was a man in the next bed to him who warned him that they had to be wary of the Americans. He said they might still try to hurt the Jews and it was possible they might put them back into camps and start killing them again.'

'That's an understandable viewpoint,' I said, sipping my beer. 'Given what he had been through, I imagine he didn't know who to trust, even his liberators.'

Hershl and the rest of the survivors in Dachau were kept in the camp until the typhus epidemic was brought under control. DDT was used to kill the lice, I told Sam. Many survivors described a feeling of numbness after liberation. I had read how they watched American soldiers in the courtyards, wearing big gloves and throwing baseballs back and forth with an energy and confidence that seemed almost superhuman. At the same time, the survivors shuffled back and forth through the camp. Most of them appeared demoralised beyond any hope of rehabilitation, beaten spiritually and physically, with no hope or incentive for the future. However, Hershl awoke in that hospital bed gripped with anger.

On a scrap of paper inserted between two folios of my notebook, I had recorded a comment from Alan about a week later. I had called him because sometimes Hershl provided different aspects of his story to each son. Alan told me: 'He was very angry at the Americans for not giving him food right away. But of course there were good medical reasons for that.'

Many of the liberated perished the day the Americans arrived, after consuming the cans of food that were distributed. The survivors were not accustomed to such nourishing fare and many died after the first mouthfuls. The former inmates called these people 'canned-goods victims'. Even when survivors knew the dangers, the food was irresistible. After weeks of eating three meals a day, many still complained of extreme hunger. Some survivors raided a local plant and devoured raw meat. Others got hold of DDT powder and used it to thicken soup. Another survivor died after consuming rat poison. These were deeply ingrained survival mechanisms that had become part of their being. Hershl hoarded food his entire life. I remembered the stacks of cans in the Sperlings' kitchen cupboards.

I saw that I had scribbled my own thoughts below Alan's remark. I had written, 'It is almost impossible for us in our modern twenty-first century western lives to imagine looking at a scrap of rotten food on the street and consider consuming it. Few of us have experienced that kind of desperation, knowing that eating it will keep you alive for a few more days, perhaps long enough to survive.'

Our meals came. 'You know that Alan probably has several months' supply of food in his house at any time,' said Sam. 'My parents did the same thing.'

As Hershl recovered in the camp hospital, he still obsessively stuffed his pockets with food, unable to forget the bread that was given to prisoners once a day. Bread equalled life. I imagined him stuffing it into his shirt and creeping into bed. I imagined him recalling the gnawing hunger of Treblinka and Kaufering, and resolving to save the bread until the following morning, because the hunger during the work period was the worst. Witnesses have told of survivors, weeks after liberation, scouring garbage cans for eggshells. In the first few weeks of freedom, Dachau's former prisoners were dying at a rate of 200 a day.

I suggested to Sam, 'Perhaps his annoyance at the Americans was also related to a panic that set in after he realised he no longer had his tin cup and spoon. I've read about how these things were like symbols of life to Dachau prisoners, because losing them meant death.'

'Maybe that was part of it. I don't know. He never spoke about a tin cup and spoon.' Paul A. Roy, one of the US commanders of Dachau, recalled:

We had 32,000 people on our hands, who for years had been treated worse than animals. Our first job was their welfare. We had to nurse them back to health and rehabilitate them mentally. Many of them had been so completely starved that the fatty tissue around their nerves had been used up, producing a kind of nervous short-circuit … they were human wrecks that needed to be salvaged.

Food shortages were alleviated almost immediately, partly because the Seventh Army provided several truckloads of food during the first week after liberation, but also, incredibly – amid the starvation and malnutrition – warehouses full of food were also discovered in Dachau itself, as were mattresses, blankets and other supplies. Fresh produce was requisitioned from the local population, although there was considerable German opposition.

Meanwhile, there were tens of thousands more survivors from Dachau's sub-camps. They also needed to be cared for, as did the stragglers who had broken away and were just now coming out of hiding and those who had collapsed, like Hershl.

'His system must have been in shock,' I said. 'Then there was the loneliness and outrage he must have felt, and the sheer chaos of liberation itself.'

'Yes, but you see, he had hope then,' Sam pointed out. 'Hope is probably the most powerful drug known to Man. I think a lot of it had to do with his age. I don't mean just physically. But I think eighteen is an age of youth and hope, and optimism against all the odds. I think people are naturally optimistic at that age.'

'So, after the initial shock, when all the rage and the desire for revenge had subsided, came a basic human faith in possibilities.'

'That's it.' After a moment he added, 'You know, he told me he had thought about going out and taking revenge after the war, just going out and killing Germans, but in the end he decided against it. In the end, it was a question of morality. He didn't want to become like the perpetrators, like the Nazis.' I sensed pride in Sam's voice.

'I think that's incredible,' I said, and I pulled from my bag the translation of his father's account, which he did not want to see, but I read him one line. 'He was talking about the people being shoved into the gas chambers at Treblinka, and he wrote, "These screams go up to heaven, demanding revenge".' I added, 'There it is.' I wanted to say something encouraging, but found myself unable. 'I've read so many things about how lost these survivors were for a long time after liberation.'

'But he did have optimism then. He still wanted to live then. He told me that he felt better for a couple of years after the Americans liberated him. His mother had told him he would survive to tell the story and that he would go to Scotland. Remember that he knew he had relatives in Scotland. Although he loved his father, he was closest to his mother, and I think he felt a certain closeness to that side of the family.'

'I guess he began the process of writing to his Uncle Louis almost right away, and beginning the immigration process as well.'

'I'm sure that he did, but it took a long time to happen.'

'It must have taken a long time for him to recover. I mean physically.'

Sam finished his meal and pushed his plate away. He took another sip of his coffee before speaking. 'I have a photograph of him from that time. I think it's at Dachau. It's weird to look at. He's painfully thin.'

'Can I see it?' I asked.

'I have it in the flat. I'll see if I can find it when we go back. I have all the photographs.' Then he added, 'Alan doesn't want any of them. He finds looking at these photographs too upsetting.' However, he didn't show me the photograph later that night. I could tell it was difficult for him. He said it would take a while to locate it. A few months later, I pestered him about it and eventually he scanned the picture and emailed it to me.

I studied it closely. In the black-and-white photograph, Hershl leans on the ledge of a large, arched window of a brick house. It must have been taken just a few months after liberation, judging by the length of his hair, full and thick, not yet thinning into the classic male-pattern baldness he possessed when I first knew him 30 years later. He stands rake-thin in a white shirt with the sleeves rolled up and an open collar. His trousers are light and slightly formal, like the bottom half of a suit. Both pieces of clothing hang from his skeletal body; they were most likely part of the allowance of two shirts, two undergarments, two pairs of socks, a pair of shoes and a 'good suit' that was given to all former prisoners before their discharge from Dachau. He has a vague smile on his face and his ears stick out slightly comically. Yet a profound melancholy haunts his expression. For Hershl, this was still a time before the ghosts came.

★ ★ ★

The idea had been to repatriate the survivors as quickly as possible to their countries of origin, but it soon became clear this could not be achieved for the Jews because their families and communities had been devastated. The policy of the relief organisation UNRRA (United Nations Relief and Rehabilitation Administration), whose task it was to care for these refugees, was useless because it was based upon the assumption that the survivors would simply pick up their old lives. As the American authorities tried to clear the camp of the former inmates, Jews rejected outright the nationality labels that were imposed on them.

Most of them, plagued by illness and exhaustion, now found themselves in a world in which they had no place. At the practical level, the way out of Germany was blocked. As Jews, most were not welcome in the countries they had come from, especially in the east. In Poland, not even the murder of three million of its Christian citizens by the Nazis had cured the country of its anti-Semitism. Many Poles even applauded Hitler, because he had taken care of Poland's 'Jewish Problem'. Except for some sick children and a few young adults, there were no offers of refuge or immigration from anywhere around the world, even Israel, where the British Mandate allowed only 1,500 survivors to enter Palestine each month. Instead, some 330,000 Jews were now categorised in Germany as displaced persons, and hundreds of D.P. camps were established to alleviate the crisis.

In Dachau, efforts were made to connect survivors. On 25 June 1945, Rabbi Abraham Klausner, an army chaplain who was assigned to one of the camp's field hospitals and later became the first Jewish advisor to General Eisenhower, published a list of some 25,000 names. This had an enormous impact on the camp, and it became a vital tool for survivors desperately trying to locate one another and their families. The names had been collected from survivors who had either seen someone or had heard that someone had been seen elsewhere. The list was typed by a group of survivors on paper that had been discovered in a warehouse in Dachau. Some 1,000 copies of this list were produced and distributed in the D.P. camps.

We know Hershl studied this list – even through he had been separated from his parents and sister only minutes before their deaths. Sam said, 'He wasn't one of the ones who didn't know what had happened to his family.'

Nonetheless, Hershl discovered names he recognised from Treblinka. These survivors were the closest people he had to a family, and he immediately sought them out. He concludes his account in the pale green book with a verification of events by naming several of these heroic individuals. His accounts ends:

> A great number of the escapees were soon killed or captured. The suffering of the others was long and terrible. Only a few escapees from Treblinka ... got to freedom ... I later met some of them personally in the American zone of Germany. They were Shmule Rajzman, from Wegrow, Kudlik from Częstochowa, Schneiderman, who now lives in Foehrenwald Camp, Turowski, who now lives in Berchtesgaden.

We know nothing of what took place at these meetings, because Hershl did not speak to his sons about them. Nonetheless, these men have emerged as extremely important figures in the history of Treblinka. Without them, the crimes and the atrocities committed at the camp would have remained a secret. The final paragraph of Hershl's account does not tell us at which camp he met Arie Kudlik, a fountain-pen expert who exchanged expensive gold-nibbed pens with the Treblinka guards for sandwiches. Nor do we know where he was reunited with Samuel Rajzman, his surrogate father and saviour. Yet I imagine there were tears of joy and sorrow. Rajzman was the only Treblinka survivor to testify at the Nuremberg trials. Kudlik later produced a map of Treblinka for the Central Jewish Historical Committee, and is listed as one of the survivors to have given evidence in 1946 in Warsaw to the Central Commission for Investigation of German Crimes in Poland.

Hershl also travelled to Foehrenwald camp, where he met Treblinka survivor Wolf Schneiderman, who later emigrated to the United States and became a butcher in New York. He also travelled to the D.P. camp in Bamberg, a Bavarian site near Hitler's retreat at Berchtesgaden to meet with Eugon Turowski, who in Treblinka worked in the metal workshop and copied the key to the armoury that made the prisoners' revolt possible. Turowski also gave evidence to the Central Commission for the Investigation of German Crimes in Poland. No more than 70 had survived out of almost a million people. Yet within this handful of individuals, this tiny sub-set of Holocaust survivors, there began a kind of conspiracy of silence. No-one else could possibly grasp the torments they had come through. Theirs was a unique, shared experience that bound them together forever.

★ ★ ★

Sam and I had a minor dispute over the restaurant bill as we stood in front of the cash register in the café. Each of us had our wallet in one hand, with the other thrusting money at the Moroccan waiter, who smiled patiently. In the end, Sam paid because he insisted more often and more stubbornly.

'How much is it?' Sam asked the waiter.

'Fifteen,' the Moroccan said.

'Fifteen million,' said Sam. 'Okay, here's twenty million.'

The waiter smiled. He took the money and dipped into the register. 'And here's five million change,' he said.

'And here's your two million tip,' said Sam, dropping two pound coins into the gratuity cup on the counter.

I laughed. It offered a moment of respite. However, there was still something disconcerting about the episode, because of how much it reminded me of Hershl – not the Hershl I remembered, but rather the person I had come to know since I had begun to write about him. I had also forgotten how much Sam enjoyed games like this, acting out his own unique brand of nonsense. In that moment, it seemed as though Hershl were speaking to me from beyond the grave, through my friend, his son, telling me that our lives and all that we cherished were meaningless, except perhaps life itself, and that nothing should ever be taken for granted. He was telling me that the mask of normality could drop at any moment.

As soon as we were outside, Sam lit up a cigarette. He smoked thoughtfully, as we walked along the street in the dark, past shuttered shop doorways. I watched him now and suddenly recalled the sadness that had overwhelmed him after his mother died and afterwards how my mother would pull him into a hug whenever he came to visit. Then she would force him to sit at our dining room table and put bowls of chicken soup and plates of meatloaf and potatoes in front of him. I remembered I had said to my mother, 'I don't think you really have to force feed him every time he comes over to see me.'

'Oh yes I do,' she informed me. 'He hasn't got a mother anymore.' And now, as we walked along this London street in the dark, it came back to me what he had said when my mother died years later, and how he had dropped everything to catch a train and arrive in time for the funeral the following day.

'After a while, you'll forget how terrible things were in the end, and the good memories will come back of her when she was younger,' he had said. 'After a while, you'll remember her in happier times.' It took a long time for that to happen, but those good memories did return eventually, and I am forever grateful for that piece of wisdom.

Now, as we walked, I said, 'It's nice to see that you're getting along so well with the Muslims. After the September 11 attacks, there seems to be so much hatred and suspicion everywhere.'

'I don't think those people in that café hate anyone. I suppose I'm hoping they don't. You know, in a lot of ways I prefer the anti-Semitism of the Muslim world, because it's not as ugly as European anti-Semitism. In Europe, the hatred is ingrained deeper in the culture. In some Arab countries, it was okay for Jews for a long time. I don't think you can say that for any European country. The culture in Europe always goes back to its Christian roots, where Jews were regarded as Christ-killers. At the same time, Jews were a minority and they had a particular way of living that was different from the majority and were easy to persecute. Even European anti-Semites today who say they don't believe in Jesus, don't understand that their hatred is rooted in their culture, and that it's passed on from generation to generation, like a disease. People still celebrate Christmas traditions, even though they're not religious, don't they? Anti-Semitism is a fundamental building block of European culture. I told you, if there were only twenty Jews left in Europe, people would still try to kill them. It's always about the hatred. Somehow, we eat away at their souls.'

I said, 'You know, there was even anti-Semitism in the D.P. camps. That surprised me when I first read about it. Actually, I found it utterly incredible after six million Jews were murdered. What does it take to stop the hatred?'

'Well, it doesn't surprise me,' said Sam. 'I'd be more surprised if there wasn't anti-Semitism in these camps. If there were no Jews left in Europe, they would still want to kill Jews, because hatred is part of their culture. The Nazis weren't particularly religious. They called themselves socialists, and in some ways they were model socialists, fighting for the rights of workers, the way a lot of Europeans are socialists now. They hide behind their fake egalitarian principles, but really nothing has changed. Outwardly, they're no longer anti-Jewish. Instead they're now anti-Israel, but they're still filled with hatred. They have all these grand ideas, with culture and cathedrals and their music, but actually they're all just hooligans who want to kill people, identical to their anti-Semitic ancestors.'

According to the records we received from Bad Arolsen, Hershl was transferred from Dachau to a D.P. camp outside the Bavarian village of Tirschenreuth, close to the Czech border, on 28 August 1945. While he was now free and the brutality of the SS had been stamped out, the conditions in the camp, especially in winter, were awful. Observers found survivors in almost every camp shivering in unheated rooms. They slept in bunks of rough, unfinished lumber. Mattresses were straw-filled sacks. Their bedding consisted of shoddy, grey Wehrmacht blankets. Two or three families lived crowded together in single rooms without privacy. The food they received was the same every day. The camp was also filled with various national groups – including Poles, Romanians, Hungarians, Russians and Ukrainians – and Jews again found themselves receiving the brunt of daily anti-Semitic taunts and victimisation.

At the same time, a rampant black market flourished amid the chaos of liberation. For much of the German population, this was yet another pretext for anti-Semitism. The D.P. camps were not only the source of much of the demand, but they were also under the jurisdiction of the US military and the local Bavarian police were denied entry, a source of resentment. However, the black market in fact was not a Jewish phenomenon – although, according to the German population, the Jews were behind all criminal activity. Data produced at the time from contemporaneous court records attempted to point an accusing finger at the Jews – but instead revealed that criminality was more widespread among the German population. The fact was that during the war, ordinary Germans experienced very little economic hardship, primarily because of the ruthless exploitation of the countries occupied by the Nazis. When food shortages occurred after the war, they were blamed on the occupying powers and, of course, the Jews, who in their view were now receiving unfair privileges. It is noteworthy that one of the first requests of the so-called de-Nazified civil governments of Germany to the Allied Control Council was that the rations of the displaced persons camps be reduced.

It is worth repeating the 1947 observation of Jewish-German writer Ralph Giodana:

> When the average German hears of the millions of graves in Treblinka, of the electric barbed wire of Buchenwald, the murdered inhabitants of Oradour-sur-Glance or the ditches filled with corpses at Babi Yar, he launches – grotesque as it may sound – into his counter-arithmetic. With a threatening gesture, he points to his stomach, demanding to know: 'And what about this?' In all earnest, he equates his empty stomach, that is to say an immediate consequence of the policy of criminality, which he, following higher orders, had defended until five minutes past midnight, with the monster crimes of Auschwitz, Lidice, Vercors and Maidanek.

In Sam's dusty apartment later that night, he told me something I found surprising. 'My father had the idea that he wanted to open a cinema,' he said. 'Did I tell you that already?'

'No, you didn't,' I said. 'Where?'

'In Tirschenreuth, I think, or maybe in the camp itself.'

Perhaps only with the kind of hope that comes with youth could a survivor of the Holocaust see an opportunity in all the misery and chaos around him. Hershl often spoke of how much time he had spent with the Americans after liberation. I wondered now if those GIs in Dachau and in Tirschenreuth had spoken to him of the great American passion for Hollywood. Then it occurred to me that Hershl had probably never seen a movie until after the war. There was no cinema in Klobuck and most likely he saw his first film – I imagine a Hollywood production from the 1930s or early 1940s – in a Dachau 'movie house' put up by the soldiers for their own entertainment. Or maybe the notion had struck him when he first awoke in the Dachau army hospital and had seen George Stevens' film crew.

Sam said, 'I guess we can speculate about what gave him the idea. Maybe he just heard about a cinema for sale in Tirschenreuth. I know he also had the idea that money was safer in bricks and mortar because currency was less secure, and people still remembered the German inflation of the 1920s and 1930s. I think he wanted something concrete and safe.'

'It was a good business idea, too,' I said. 'There were thousands of people there, who were starved of any form of cultural relief. Some of the camps had cinemas, but not all of them, and there was none in Tirschenreuth. It was a business opportunity to be seized, a captive audience, so to speak.'

Back at my desk, as I looked over my notes of the conversation, I remembered how years later Hershl had gone alone one night to the cinema in Glasgow to see *The Killing Fields*, the film about Cambodian journalist Dith Pran, and his journey to escape from the death camps of Pol Pot's Khmer Rouge. I remembered there was a sequence in that movie in which Pran escaped and stumbled upon the infamous killing fields of the regime, where millions of Cambodian citizens had been murdered as traitors to the new order. I also remembered how Sam had said to me that Hershl had 'felt bad' for Pran. An image now came to me of Hershl standing in that dumping ground of human remains, surrounded by bones and skulls amid the terrible stench, alone, as if in Treblinka, as if he were the last Jew on earth.

★ ★ ★

Hershl had no money, save the special currency that was issued in the camps and which could only be spent in camp food stores. There was only one possibility for him to get his hands on real money quickly and enter the cinema business. His plan was to reclaim his grandfather's land in Klobuck and sell it. It was good, fertile ground, where horses and cattle once grazed. He knew he could not return to Poland to live, and he had no desire to do so. Everything for him there was gone. He only wanted his rightful inheritance and then to leave. He had no difficulty persuading the officials at UNRRA to provide his ticket. One day during the early fall of 1946, he walked out of the D.P. camp in Tirschenreuth and headed for the train station.

'I remember a story I think he told me about riding on top of an American tank,' I said to Sam.

'Maybe that was the time,' he said. 'He was also selling things on the black market then. My father said the Americans felt sorry for him and gave him things to sell.'

'I guess he took a train from Tirschenreuth – where there was a station then – to Wiesau, about ten miles west, and then east to Prague, and on to Poland. He would have had to be careful.'

'Why?'

'It was a crazy time on the roads in Germany, just after the war. The confusion and population movement were incredible. The roads were jammed with a tidal wave of refugees – and not just Jews, who'd been forced inside Nazi Germany towards the end of the war. There were foreign conscript workers and freed prisoners, as well as Germans, expelled from various territories in the east, heading west. Millions upon millions of migrating, disoriented people trekking this way and that.'

Jews who left the relative safety of the D.P. camps put themselves at risk. Officially, the US military that controlled Germany had stamped out Nazism and its ideology by banning Nazi organisations and removing known Nazis from public office, but the anti-Semitism could not be removed. In the archives of the London *Jewish Chronicle* I found the story of a German ticket inspector who tried to throw an Auschwitz survivor from a moving train in September 1946. A Parliamentary Foreign Affairs committee in Britain also reported that when cinema newsreels showed footage of a Munich synagogue re-opening in 1948, someone in the audience called: 'Not enough Jews were killed.' Jewish cemeteries continued to be ransacked.

Nonetheless, Hershl made it to Czechoslovakia unscathed. 'Both my parents spoke very fondly of the Czechs,' said Sam. 'I think they were nice to them and made them feel welcome.'

I found numerous testimonies in which survivors spoke of their return to Poland through Czechoslovakia, where they had been showered with food, warmth and sympathy by Czechs. Others recalled how people at Prague's Hlavni Nadrazi, the main train station, threw flowers as they came through. However, it was a different story when they crossed the border into Poland. Here, returning Polish Jews encountered unrelenting anti-Semitism. At the same time, those Poles who had sheltered Jews during the war – and there were many – begged to remain anonymous for fear of reprisals from neighbours. One image I saw in the Jewish Historical Museum in Warsaw in February 2007 has continued to haunt me. It showed an aerial view of Treblinka in September 1945 – a moonscape of craters, where Poles had dug thousands of holes searching for gold fillings amid the bones and ashes.

A particularly horrific episode of anti-Semitism occurred in Poland in July 1946, just before Hershl returned. The incident was triggered by an eight-year-old boy who falsely claimed he had been kidnapped by Jews. Residents in the Polish town of Kielce, among them soldiers, policemen and boy scouts, murdered 80 Jews with iron pipes, stones and clubs in a day of carnage. The pretext for the savagery was the medieval charge of Jews killing Christian children for their blood. However, this time, there was a new and grotesque twist – Jews now craved the child's blood not to make matzo, but to fortify their bodies, which had been emaciated in Nazi camps.

At some point he arrived in the city of Częstochowa. I imagine him walking instinctively toward the old ghetto, alone in his 'good suit', like a being from another planet. I imagine people staring at him, and their expressions asking 'Why did you return? You were supposed to die.' I recalled the echo of my own steps on the streets of the old ghetto in 2007. What did Hershl think when he crossed the railway tracks, where five years earlier he had been among 35,000 Jews crammed into boxcars and taken to Treblinka?

He either walked the ten miles to Klobuck or hitched a ride. Upon arrival at the town's market square, he passed the church where Jews had hidden during the Gestapo round-ups, and – according to Hershl in later years – were betrayed by the priest. He went to his old house, where Poles lived. Were they sitting at his father's table and eating from the family crockery?

Sam said: 'I don't know exactly what happened. There was some kind of incident. I know that he went back to sell his grandfather's land. Presumably the ownership papers were still in the Szperling name. At some point, while he was in Klobuck, Poles threatened him. They told him leave or they would kill him. So he left, and he never went back again.'

However, on his return to Germany, something extraordinary happened once he crossed back over the border into Czechoslovakia. Sam told me, 'The story Alan and I got was that my father was standing on a railway platform somewhere in Czechoslovakia – I have a feeling it was Prague – and that was where he met my mother. She said he was so emaciated he was barely alive. At the time, she was living in a former porcelain factory in Tirschenreuth with some members of her family that hadn't been killed in the camps. There was Cheskel – I suppose that's Charlie, in Yiddish – my mother's younger brother, her older sister, Regina, and Mundich, Regina's husband. I think that my mother may have felt sorry for my father and she brought him back with her to the porcelain factory.'

There, Hershl became part of this depleted family of small-time, Jewish black marketeers.

'Of course, we can't know for certain,' I said, 'but I imagine the minute Hershl laid eyes upon the beautiful Yadwiga Frischer, he was smitten.' Sam agreed.

'I know they loved each other,' he said. I remembered them again walking arm-in-arm past the window of my parent's home in Glasgow, and the tender and desperate way they clung together.

The records from Bad Arolsen reveal that on 7 October 1946 Hershl registered a new address as Marktplatz 157, Tirschenreuth, the location of the old porcelain factory. The factory had been requisitioned by the American authorities to help alleviate overcrowding at the camp.

Hershl told them about what had happened in Klobuck, and in their innocence and hopefulness the group now agreed that they would join forces and buy a cinema together. It was the beginning of the happiest period in Hershl's adult life.

★ ★ ★

In the porcelain factory, they were a gang of six – Hershl, Yaja, Cheskel, Regina, Mundich and a man they called Michah. Perhaps there were others. From their base in Tirschenreuth, the men would carry out black market excursions across the border into Czechoslovakia and Poland, against the flow of the refugees fleeing westward into the American and British zones. They had various schemes by which they were able to accumulate money, most of them involving acquiring goods from the Americans and from UNRRA, and selling them in countries that were under the jurisdiction of the Soviet authorities, where the shortages were even more acute than in Germany.

I looked again over the notes from my meeting with Sam. I remembered now that he had gone into the kitchen to make himself another cup of coffee – it was his fourth in the past hour – and lit up his umpteenth cigarette.

'You want more coffee?' he asked.

'Why not?' I said, meandering into the kitchen while he waited for the kettle to boil. 'I might as well be as jittery as you while I'm here.' He laughed.

'I remember when I was young and we were in New York, my parents and Regina and Mundich were all laughing about their time in this porcelain factory in Tirschenreuth. I was there in the room when they mentioned this guy, Michah. I remember asking who

Michah was, and they all started laughing. They said things like, "Oh, you don't want to know Michah." One of them said he was a barbarian. I don't think he was Jewish, but he lived with them in the factory. I got the impression he used to pretend to be Jewish, probably so he could get things from the Americans and UNRRA.'

Sam said Hershl gave the impression that he knew his way around all the networks of various UNRRA or International Relief Organisation offices. 'I know they had one scheme where they would go from office to office and tell the authorities they had no clothes, and they were given suits which they would then sell on the black market.'

'You can't blame them,' I said. 'It was still about survival.'

'Of course it was.'

It was not just suits, however. Hershl also somehow managed to acquire large quantities of fish, which he smuggled out of the country by the truckload in barrels into Czechoslovakia and Poland. And Mundich had another scheme: he would dip his hands in a vat of olive oil, rub them on his clothes and later ring out his clothing and sell the oil.

'I think Mundich might have actually worked in an olive oil factory at one point,' said Sam. Sometimes they would be gone for long periods of time. On some occasions, Hershl would go by himself. 'My mother told me he used to disappear for weeks on end, and that she was worried about him a lot.'

During one smuggling excursion to Poland with Cheskel, Hershl was arrested and ended up in a police cell. 'He didn't say what he was smuggling into Poland, but I know he got arrested and found himself in a Polish jail,' Sam said. To be sure, a Jew, alone in a Polish police cell in 1947 was in a highly dangerous situation. He would likely be beaten up or possibly murdered. 'This was one of his crazy stories. Apparently, Cheskel arrived at the jail dressed in a Polish policeman's uniform. I don't know what was said, but he escorted my father out of the cell and the two of them escaped. Perhaps he said he was going to beat him up or kill him.'

Nonetheless, this story was also significant because Hershl had lost a sizeable sum of money during the incident, and with that loss the dream of buying a cinema came to an end. Shortly afterwards, Hershl and Yaja were married in Tirschenreuth.

'I have the picture,' said Sam. 'I'll show it to you some time when I can dig it out. It was somewhere in Germany. There are a lot of people at it. My mother was wearing a big white wedding dress, and the men were dressed like gangsters, with suits and trilby hats. It's a funny picture. That whole period for my father seems like it was a big adventure, at least that's the way he would tell it to us.'

I lay that night on Sam's fold-down couch in his TV room, and I turned over and over in my head the images of Hershl's fearless smuggling adventures and his marriage to Yaja. I tried to reconcile that with what he must have felt towards the end. I found myself trying to visualise him during those difficult but essentially happy times, and all I could do was grieve for all that lay behind and ahead of him, and I supposed that was what he must have felt, too.

The happiness was all a diversion; I knew it now and he had known it then, a little digression that had allowed him to live without focusing incessantly upon what had happened to him and his family.

CHAPTER NINETEEN

MEMORY

I decided to visit the United States Holocaust Memorial Museum in Washington DC in another attempt to get to the bottom of the enigma of Hershl's written record of Treblinka. My own research had revealed scant information about what lay behind the writing and publication of this journal that contained Hershl's account. My email enquiries to professors and experts at the Yad Vashem Holocaust Museum in Jerusalem and various universities around the world had yielded little fruit. This extraordinary historic journal always raised more questions than answers. Why had it been published? How had it been published? Where had they found the machinery to typeset and print such an account with Hebrew characters amid the chaos and destruction of post-war Germany? Also, why had Hershl kept in his possession a journal that had not included his own account – but was instead something similar, but different? Sam and I had concluded that the actual book Hershl had so obsessively guarded was nothing more than a red herring. It contained no information specific to Hershl's story. Had he carried it with him because he wanted to have something that was connected to what had happened, but the real thing was too much? There were also questions about content. His account contained a number of peculiar errors – discrepancies in time and the appearance of the sadist Kurt Franz during the uprising, who had not been in Treblinka at that time. I was concerned these discrepancies would be seized upon by Holocaust deniers and the overall truth of his record would be ignored. Also, for what purpose had Hershl written his memoir and under what circumstances? Why had he included only his ten months in Treblinka? Why was there no mention of Auschwitz, Radom, Dachau, Kaufering, Sachsenhausen, or his extraordinary experience with Mengele or his time as a secret Jew in the *strafkompanie* of Birkenau? And what precisely was this series of eight journals called *Fun Letzten Hurban* – or 'From the Last Extermination' – of which it was part, and where did Hershl's story fit into it? These were some of the questions that had sparked my journey into his life.

The best information I had found so far came from the descriptions of online antiquarian booksellers, several of whom offered either all or some of the journals in the series at prices that ranged from $85 to $125 apiece. They were clearly semi-rare and collectable. Only a couple of vendors seemed to have the particular journal in stock – Number Six – that contained Hershl's story. There had only been 8,000 copies printed when it was published in August 1947, according to the journal's inside sleeve.

The third and fourth volumes appeared to be the most common. The fullest description I found among these online antiquarian booksellers stated:

> One of 8,000 issued. In Yiddish, with English cover, table of contents, and photo captions. Important journal lasting ten issues, which was written and published by Jewish D.P.s themselves to document crimes and survival in the Holocaust. The publisher's decision to include the English table of contents, probably in part to ensure the journal's use in future war crimes trials, makes these first-hand accounts especially user-friendly today, almost sixty years later.

At this stage, that was the full extent of my knowledge about these journals.

I called Sam that night and asked him if he had any more thoughts about this apparent mystery. He didn't seem interested.

'This book thing is strange,' he said. 'I'm not sure it's really that important. I suppose the book is a bit like looking back at the Holocaust itself. It's like a metaphor for trying to find out anything about the Holocaust, especially from authentic sources. It's also a metaphor for how difficult it was to find out about the Holocaust from my father.'

'Well, he certainly didn't make any of this easy.'

Sam said, 'I was thinking the other day that because it seems to contain only partial information and some odd time sequences, it would be very easy for the Holocaust deniers to get hold of it and claim that the whole thing had never happened. The point is that you and I know it happened – we know my father was there in Treblinka – in spite of the discrepancies – unless of course I've been lying to you, or my father and all my relatives have been lying to me for their entire lives. As you've said, there is too much that's right, authentic and corroborated about it to make it untrue. You see, if it weren't true, the whole world would have to be in on the conspiracy.'

Yet there had to be some practical answers, a real history to this testament. So I booked two tickets to Washington – one for myself, and one for my twelve-year-old daughter. I decided she was old enough now to learn about the Holocaust. She had already experienced anti-Semitism. In a strange and terrible way, our trip to Washington would be a variation on a rite of passage taken by all Jews, at one time or another, everywhere – a way of explaining to my daughter that she too was a Jew and, terrible to say, the reality was that half the world wanted to kill us, and too many of the other half didn't care whether we lived or died. The Holocaust for all Jews was irrefutable evidence of this truth. Those images she would see at the museum might have been pictures of her or me, and by extension anyone. But aside from these considerations, I knew that I'd be grateful for her company. At the same time, I decided to combine our trip with a visit to Rubin Sztajer, the former Klobuck resident, and his wife Regina, who lived in nearby Baltimore.

I had discovered Rubin through an online article from 2005 I found in the *Baltimore Jewish Times* when I was first searching for information about Klobuck. I had contacted him through the reporter who had written the article and Rubin replied – via Regina – almost immediately. We had corresponded for several months until I had been able to construct a full picture of life in the Klobuck shtetl. Although Rubin, who in 1939 was the thirteen-year-old son of the town's Mikvah keeper, did not remember Hershl, he recalled the Szperling family's presence in the shtetl. He had also put me in touch with his cousin, Rebecca Bernstein, who had lived across the street from Hershl in Klobuck and she remembered him very well.

From the beginning, I was struck by how different Rubin's fate had been to Hershl's, in spite of similar beginnings. Rubin had been spared Treblinka because his family had not fled to Częstochowa. Instead, he had remained in the Klobuck ghetto. Had he escaped to Częstochowa he would almost certainly have been murdered. At some point later, however, Rubin's two younger sisters ended up in the Częstochowa ghetto, and they died in the gas chambers of Treblinka. Later, when the Klobuck ghetto was emptied, Rubin was transferred from one camp to another until, close to the end, he was death-marched and dumped at Bergen-Belsen. He, too, was lucky to be alive.

Yet, while I understood the survival of Hershl Sperling had really been no survival at all, Rubin's was a success. He had made it his life's work to talk about his Holocaust experiences, and each year he spoke to students at 80–100 venues. It was therapeutic and cathartic for him, and enlightening for his students. When I emailed him to tell him I would be conducting some research at the USHMM in Washington DC and that I was coming with my daughter, he insisted we base ourselves in his home and said he would drive us to the museum and help in any way he could. He also insisted on picking us up at Baltimore-Washington International Airport, and he asked me to send a photograph so he and Regina would recognise us when we got off the plane.

'Your daughter is adorable. Love her freckles,' Regina wrote back, after I sent our photograph. 'Rubin will take you to the archives at the museum and help you get any information you need. By the way, Rubin is not computer literate, so it is Regina, his little wife, who does the typing.'

★ ★ ★

It was evening when our plane landed. They greeted us with hugs and took us directly to dinner at a Chinese restaurant near their apartment. Rubin was a small, stocky man with kind eyes, who a few months earlier had turned 80. He was thirteen months older than Hershl. Regina, a former advertising artist and now a political blogger on the internet and writer of World War II history, was a few years younger. She was originally from Brooklyn and had a pronounced New York accent. His accent was Yiddish and his voice was gruff, as though something were permanently caught in his throat. On the way to the restaurant, she prodded him with persistent reminders about things, such as directions and his medication, and each remark prompted the deadpan response, 'What do you want from me?' The talk between them was laced with an underlying humour. It was a tenderness that reminded me of Hershl and Yaja, and I found myself wondering about the divorce rate among Holocaust survivors. Later, I researched the subject and discovered numerous references to studies. One such study noted that divorce occurred among about 11 per cent of survivors, compared with 18 per cent of American-born Jews and some 50 per cent of all Americans.

'Why Baltimore?' I asked from the backseat, as the car sped along the highway.

'Baltimore is where I first came when I got to America,' Rubin said. 'I'd wanted to go to New York, but what are you going to do? After a while, I went to New York, but when I saw it I turned around and came straight back to Baltimore.' He chuckled.

After we parked and walked half way across the parking lot, Rubin realised he had forgotten his sweater and went back to get it. He was wearing short trousers and as he jogged back to the car I was surprised to see how quickly he moved and how muscular his legs were. In the restaurant he ordered a large unfilleted fish, whose head and tail extended over the sides of his plate. He laughed when it arrived and he picked up his knife and fork with glee. 'If you eat a fish like this every day, you'll live to be 100,' Rubin said.

Over dinner, Rubin told us his story. He spoke about how the Germans had torched the prayer books and Torahs in Klobuck and then turned the town's only synagogue into a stable for their horses. Although, like Hershl, he had lost his faith in God in the camps, the memory of that act continued to offend him. He also spoke about the spring of 1940, and how the Jews of Klobuck were forced out of their homes and into a ghetto.

'I take it that you have no truck with modern Polish historical teachings, which claim that Poles tried to help Jews, but could not do so for fear of punishment from the Germans,' I said.

'I never saw any kindness or help from the Poles, and they did not risk their lives to sell anything to the Jews. We traded things with them and they paid us for them,' Rubin replied. He carved at the fish, skilfully and speedily stripping away the bones. 'I'm surprised to hear you say that.'

'I was just putting it to you,' I said. 'I know this Polish version of events is not true, from what I know of Hershl's life.'

'Good,' he said. 'Let me tell you, as children in Polish schools and in the Catholic Church they were taught the Jews killed Christ and therefore should be hated. I remember anti-Semitism from infancy. The church was across from the ghetto and every time a Jew ran up to hide in the bushes, the priests pointed them out to the Nazis. Of course, today the Poles will insist there was no anti-Semitism during World War II and that they were only trying to protect themselves by turning in the Jews. Hogwash!'

He also told us that on 12 April 1942 he was sent from the Klobuck ghetto to a concentration camp near Niederkirchen in Germany. He was put to work with a shovel, levelling the ground for an ammunition factory. He was marched for an hour and worked all day each day and then marched back to the camp. During the summer he baked and in the winter he froze. In the evening, he received the day's only meal – a tin cup half-filled with soup made from turnips and a small portion of bread. A bucket in the barracks was the toilet. He did not know how many camps he was in after this one, over the next three years, except that it was 'many, many'.

'The Nazis intended to work us to death or to starve us to death. Our death was what they hoped to achieve eventually. I do not know what happened to my parents and my three younger siblings. I can only assume they were murdered by the Nazis.' He then turned to my daughter and said, 'You can ask me any question you like. Any question at all, and I'll answer.'

My daughter smiled, and thought for a moment. Then she asked, 'Do you miss them?'

'Every day,' he replied. Then he turned to me. 'But I don't believe these things they write in Holocaust books about guilt. What does it say – that I'm guilty because I survived and my parents died? My parents would have wanted me to live. It's insulting to them. If I could tell my mother and father that I wanted to die instead of them, they would slap me in the face.'

I knew now that I had come here for more than research into the origins of Hershl's book. I had also come to ask Rubin, a fellow Holocaust survivor who had grown up just streets away in the same Polish shtetl, why he thought a man who had survived Treblinka – let alone Radom, Auschwitz, Birkenau, Sachsenhausen, Kaufering and Dachau – would throw himself into a river more than 1,000 miles away, 44 years after liberation. I had already asked him the question by email. He had replied 'I happen to be fortunate to be able to have coped with my past. That's why I've lived for almost 81 years. Speaking to schoolchildren has been a help to me. It is a way for me to deal with the subject. Each and every one of us came out differently.' But I wanted more.

After dinner, we went directly to their apartment building and their front door opened into an orderly living room, lined with pictures of their children and grand-children. It was late and we were tired. Regina showed us to the spare room and pointed out the bathroom.

In the bedroom, I asked my daughter, 'So, what do you think?'

'She's a bit strict,' she said. 'But he's funny.'

'They're both nice,' I said. 'They're good-hearted people.'

My daughter fell asleep almost as soon as she got into bed; it had been a long day. I lay awake for a long time and thought about Rubin in the camps. In my mind, I saw him toiling. I imagined his misery and physical suffering.

Something I had read a few weeks earlier suddenly came back to me. While I was conducting an internet search on the German town of Wiesau – from where Hershl had taken the train connection to Prague during his time at Tirschenreuth – I had stumbled upon the 14 October 1946 testimony of one Sebastian Herr, an ethnic German from Romania who had, according to the report, worked as a tailor for the SS in Leitmeritz in Czechoslovakia. His testimony related to events that had occurred in May the previous year in Prague, just after the city had been liberated by the Red Army. Herr had been incarcerated in Pankratz prison. He told how he and a group of prisoners were forced to dig up the bodies of SS men who had been killed during the Soviet liberation and had been buried in mass graves. I recalled Herr's terrible description.

> I saw from the dug-up corpses their ears and noses had been cut off, their eyes were gouged out and their hands had been scalded … There were 60 of us who had to do this exhumation work, and while working we were beaten so dreadfully that many of us lost consciousness.

This was clearly not an isolated incident. The website contained numerous testimonies relating to atrocities committed against ethnic Germans in the aftermath of the war. I felt ashamed as I read these accounts. This was not the way victors should behave and it was not justice, even if the SS had committed atrocities of their own, and I was in no doubt that Hershl would have agreed with me.

As I lay there, in Rubin and Regina's spare room, with my daughter sleeping beside me, it came to me that Hershl's story was not just about Hershl. Nor was it only about the terrible and tragic plight of six million murdered Jews or those who survived and were doomed to suffer for the rest of their lives. It was about the irrational hatred that had made it all possible, the same raw hatred that had gouged the eyes from SS men and beat desperate individuals into the gas chambers of Treblinka.

I fell asleep that night thinking of the millions of people like Hershl through history and that there must be thousands upon thousands of new Hershls in the world today. The root cause of it all is the hatred that is breathed into the crib and is nurtured and grown into a virus that consumes and destroys everything it touches. It can never be destroyed completely. There is always a remnant that lives to pass on the disease. This, I was certain, is what former Israeli Prime Minister Yitzak Shamir meant when, speaking in 1989 of anti-Semitism, he said that Poles 'suck it in with their mother's milk,' adding, 'this is something that is deeply imbued in their tradition, their mentality.' What happened on Polish soil during World War II will accompany the history of Poland and all of humanity until the end of time. I fell asleep listening to the rhythmic breathing of my daughter, and eventually I stopped thinking about how brutal and beastly the human race is to itself.

★ ★ ★

Rubin, my daughter and I set off early the next morning. Before turning on to the highway to Washington, we pulled into a drive-through McDonald's, just minutes after getting started.

'I've got to have my Prozac,' said Rubin. I was aware that I was looking at him curiously.

'Coffee,' he said, laughing to himself.

'You never know,' I said. Rubin chuckled again.

'That's true.'

At the service window, Rubin ordered a couple of half-price 'senior-citizen' coffees and asked the teenager who served us 'How are you today?'

The young man smiled. 'I'm a little tired,' he said.

'Come on now,' said Rubin. 'What are you going to do when you get to my age?'

Moments later, we turned on to the Baltimore-Washington Parkway. Rubin said to me: 'That's what I tell the kids when I talk to them. The message is always the same. I don't care what kind of background you come from – if someone like me can make it, anybody can make it.' After a pause, he added, 'You know, if somehow I couldn't speak, if I couldn't tell the world what happened, I'd go out of my mind. I've spoken to more than 100,000 people in 25 years of doing this.' We chatted more about his classroom talks and about his disappointment at the limited interest in the Holocaust among America's Jewish community. 'I'm disappointed in the world,' Rubin said. 'But

I'm also disappointed in America's Jews. In all the years I've been speaking, I've never had a rabbi come listen to me once, and it's increasing all the time, because every year there are fewer of us available, so to speak. I think it's important to learn what to do when the next Holocaust comes. I only had six years of formal schooling, but I have a lot of common sense after what I've been through. For me, the whole business is political. Evil flourishes when good people do nothing.'

We cruised along the busy highway, and we also spoke about Hershl, about his life and about the tragedy of his suicide. Rubin was silent as I spoke, and asked almost no questions, except occasionally to clarify the details of a few minor specifics. Hershl's story appeared to disturb him. His lips pursed and his head shook at times when I spoke. As we approached the outskirts of Washington DC, Rubin said, 'Tell me what it is that you want. Why have you come to see me?'

'Apart from accompanying me to the museum?'

'Yes, apart from that.' I hesitated for a moment, but then blurted it out.

'I want to know why you, as a fellow Holocaust survivor, think Hershl Szperling killed himself.' Rubin took in a deep breath.

'In the end – and I'm sorry to say it – he was a coward,' he replied, not without sympathy. 'You asked me what I think, so I'm telling you.' His response disturbed me, and I could see he knew it. I profoundly disagreed with him.

'You know, I knew him quite well when I was a teenager. He was the father of my friend. I've also studied his life now for more than a year, and I've discovered things about him that seem to me absolutely extraordinary and often brave. Never once did it strike me that anything he did was an act of cowardice.'

'Well, I think it was cowardly, and it was selfish. Just look at the pain and the suffering he left behind for his two sons to carry.'

'I think – in fact, I know – that they were suffering long before Hershl killed himself. I suspect their problems stem more from Hershl's inability to cope with life after the Holocaust and its lasting trauma, than from his death.' I now saw that Rubin was uncomfortable with his own conclusion.

The museum loomed up before us, a massive ornate stone block – a mix of limestone and brick, mimicking Jerusalem stone – with a large brick courtyard, just off Capitol Mall, in the centre of Washington. A sculpture stood in the museum's plaza, entitled, 'Loss and Regeneration'. It was 10.00am and there were already long lines forming, but we were able to circumvent the crowd with Rubin's privileged 'survivor' status. Once inside, my backpack was sent through an x-ray machine. My laptop was removed from the bag by a large, female guard and the keyboard was dusted for traces of explosive. Afterward, we went straight to the museum's archive department on the fifth floor. I had arranged to meet Severin Hochberg, a historian whom I was informed knew something about the testimonies written immediately after the war. Rubin joined me, but he did not come in for the interview. Instead, he made sure I got to where I needed to go, and then took my daughter downstairs for a tour of 'Daniel's Story', a special children's exhibition. I shook hands with Hochberg, a bespectacled, grey-haired, scholarly man. He led me into his office, which was piled high with papers and books.

'Please, sit down,' Hochberg said.

I took my notebook and a pen from my pocket. I saw that he had printed out some of my emails and had placed them in front of him on his desk. 'So,' I said. 'What can you tell me?' Hochberg picked up a thick wad of papers and handed them to me.

'This may help,' he said. 'I did a little research for you.'

They were academic documents, the first of which had been published by the Johns Hopkins University Press in 1997. It was entitled, 'Our Eyes Have Seen Eternity: Memory and Self-Identity Among the She-erith Hapletah'. I knew that She-erith Hapletah translated from Hebrew as 'saved remnant', and it was the name the Jews of the D.P. camps gave to themselves. Hershl was a 'saved remnant', as was his pale green book.

A line from the document jumped out at me. I underlined it in red ink. 'Survivors are obsessed with the need to keep memory before our eyes, to be a bridge to the memory of future generations. Do not let the world forget.' This was also part of Hershl's burden. I saw now that the article also quoted renowned survivor-writer Elie Wiesel: 'What survivors wanted was to transmit a message to the world, a message of which they were the sole bearers. Having gained an insight into Man that will forever remain unequalled ...'

'What do you know about the Central Historic Commission?' I asked Hochberg. 'The name of this organisation appears at the front of the journal.'

'Well, there's a lot of information in those articles. The Central Historical Commission was created by the Central Committee of Liberated Jews in the United States Zone of Occupied Germany. It was one of the first organisations allowed in the D.P. camps and was a coordinated effort to collect material from survivors. The idea was to leave a historical record, so it all didn't just disappear into history, and also evidence for future war crimes trials. There were thousands of testimonies taken, some written by the survivors themselves, some dictated to people from the commission. Not all of them were published.'

'I don't think any of this is particularly well-known. I suppose among scholars it is,' I said. Hochberg smiled.

'There is a huge amount of information that not many people know about.'

'Do you think that behind it all, there was also the Jewish idea of leaving a body of text behind, a kind of cultural reverence for the written word? You know, like the exhortation of Simon Dubnov, the Jewish Historian from Riga, 'schreibt und farschreibt!' – write and record?'

Hochberg smiled again. 'Absolutely,' he said. 'I think you'll find in those articles there were survivors who believed that allowing even one piece of information about the death camps – its murders and its victims – go unrecorded was tantamount to giving Hitler a victory. There was a lot of writing going on in those camps. There were eleven Jewish newspapers in the deportation camps in the American zone in Germany in the first years after the war. That is where a lot of the survivor testimonies were first published.'

'I see,' I said. 'I also wanted to ask you about some of the discrepancies in Hershl Sperling's testimony. Some of them are strange, like the timing of the Treblinka revolt. Hershl says it began at 4.00am. In fact, it began at 4.00pm. He's exactly twelve hours out.'

Hochberg shrugged. 'After seventeen years of reading survivor accounts, I can tell you that time errors are common. Time is often confused by survivors, as is day and night. First of all, you have to remember that time was not the important thing to them.'

'Presumably, he knew that it was afternoon, not morning,' I said.

'You know, it's also possible that what he wrote down or dictated was printed incorrectly. I've come across several instances of this. As I've said, many of the testimonies are full of little discrepancies, which can be put down to all kinds of things. I don't think any of them detracts from the overall truth.'

'I believe he wrote it himself, simply because he told one of his sons that he had "written something". But I have another question.'

'Go ahead.'

'I wanted to ask about the names Israel Kaplan and Joseph Kas? Do they mean anything to you? Their names also appear at the front of the journal as editors.'

'There's some information on Kaplan in one of the articles I gave you.' Hochberg looked at his watch. I could see he was anxious to end our meeting, so I stood up and shook his hand. Once at the door of his office, he called out, 'Good luck with the book.'

'Thanks,' I said, and made my way down to the main floor of the museum.

I found a bench and sat and read through the articles. As I read, I remembered a poster I had seen years ago in the library of the Holocaust research centre at the Yad Vashem in Jerusalem. It showed a camp inmate holding aloft in his arms a scroll, and above him were the words: 'Help Write the History of the Last Destruction.' The poster was made in 1946, and was one of several that were put up throughout the D.P. camps. It was designed to attract attention, and it did. I suddenly connected this poster with the journal containing Hershl's testimony, entitled: 'From the Last Extermination'. The Yiddish words, *Fun Letzen Hurban*, translates precisely into 'from the latest destruction,' according to standard Yiddish dictionaries. Contained within the title, there was also the sense that something, an entire culture and human existence, had been lost and could never be recovered. Yet it also seemed to imply that more was to come. I tried to imagine Hershl seeing this poster and responding to it, determined to write and record.

I sat on the bench, amid a throng of museum visitors and read further into the papers. I learned that during its three years of existence, the Central Historical Commission collected more than 2,500 written testimonies and almost 10,000 questionnaires in the American Zone of Germany. Shmuel Krakówski, the director of archives at the Yad Vashem Holocaust Documentation Centre, noted:

> Hundreds of Holocaust survivors, both the educated and the ordinary folk, set down their recollections immediately after the war, even before they rebuilt their homes. Many of these compositions are hundreds of pages long and relate not only to what befell the author and his family but also the history of many communities in the Holocaust.

I also read that Israel Kaplan, a teacher from the devastated central Lithuanian community of Kovno, had been appointed to head the Central Historical Commission, along with accountant Moshe Figenboim. Through their leadership and a pool of employees, all unpaid, 2,500 testimonies were recorded and 8,000 questionnaires were filled out.

However, Hochberg shed little light on the practical considerations of where Jewish printing presses had been found. Weeks earlier I had written to the Yad Vashem in Jerusalem for information, and Dr David Silberklang, director of *Yad Vashem Studies*, the scholarly annual journal of Yad Vashem, answered me. Coincidentally, his reply came the day before I had flown to Baltimore. I called it up and re-read it: 'I don't know where the commission obtained a Hebrew-character typewriter, but these were around. The Nazis had not destroyed every one.'

I also discovered the commission had published the first issue of the monthly *Fun Letzen Hurban* in August 1946. Hershl's story appeared in August 1947, although we cannot know when it was written. I imagined Hershl now, grief pressing down through the tip of his pen, writing his story in the empty porcelain factory in Tirschenreuth.

★ ★ ★

My concentration was broken by the sound of my daughter's voice. I looked up and saw her running toward me. She ran into my arms and embraced me with what seemed to be extraordinary strength.

'Dad, we've been looking everywhere for you.'

'How did it go? Did you like Daniel's Story?'

'We didn't go to Daniel's Story. Rubin said I was old enough to see the whole museum.'

'Well, if Rubin said it was OK, that's fine with me,' I said.

'She was very interested,' said Rubin. 'Did you get what you needed?'

'It's another piece of the puzzle,' I said.

'Can you come round again with us?' my daughter asked.

'Come,' Rubin said. 'I want to show you the boxcar they got from Poland.'

We walked together through the three floors of photographs, artefacts and models depicting streams of Holocaust memory and open theatres of looping film footage. The museum was divided into three parts – Nazi Assault, Final Solution, and Last Chapter – and we passed image after image of ghetto round-ups, beatings, murders, deportations, medical tortures in Auschwitz, emaciated corpses of survivors and mountains of dead, twisted bodies.

On the third floor, a procession of visitors moved along a corridor that led through a wooden railcar. It was the same kind of railcar that had taken Hershl to Treblinka.

'They made a big deal about this coming from Poland,' Rubin said. 'The Polish government was supposed to donate it, but I think the museum ended up having to pay for the wagon.' We moved inside the boxcar. 'This was it,' he said.

'Was this the same car you were in?' my daughter asked.

'It was one just like this,' Rubin said. '100 people were packed in. Ten came out alive.'

We were holding up the flow of traffic through the railcar and some of the people in the line were becoming irritated. Rubin ignored them. Others, however, had gathered around and were trying to listen to him speak, as though he were bringing word from another planet. A young black woman came over to us.

'Excuse me,' she said. 'Did you say you were in a railcar like this?'

'Yes, I was.'

The young woman lifted a pad. 'How old were you? Can you describe it?'

'Where are you from?' asked Rubin.

'Washington,' the woman said. 'I'm a sophomore student at American University. Can you tell me what it was like?' She was poised to write. Rubin studied the pad.

'Can I describe it? There were 100 people in our car, all men. The women and children went in another car. I went to Bergen-Belsen, but I can't tell you where I was coming from. I don't know. There was no room to sit. It was only after a few hours, when people started to die and we put their bodies in the middle of the wagon, that we were able to sit. We travelled for four days and three nights. There was no food or water. They threw in one bucket for us to relieve ourselves. It wasn't long before it was overflowing. At Bergen-Belsen there were only ten of us left alive. How I survived, I can't tell you.' Then he added, 'This is what happens when you don't protect the free political processes we have in this country.'

The young woman scribbled furiously in her pad as Rubin told her his story. I was scribbling in my pad also, and I watched her face at the same time, the way the sadness and emotion crossed her expression with each tragic nuance of Rubin's story. I noticed now that a crowd had formed around us, each person listening intently.

'Which camp were you liberated in?' she asked.

'I was liberated in Bergen-Belsen. After the train, they sent us on a death march. We had to wear wooden shoes, like clogs. We walked through fields and along forest tracks. We came from the east. That's all I know, and we walked in fives. When somebody fell they were shot and trucks came behind to pick up the dead bodies. It must have been winter. I remember there was snow on the ground and we were freezing.'

'And what can you tell me about Bergen-Belsen?'

'I'll never forget the bulldozers moving piles of naked dead bodies and crushing their bones as they were pushed into the big pits. So inhuman to treat the dead like that. That is something I'll never forget. We were treated worse than animals. How they came up with some of the things they did to people I'll never know. Bergen-Belsen was where they dumped you when you couldn't work anymore. It was the last stop.'

'Can you give me your name?' the young woman asked.

'What do you want my name for?' Rubin asked.

The young woman smiled again, embarrassed. 'Because I want to write something about you,' she said.

'You want to write something about me. For you, I'll tell you my name. My name is Rubin Sztajer.' He spelled it carefully.

'And how do you spell the name of that town you were from?' He spelled out Klobuck for her also, and she wrote it in her pad. 'Thank you,' she said, her voice broken with emotion. Then, suddenly she learned forward, put her arms around Rubin's neck and embraced him tightly. Rubin smiled in embarrassment.

'Wherever I go, people want to hear my story. That's why I think it's worthwhile what I do.'

That evening, on the way back to Baltimore, there was little conversation in the car. I offered to drive, but Rubin said no. My daughter had fallen asleep in the back seat. Suddenly, after a long while, Rubin suddenly said to me, 'I'd like the right to change my opinion.'

'Of course. About what?'

'I've been thinking, and I've changed my mind about Szperling. He wasn't a coward.'

'OK,' I said, pulling out my notebook and pen. There was a pained expression on Rubin's face.

'I think what he needed was to talk to someone – I mean after his wife died – but he didn't know where to start. I think he was afraid that if he started he would never be able to stop, and the memories would flood back out and destroy him.'

'Maybe, in the end, that's what happened.'

★ ★ ★

Back at the Sztajers' pristine apartment Rubin told me more of his story. We sat on his sofa and I scribbled notes as he spoke. He picked up his story the day the camp was liberated.

'I was close to death,' he said. 'After liberation, the same day, I collapsed. It was the end for me. I was naked and in pain. There was nothing left of me. I don't remember. My sister, Gussie, knew what happened, but she wouldn't speak. She would never speak about what happened.'

'You never talked to her about her experiences?' I asked.

'You know, a woman survivor in the Holocaust, I don't want to ask. I don't know and I don't want to know. But I had been asking her for years to come to see what I was doing in the schools. I said, "You're not going to have to speak. Just listen and watch." I had to promise. So she agreed to come and sit at the back of the class.'

'What happened?'

'Well, I told my story the usual way in the classroom. They were very good kids. At the end, when I asked if there were any questions, this one kid put his hand up and asked about liberation. I said I didn't know, but that my sister did. So I introduced her at the back of the classroom. "Gussie," I said, "I know I promised you, but this student is asking a question that I want to answer, but I can't." Then, after a moment, she stood up and, very bravely, began to speak. "Just this one time," she said, and she told the story of how we had both been in Bergen-Belsen, but hadn't known it. After liberation, someone recognised me lying on the ground and went to tell Gussie. The first thing she did was to take off her underwear and put it on me, to give me some dignity. Then, somehow, she and some of the other women carried me into the women's barracks where they nursed me back to health. They saved my life.'

'That's quite a story,' I said. Rubin sprang from the couch with astonishing agility.

'I'm going to phone Gussie in New York.'

He spoke first to her in Yiddish, and then handed me the telephone.

'Hello?' I said, tentatively.

'Hello,' she said. Her voice was accented and soft. She sounded much younger than her 83 years. There was something gentle in her tone, and I immediately warmed to her. I started to tell her about the book I was writing, but she quickly interrupted and said, 'Rubin told me.'

'I wanted to ask if you remember anything of the Szperling family in Klobutsk.' I used the now-defunct Yiddish rendition of the town's name. 'Do you remember anything of Hershl?'

'Yes,' she said. 'I was two years older, but I remember a lot of girls in town had a crush on him. He was so cute and so likeable. Everybody liked him.' I had heard this before from Rebecca Bernstein but it was wonderful to hear again.

'Anything else?' I asked.

'I remember his mother was very tall and the older brother that died was very tall also.' There could be no doubt she was talking about the same Szperlings. 'But I didn't see much of him, because I was older. I do remember his mother was a Goldberg, and they had family that moved to Scotland. They wanted to get away from Poland, from all the anti-Semitism then. I remember when they went it was a big deal in the town. Everybody spoke about it. There was also a Goldberg sister, I think, who went to Israel.'

'Did Rubin tell you what happened to Hershl?' I asked.

'I was surprised when I heard,' Gussie said. 'I can't understand it. I'm a survivor also – I can't tell you the hell I went through – but I want to live.' She drew breath and repeated: 'I want to live!'

I thanked her and said goodbye. I felt terrible. The last thing I had wanted was to upset her, but I knew that I had.

The next morning, as my daughter and I took our seats on the plane, I had the strangest sensation of seeing Hershl again in Tirschenreuth, writing his story. He was nineteen and still thin as a rake, but his eyes held the pain of a thousand years.

CHAPTER TWENTY

THE SEARCH FOR LIFE

A few weeks later I was back in Scotland and the rain was beating down in sheets. It was a Tuesday afternoon and I took a break. I had been re-reading the few testimonies of other Treblinka survivors. I had also gone back over the papers that Severin Hochberg had given me in Washington. My head felt heavy. I stood at my back door and watched the rain push across the hay field behind the house. The Campsie Hills stood above and beyond them but they were shrouded in thick, grey clouds and half the hill was obscured. Suddenly, the rain stopped and a rainbow appeared. A jet's vapour trail became visible. Within minutes, the sky was a clear blue and the clouds lifted off the top of the hills.

I scribbled, 'Natural beauty affirms life.' I knew that when Hershl needed nature he went to the coastal town of Ayr, where seagulls squawked on the pier as he stared out at the choppy waters of the Firth of Clyde and the hills of the Isle of Arran in the distance. He always seemed so solitary, and his presence on that pier perilous. One line from Hochberg's papers kept returning to me. 'You understand,' a survivor had written, 'the concentration camp experience is nothing that endears you to people.'

I checked my email for the first time that day. I was suddenly excited. A note from my sister told me that Haddas, an Israeli friend in Los Angeles, had made contact with Treblinka survivor Samuel Willenberg in Tel Aviv for me. I had understood that Willenberg was the last Treblinka survivor alive, and I desperately wanted to speak with anyone who remembered Hershl beyond his childhood in Klobuck and to confirm his existence among his peers. I had obtained Willenberg's phone number from his daughter, but because he did not speak English and my Hebrew and Polish were virtually non-existent, my sister arranged for a translator. It turned out that Willenberg's wife spoke English and they very much wanted to speak to me. Later in the afternoon, when I called Haddas, there was another piece of good news.

'Willenberg is not the last Treblinka survivor,' she said. 'He told me there are four others and I have the phone numbers of three of them. The fourth one you can't call, because he has Alzheimer's and doesn't remember anything. If you need me to call them, just let me know. But I'll give you the numbers.'

She gave me the telephone numbers of survivors Kalman Teigman, Pinchas Epstein and Josef Czarny. I wanted to call them immediately, but because of the time difference I would have to wait until the following day. I began also to think about

Hershl's life beyond Treblinka. Who was alive who could give me their impressions of him as a twenty-year-old refugee amid the smoke-blackened brick and rain of industrial Glasgow in the 1940s? There were civic documents that verified he was there, and there was further documentation from the International Tracing Service archives at Bad Arolsen in Germany, which noted first that Hershl had 'emigrated on 4 September 1947, coming from Munich, from France to England by train and ship'. But I wanted human corroboration.

I telephoned Sam and told him about the Treblinka survivors. I also asked him if there was anyone who might remember his father when he first arrived in Glasgow.

'You could try my cousins, Sylvia and Felicia,' he said. 'They're the daughters of Louis Goldberg, the brother of my father's mother. They changed their name to Gilbert when they got here. They must remember my father when he first came from Germany. They were children when my father went to live in their house. I'll speak to Alan and try to think of others.'

'Where do they live?' I asked.

'Somewhere in Glasgow,' Sam said. 'I have phone numbers and addresses. I haven't seen them in years.'

As soon as I ended my call with Sam, I called Sylvia, the younger of the sisters – both of whom were in their late sixties – and I arranged to meet with her at her house on Saturday. She seemed happy to help me.

★ ★ ★

The following day, at around 11.00am, I telephoned the survivors. I began with Josef Czarny. Like Hershl, he was born in 1927 and had been fifteen when he was deported from the Warsaw ghetto. He was penniless and desperately hungry. His family were already dead from starvation. When the order came to report to the Umschlagplatz, he went of his own free will for the three kilograms of bread and one kilogram of marmalade promised to those who reported voluntarily. He and thousands of others were then placed in cattle cars. In Treblinka, he was selected to live and ended up working in the camp zoo. There was a time I might have been reticent to question Holocaust survivors for fear I might upset them and dredge up unwelcome memories, but I now understood that most survivors wanted to talk. They wanted to tell the world. It was just that the world didn't want to listen to them. Anyway, if he didn't want to talk, he would say so.

'Josef Czarny?' I asked when he picked up the telephone.

'Ken,' he said, using the Hebrew word for 'yes'. His voice was like gravel.

'Do you speak English?'

'No,' he said, forcefully. But then he added, 'A little. How can I help you?' I explained to him why I was calling. 'I don't understand,' he said.

'Do you remember Hershl Sperling in Treblinka?'

'Szperling?' he asked.

'Yes,' I said.

'No,' he said.

'Hershl Szperling?'

'No. Do you speak Hebrew?'

'No, I'm sorry,' I said.

'Find someone to call me in Hebrew. Goodbye.' He hung up the phone.

I put a mark beside his name and number in my notepad to have Haddas call him in Hebrew. I moved on to Kalman Teigman, born in Warsaw in 1922, whose testimony, coincidentally, I had been reading just that morning. Teigman had been one of the planners of the Treblinka revolt. He spoke good English, but only after expressing disappointment that I did not speak Yiddish. He did not recall Hershl either, but he became very interested when I told him about the pale green book containing Hershl's testimony.

'Maybe if I saw a picture of him, I'd recognise him,' he said. 'Tell me, does he mention any names in his testimony?'

I opened it and went to the last paragraph, which contained the list of names. 'Maybe you know some of these people. Did you know a Samuel Rajzman?'

'Rajzman, no.'

'Schneiderman?'

'No.'

'How about Kudlik from Częstochowa?' I asked.

'Kudlik? Kudlik's a good friend of mine.'

'Is he still living?'

'No, he's gone. His son is in Israel, but he doesn't know much.'

'He also names Turowski. Do you know him?'

'Turowski's also a friend of mine.'

'Is he living?'

'He's gone, too. His wife lives near here, but he's gone a long time ago now.'

'And you definitely don't recall Hershl Szperling?'

'You say he was fifteen. You could maybe try Czarny or Epstein. Or maybe Willenberg. And you're writing a book about Treblinka?'

'Treblinka and Hershl Sperling,' I said. 'There doesn't seem to be much written about Treblinka. Everything is about Auschwitz.' He suddenly became agitated.

'Treblinka was not the same as Auschwitz. In Treblinka, there was nothing, just gas chambers where they murdered people, the workers and the guards.'

I thanked him and promised to send a copy of Hershl's testimony, which he had requested.

'It was very nice talking with you,' I said, and I meant it.

'Don't forget to send me the book,' he said before he hung up.

Next I tried Pinchas Epstein, the Częstochowa-born Jew whose job in Treblinka was corpse-carrier in the death camp.

'Mr Epstein?'

'Ken.' His voice sounded older and more frail than the previous two, and I could hear him breathing very heavily.

'Do you speak English?'

'No … a little.'

I told him about Hershl's testimony and that I was writing about his life.

'I don't understand. You speak Hebrew? Yiddish?' His English was slow and broken.

'I'm sorry,' I said. 'I want to ask you if remember a Hershl Szperling in Treblinka.'

'Szperling?'

'Yes. Hershl Szperling in Treblinka.' His breathing became louder.

'Yes. I remember him.'

'You do?'

'I remember Szperling.'

'Can you tell me what you remember?' I asked. After several stops and starts, he said 'My English not good. If someone calls and speaks Hebrew ...' I had to wait a few hours before calling Haddas, because of the time difference between Scotland and Los Angeles and by the time I got hold of her it was too late to call Israel. However, she promised she would call the next day. Finally I called Samuel Willenberg's wife. She was friendly and helpful. We spoke for a while about Hershl and Treblinka, and she translated for her husband.

'My husband says he doesn't remember Hershl Szperling, but he has his name on the list of people who survived the uprising,' she said. 'So he's definitely one of them. You should come to Israel and visit us if you want to know more about Treblinka.'

'I know,' I said. 'It's expensive.'

'Well, if you come, you should hurry.'

'Why?' I asked.

'Because we're 85. Things can happen. You know, my husband is supposed to be in Warsaw now getting a medal from the Polish president, because he was also in the Warsaw uprising, not the ghetto, but the Polish uprising. But he fell and broke his leg. Now he's sitting here with a cast.'

'I'm sorry to ask this question, but I'd like to know why you think a Treblinka survivor would kill himself, after so many years.'

I heard her translating the question for her husband. Then a short discussion in Hebrew followed. At last she said, 'Maybe he became crazy. You know none of us came out the camps 100 per cent.' She too wanted me to send a copy of Hershl's testimony – 'This is a very important historical document' – I promised I that would.

★ ★ ★

The next morning, I drove my car across Bridge Street in Glasgow, the old road over the River Clyde, on a rare sunny morning and entered an area known broadly as the South Side. I glanced over at the rail bridge on my left as I passed, and looked into the darkness of its iron-girder interior, where Hershl had been before his death. I wanted to stop, but the flow of traffic made it impossible and I pushed southwards, my mood sorrowful.

Once over the river, I drove through a district called the Gorbals, a knot of streets tucked into the shoulder of a bend in the Clyde. This was where the Glasgow journey began for the thousands of Jews who had arrived in Scotland, desperate and poor, fleeing the pogroms of tsarist Russia in the late nineteenth and early twentieth centuries, some of my own relatives among them. Its grid-iron layout of four-storey brick tenement buildings – home to Jews, Scottish Highlanders and Irish Catholics forced from their own lands by famine – has long been demolished. In the many memoirs of Jewish life in the Gorbals during this period, most go to great lengths to stress the absence of anti-Semitism. It is an urban wasteland now of crime and crumbling high-rise tower blocks.

I followed Pollokshaws Road, the main artery leading south from the river, out of the Gorbals. This was the same route most of the Jews had taken on their upwardly mobile, southward journey out of poverty. During the inter-war years, building decay, overcrowding and sanitation conditions grew worse and many Jews began to move down into adjoining districts with names such as Govanhill, Strathbungo, Crosshill, Crossmyloof and East Pollokshields.

The wasteland between the Gorbals and Strathbungo gradually gave way to a few shops with names that reflected the fact they belonged to later waves of immigrants – mostly Pakistani and Indian. I turned left on Allison Street and drove past rows of Victorian sandstone tenements. The streets were full of people. I turned right on Niddrie Road and passed an old synagogue, built in 1927, around the time Jews were beginning to relocate to the area. I was looking for Westmoreland Street, where I knew Hershl, Yaja and Alan had lived before the birth of Sam.

I crossed Victoria Road, and turned right on Westmoreland, a quiet backstreet between two main thoroughfares. I didn't know the street number, but it didn't much matter because it was a row of four-storey, sand-coloured stone tenements that were all the same. I drove to the end and turned around, and crossed back over Allison Street until I reached the other end of Westmoreland. The number 21 suddenly popped into my head. Perhaps Alan had mentioned it during one of our telephone conversations. The street probably hadn't changed much since he and his parents had lived here. I stopped the car and looked across at 21 Westmoreland Street. A young Pakistani woman wearing a red sari and multi-coloured scarves pushed a baby carriage along the pavement. I tried to imagine Hershl here before setting off again.

Back on Pollokshaws Road, I passed pubs, South Asian fast-food restaurants, fruit sellers, specialist meat vendors and clothes shops. At Shawlands Cross, Pollokshaws Road became Kilmarnock Road, and tenements gave way to handsome old residences with large, manicured lawns and trees. Another mile or so, and I was in the heart of Giffnock, now home to most of Glasgow's remaining 7,000 Jews. People were out walking their dogs. A jogger went by. I turned left into Otterburn Drive, where Sam's cousins, the Goldbergs – now Gilberts – had once had a home and where Hershl had lived when he first arrived in Scotland. Large, affluent two and three-storey villas dominated the street. It must have appeared extraordinary to Hershl.

Another few minutes' drive south and I was in Whitecraigs, one of the richest enclaves in Glasgow and then passed into the neighbouring suburb of Newton Mearns. After studying Sylvia's directions I found her house fairly quickly. I headed along a wide driveway and up to the door. I saw a woman get up as I walked past the large front window. She opened the door as I arrived.

'Are you Mark?' she asked. She was a small, middle-aged woman with large glasses.

'Yes. Sylvia?' We shook hands as I entered the house.

'Come into the living room,' she said. We entered a bright, tidy room with comfortable-looking chairs and couches. As I turned, I was surprised to see another woman rising out of a chair in front of the window.

'This is Felicia, my sister,' Sylvia said.

'Hello,' Felicia said, and shook my hand weakly.

Sylvia offered coffee and I settled on black tea. I noted that Felicia was more confident than her younger sister. Sylvia invited me to sit and went off to the kitchen. I explained to Felicia what I was doing, although I assumed she already knew, and she nodded and smiled. I told her that I was missing a good deal of information about her cousin's arrival in Scotland. I told her I was interested in his behaviour – how he reacted and how people reacted to him after what he had been through. I wanted to know if there were already signs of his ultimate fate. I also told her about my trip to Poland earlier that year and I pulled out my laptop to show her photographs of what was left of the shtetl her father had come from. She smiled, but seemed quite unimpressed – although perhaps she was also unimpressed that I was delving into family matters that were none of my business.

Then she surprised me. Felicia told me she did not know Hershl had been in Treblinka.

'I knew he was in a concentration camp, but that was all,' she said. I concluded, privately in my notebook, that in spite of being cousins she and Hershl could not have known each other very well. She was hard to gauge, because her responses were guarded. I wondered if Hershl's suicide disturbed the sisters; perhaps they harboured some guilt about the way Hershl's life had unfolded and the way he died.

Sylvia came back with the tea. She too looked at the photographs of pink and brown houses amid the Polish mud. She seemed more interested than her sister, and appeared genuinely pleased when I offered to send her copies of the pictures.

'I was hoping you might remember something of Hershl when he came to Scotland,' I said.

'You mean Henry,' said Felicia.

I had forgotten Hershl was the Yiddish rendering of his name, and that he only spoke Yiddish in his home and to his immediate family.

'Yes, Henry,' I said. 'Do you speak Yiddish?'

'We spoke English only in the house,' said Felicia. 'Yiddish was very much considered the language of the past.' She smiled, but seemed uncomfortable. 'We didn't see much of him, you know. So I don't know how much help we'll be.'

'How old were both of you when Henry arrived?' I asked.

'Oh, I would have been eight,' said Sylvia. 'And Felicia would have been nine.' Then she added: 'It's funny that you mention Yiddish, because I remember my father lying in bed, writing letter after letter in Yiddish when I was very young. He must have been writing to Henry and maybe to the authorities for permission to bring him here.'

'I don't suppose you have kept any of that correspondence?' I asked.

'I'm afraid we wouldn't keep that kind of thing,' said Sylvia.

I told the sisters how after liberation the survivors – about 300,000 people – had been housed in displaced persons camps in Germany because they could not go home and every country had more or less closed their doors to immigration. However, following a statement in the British Parliament in late 1945 and a slow start in 1946, the official machine swung into action. In 1947, reports from the time reveal that more than 10,000 applications for British citizenship for refugees from Germany, Austria and Czechoslovakia were granted. Hershl was among them. He left Yaja, his young wife, behind in the D.P. camp in Tirchenreuth and promised her they would reunite as soon as it could be arranged. Their parting must have been painful, knowing as I did how deeply they loved one another.

I imagined him on the deck of a steamer, thin as a coat rack. He carried with him a fragile hope and the clothes on his back, plus a few possessions in a bag he clutched, among them the pale green book – proof-positive of the unthinkable mass murder he had witnessed – his naturalisation papers, and the sponsorship details from his Uncle Louis. He was twenty years old, but he had lied about his age so he could be legally adopted as a minor. He was still painfully thin and could have passed for a boy considerably younger. A few hours later the shipped docked, where he passed through immigration and using pidgin English learned from listening to Americans, he made his way by tram to Liverpool Street station in London. From there, he travelled on to Newcastle, where the eldest Goldberg brother, Sam, now lived. Hershl stayed only a few days before making his way north to Glasgow, where Louis was waiting for him. The train arrived early in the morning.

Sylvia said: 'He just appeared one day at the dining room table. I remember waking up that morning and going downstairs, and there he was, sitting and eating breakfast.'

'And how long was it before Yaja arrived?' I asked.

'You mean Yetta?'

'Yes, Yetta.'

'I suppose about a year, but I think they moved out soon afterwards.'

'What else do you remember?' I asked.

'I suppose I remember he was very thin, and he was wearing a white shirt,' Sylvia said. 'I remember feeling a bit annoyed also, because my sister and I were never allowed to eat breakfast at the dining room table, but here was this stranger doing just that.'

And what must Hershl have observed, this young man, whose childhood had been obliterated and whose experiences were already far beyond those of any age? I remembered Sam had told me Hershl had felt the loss of his mother most acutely and therefore felt naturally close to her side of the family. He had expectations of them, as they did of him. Hershl had also told Sam that Sylvia was cute and had reminded him of the sister whose name he could not utter. Sylvia had been the same age as Frumet when she died. Yet he must have felt like an alien at this table, in this house, in this affluent neighbourhood – or anywhere in the outside world after all he had been through.

By the time Hershl arrived in the autumn of 1947, Louis had already made his fortune in a dress factory that during the early part of the decade had become connected to the war effort. Louis had originally called his factory Goldberg's, but changed the name to Gilbert because Goldberg's was already the name of a busy department store in the city. In 1947, with the hardships of rationing still in place, bartering became a way of life throughout Britain, and Louis grew richer on the rampant black market.

'Did your father explain to you what was happening at the time, I mean with Hershl?' I asked.

'He just said, "This is Henry, your cousin, who has come from Germany and he's going to be staying with us for a while." And that was that,' said Sylvia. 'We just accepted it. I think his English was understandable, because we didn't speak a word of Yiddish in our house.' Another testament to Hershl's language skills, I thought.

Before long, however, it was clear that things were not going according to plan. It was obvious that neither Hershl nor the Gilbert family had the remotest understanding of each other. How could he understand these people? How could they possibly understand him?

Felicia said: 'We were a house of three girls, including my mother. I think Henry was the son that my father never had, but because of his circumstances, he couldn't give back. My father did everything for him. He fed him, clothed him, gave him work in the factory and paid him. He even bought him a flat. Later, he even helped him set up in business.' I asked her about her relationship with Hershl – I wanted to know if it was close or distant. 'We didn't really have a relationship with him. How could we? I mean, the way he was.'

I also asked her about a dispute that Sam told me had occurred over Hershl's education. Soon after his arrival, Hershl enrolled himself in Stow College in Glasgow to improve his English – which he did, very quickly. Sam told me that after a week or two in college, one of the teachers came to the house to see Louis. He told him Hershl had shown some educational aptitude, and that he had expressed interest in becoming a doctor or a dentist. The teacher said he would help as much as he could, but funding was required for the tuition fees. Louis refused.

Felicia turned her head to one side as if she were slapped. 'I don't know anything about that,' she said, coldly. Then she said, 'If he hadn't got that money from South Africa, I always thought that maybe he would have tried harder to make it.'

'What money from South Africa?' I asked, slightly stunned by the response. Sylvia and Felicia looked at each other. Between them, they told me a story about how the Sperling family's financial fortunes had changed in 1956 with the death of their Aunt Florie, younger sister of Hershl's mother. Florie had emigrated from Klobuck to Umtata in South Africa, after an arranged marriage in the early 1930s. Following the death of her husband, she came to Glasgow and moved in with her brother, Meyer. When she died, in accordance with her will, Florie's inheritance was split between Hershl and his Uncle Meyer. Childless Florie had divided her inheritance – a sum of about £50,000 – between the two neediest members of the family.

Felicia, speaking about one of the Sperlings' trips to Israel, said, 'I can tell you, Henry didn't get on very well there. He went there and spent money like water. Israel was a much poorer country in those days, and that kind of behaviour just upset people. Henry was always emigrating or going somewhere, but he always came back to Glasgow. I think he felt safest in Glasgow, because it was the place where he had first come.'

Conversations with Alan and Sam later revealed that Hershl, who was always by nature generous, had distributed some of his inheritance to Yaja's family in Israel. This may well explain Felicia's accusation that Hershl had spent money like water. Meanwhile, Sylvia added: 'I think he also didn't get the sympathy he was looking for, because of course there are a lot of Holocaust survivors in Israel and no-one was interested in his story.'

'Maybe there could have been a better support system in place for survivors,' Felicia conceded.

'Well that must certainly be true,' I said. 'He'd been through a lot. He always struck me as an intelligent man, whose attempt at living life was crushed at the get-go. He never had a chance.'

'It's funny,' Felicia said. She tilted her head. Her eyes looked straight at me. I was struck by the harshness of her stare. 'I never thought of him as intelligent,' she said, 'but in those days people associated education with intelligence, and of course he had had no education. I always thought of him as more cunning than intelligent.' I asked for a specific example. 'I wouldn't tell you – even if I could remember. I don't want anything bad written about him.'

How was it possible to survive Treblinka, Dachau and Auschwitz, where he had managed to pass himself off as a gentile, and not be cunning? I now realised that it must have been apparent to him that if his closest living relatives could not understand him or the terrible fate that had befallen the millions of others, the rest of the world could not grasp it either. Perhaps they understood the dead, but it was the living they could not fathom. Did they not wonder at his tortured cries in the night, even though, to them, he was normal and 'cunning' during the day? They could not have known about the horrific images and the all-encompassing loneliness that engulfed each moment of his life, about the fires of burning flesh, or the man begging to die beneath him in the forest, or the terror he still felt when he remembered the eyes of Mengele, or even about the adrenaline rush he felt when he held stolen goods.

Sylvia's husband arrived. We shook hands, and he flopped on the couch.

'Well,' he said, cheerfully. 'Any buried family treasures?'

'Not in this family,' said Sylvia.

On my way home, I detoured again past the sandstone tenements of Westmoreland Street, and I imagined I saw Hershl standing on the corner, his pale green eyes gazing helplessly at the world.

★ ★ ★

The following day, I called Sam. As I was reading some of my notes on my conversation with Sylvia and Felicia to him, he interrupted. 'I think I know where their bitterness comes from.'

'Where?' I asked, then tried to answer my own question. 'I got the impression that neither Hershl nor Louis lived up to one another's expectations, and that there was tension between them. Maybe, from their point of view, they were kind and generous relations to him, but he shrank from them and they shrank from him. It must have been difficult to have a disturbed Holocaust orphan in their home – who must have suffered, but, save an Auschwitz tattoo, showed no outward scars.'

'For sure,' said Sam. 'But I think Louis had other plans. I think he wanted my father to become more involved in his business. I can't prove any of this, because it's just what my father told me. There was also a story about Louis wanting him to marry some distant female relative, which astonished him, because, you know, he was already married. I think Louis wanted him to forget about my mother and leave her in Germany, but he wouldn't do it.'

Louis died in the mid-1950s and was therefore unable to defend himself against these claims of what appear to be perhaps benevolent manipulation. When I told him that Felicia had described Hershl as 'cunning' rather than intelligent, and she had 'associated intelligence more with education', he laughed.

'When did he have the time to go to university? He didn't even make it out of primary school.'

'What about your father's life in the years immediately after he left their home? How much do you know about that? I know it was still before you were born.'

'You need to talk to Alan about that,' he said. 'He was there.'

★ ★ ★

Hershl and Yaja were married for the second time on 6 February 1948, shortly after her arrival from the Hook of Holland. I purchased a copy of the marriage certificate from the Glasgow City registry offices. Their address is given as 6 Otterburn Drive, the Gilbert residence. His age is recorded as eighteen, even though he was twenty, and his occupation listed as 'furniture warehouseman'. Her occupation is 'domestic servant'. Louis Gilbert and his wife Annie are named as the witnesses. Unlike the first wedding in Germany, this was merely a civil formality. Yet it must have been a happy day. I imagine Hershl finding the proceedings vaguely ridiculous, because neither thought much of national laws. He laughed about it later.

After the wedding, they moved out of the Gilberts' home into the apartment in Westmoreland Street. It had probably been bought by Louis, to whom Hershl and Yaja paid rent from the small amount he earned as a travelling salesman for his uncle. Nine months after her arrival from Holland, a son was born, whom they named Alan. He was supposed to have been called Isaac, after Hershl's father, but they thought it did not sound very English and that he would get teased.

I hadn't seen Alan in about twenty years. I remembered him with jet-black hair and a beard, which Sam told me was now white. Like Sam, Alan's life had also been permanently altered by his parents' experiences. I wanted to know about his father's life in the 1950s. Was he happy? Were there early signs of the lasting suffering that would one day engulf him?

Alan recalled: 'Nothing could be calm when my father was around. I don't have any happy memories at all, but maybe that's a reflection of me and the way I saw life then, rather than a reflection of the way things really were in the house.'

'Really, none?' I asked.

'I suppose in his better moments, my father could be funny, but in a crazy way. That of course wasn't true of my mother, but it was my father's suffering that was always at the root of everything.' There was a long silence. 'I don't think my father was capable of dealing with a child. I don't know whether I was planned or not, but I felt like my very presence chained him down. But I understand now why he wanted to be free. Even when he was calm he was disturbed.'

'What do you mean?'

'Sometimes we would be sitting watching television, something entirely unrelated to his experiences, and he would turn and say, "You know, I still can't believe what happened."'

As was often the case in the Sperling household, things were rarely what they seemed. In spite of first impressions that Hershl was running things, an astute observer would have seen that Yaja was the family's anchor. Both Hershl's sons agreed that had it not been for their mother, Hershl's collapse would have come much sooner. At night she cooked special meals for him – gala meat jelly, spicy tomato soup, borsht, potato soup, tzimis, cabbage and halvah – that reminded them of their childhoods in Poland. Then, after dinner, she brought him his glass of lemon tea.

When the memories became too much for him, she would embrace him and whisper soothing Yiddish words in his ear. They embraced often, and kissed and held hands publicly. For all the difficulties of living with his suffering, perhaps his neediness pleased her. Together, they were up against the world in their little apartment, and they were still surviving against the odds.

Alan described their relationship as 'too close'. 'It was intense. They seemed to talk to each other incessantly. It was very intimate, and they kissed and held hands all the time. I remember my mother telling me you could catch germs from kissing strangers, because when I was young I started to copy them and I was kissing almost everyone. But I also remember how desperately they both reacted when one of them became ill.' He paused a moment. 'I've never allowed myself to get that close to anyone. You pay a very heavy penalty for that kind of love.'

During the early 1950s, the acrimony between Hershl and Louis continued, and he quit his job as a salesman for the Gilbert factory. He held several jobs, usually selling or managing clothing shops, but he was never able to keep any of them for very long.

Alan said, 'He was always giving up on jobs.'

'Anything else you remember?' I asked.

'It was a life of poverty. I remember my father was paid every Friday and on Thursday my mother literally didn't have two old pennies to rub together. One time – I think I was about five – I wanted a lucky bag that cost tuppence, but she literally didn't have it.'

'Anything else that you think is important?'

'Rajzman,' he said. Throughout these years, letters were sent back and forth between Hershl and his surrogate father from Treblinka. The letters had a calming affect on Hershl. 'Sometimes, there were telephone calls, in spite of the fact that international calls were at a premium in the 1950s and were considered a luxury. You should call Benny Chininzon.'

'Who is he?'

'He was a lodger my parents took,' Alan said. 'He had an enormous stabilising effect on the family. I thought of him like a grandfather. I don't know exactly what his background was, but I think his wife and children had been killed by the Nazis in Poland and he had spent time in Russia, possibly in one of the camps there. But my father spoke to him a lot about things he wouldn't talk to us about.'

★ ★ ★

There appears to have been several months between Florie's death and Hershl's receipt of his share of her inheritance. Hershl borrowed money – possibly from Louis or the Goldbergs in Newcastle – against the roughly £25,000 he knew was coming. With the borrowed money, Hershl acquired an automatic-laundry business near the apartment. He also bought a plane ticket for himself and his family to New York. It was the first of many overseas trips for the Sperlings. In New York, they stayed with Regina and Mundich in Brooklyn and socialised with other Holocaust survivors.

Alan, who was five or six years old – but whose memory of those years remains clear – has no recollection of his father meeting with other Treblinka survivors, but said: 'If he knew they were there – and he must have known – he would have sought them out. The survivors know each other and they talk among themselves the way they don't talk to other people. But then, that's hardly surprising. Their shared experience is unique.' During that trip, the family also went north and stayed at the famous Grossinger's Hotel in the Catskills, whose maitre d', coincidentally, was Joe Seildeki, another Treblinka survivor. Alan said, 'If my father had known he was there, he would have gone to find him.'

Two weeks later they returned to Scotland. The Sperlings worked and waited. As soon as Florie's inheritance was in his hands, some time during 1959, Hershl gave up the laundry business. He packed up his family and they moved to Israel for the summer. It was to be a calamitous season. Alan recalled it as one of the happiest times of his life. They moved into a small rented apartment in Tel Aviv and made regular visits to the Israeli contingent of the Goldberg clan. Hershl's mother had been one of ten siblings in Klobuck. Half of them were now in Tel Aviv, those who had emigrated to Israel as pioneers from the Zarki training community near Częstochowa in the 1930s. They also visited Alta, Yaja's eldest brother and an orthopaedic shoemaker in Tel Aviv, and his family, to whom Hershl gave money. During the visits a friendship began to develop between Hershl and the wife of one of the Goldberg cousins. The friendship bloomed into an affair, the motivations for which can only be guessed at. It seems surprising given Hershl and Yaja's intense mutual devotion.

In any event, it soon became public knowledge. A family scandal erupted and it became impossible for them to stay in Israel. Some time before they left, their second son, Sam, was conceived.

'Maybe I was a consolation prize for my mother,' Sam told me, and laughed.

They returned to Scotland, resolved now to make a life for themselves. They bought a four-room bungalow on Brora Drive in upmarket Giffnock, farther south from the tenements of Westmoreland Street. They paid £2,900 for the property. Hershl also paid £500 for a diamond ring that Florie had left to Meyer's daughter in her will.

Alan told me, 'My mother had admired the ring, and Meyer's daughter didn't like it. So they had it valued and my father made her an offer. I still have the receipt, signed and witnessed.' Perhaps, like Sam, the diamond was a part of Hershl's atonement. That night, I kept thinking about Felicia remark – that if Hershl hadn't got the money from South Africa, he would have 'tried harder to make it'. I feel now, after more than a year of investigation into this man's life, I can say with certainty that if anyone had tried hard to 'make it', it was Hershl. I do not honestly believe he could have tried harder.

The telephone rang just as I was drifting off to sleep. It was Haddas in Los Angeles.

'Did I wake you?' she said.

'It's all right. What is it?'

'I wanted to tell you. I spoke with Pinchas Epstein in Israel.'

'And?'

'He didn't want to talk. Now he says he doesn't remember Szperling.'

'Well, if he doesn't want to talk, he doesn't want to talk. What can I do?'

'Willenberg had him on the list. At least you got something,' she said.

The following day, my efforts to contact Benny Chininzon, the Sperlings' former lodger, also came to nothing. I discovered that Chininzon had died two years earlier.

CHAPTER TWENTY-ONE

SHOCK TREATMENT

The following week I drove back to Giffnock. I was looking for Lothian Drive, where the Sperling family had lived between 1965 and mid-1967, an unremarkable residential street in this middle-class Glasgow suburb. It was spring and the Scottish sun shone intermittently. The wind was cold. I had come here simply to observe. A terrible, private incident had occurred on this street one day in 1966, and I needed to get a sense of the place.

As I sat in my car, I realised that what the world had expected of Holocaust survivors – and indeed the survivors of all mass human barbarities – was delusional. The survivors had been liberated from the camps and then somehow they were expected to go off to live their lives as normal citizens. I supposed it was much easier to think of things that way. Of course, it was terrible about all the dead; but it was fine for the survivors, because they had survived, and soon they could become like everyone else again. Numerous books and television programmes reinforced this version of events. There is always the urgent and melancholy sound of a lone violin playing and scenes of thousands of Jews being driven along streets into cattle cars. Yet this is also a world where children creep out of hiding places, families miraculously reunite, chess games save lives, musicians spend the war in camp orchestras that play Bach while death reigns all around them, and people survive, inspirationally, because of their overriding faith in God and humanity and their love for life. This is the acceptable, life-affirming face of the Holocaust. While these extraordinary stories should be told, they do not represent the experience of most who emerged from the nightmare. Most survivors could not reunite with their families because their families had been killed. The orchestras saved a handful of musicians against a backdrop of six million deaths. The suicide rate amongst those who played Bach for the killers, or to drown out the screams of the dying, was high. The children who came out of hiding did so after the murder of one and a half million other Jewish children. In the everyday world, most of the survivors who lost everything emerged with their faith in God and their love for life buried beneath mountains of corpses. I recalled Rubin Sztajer's words to me a few months earlier. 'If there is a God, he fell asleep at the wheel.'

The truth was that the Holocaust did not end with liberation. Every survivor emerged traumatised, although some more than others. Those who were driven closest to the evil, the true witnesses, perished in its gas chambers. But there were also those who came almost as close and survived, and they were doomed to taste and smell the evil for the rest of their lives. Add to this the separation from parents and family, the memory of their last moments with them, the unbearable loneliness, the countless hours of backbreaking labour, and the psychological warfare waged on them cease-lessly by the SS, which made them fearful and at the same time utterly dependent on the killers. Those who remained alive after the selection could either become a cog in the machine or join the dead. And in the years after liberation they unconsciously transmitted their trauma to their children, an innocent generation also tainted.

I understood now how Treblinka had killed Hershl Sperling. I knew now that each memory of the trauma he suffered was traumatic in itself, because memories were wounds that repeatedly re-opened. When survivors admonish us to 'never forget', perhaps they are also telling us that they, too, can 'never forget'. No inspirational tale could ever alter that. When Hershl emerged from the camps, no one could have pos-sibly understood him. No wonder he had been silent.

It was on this street, in the late summer of 1966, that Hershl had reached a turning point in his life where his body and mind could take no more. In the previous months, he appeared no stranger than usual. From the outside, it even seemed that a measure of stability had come to the Sperlings' lives. Hershl had been working for some time as a store manager at Grafton's clothing shop on Argyle Street. It wasn't exactly what he had wanted, but the money was reasonable. Yaja also worked, which added to the household income. Alan and Sam were on school holiday, and sometimes they all went out to a restaurant or the cinema, or to the seaside at Ayr or Prestwick. In July, Yaja's sister Regina came from New York to stay for a few weeks, and they cheered as England thrashed West Germany 4–2 in the World Cup – although Hershl refused to watch, as he often did when a German team were playing. Normal life continued, apparently.

Hershl's mania manifested itself in other ways. He was an adrenaline junkie – doubtless a consequence of his years having to manoeuvre between life and death to survive the camps. He often drove at high speed with his hands off the steering wheel, and he would play a game with himself to see how close he could drive to the kerb. He also occasionally shoplifted – not for the item itself, but for the thrill.

'It was like sitting on top of a volcano, admiring its beauty, but knowing that it could erupt at any moment, that there is something bubbling and violent beneath the surface,' Sam had told me the previous night. 'There was normal life going on, but there was always an anxiety and tension going along with it at the same time.'

As I sat in my car, I looked back through my notebook and found our conversation.

'What about this incident? Can you remember any of the detail?'

'You mean my father's breakdown?'

'Yes.' There was a long silence.

'It's funny, I don't remember the breakdown at all, but I must have been around. My mind has blocked out moments that are particularly distressing, so I have gaps in my memory – things that I know I must have witnessed, but I just can't remember.' His voice suddenly sounded nervous, and he added, 'I need to think about it. You could call Alan, because he was older and might remember more.' I telephoned Alan.

'I want to talk about your father's breakdown,' I told him, 'Is that okay?'

'Look, I've told you before that I'm happy to talk to you about anything. I have to say, I don't feel particularly good after our conversations, but I'll feel worse if I read the book and there are things you should have asked but didn't.'

'All right, then,' I said. 'I appreciate that very much.' I asked if there had been any particular trigger. There was a moment's silence and I heard him breathe as though he were bracing himself. At last, he said, 'The trigger could have been something as insignificant as spilling a cup of coffee on the carpet. It doesn't matter what it was, because things had been bad for weeks.'

'What do you mean by bad?'

'Did you know he was seeing a psychiatrist?' Alan asked me.

'I didn't.'

'Well, he had been seeing Dr Shenkin, who was based at the Southern General Hospital in Glasgow, but my father saw him for private consultations at his home in Whitecraigs, because there was, and still is, a stigma attached to seeing a psychiatrist.'

'Had he been seeing Dr Shenkin for long?' I asked.

'I don't know exactly – a few months, a year perhaps.'

'So he recognised that he had problems?'

'Yes, I would say that he did.'

'Now, on this day in 1966, was there anything that might have set things off? I understand generally things were never very good, but can you actually think of anything specific?'

'He was having problems at work. There was one person in particular there, whom he seemed to be in constant disagreement with. During that time he also became fixated on the idea that my mother was having an affair. It was delusional, because it just wasn't possible. She was so devoted to him. It was just crazy.'

'It couldn't have been very pleasant at home,' I said, unsure of precisely how to respond to this. I was uncomfortable and so was Alan. It seemed intrusive delving this deep into a man's private madness and memories of those who loved him.

'Well, it was never pleasant in our home. But, yes, there was a lot of arguing in the house. He was difficult to live with when he was like that, and I imagine he was equally difficult to work with. But I know enough about how the mind works to know that when people argue that way, it is rarely about the thing they're arguing about. There is usually something else behind it. Quite selfishly, I remember being annoyed because I was studying for exams.'

'Can you tell me anything about the day of the breakdown?' I asked. There was a momentary panic in his voice.

'Listen, can you call me back in, say, one hour. I need to attend to something in the kitchen.'

'Of course,' I said, and we hung up.

A dog barked on Lothian Drive and I looked up from my notebook. I looked at the dashboard clock and saw it was almost 4.00pm. I had been sitting there for almost three hours. I looked back down at my notes. I remembered that almost as soon as I had ended my conversation with Alan, the phone rang again. It was Sam.

'I've been thinking,' he said, 'I've remembered something.'

My friend had dredged up a memory of a summer day more than 40 years earlier. He was six years old. There was a panic in the house. His mother seemed to
be fighting hysteria. Sam recalled her pacing the hallway. Her reaction was unusual,
because she was normally calm and collected. Sam was in the living room, watching
his mother through the open doorway. He saw the dread in her expression and he
also began to feel worried. She began to cry, and she was repeating the words: 'I don't
know what to do. I don't know what to do.' Suddenly, she went into the living room,
took Sam by the hand and pulled him out. Together they went outside and ran up the
incline of Lothian Drive, hand in hand.

'It was the middle of summer,' Sam recalled. 'I remember it was warm, one of those
long evenings. I remember her taking me up the street to a house that was at the top
of the little hill. A Jewish family called Goldberg lived there, but they weren't related
to us. Anyway, I remember we went into the house. But after that I don't know what
happened.'

I asked Sam where his father was at this point, and there was another long, painful pause as he dug deep into his memory. 'He wasn't there. This must have been the
night that my father had his breakdown, or at least around that time. My sense is that
it was that night, but I couldn't say for sure. You understand that no-one said anything
about it, and I was six.'

'Okay,' I said.

'I remember when I was young that I had it in my head that my father had gone
to prison, because he was away for a few days. But he must have gone to the hospital.
I don't know where Alan was. I don't remember. He must have stayed in his room,
which is something he often did.'

Between the two Sperling brothers it is possible to piece together what occurred
that summer evening. When I called back an hour later, Alan told me that Hershl
had been off work for several days, and on that particular morning he called in sick
again. At home he shuffled his feet from room to room, separated from the world.
He had not shaved in days. Later, when he lay down on his bed in the middle of the
afternoon for a nap, memories of Treblinka assailed him – as he slept he howled. His
sons remember this. When he woke he was disoriented. An expression of horror was
frozen on his face. For once, Yaja's tender words could not calm him, and he resumed
the accusations against his wife.

Alan told me, 'Certainly, something pushed him over the cliff, but it would have
been insignificant. He was already in a precarious situation. Because of the way
mental illness works, I would say my father's breakdown was a long gradual process
that took 21 years. When it comes, you just rant and rave until you finally collapse
from exhaustion.'

'So what happened next?' I asked.

'My mother called Dr Shenkin and pleaded with him to do something. He came
to the house and managed to subdue him with medication. The medication in those
days was primitive, compared with what they use today. He probably gave him a
heavy dose of barbiturates – he had been prescribed barbiturates already.'

'Then what?'

'Shenkin called an ambulance. I remember the ambulance taking him away.'

Given Hershl's situation, what followed seems barbaric in the extreme – and certainly that is the opinion of his surviving sons. Arthur Shenkin, a pioneer in bringing psychiatry into general hospitals in post-war Glasgow, had already diagnosed Hershl with severe clinical depression. I discussed this diagnosis with both Alan and Sam and we concluded Shenkin probably had no idea what was wrong with their father. Hershl was not mentally ill. He did not have an imbalance in his brain chemistry, but was deeply traumatised, and no medication or treatment could ever cure him.

'He was treating a Holocaust survivor without addressing the Holocaust,' I said.

'Well, exactly. I told Dr Shenkin later that I thought the way he had dealt with my father was shameful.'

Shenkin, in his misdiagnosis, arranged for Hershl to be given the only treatment that was then available for clinical depression – electroconvulsive therapy, or ECT. That evening Hershl was administered with a short-acting anaesthetic and muscle relaxant, probably suxamethonium chloride, a substance also used as a paralysing agent for executions by lethal injection. Its purpose was to ensure complete muscle relaxation so that when the electricity-induced convulsions came, Hershl would not flail wildly from the physical shock and break bones. Once under anaesthetic, the electrodes were placed on either side of his head. In order to produce the desired convulsion, the stimulus levels used during ECT are held at about twice an individual's seizure threshold, a level that can only be defined by trial and error. Some ECT subjects have recalled a searing light, noise and sometimes pain surging through their brain during treatment.

Another two or three treatments were given to him during a week-long stay at the psychiatric unit of the Southern General Hospital, under the control of Dr Shenkin. I was surprised to learn from Alan that Hershl had consented to the treatment.

'When you're suffering that much, when you're that desperate, you'll do anything,' Alan said. 'I remember that when he came back the first time, after that week in hospital, he looked completely blank and when he looked at me, there was no recognition at all. He didn't know who I was. You can't imagine how disturbing that was.' At the end of the week, he was sent home and allowed to continue his treatment as an outpatient. 'I remember my mother going with him in a taxi to the hospital and him coming home with that blank look on his face,' Alan said.

It was getting late. I pulled out of Lothian Drive and began driving back through South Side. The traffic began to get heavier as I moved toward the city centre. I was stuck at a traffic light in Shawlands when it came to me that Shenkin may have been trying to erase Hershl's memory. I had read that temporary short-term memory loss was common among patients who had received ECT treatment, and sometimes also long-term memory loss. But I understood the treatment was doomed to fail. Although memory tortured Hershl, it was also the weapon he had used to confront the truth. Removing his memory was equivalent to emasculating him, and the whole episode was just another barbaric ordeal he had to endure.

I found myself at the River Clyde. I parked my car under the bridge and got out. I wanted to take another look. I hadn't been back in more than a year. I pushed open a creaking metal gate that led down to the southern bank, directly beneath the bridge. The city centre across the river glistened in the afternoon sun. Some impulse drew me toward a weather-blackened metal ladder that was cemented into the concrete bridge supports. The place was empty except for beer cans, broken bottles that had held cheap wine and discarded syringes.

I put my foot on the first metal rung and began to climb. My heart was pounding. I climbed higher and higher until I reached a small platform, from which I pulled myself into the bridge. Instinctively, I called out warily, 'Hello.' My voice echoed into the dimness of the bridge's metal innards.

There was no reply. Two wooden ramps stretched along the length of the bridge, one on each side, placed there to provide access for maintenance. Wavering streaks of light shot through the spaces made by the criss-cross of iron supports, strangely illuminating pockets of the interior. I could see an old blanket rolled up against one of the supports. As my eyes grew accustomed to the dark, I picked out other remains of human habitation – more cans, newspapers and empty wine bottles. I made my way along the eastern ramp, toward the middle of the bridge, on the side that Hershl had tumbled from. My footsteps echoed on the board as I walked. I heard the sound of a low humming that grew quickly louder, the sound of an approaching train. The roar was deafening as it passed overhead, as though I were directly beneath the jet of an ascending aircraft. The air was ripped from me. The entire bridge shook and swayed and rattled, and I held fast to one of the supports to steady myself until the train crossed the bridge and its sound became a distant moan. I felt suddenly terrified to be here, in the empty shell of this bridge and in the place where Hershl had spent his last moments.

I made my way slowly to the centre of the bridge, and stopped at an open space between two sets of supports. I reasoned that if Hershl had been sleeping along this horizontal bar, he might easily have rolled over and fallen. It was a risky place to sleep, but Hershl liked taking risks. There was also something about the confinement and the austerity, and the company he had kept here that may have taken him back to the Treblinka barracks. I crouched down and edged myself on to the bar. I touched the metal above my head, as though I were seeking an answer from it, as though this ancient iron might remember what had occurred eighteen years earlier. I looked down at the water below and I suddenly began to feel very dizzy. An image of Hershl falling entered my head and I imagined myself floating in the water below. I felt a sudden urge to see my children. I realised I had been too long away from my family.

It was after 7.00pm by the time I arrived home. I could smell the chicken my wife was cooking. My ten-year-old son saw me from the hallway and rushed in to greet me. 'Daddy's home,' he called. As he was hugging me, my daughter ran in and did the same. 'Where have you been?' she asked.

'I was just out for a little while,' I said. 'Stuff to do with my book.' Then my wife came in. I leaned over to kiss her and we all embraced. My son called out with glee, 'Family hug.'

'We've been trying to call you,' my wife said.

'Cell phone's out of batteries. Sorry.'

'We were starting to get worried.'

'I went to the bridge,' I said.

'Are you okay?'

'I'm glad to be home.'

I poured myself a long shot of whisky. I went out to sit on the back step and watch the red sunset over the hills. It was beautiful. Then my daughter came out and hugged me again.

'I forgot to tell you, your friend Sam called.'

'Oh yes?'

'He made me write down this name on a piece of paper.' She handed me the note, and the name on it was Flora McInnes. 'He said he didn't know the number, but her son owns a cafe called –' her voice rose up at the end of the sentence to make a question – 'Gandolfi? And that you can get the number from him.'

'Café Gandolfi. Yes, I know it. It's a place in Glasgow. What else did he say?'

'That she used to live on the same street and that she was friends with his mother and she might know some things.'

'Which street?'

'It's on the other side of the paper.'

I turned over the piece of paper, and saw that it said 'Lothian Drive' in big letters. 'Thank you very much,' I said, and kissed her.

The following day, as instructed, I obtained Flora McInnes' telephone number from her son Seumus at the cafe. Seumus remembered the Sperling family well. He told me he had attended Sam's bar mitzvah. He called him 'Sammy' and he called Yaja 'Yetta'. I also learned that his mother, a world-renowned traditional Gaelic singer, was better known by her 'Barra name' Flora McNeil, and that she was now 85 but 'still going strong'. It occurred to me that Hershl, too, should have been still going strong. I phoned Mrs McInnes.

'She called on me a lot,' Mrs McInnes said, her soft Western Isles accent lilting gently upward. 'But it was a long time ago.'

'I know,' I said, 'and it's difficult to remember the things she said. But I was wondering if you remember anything she might have said about her husband.'

'Well, I remember that she used to come to the house at all times of the day, sometimes in the morning and sometimes again in the afternoon. Sometimes she was upset and a bit disturbed. But we spoke about her upbringing and I spoke about mine. They were very, very Orthodox, you know, and we developed quite a taste for Jewish cooking in our house, because she would always come around with challah or gifilte fish. My son still makes them in his restaurant. We used to swap recipes. She used to say that she understood me and that I understood her.'

'But nothing about what was going on in their house?'

'It's so difficult to remember. It is so many years ago. I do remember she used to say that the Jewish people in Glasgow didn't want to know what they had gone through. And there were plenty of Jewish people in that area, even on their street. But she used to come to me, and if I was doing the ironing she would tell me to sit and she'd take over the ironing herself. She was a lovely woman. I was very fond of her. She was the strong one in that family, I'll tell you, but she never got a chance, what with everything that happened to her and the way her life was then. But she was very proud of her boys.'

'I know she was,' I said.

'I remember one time I was going to a dance and I was all dressed up. We were just about to go out when the doorbell rang and it was Yetta. I can still see her now standing in the hallway. She said, "Here, you can borrow this ring." I had seen her wearing it and I'd only mentioned in passing that I liked it. It had a big blue stone and, you know, everyone admired it that night.' It was Florrie's ring.

'Did you ever meet Hershl – or Henry, I suppose you would have called him?'

'Yes, Henry. No, I didn't see very much of him. He was always very quiet. I think he was a client of my husband, who was a lawyer. It was conveyance work and maybe some other business when Henry had a shop.' I told her a little about Treblinka, and what he had been through. Her voice seemed to fade. 'How little one knows about what's in people's hearts,' she said.

★ ★ ★

Over the next few days, further conversations with Sam and Alan filled in more of their father's story. A few weeks after the ECT ended, Hershl began to pick up – although he always did; his suffering came in cycles. He resumed his work at Grafton's Fashion Centre, although the situation was still difficult for him, Alan recalled. Hershl and Yaja also now seemed closer and more dependent on one another than ever before. They resumed their after-dinner walks, with their arms entwined and their whispered Yiddish. Sometimes, the suffering returned, and it seemed these walks along with regular calls to his surrogate father, Samuel Rajzman in Canada, were all that held him together.

During the early summer of 1967, Hershl decided to take drastic action – he packed up his family and moved them to Montreal. He had flown to Canada two or three times over the past few months to see Rajzman and make preparations for a new life. The trips occurred before Rajzman gave his interview to journalist Gitta Sereny in the early 1970s for *Into That Darkness*, her book about Treblinka commandant Paul Franz Stangl. According to the descriptions of Sam and Alan, Rajzman's situation appears to have been similar when Hershl arrived.

Rajzman had emigrated to Canada shortly after the war and had become prosperous and well-established in a quiet residential district of Montreal, from where he conducted a flourishing lumber business. He lived with his second wife and they were a quiet and gentle couple, who had found each other after the war. Both had lost everyone they had loved during the Nazi terror in Poland.

Hershl quickly found a job, with Rajzman's help, as a manager at Steinberg's Miracle Mart, a discount department store chain carrying clothing, toys, appliances and other goods. Rajzman may also have helped with the immigration process for the Sperlings, because he counted Pierre Trudeau, the flamboyant Canadian justice minister who the following year would be elected as the country's prime minister, among his close friends. Trudeau at times also turned to Rajzman for advice, and did so by telephone on several occasions in the Sperlings' presence. Privately, Rajzman boasted he had given Trudeau his first job after he graduated as a lawyer.

In the summer of 1967, the Sperlings arrived by ship, the *Empress of Canada*. For Hershl and Yaja, much of the time aboard was spent listening to the BBC World Service for news of the Six-Day War in Israel. They will have heard the first reports on the morning of 5 June 1967, the immediate aftermath of the moment when a fleet of low-flying Israeli jets surprised the Egyptian air force on the ground and destroyed it, in response to the threats by its Arab neighbours to 'wipe Israel off the map'.

'It was like a floating hotel,' Sam told me one night. 'Very luxurious. I remember going past Newfoundland and how huge and exciting Quebec port was, at least to a seven-year-old.'

It was a happy and hopeful time for the Sperlings, and Hershl loved a new beginning. He was addicted to hope. He and Yaja strolled the deck of the *Empress of Canada* arm-in-arm during the voyage. Hershl was also pleased that he would soon be nearer to Rajzman. While young Sam explored the decks of the ship, only teenage Alan was sullen. He had already enrolled in a pre-law degree at McGill University in Montreal and was miserable at the prospect. During the course of my research, I came to understand this was not an isolated phenomenon. Like so many other survivor parents, Hershl and Yaja's expectations of Alan, born in the first years after liberation, were extraordinarily high. In response, Alan spent much of his life rejecting the special role he had been designated – to fill the emptiness left behind by those who had perished. I wondered if Hershl had looked at his first-born son and in some way dreaded what he represented – the pull toward life and the future, which for him meant abandoning the past and all those who had died.

When they arrived in Montreal, they stayed at first with a family called Osczega, whom either Hershl or Yaja had known from long ago in Poland. They had a daughter, who was around ten years old, with whom Sam recalled fighting furiously. Eventually they moved into the top floor of a duplex owned by a Greek family. Hershl bought himself a Chevrolet and drove to visit the Rajzmans once or twice a week. This was the home of the man who had kept Hershl alive in Treblinka. Being once more in his presence was a haven.

I asked Sam what he remembered of that time.

'It was a clean house,' he said. 'Thinking back, I'd say it was fastidious and over-tidy, very old-fashioned. He used to give us tea in china cups. I remember there wasn't much to do. I was seven and he seemed very old. Then, I would have said he was about 90, but I guess he was in his sixties. Even then, I knew very well he was very special to my father.'

'Did you like him? Was he friendly toward you?' I asked.

'I liked him, but he was never someone who bounced me on his knee and, when I think about it, he never gave me any presents. He didn't seem overly interested in me. The first time I met him, he took me into a room with an aquarium and fish, and he showed me squirrels out the window. I used to stay in this room while he talked with my parents. I got the impression they spoke about everything. Once you've been through Treblinka with someone, when you've been naked with someone– both physically and emotionally – I don't believe anything is barred.'

In August 1942, during the deportations from the Warsaw ghetto, Rajzman and his first wife had tried to hide their twelve-year-old daughter, as related to the writer Gitta Sereny. I read Sam a section over the telephone from Sereny's interview. 'My wife and I had only one thought – to hide our little girl,' Rajzman said. 'In the street where both my wife and I worked at a factory was a cellar. And in that cellar was a coalbunker. We took about twenty children and hid them in there and locked the door. Even though we were considered essential workers, the Gestapo came the next day and we were all driven to the assembly square.'

Rajzman managed to get away from those assembled after two days and went straight to the cellar to find his daughter. 'The door was open and the children were gone. A neighbour said the Germans had come the day before and taken them.' Then it occurred to him the children might still be in the square, because the transports were often kept waiting for days. He enlisted the help of a Polish friend and the two of them raced to the Umshlagplatz. Miraculously, the children were still there. 'We managed to get my little girl and a boy whose parents were friends of ours and we took them back to our factory. They stayed hidden for several days, but in the end they took them away. Since that day, I cannot bear to look at a child.'

A long silence followed. Eventually, Sam said: 'That makes me sad to think that my presence there might have upset him, because I was there and I was seven, while I was playing in his living room. The very last thing I'd want to do is to upset him or cause him any more suffering.' He stopped again, and I could hear him puff deeply on a cigarette. 'I think that when they were in Treblinka, they found each other. For my father, Rajzman would become his father, and for Rajzman, my father became the child he had to save.'

Sometimes, during these visits, Hershl had in his possession the green book and he and Rajzman would discuss its contents for hours. The exact nature of these discussions cannot be known of course, but Rajzman did hold copies of other volumes in the series, 'From The Last Extermination'. I still had come no closer to solving the mystery of why Hershl had held in his leather briefcase a volume in the same series of journals, but one that did not contain his account. I wondered now if it were possible that at some point during these discussions with Rajzman the pair had exchanged books.

'It's possible,' said Sam. 'As I've said, I think essentially my father wanted to keep something that was connected with Treblinka, but he could not handle having the real thing. It was probably too painful for him. It was enough for him to have something that was closely associated with the things he had written about.'

'There might be another possibility,' I said. 'What if he never had the journal that contained his account, volume number six, in the first place? It was printed in August 1947, and he left Germany in September that year. Maybe he just wasn't around to get a copy when they were distributed. The book your father had was volume four and it was published in May 1947.'

'But you see, I think if he wanted to have volume number six, he would have found a way to get it,' Sam said. 'I think he just couldn't bear to have it.'

Life went on for the Sperlings in Montreal. Hershl's job at Steinberg's Miracle Mart worked out well. Sam went to school and Alan began pre-law at McGill. Hershl seemed happier also, and so did Yaja, because Rajzman had taken the pressure off her to be the rock on which Hershl was anchored. The trauma now manifested itself in unusual ways.

'When I look back at our time in Canada, some things stand out,' Sam said. 'I remember being in a store with my father and I wanted one of these jackets they called wind-cheaters. I wanted it in blue, but he wouldn't let me. I could have it in any other colour except blue. He became very angry, because I wouldn't accept that. Even at seven I knew that blue must have reminded him of something in the camps, but I don't know what. I also knew this wasn't normal, and that there was something very, very wrong with the way he was reacting.'

He asked me if I knew of anything about the colour blue that might have reminded Hershl of the camps, but I could not think of anything, except perhaps prisoners' striped uniforms in Dachau, which the Americans dyed blue to change their appearance. Sam sighed deeply, as though he were utterly drained. 'I remember deciding then and there, when I was seven, that I didn't want to have children, because I thought all fathers must surely be crazy like him. There were other things, too. I remember a lot of toys disappearing, and clothes, and some things that other people had bought for me. I learned later that he would go around the house and if he discovered that something was made in Germany, he would just throw it out, without saying anything.'

There was strange behaviour. On one occasion, the family were driving back to Montreal after spending a few days with Yaja's relatives in New York during Passover, in the spring of 1968. During their stay in Brooklyn, the Sperlings had bought various electrical goods. Alan had bought a cassette player, a technological wonder in those days, of which he was particularly proud. However, Hershl decided he did not want to pay the tax on the goods on re-entering Canada. Driving north on the New York State Thruway, close to the Canadian border, Hershl attempted to avoid the main border crossing on the Northway and veer west, probably at Plattsburg, into the back roads of the Adirondacks. He was determined to cross the border undetected. It was April, and there was probably still snow on the ground. He drove north on the old Military Turnpike, and then veered off the beaten track again on to the remote, twisting small roads that cut through the region.

Sam recalled: 'Some of the roads he took were really back roads. I remember Alan getting very nervous. He kept saying that this was going to end in disaster, but my father just waved away all his objections. Eventually, he found a road that crossed in to Canada. But, of course, as soon as we entered Canada, we were pursued by the border authorities and when they stopped us they wanted to know what the hell we were doing. My father started speaking Yiddish at them. Then he went into this method-acting performance of the innocent tourist. It was very convincing, but they took us all back to their headquarters, and they kept us there for something like ten hours.'

'So what happened?' I asked.

'I remember my mother was wearing this very colourful sweater and for some reason the customs people were very interested in it, and I remember the customs officials made her keep taking it off and putting it back on, which my father found hysterical. He was the only one there who seemed to be enjoying himself. I'm sure he liked the risk and the danger of it all. He took the attitude that this was a safe kind of risk, because these guards weren't Nazis, and although they had guns, they weren't going to shoot us for trying to get some radios and a cassette player over the border. Alan, on the other hand, was going crazy, and ranted on about the customs having authority to smash everything with a hammer. Alan didn't want his prized cassette player destroyed with a hammer. But my father stuck to his story, continuing this guiltless face, and eventually they let us go. I'm sure he got a really big adrenaline buzz from the whole episode.'

Meanwhile, back in Montreal, Alan began to struggle at McGill University – not academically, for Alan never scored less than 90 per cent in any exam he sat, but he was bored. He was also unhappy over the fact he had to pass a pre-law degree, in keeping with the North American university system. He wanted to go straight to the law degree, as in the British university system. This was a teenager with an IQ over 160. The previous year, he had achieved the highest mark in the country on a high school history exam. One afternoon, during a family visit to the Rajzmans, Alan suddenly announced that he was desperately unhappy and that he no longer wanted to become a lawyer. An argument erupted. Hershl was particularly upset. Then the patriarchal Rajzman spoke out amid the melee.

Alan told me a few nights later that Rajzman had said, 'So the world will have one less lawyer. It's not the end of everything.' Amid the silence that prevailed, Hershl threw his hands in the air and accepted.

'He had extraordinary influence over my father,' Alan said. 'He was an enormous calming power and had an ability to take him back to reality.' Arrangements were made for Alan to return to Scotland alone, and the family would follow a few months later, albeit against their wishes. They returned in the summer of 1968. In Hershl's hand was the briefcase, possibly now containing the switched book. It is possible that Hershl's original book is now held in the Jewish Public Library in Montreal. I made several enquiries by telephone and email, and a few weeks later received a reply from Eddie Paul, the head of Bibliographic & Information Services at the library.

'Since we seldom take note of the provenance of book donations – we do with our archival collection – it would be difficult to confirm how we obtained any of the items in our collection. However, since the estate of Samuel Rajzman did leave the JPL an endowment fund to fund books on the Holocaust, it is entirely possible that the journal was obtained through his collection.'

CHAPTER TWENTY-TWO

THE FINAL STRUGGLE

Sam and I must have been about fifteen. I remember it was late morning on a Saturday. The weather was typically dull and chilly. I remember the sky over Newton Mearns was low and steely grey. Sam's house at 63 Castlehill Drive was just around the corner from mine, and I went to meet him. Alan was upstairs, the reclusive genius in his bedroom busying himself with cricket statistics, crossword puzzles and impossibly difficult Mensa enigmas, or at least that was what I assumed. Sam got his jacket and we set out through the quiet suburban streets, past the affluent homes with their new cars in the driveways and their neatly mown lawns. We were not exactly fearful of anti-Semitic youths, the way we might have been had we been walking through the streets of Klobuck 40 years earlier, but we were still vigilant. Anti-Semitism in Newton Mearns was widespread, but it was a kind of subdued anti-Semitism that existed overtly in the school playground and behind closed doors. We reached the bus stop on the Old Mearns Road without incident and made our way into the city centre. Hershl had driven into Glasgow much earlier that day, and we were going to meet him. This was a big day for Hershl. That morning he had opened his own men's clothing retailer. Its name, Catch 22, after the popular Joseph Heller novel, had been Alan's idea.

We arrived in Glasgow around noon, but we first stopped off to see Yaja. She gave us money for lunch and we bought something on the run. Then we went east along busy Argyle Street and on to Stockwell Street, and finally into Catch 22. I remember thinking when I first saw Hershl how incredibly happy and proud he looked. He was dressed in a striking new brown suit, which matched the colour of his thinning hair perfectly. He also had on brown shoes and he wore an impeccable white shirt and patterned tie. But most striking of all, I remember, was the genuine happiness on his face as he strode through the aisles of clothing, past Glasgow's Saturday shoppers and racks of new shirts and suits. His pale green eyes sparkled with joy as he shook hands with customers and asked if they had found everything they were looking for. He was at that moment neither desperate nor sad, but everything a man should be in the world outside his family. When Hershl caught sight of us entering his new shop, already heaving with customers, his smile grew wide, and I remember clearly the way his arms swept out before him, his hands open, telling us to survey his new kingdom. 'What do you think?' he called to us through the crowd. He strode over, so proud it was a veritable swagger, and he put his hand on his son's shoulder and smiled. Then he patted me hard on the back and asked: 'Boychik, you like it?' I smiled and said, 'Yes,' unsure of what else I should say in that moment of glory.

Perhaps it was that same day, I cannot recall, but I have a clear memory of Hershl collaring two thieves near the shop's door. I remember both of them were at least a head taller than Hershl's five-foot-seven-inches, yet he gripped them both by the ear and threw them out. It was impressive to see that this little man had no fear in a city where knife crime and violence was common. When I think back now, it is difficult to think of him as being afraid. He seemed to fear nothing. For a man who had looked Mengele in the eyes and survived, what were two Glasgow delinquents?

In the end, a little more than a year later, Catch 22 failed because of repeated break-ins. Several nights each week, the family were woken up in the early hours of the morning by police calls demanding that Hershl come into the shop and board up the premises. Once, thieves had even tried to enter the shop through the roof. Perhaps he could have improved security and persevered, because the business was highly profitable, but after the initial thrill of opening, his interest waned and he was bored again.

I remember, when I came to visit Sam in the evening, even during the time when Catch 22 was still operating, Hershl was often restless in his house. I recall the way he used to pace. Sometimes, bored with television and domesticity, he would suddenly jump up from the couch, impatiently grab for a packet of cigarettes on the coffee table, light up and leave. Then, still smoking his cigarette, he would re-enter the living room, and sit down for just a moment before jumping up again.

Sam said, 'Everything was approached as though it were a terrible crisis, from the smallest, insignificant, trivial thing, such as deciding what food to buy, to real crises, like sickness and death.' Sometimes, he would begin annoying Alan. He might begin an argument, or start making noises, and when Alan got up to leave, Hershl would chase after him up the stairway and continue his efforts through the closed door of Alan's bedroom. I remember once he chased Alan up the stairs while mooing like a cow, and he continued to moo for some twenty minutes after Alan had banged shut his door. I did not understand then that, for Hershl, everything really was a crisis. For the purposes of survival, Hershl had marshalled all his powers, both physical and psychological, in the camps, and that state of mind had become part of him forever. It seemed as though some chemical change had occurred in Treblinka that could never be reversed.

'Living in a house with two Holocaust survivors was not exactly like growing up in a normal British household.' Sam told me. 'From an early age, it was made very clear to me that the outside world was a very dangerous place, and that there were people out there who wanted to kill us, and that there were these other people called Nazis, who had killed millions of Jews like us and who had tried to kill my parents.'

I remembered Hershl and Yaja having dinner with my parents in our home. Hershl had liked my father because he generally liked Americans. American soldiers had liberated him, and his experience in the American Zone of Germany after the war was generally positive. During the course of the evening, while Yaja and my mother conversed happily, Hershl said almost nothing. My father's well-meaning efforts to make conversation were met with nods, short, polite replies and the occasional strained smile. I remember Hershl sitting on our couch after dinner, with an impenetrable look on his face. Was he remembering Treblinka then? I understood his utter inability to relate to those who had not suffered as he had done and had not witnessed what he had. His capacity for empathy was smashed, and with that came an inability to make friendships. But then something unusual happened. Out of the silence, when no-one was paying attention, he looked up at me and winked. It seemed as extraordinary now as it did then, an act of complicity; for just a second he had let me into his world. I wondered, illogical as it was, if Hershl might have been giving me a sign. Was he giving me permission to sift through layer upon layer of his tormented psyche and one day write his story? Out of the reverie, I stared through the canopy of branches into the great reddening of the sky, and I realised then that the story of his life – a story that needed to be told – was a gift not from him at all, but from my friend, Sam, and his brother, Alan, both of whom were the last keepers of Hershl's memory and his suffering.

After Catch 22 finally closed, Hershl pottered around the house, smoking and sleeping. On Shabbas, he and Yaja said prayers and observed the holiday faithfully. Hershl knew every nuance of the service by heart. For them, their Jewishness was everything. It was the link to all he had been before the Nazis came and all that had been lost.

★ ★ ★

Disaster struck during spring 1977. Yaja had previously been diagnosed with cervical cancer, but it had spread to her bones. The cancer had first appeared three years earlier, but she had responded well to treatment and it was beginning to look as though she had beaten the disease. Yaja was also kept willingly in the dark by her family; she may have suspected her illness – indeed, she must have known – but she asked no questions and sought no confirmation. There was a deep-rooted mistrust of doctors in the Sperling house; in the camps becoming ill and being sent to a doctor was often the equivalent of a death sentence. I asked Alan what he remembered about this period.

'Like so many things in our house, we knew nothing about them until the shit hit the fan, if you'll pardon my language,' Alan said. 'All sorts of things happened in secret. You have to remember that in our house, doctors didn't exist, illness didn't exist and death didn't exist. Anyway, my mother went into the hospital for an operation and things seemed to go quite well. I had no idea there was anything wrong until the day before she went into the hospital.'

Over the next year-and-a-half, Yaja's condition seemed to improve. Then, some time during the middle of 1977, she began to experience excruciating pain in her back. I was in and out of the Sperling home often during that time, and I remember Yaja very clearly smiling as affectionately as ever at her family – and at me, also, when I was there. I recall no instance of her succumbing to pain or losing patience. One night during the winter of 1977, Yaja was in the hospital undergoing tests, and a call came. The doctor gave no news on the telephone, but asked that Hershl come in the following day.

Alan said, 'My father didn't have to say anything to us. A phone call from that particular doctor was enough. He simply asked that my father come in the next day and see him. What he would tell him was that my mother's condition was terminal.'

'Do you remember how your father reacted?' I asked.

'I remember his reaction after that phone call very clearly. He hung up the phone and proceeded to consume a large quantity of whisky. I remember being shocked by that, because I had never seen him drink like that before. Then he retired to bed without saying a word. It was a pivotal point. From the moment of that phone call, my father utterly lost the will to live. It was downhill from there.'

Yaja came home after treatment. Occasionally I would visit Sam and she would be there, moving between the kitchen and living room, smiling, sometimes affectionately touching Sam's cheek as she spoke to him in a soft Yiddish. He would answer her in English.

Meanwhile, the talk between Sam and I in those days was black as death. I remember feeling helpless. Sometimes, at the front door, Sam would tell me that this was not a good time – never because his mother was not feeling up to having his friend in the house, but because Hershl 'wasn't feeling well'.

In the middle of it all Hershl struck upon the bizarre and untimely idea of opening another business – a rival suede and leather shop in Glasgow's prestigious Argyle Arcade, near Skincraft, the shop where Yaja had worked before her illness.

'It wasn't so much a business idea as a distraction and a fantasy. The whole thing was mad, and what's even crazier is that he managed to persuade a partner that it was a good idea. It went as far as them signing a lease on the property in the Argyll Arcade, which as you can imagine cost a lot of money. That was where Glasgow's most exclusive jewellery shops were located, and still are, I believe.'

'What did you and Sam think about it, in the middle of your mother's illness?'

'It was just something else we didn't know about. I knew nothing about it, until one day an envelope arrived from the partner's lawyer. I remember when my father saw it, he just went to bed. Soon, we started getting frantic phone calls from the partner and his lawyer, and I realised how serious the situation was.'

'So what did you do?'

'I took the package and went to see my father's lawyer immediately. We spoke generally at first, then he said he understood fully how my father and I had arrived in this state. It was a bit of a relief. You see, the lawyer was also the son of a Holocaust survivor. He said that although he had problems he was lucky because only one of his parents had been in the camps. Anyway, he looked over the lease, and the situation appeared to be hopeless. I was extremely worried, because the following week the landlord would begin taking a large amount of rent money out of my father's bank account and there was no way he was in a state to operate a business. We would run out of money in a very short time. I had visions of us all being thrown into the street as my mother lay dying.'

'So how did you get out of the situation?'

'The lawyer gave me a copy of the lease, and he asked me to look over it to see if I could spot anything, and he said he would do the same. The missives had not yet been signed, so the contract was not formalised. When I took it home and read over it, it became clear that the landlord had missed one of the deadlines. I forget precisely what it was about – it was a long time ago – but in the end we were able to nullify the contract. I don't want to make myself out to be a hero, but I will say that was the most valuable thing I have ever done in my life.' I asked him how his father had responded to this sudden reversal of events.

'He was so depressed, it didn't matter. He simply acknowledged it and went back to bed when I told him. I still have questions about the way the so-called partner acted. He must have known what kind of condition my father was in. Anyway, thankfully, it ended there.'

In the weeks before Yaja's death, the despair of the Sperling family was unconquerable. Sam disappeared to a friend's house to sleep, and although he sometimes ate with us, I saw little of the Sperlings for three months. In September, Yaja went into hospital and died.

'My mother did not have private medical insurance, but one of the consultant doctors there was so impressed by her that he made sure she got a private room,' Alan said. 'Unlike my father, there was no-one who wanted to live more than my mother.'

I remembered that Felicia had told me that Hershl had prevented people from visiting his wife in hospital – although that edict may have only applied to certain people. During my conversation with Flora McInnes, the Sperling's former neighbour, she told me that Hershl had called her.

'I remember it was Henry who called. I hadn't heard from them much since they moved away from Lothian Drive, but he said she was very ill in the hospital with cancer and that she wanted to see me before she died. So I went up to the hospital. I could see she was being well looked after, but it was very sad. I don't remember the exact conversation, but I do remember that she said she was very happy to have known me and that I was to give her love to all my family. She was a remarkable woman, you know,' she added, 'really a remarkable woman and she never got a chance in life.'

Yaja died on 7 October 1978. Hershl took the call at 2.00am on Saturday morning. I went to visit Sam the following day and he gave me the news at the front door. I remember the moment very clearly. 'My mother died last night,' he said matter-of-factly. I left them to mourn. I remember sitting in the back seat of my parents' car driving to her funeral. I was eighteen, and I was very upset with them. I remember lashing out, saying that they should not go to the funeral of a woman they had made no effort to befriend in her lifetime and that it was hypocrisy. My words upset them and I remember the way they looked at each other. Of course, I was wrong. Sam was in our house as much as I was in his. My mother had treated him like another son. I later apologized.

The funeral is a blur. I remember walking with Sam beside the coffin. His face was a mess of tears. It is the only funeral I have ever attended in Scotland at which it did not rain, although I remember a cold wind ripped through us. He shovelled earth on the coffin in the grave, and recited the Kaddish. I also scattered earth. I remember looking at Hershl. His eyes were closed and his mouth was unnaturally open, as though he were dead himself. I remembered I was ashamed to be staring and I turned away with tears in my eyes.

The following day, Sam checked himself into Leverndale Psychiatric Hospital in Glasgow, then changed his mind and escaped over the wall the following day in his pyjamas. That night, he came to our house for dinner.

★ ★ ★

I found an article on the internet from the *American Journal of Geriatric Psychiatry* from 2004. It was about suicidal tendencies among ageing Holocaust survivors. The study found that amongst depressed older adults, survivors of the Holocaust were 87 per cent more likely to contemplate suicide than anyone else in that age group. Moreover, the article noted that the loss of a spouse often reactivated Holocaust terror. The reactivation of the terror in Treblinka was amongst the worst possible. I remembered that Treblinka survivor Richard Glazer had killed himself after the death of his wife in 1998 and I noted that the wives of the four Treblinka survivors I had spoken with in Israel were still living.

The years that followed Yaja's death marked a slow and tortuous decline for Hershl. After the closure of Catch 22, he never worked again. He was lonely and there was no-one left to bring him back and to whisper soft Yiddish in his ear.

Letters and phone calls came often from Samuel Rajzman in the months just after Yaja's death, perhaps more than usual. Hershl read them with relish and replied quickly and with equal fervour. Then he would return to bed, where he spent much of his day. He consumed disturbing cocktails of Scotch and Valium, and smoked cigarettes incessantly. He rarely went outside, except to the local shop to replenish his whisky and cigarette supply.

Sam had by now moved to a kibbutz in Israel. Hershl and Alan remained alone in the house at 63 Castlehill Drive, each in their own precarious psychological state. Alan cared for Hershl and they alternately bickered and ignored one another.

Then one day the letters from Rajzman stopped. Their absence left a gaping hole in what had been, through the years, through all Hershl's suffering, one of the few constants in his life. Hershl called Sam in Israel to tell him that he feared something had happened to his surrogate father. A few weeks later, an article in the now-defunct *Jewish Echo* reported his death. I found a listing through the JewishGen website, in the death records of Quebec, which noted the burial of one Sam Rajzman on 16 September 1979 at Baron de Hirch – De la Savane Cemetary, Montreal, Line 10, Grave 332. A separate listing noted the burial of a Rosa Rajzman at the same cemetery in November 1992, at Line 10, Grave 331, beside her husband.

A string of house moves followed, all of them just a few streets from each other. It was the only way Hershl knew how to keep going. Alan told me, 'Whether it was moving house, moving street, or moving country, he always thought he could start again and everything would be better. But they were all just distractions. It meant he was doing something. But of course you can't run away from yourself, no matter where you go.'

In 1980, Hershl suffered a heart attack. All those years of gut-wrenching stress, anxiety and inner turmoil – not to mention his heavy smoking and alcohol addiction – had taken their toll on his body. Nonetheless, he recovered from it. Then, a few years later, came his first suicide attempt.

'I think it was in 1983 or 1984. He had gone to Israel for a holiday,' Alan told me.

'I guess Sam was still in Israel then.' I said. 'Is that why he went back to Israel?'

'It was just a holiday. Sam had met a girl on a kibbutz and had moved to Denmark. Anyway, about 48 hours after my father left Glasgow, I got a call from the Israeli police, who said there had been an incident and that he may have tried to kill himself. After another 48 hours, he was back at home and he refused to talk about what had happened.'

Other disappearances and suicide attempts – whether real or half-hearted – followed. For the most part, Hershl remained in bed in a haze of alcohol, Valium and cigarette smoke.

Alan said, 'I tried to cook for him, but it seemed he hardly ever ate. He seemed to go for years without eating. He just drank all day and smoked. I imagine he was trying to kill himself like that. I remember one time walking into the bathroom while he was in the bath and he was so skeletal, like he must have been in the camps, or at least that's what I thought. I knew he was dying, one way or another. Nothing could erase the past or bring my mother back to him. That was what he needed, impossible as it was. Whenever he went out, I used to worry that he might kill someone else. I used to wrestle with my conscience about calling the police, because he was driving drunk all the time. If he had killed someone like that I don't know how I would have continued to live with myself. But miraculously it never happened.'

It occurred to me now that it must have seemed to Hershl that he could not die. Treblinka had not killed him, nor had Auschwitz, Dachau or any of the other camps. He had survived death marches, starvation, even a heart attack. Now he was surviving all this whisky, and the madness that plagued him. The drunk and careless driving and all the crazy risk-taking had not worked either. Over the course of the next few years he took at least five overdoses and on each occasion his stomach was pumped and he survived. On two occasions, after being reported missing by Alan, he was discovered unconscious by police in a hotel in Ayr with whisky and Valium at his side.

I telephoned Sam and asked about his impressions of his father at that time.

'Maybe he was so scared of the past, maybe the things that happened in day-to-day life, all the risks he took, meant nothing to him. Alan once said "if the devil suddenly came out of the carpet, my father wouldn't bat an eyelid." Maybe he was convinced that he could survive everything, although I think sometimes he was annoyed that he couldn't die.'

In early 1987, Hershl's condition picked up a little after a phone call from the American Embassy in London. They had wanted him to identify John Demianiuk, a retired autoworker from Cleveland, Ohio, who had been deported to Israel and was about to be placed on trial in Jerusalem under the allegation that he was really Ivan the Terrible, one of the most notorious, sadistic and malevolent practitioners of genocide at Treblinka.

Alan told me: 'He was in absolutely no doubt that he would recognise him. He said he would be able recognise him no matter how old he was or even if he had undergone plastic surgery.' Shortly afterwards, two men from the US State Department came to Scotland to interview him.

'Were you there when the men arrived?' I asked.

'Yes I was,' Alan said.

'And what did your father do?'

'Well, he got out of bed, which was a big thing for him. They spread out a lot of photographs for him to look at. My father studied them all closely. After a while, he said, "You haven't shown me a picture of him yet." The men appeared disappointed, but they were not as disappointed as my father. He would have liked nothing better than for Ivan the Terrible to have been brought to justice, but none of those pictures were him.'

It turned out that Hershl was right. Demianiuk was not Ivan the Terrible after all. In 1993, four years after Hershl's death, the Israeli Supreme Court concluded from evidence that had recently become available from Russian archives that another man, Ivan Marchenko, was in fact Ivan the Terrible. However, in 2002, a US judge ruled that documents from World War II proved that while Demianiuk had not been in Treblinka, he was indeed a Nazi guard, who had trained at the Operation Reinhard training camp at Trawniki and that he had been a willing participant in leading Jews to the gas chambers at Sobibor. The judge also concluded that he had served as a guard at Majdanek in Poland and Flossenburg in Germany. In early 2008, the United States Court of Appeals for the Sixth Circuit rejected a challenge from Demianiuk, then 87, to a final deportation order by the nation's chief immigration judge. The order was finally given to send Demjanjuk to Germany or Poland if his native Ukraine would not take him. At the time of writing, the matter is still unresolved.

As Demjanjuk's trial proceeded, even as it brought Treblinka back into the public light, Hershl's condition deteriorated further. There was another incident when he went back to Israel for a holiday in the late 1980s and gave himself hypothermia from sleeping on the balcony of a hotel. Back in Glasgow, he took another overdose of sleeping pills.

Alan said: 'I went round to his house to see him. By this time he had more or less kicked me out, so I was living in my house around the corner. He said he was better off without me. He accused me of being like a camp guard, so I left. But I was checking up on him all the time – even though when I went there he didn't want to see me, but when I didn't come he later accused me of not caring. Anyway, I went to see him that day, and I found him unconscious. I couldn't wake him, so I called an ambulance and they took him to the Victoria Hospital, where they pumped his stomach again.'

'This is awful,' I said. 'I can hardly bear to listen to this. It must have been terrible for you.'

'He was extremely angry because he wanted to die,' Alan said. 'Actually, angry doesn't come close to describing it. While he was getting his stomach pumped he was screaming at me. He was abusive and furious that I had found him and that he had survived again.'

'I'm sorry,' I said.

'You know,' Alan said, 'when he did finally die, I didn't believe it until I had actually seen his body.'

CHAPTER TWENTY-THREE

THE END

On Friday morning, 23 September 1989, some time around 10.00am, Alan Sperling, the eldest son of a man who had survived two Nazi death camps and four concentration camps, was observing his father with suspicion. It was an unusually clear and beautiful morning in Glasgow, and sunlight streamed in through the windows of Hershl's latest home on Laigh Road, in Newton Mearns. In spite of having his own home around the corner, Alan had moved back in with his father. Hershl was already out of bed and dressed, which was unusual in itself for this time of day, and he informed Alan he was going out to buy a pack of cigarettes.

'I thought that he was planning something, so I said I would go with him,' Alan said. 'He accused me again of being like a camp guard and a kapo, which I found particularly insulting – but I went anyway, because I was worried about him.' Father and son got into the car together. Instead of turning left at the end of Laigh Road to go to the nearest store, Hershl turned right and pulled into the service station on the Old Mearns Road. Alan got out and filled up his father's car with petrol for him, and then he got back into the passenger seat.

'He had obviously worked it all out in advance,' Alan said. 'As soon as I got back in the car, he told me that he had forgotten his wallet. So I got back out of the car and went inside to pay for the petrol.'

'Then what happened?' I asked him.

'Well, by the time I'd come back out, he had driven off. Even in the terrible condition he was in, that cunning was something he never lost. It was something ingrained in him from his time in Treblinka. I ran back to the house, normally about a ten-minute walk, even though I knew he wouldn't be there. I'm not sure he'd worked out what he would do next, but certainly his immediate plan was to separate himself from me.'

The terrible last few months that preceded that day in 1989 was a period of torment for Hershl and sorrow for his sons. Before their eyes, their father was transforming from suffering survivor into a *muselmänner*, the term Hershl had used himself when referring to those emaciated souls in the camps who were in the final stage between starvation and death. Hershl might have once been a muselman himself before liberation, when he had been on the brink of death. Now, here he was again, his life hanging by a thread. I asked Sam what he remembered of his father in that condition. The last time Sam saw his father was around two months before his death. He had travelled up from London, where he was living, and had been shocked to discover how much his father had deteriorated in the months since his last visit.

'I can tell you about my last image of him,' Sam told me. 'He was sitting in a chair, a distance from the television, but he wasn't really watching it. There was no movement in his body. His head didn't move. His eyes didn't even move. It's difficult to explain. They were completely empty.'

'Like a *muselmänner*,' I said.

'Exactly. There was something that he was absorbed in, but it wasn't here. He had gone back to the camps. I could see that clearly. It was very disturbing. I remember getting very angry and shouting at him. I remember saying that he should never have had children, that he had had no right, and after a while he just said, 'You're right.' I was getting angry to try to get a reaction out of him, but even those two words were an effort. Eventually I just left; I thought he might snap out of it, because we were used to the cycles of depression he went through.'

But there was no recovery this time. Over the next few weeks, he sat, drank whisky, popped pills, gazed into emptiness and slept. Sometimes, he lifted his head in flashing moments of lucidity and told Alan: 'This is worse than Treblinka.' I asked Alan what he remembered about the final disappearance.

'You know, the whole business lasted for three or four days, but now it has merged into one for me.' I could hear the emotion crack his voice.

'If you want me to call back another time I can. I know this is difficult for you.'

'I think I called the police immediately and I explained the circumstances to them. I can't stress to you enough the inevitability of this. He had tried to go off somewhere and kill himself before, but more recently he had simply stayed in bed and taken overdoses of pills and I had always been there to call the ambulance.'

The police arrived at the house 'fairly rapidly', Alan recalled. They were told about Hershl's condition, about how he had suffered in Treblinka and Auschwitz, and his previous suicide attempts. Alan also gave them the name and telephone number of Hershl's doctor, so they could verify his psychological state. Then the police left. In the afternoon, when still no word had come, Alan telephoned Sam in London.

'I was going to come up to Glasgow, but we decided that I'd better stay put, in case my father had decided to drive to London,' said Sam. Later that day, the police called Alan to report that Hershl had not yet been found and they asked if he was agreeable to a missing person alert and a photograph being shown on the local television news. Alan agreed. A series of small articles also appeared in the local *Glasgow Evening Times*, complete with Hershl's physical description, an inaccurate age and a dubious paragraph about frogmen searching the waterways and coastline at Ayr. And so began the long hours and days of waiting and worrying.

Sam recalled, 'The longer we waited and because the police hadn't found him yet, the more we became afraid that maybe he wasn't dead, but had somehow damaged himself.' On the second day, Hershl's car was discovered in the parking lot of the Whitecraigs Golf Club, 500 yards from Whitecraigs train station. That day, the police also received a call from someone who had recognised Hershl on the station platform two days earlier, possibly from the photograph on the missing person alert on the television news. Then something strange occurred. The following morning, several police arrived at Alan's house and asked for permission to search his premises.

Alan said, 'They searched the house and went up to the loft, but of course my father wasn't there. Then they asked if they could remove the carpets and lift the floorboards. It was obvious now that I was under suspicion. But I'd had enough of this. I told them if they wanted to lift the floor, they would need a warrant. So they left and didn't come back again. But I know they also talked to the neighbours, because some of them spoke to me later and told me the police had made it clear to them that I was under suspicion.'

'That does seem a little odd,' I said, 'given your father's history.'

'I was extremely irritated by their attitude. They were utterly unsympathetic and suspicious. Considering what my father had been through and his mental condition, their attitude was ludicrous. I had even given them the name and address of his doctor, so they could verify his psychological state. They appeared incompetent. They were just wasting time, especially now that I know he didn't kill himself right away. Until you told me, I hadn't known he'd been in Glasgow for four days. The fact that they didn't find the car for two days, even though it was parked just yards away from the train station, says it all to me. In spite of all this, I already knew what the end would be.'

★ ★ ★

I began to wonder why Hershl had not killed himself right away. Did he still feel that he was immortal? Now, at 62 years old, it was as if he had lived a thousand years and more, and so much of it in unfathomable loneliness. I was trying now to imagine how empty my world would be if it had been revealed to me at fifteen how truly terrible and murderous the human race was.

In the end, he may simply have concluded that hope was useless. It was a virus that had been transmitted to his sons. The fragile optimism Hershl felt after liberation in Dachau turned to bitter disillusionment when it became clear that the world had not changed and it had not learned. The old order had remained in place. There was still anti-Semitism, although it was cloaked in anti-Israel sentiment. There was still the hatred that had been behind every kind of cruelty imaginable. Maybe Hershl's brooding thoughts and his memories simply drove him insane. Only those who had the ability to forget and pretend were allowed to live. Numerous Holocaust studies suggest this. Because Hershl remembered, he was doomed.

There was one final task that needed to be accomplished. I had the strongest sense that he had wanted to return to Treblinka and to bear witness one last time. Yet only the *muselmänner*, the living dead, could truly bear witness, because they had been closer to death and had still lived. And so, he made his way to the Caledonian Rail Bridge and climbed inside, where he could be near to people who were closest to those in the camps – the dispossessed, the lonely and the desperate. We do not know if he conversed with any of them, but he could see them, hear them and be close to them.

He wandered the city streets and slept for four nights in the belly of the bridge with the other vagrants. The thought of him there, and wandering the city, in a drunken and drugged haze for four and a half days still comes back to me at unexpected hours, if only because it continued to disturb his sons. I wondered now if it meant that he agonised over the final decision? Or did it mean that his intention was not to kill himself, but simply to 'go back'?

Alan asked me, 'Did you know that my father was a strong swimmer?'

I had not known. Although strong swimmers are less strong when fully clothed in cold water, and even less so when under the influences of whisky and Diazepam, the bridge from which he tumbled spanned a distance of no more than 200 feet over calm waters. This suggested to me he had not died in the water by accident.

At 3.30pm on Tuesday 26 September, Hershl fell from the iron girder he was lying on. If he was conscious his natural instinct would have been to swim, to raise his head and gasp for breath. Perhaps what followed was an act of courage – Hershl kept his head down in the water. Perhaps the exhaustion he felt, the effect of the pills and the alcohol made it easier for him to make peace with death. I wonder if he felt a sense of pleasure as he abandoned the struggle for life. He no longer had to hold on.

Although George Parsonage, the lifeboat officer of the Glasgow Humane Society, was alerted by the city's police about 4.00pm and he later concluded that Hershl's death had occurred a half-an-hour earlier, Alan was not notified until later that evening. It was already dark when the phone call came from the police, marking the end of four-and-a-half terrible days of worry. 'It seemed as though it was late at night when the police called me, but it is difficult to be exact about the time during that period,' Alan said.

'The exact time doesn't matter,' I said. 'It's all right.'

He proceeded in staccato sentences. I knew it was a strategy to fight back the sadness that now seemed to overwhelm him. I felt terrible for putting him through this interview.

'I remember it was dark,' Alan said. 'A police car came to the house and took me to the morgue. It was somewhere on Pollokshaws Road. I was taken to a glass or Perspex window, where I identified the body. Only his head was showing. The rest of him was covered up. It was enough. I turned and walked away down the corridor. I was immensely sad, but to be honest I was also ambivalent. When my mother died, I was devastated, destroyed. No-one wanted to live more than my mother. But with my father, well, again, I cannot stress enough the inevitability of it. He wanted to die. I remember thinking as I walked away that it was such a huge irony that he had survived the camps and now here he was lying in a morgue in Glasgow.' The emotion now completely overwhelmed him and Alan began to choke on the memory. He began to speak, but then stopped himself. 'I'm sorry,' he said. 'This is difficult.' Then he added: 'I remember that he used to tell me how he wanted to die in the camps.'

'Did he say anything about the circumstances surrounding those feelings then?'

'When planes flew overhead,' Alan said. 'I suppose it must have been in Auschwitz or Dachau. The prisoners hoped they were Allied planes, and that they would bomb the camp. It didn't matter if they were killed too. They were prepared to die, because all they wanted was to put an end to the camps. It was worse in Treblinka. Now, when I think about what he saw in Treblinka and the things he had to do to stay alive …' Alan's voice broke, then suddenly he became silent. 'I'm very sorry,' he said again. 'I still find this extremely upsetting. But I believe I have to tell you these things.'

I understood how the sight of Hershl in the morgue had aroused terrible conflicting emotions in Alan. Death was what his father had wanted – but how wrong it is and how unjust is the world we lived in.

The following night, Sam said to me, 'I think it's probably the same for all the people who died in the Holocaust. People cared at first, for a little while, then they forgot about it. It's the same as the way people might see a car accident on the road. At first, they're disturbed by the carnage, but then they pass by it and it's gone.'

★ ★ ★

There is no clear Biblical or Talmudic law against suicide. The Bible mentions only two suicides – King Saul on Mount Gilboa and David's counsellor, Ahitophel. In Saul's final battle, he faced certain defeat and suffered terrible despair. According to the Biblical account, what followed was an unsuccessful suicide attempt, in which the first king of Israel fell on his sword. In terrible agony, Saul asked a nearby soldier to slay him. The soldier finished the job, and thereby assisted Saul's suicide. In Jewish thought, Saul has been a pardonable prototype for suicides under stress ever since. Nowhere does the Talmud speak of suicide as a sin, although the post-Talmudic booklet Semachot states that those who commit suicide should receive no burial rites. Nonetheless, only those who take their own life with a clear mind should be treated as a suicide, while at the same time suicide as a freely chosen act has more or less been defined out of existence by mental health considerations. And while suicide remains a heinous offence in Judaism, Jewish law insists there must be absolute certainty. The presumption of suicide is not enough.

The funeral took place the following day, according to Jewish law, and Rabbi Philip Greenberg, who conducted the ceremony, made no mention of suicide – or even the overwhelming likelihood of suicide. The sun still shone, extending the rare Indian summer in Glasgow for one more day. The grave had already been dug by the time the mourners arrived. Felicia and Sylvia were there. All the mourners gathered in the small room near the entrance to the cemetery. It was a much smaller group than had attended the funeral of his wife eleven years earlier. The closed casket was just a simple pine box, for ostentation is not permitted at the funeral of a Jew. My people believe that, even after death, the body, which once held a holy human life, retains its sanctity.

Rabbi Greenberg, who was then the rabbi of Giffnock Synagogue, tore the garments of Sam and Alan, and recited a blessing – 'Baruch atah Hashem Elokeinu melech haolam, dayan ha'emet'; 'Blessed are you, Lord our God, Ruler of the universe, the true Judge.' Later, the same blessing was recited by all mourners at the graveside. Hershl had not believed in God for many years, but he would have been familiar with, and perhaps even comforted by, the ancient practice. He had lived as a Jew, suffered as a Jew and would be buried as a Jew.

Alan said: 'If there had been even the slightest suggestion that he was going to be buried differently because of the likelihood of suicide, I would have gone crazy. I would have seen to it that nothing like that ever happened.'

'Do you remember much about the funeral, or was it all a bit of a blur?' I asked.

'No, I remember it quite well,' Alan said. 'Before the burial, Rabbi Greenberg gave a eulogy in the waiting room at the cemetery. It was ridiculous, because he had not known my father at all, and he seemed to have just picked up a few things about my father from the people there. At one point, he even forgot my father's name for a period of time – I don't know how long it was, but it was embarrassingly long. It was a very long silence, before someone reminded him.'

'Do you remember what was said?'

'He started to speak about the war and the camps, and about some of my father's experiences, but only in very general terms. I remember he said that the fact that my father's two sons were present at the funeral was evidence that, in spite of all his suffering, Hitler had not won.'

'I see,' I said.

'I remember thinking, given the way I was feeling and the way my life had been up until now, how hollow his words were.'

The following day, I called Sam and asked him about his recollections of the funeral. 'We're almost finished with these questions.'

Sam sighed deeply. 'It's all right,' he said. 'I felt nothing.'

Hershl's body, dressed in a simple white shroud and ritually cleansed in its wooden casket, was wheeled out of the room and into the cemetery. The mourners followed. At last, the body was lowered into the grave. The Kaddish, the Jewish prayer for the dead, was said. Earth was shovelled on to the casket. The back of the shovel was used, which, according to Jewish tradition, shows reluctance to bury a loved one. Covering the casket with earth is considered an honour, because it is something that can be done for the deceased but cannot be reciprocated. It is considered a selfless act.

Sam said: 'I remember the feeling of emptiness, but there was also relief. My father had wanted to die.' Hershl's long years of suffering had come to an end. I wondered now about all the ghosts that he carried on his back for so many years. What would become of all those memories and where would those ghosts go now? Sam and Alan did not deserve them.

In spite of Rabbi Greenberg's insistence that their presence at their father's funeral was evidence enough that the Nazis' plan to annihilate the world's Jews had failed, he appeared deeply disturbed on the journey from the cemetery. He was riding in a car with Felicia and Sylvia and they were discussing Hershl's tragedy. After a long silence, the rabbi shook his head and, according to Felicia's recollection, he said: 'Maybe Hitler did win after all.'

CHAPTER TWENTY-FOUR

HOPE

During my visit to Warsaw in February 2007, I went to visit Michael Schudrich, the chief rabbi of Poland, at Nozyk Synagogue on Twarda Street, on a brutally cold, white winter's day. I had come with the dual aim of researching Nazi terror for this book and to write a newspaper article on an extraordinary Judaic revival that was occurring in Poland. Nozyk, the only synagogue in Warsaw not destroyed by the Nazis, was now the epicentre of the revival. It seemed to me a phenomenon that defied Hitler's vision of a Jew-free Europe – especially in the country that had once been the beating heart of European Jewry and where the slaughter had been keenest.

I arrived at the synagogue as Warsaw dragged itself to work. Outside, commuters pushed into tramcars. Except for the old town, which has been meticulously re-made, brick by brick, it was hard to imagine the beautiful and vibrant city it once was.

Earlier that morning, I had taken a stroll through Praga, a district on the other side of the Vistula. This is one of the few places in Warsaw that retains the physical touch of history. I entered a Communist-era milk bar, housed in a 1920s or 1930s building, stoned-faced and pockmarked. While ordering a drink, the waitress disconcertingly referred to the old town as the 'Ayrian side' and I wondered what she meant by the remark – whether it was a pejorative view of the old town or a comment on the growing sense of 'cool' of Praga itself. A Jewish community had established itself in Praga in the eighteenth century, and was centred around Szeroka and Petersburska streets – now Jagiellonska and Klopotowska streets. Praga's famed stone synagogue was built in 1836 and was one of only six circular masonry buildings in all of Europe. The Nazis turned it into a delousing centre. After the war, the building housed the offices of the Central Jewish Committee in Poland – the sister organisation of the group that published Hershl's testimony in 1948. In 1961, the building was demolished amid considerable Jewish protest. A public high school now sits on the site.

With the murder of its Jews, Warsaw and the entire country ultimately lost the multi-national character that had been its treasure for centuries. In 1939, there were almost 400,000 Jews in Warsaw alone, around one in three of the population. A decade ago, there didn't seem to be any at all. But there were now more than 500 who apparently had always been there, and that number was increasing.

Almost every week, another secret Jew came out of the closet and appeared before Schudrich in a state of turmoil. Here in Warsaw, and also in other Polish cities, this had become such a recurring event it led Schudrich to conclude he was in the middle of an important historic phenomenon. Yet the circumstances that brought these people to him were always extraordinary and shocking.

The month before, two teenagers came to visit Schudrich. They were a brother and sister. A few weeks earlier, their father had been hit by a car while crossing the street. He was taken to a hospital, where he subsequently fell into a coma. A few days later, surrounded by his family, he awoke and began singing a song in Yiddish. Then he died. His astonished children began probing relatives, who eventually confirmed that, yes, they were secret Jews – their parents had concealed their heritage and faith from their own offspring.

A few months earlier, an 80-year-old man wandered in off the street and into the rabbi's office. He then proceeded to drop his trousers and revealed that he had been circumcised. He, too, was a secret Jew. On another occasion, a 22-year-old skinhead named Pawel, an adherent of extreme right-wing Polish nationalist politics, informed Schudrich – rather embarrassedly – that he had been privy to the deathbed confession of his grandmother. The former skinhead, whose grandmother had also been a secret Jew, was now one of Nozyk Synagogue's most observant congregation members. His parents had turned their back on Jewish life and they had never told him about his background.

Yet another was Mati Pawlak, Schudrich's assistant and the country's first Polish-born ordained rabbi since the 1930s. He did not learn until he was fourteen that his family was Jewish, in spite of some early clues. He was the only child in his school whose mother kept him out of Catholic religious classes.

Schudrich now swept into Nozyk, this imposing, but almost hidden one-hundred-year-old building that survived the war only because the Nazis had used it as a stable for their horses. There was an air of mayhem about him. The rabbi's long scarf and overcoat flew behind him as an entourage of secretaries and well-wishers tried to keep pace. I joined the train and followed him up two flights of stairs into his study. His cell phone rang incessantly. He seemed to switch between English, Polish, Hebrew and Yiddish without thinking. Schudrich switched off his cell phone and put it on his desk.

'That was another one,' he said.

'Another secret Jew?' I asked.

'It really is like they're coming out of the closet. Now sit down.'

I looked around a room, cluttered with books, documents, scraps of paper and items of clothing, and saw nowhere to sit. On the wall by the door, a photograph of Schudrich shaking hands with the Polish Pope, John Paul II, drew attention to itself. He swept a crumpled bundle of clothing onto the floor and gestured to me to sit.

'I just flew in from New York and my arms are killing me,' Schudrich joked, loosening his tie and removing his overcoat, before collapsing in a chair in front of me. A rabbi needs a sense of humour here, I thought. 'Actually,' he added, 'my ankles are swollen. Now, what can I do for you?'

I wanted to know what was happening in this country more than half a century after the Holocaust. Why, of all places, was a revival occurring here? I also wanted to know what the future held for this fragile but ancient community of Jews. While the vast majority of the world's Jews can trace their ancestry here, Poland is a country where anti-Semitism was – and, to some extent, still is – virulent. For many, Poland is a graveyard, even cursed ground. In 2008, there were an estimated 15,000 Jews in a total population of 40 million, a tiny fraction of one per cent. Yet they continue to loom large in the Polish psyche. I still saw anti-Semitic graffiti on the walls and, the previous year, Schudrich was punched in the chest and sprayed with pepper spray by a young man shouting 'Poland for the Poles' in central Warsaw. The incident made national headlines.

'There was no question that it was an anti-Semitic incident. But what the papers didn't report was that I punched the guy back. I'm a New Yorker,' Schudrich said.

'Where have all these new Jews come from?' I asked him.

'In the very beginning, I became fascinated by the question of what was really left in Poland after the war,' said Schudrich, who first visited this former Eastern bloc nation in 1973 as a student, decades after his grandparents had left the country. 'Everyone said there was nothing, just a few old Jews. I felt it didn't make sense, there had to be something. Imagine going back to Spain in the 1540s, 50 years after the beginning of the inquisition. How many of the hidden Jews could you prevent from disappearing into history? This is the exact modern-day equivalent. When these people come to me with their family histories and their secrets, I don't tell them they're Jewish and they have to come to the synagogue. How could I? All I can do is give them choices. If they want to become part of the community here, they're welcome.'

'How about Polish anti-Semitism? I can't help wonder how these Jews can continue to live among it, after all that has happened here?'

'There is anti-Semitism in every country, but citizens here are not desecrating Jewish cemeteries or attacking Jews in the street, the way they have done recently in Germany, France and in Britain. Of course there is anti-Semitism in Poland. But you have to remember 50 years ago, 95 per cent of Poles were anti-Semitic. Now that figure is probably down to fifteen per cent.'

'Can you tell me how this happened?' I asked.

'There are two different phenomena going on – both parallel and complementary,' said Schudrich. 'The first phenomenon is this. Until September 1939, Poland was the centre of the Jewish world. It was a huge and vibrant community – religiously, culturally, socially, you name it, everything. You couldn't go twenty feet in the street without bumping into a Jew. They were part of the landscape, and like any large group of people – there were about three-and-a-half million of them – some were good and some were bad, some were religious and some assimilated, but they lived in a normal multicultural society, where the various groups all had contact with each other.

'Then the Nazis came and killed 90 per cent of them. That means ten per cent survived, about 350,000 people. But then after the war, Communism came, and it was made clear that if you wanted to stay Jewish you had to leave the country. In the 25 years after the war, about 250,000 Jews left. That means 100,000 stayed, but they went underground and they kept their religion, their culture and their heritage a secret.

'That was one or two generations ago. The steady stream of people we are seeing now are the children and grandchildren of Holocaust survivors, who feel more free and are gradually discovering their roots since the fall of Communism at the end of 1989.'

'And the second phenomenon?'

'Pope John Paul did an extraordinary thing – he declared that anti-Semitism was a sin. They even have a national Judaism day in Poland now. I can't begin to tell you the impact that had. Almost overnight, centuries of hatred were reversed.'

'This is an extraordinary community you are nurturing here,' I said.

He looked squarely at me, and said seriously, 'It's a victory over Hitler.'

I wondered what Hershl would have thought of it all. I suspect he would not have trusted it; Alan is certain of it. I suspect he would have told me that human beings always behave decently during times of social and economic stability, that they could afford to be magnanimous in the good times, but the real test of human nature is how they behave during times of hardship. It was then that all the old hatreds and jealousies manifested themselves. Yet Schudrich's parting comment seemed to evoke Felicia's recollection of Rabbi Greenberg's remarks during the funeral and then the reversal he made later in the car. 'Maybe Hitler did win,' Greenberg had said.

It struck me now, as I sat in front of my computer in Scotland, that Hershl's suicide – that he should have survived one of the worst of all possible Holocaust experiences and then throw himself in the river so many years later – was proof that Greenberg had been right. Yet, from the outset of my investigation, I was driven by the ancient words of the Jerusalem Talmud: 'Whoever saves a single life, it is as if he has saved the whole world.' This maxim was pinned to the wall above my desk during the many months I worked, and sometimes at night it assailed my dreams. I could not face the idea of victory for the murderer.

I had desperately wanted to know if anything could have been done to save Hershl's life. I became obsessed with the idea that, even hypothetically, if I could discover a way to save Hershl's life, I could save others in a similar situation and ultimately save the world. At the same time, I entertained the notion that somehow, by filling in the details of their father's life and by drawing the right meaning from it, I could also save Alan and Sam. Their survival, too, had hung in the balance in recent years and their attempts to take their own lives had been evidence enough for me that the evil of Hitler's legacy persisted. Yet I now understood that my hopes were nothing more than the naïve ambitions of a dreamer who could not understand, because he had not been touched personally by the Holocaust. If the tyrant's primary ambition had been the annihilation of the Jewish people, what further proof of victory did we need than the attempted suicides of a victim's children more than half a century after Hitler's own death? As if to compound my failure, I remembered Alan had warned me a few weeks earlier. 'No book can ever save a single human life,' he said.

A few weeks later, I lay awake late at night. I remembered trudging through the snow at Treblinka, the thousands of stone monuments like hunched victims. I thought of all the suffering that place had seen. How could I have been so naïve as to imagine Hershl's story could change anything? I thought of Barry, the dog that had belonged to Kurt Franz, Treblinka's sadistic deputy commander. I recalled the accounts from former prisoners about how Barry would mangle prisoners on the order, 'Man, get that dog'. Franz no doubt considered the command to be appropriately dehumanising and amusing; it expressed the depth of his hatred of the Jewish *Sonderkommando*, and all Jews and other so-called enemies of the Reich. To Franz, a dog was better than a Jew. I had been surprised to learn Barry had been a St Bernard, a gentle-natured breed most often asso-ciated with the rescue of human lives. In Treblinka, the animal was a monster.

I got up and drew aside the curtains. In Treblinka, Hershl had seen the potential monster in all of us, borne of hatred. I recalled a line from F. Scott Fitzgerald's *The Great Gatsby*: 'So we beat on, boats against the current, borne back ceaselessly into the past.' In the decades that have elapsed between Treblinka and the time in which I write these words, the world has changed very little. Anti-Semitism, in all its irra-tionality, persists. Hatred persists, too. The Holocaust did not prevent the genocides of Cambodia, Rwanda, Darfur or Srebrenica. Every mass human slaughter has been achievable only by harnessing the ever-present hatred of many individuals. In Darfur and Rwanda and in the Balkans, there must be thousands of Hershl Sperlings and thousands of Alans and Sams. We now live in a world where bloodthirsty dictators are brought to justice in courts of human rights, where war criminals are hunted and where responsible nations monitor the movements of tyrants and deploy UN peacekeepers. Our world is one of increasing global scrutiny. But, in the great tally of human suffering and the towering heaps of dead, none of it has made one blind bit of difference. In that moment, as the storm raged over the Campsie Hills, it felt as though the whole world had killed Hershl Sperling.

I went into the living room and sat in the darkness for a while. It was cold and late, and I wrapped a blanket around me. It was the middle of the night, but I felt an overwhelm-ing desire now to talk to my friend. I looked at the clock and saw that it read 2.20am, yet I found myself dialling Sam's number. He picked up almost as soon as it began ringing.

'Hello,' he said, slowly.

'It's me,' I answered. 'Did I wake you?'

'No, it's all right. I was just listening to music and reading.'

'I can't get your father's story out of my head,' I said. Then I blurted out the absurdly massive question that now plagued me, 'Is there no hope for humankind?' I asked.

Sam puffed on a cigarette, 'I think all you can do is tell people what they are,' he said. 'There doesn't necessarily have to be hope.' He continued, 'If you were to ask me if I thought that the human race would still be in existence in, say, another 50,000 years, I would have to say no. We haven't been on the planet very long, and look at what we do to each other.'

'I just can't understand why it has to be that way,' I said.

'Now you're starting to sound like my father,' Sam said, 'Maybe it's something to do with Treblinka, the way the place infects you. Maybe it's the way anyone feels who has been touched by the Holocaust.'

Hershl's suicide should not surprise anyone. I thought now of the other post-Holocaust suicides I had read about over the past year. I recalled Treblinka survivor Richard Glazer, who wrote of the 'little death' he died every day during his years of freedom. Glazer committed suicide in Prague on 20 December 1997. I also thought about the better-known suicides of Primo Levi and fellow Auschwitz survivor Jean Amery, whose experiences had been less appalling than Hershl's.

'What if each of us is born not with innate hatred in us, but merely the capac-ity to hate, like a cup not filled? What if this cup can only be filled by our parents?

What we experience as children makes us what we are as adults. Isn't that your father's story? He was only twelve when the Nazis marched into Klobuck. He was fifteen in Treblinka. I have a strong feeling that anti-Semitism, and all other racial hatreds and intolerances can only be passed from our parents. It just seems to me that all we have to do is teach our children not to hate. Every time we resist hatred and each time we teach tolerance to our children, we make the future of the world that much better.'

'I think that's too much to hope for,' Sam said.

'How can you be sure?' I asked – but as I posed the question, I thought about Sam and Alan's difficult, troubled lives, and how Hitler's murderous and hateful legacy had not ended for their father and neither could it ever end for them. I had always understood that in return for the Holocaust nightmare – particularly the experience of Treblinka – Hershl had been granted the gift of deep human knowledge, which, from the moment of their births, had been transmitted to his children. Sam and Alan both understood intuitively that men are beasts and that our civilisations are mere facades.

Sam said, 'I think each of us have cups of hate and cups of good, if you like, which are already full when we are born. It just depends on what kind of person you are and the extent to which we use the contents of these cups.'

'But aren't children born innocent, with a world of hope before them?' I argued.

'I think of it all like a bell curve,' he said. 'The great mass of the human population appear to occupy the middle. These people represent the herd, and seem to be capable of being persuaded toward either direction, toward good or evil. Only a few people seem to be inherently good or evil, and these two extreme groups sit in those little bits that flick out at either side of the bell curve.'

'If what you say is true, then there is nothing anyone can do about truly evil people – people like Hitler and even Franz Stangl, people who may not even have killed anyone personally but were responsible for millions of murders – apart from perhaps try to stop them.'

'That's it,' said Sam. 'But we also need to think about the people on the good side of the bell curve, like the farmer who helped Rajzman, or that SS officer my father mentioned, the one who came to Treblinka and couldn't believe what he saw? In the end, he was probably killed or sent to the Russian front because he refused to participate. Both of them behaved in a way that was contrary to the logic of survival, probably because they were simply good people.'

'But those people who are naturally evil still need the great mass of the population in the middle of the curve to carry out their evil acts. What if the cup is what the masses get from nature and the hate that goes into it is what they get from nurture?'

★ ★ ★

The next morning, I went for a walk in the hills near my house. I recalled a telephone conversation I'd had with Alan a few days previously.

'I'm sorry, I should have told you about this before,' Alan said, 'but I've just worked this out.'

'Tell me,' I said.

'Well, there was a period of about ten days – I think it was 1961 – during which my father went away on a trip,' Alan said. 'Sam was very young. I remember he was still in his pram. My mother was in an absolute panic and fraught with worry, which was out of character for her. My father said he was going to testify at a trial in Switzerland, and there was all this talk about him having to be careful because it was the middle of the Algerian War and he had to travel through France.' He paused for a moment, as if struck by sudden emotion.

'Go on, please,' I said.

'Well, I don't know if he went to testify at a trial. The more I think about it, I'm almost certain he went back to Treblinka. When I think about how worried my mother was and my father's reaction when he returned …'

In spite of weeks of digging, I could find no trial in Switzerland, or anywhere else for that matter, at which Hershl could have testified.

'What was his reaction?' I asked.

'He was down,' Alan said, quickly. 'He was very down.'

'I see. Can you tell me why you think he went back?'

'I'm sorry I didn't tell you this before,' he repeated.

'It's OK,' I said. 'You can tell me now.'

'I think he went to pay his last respects and to say he was sorry to the people he could not save. It's the only thing that makes any sense.'

'Do you think going back to Treblinka might have helped him in any way?' There was exasperation in his voice.

'Look,' he said, 'nothing could help him.'

Not long after I returned home from my walk, Sam telephoned.

'I called to talk to you about hope. I was thinking about what you said yesterday, about how you wanted to end your book with hope. The only hopeful thing I could think of that may have come out of the Holocaust is that maybe guilt about the Holocaust has helped save lives.'

'Do you believe that's true, given all the genocides that have occurred since the end of the World War II?'

'I think you have to be clear about European guilt, which is special because of its history. It's possible that it saved lives in the Balkans by forcing international intervention – like NATO's bombing of Serbs in Bosnia and Kosovo, for example – earlier than might have otherwise been the case.'

'But Sam, what about your life? And what about the life of your brother and your father? What about the lives of all those family members who died in the gas chambers? I have to ask you directly: Did Hitler win – maybe not in the context of all the world, but for you and your family?' I heard the flick of his cigarette lighter at the other end of the line, and I waited in the silence that followed. The pause seemed longer than usual.

'I think the only way Hitler could have won was to have succeeded in the complete annihilation of the Jewish people, and he didn't do that. I suppose you could argue that he succeeded at a personal level, because Alan and I have decided not to have children.'

'Alan told me that you both decided independently long ago not to have children, that it was because of the suffering your father had passed on to you and Alan, that neither of you wanted to pass that on to your children.'

'That's true,' he said. 'But we have cousins and friends, like you, who have children. And to know that is enough for me. It's enough to defeat Hitler.'

'And what about your father? Was his suicide a victory for Hitler?' I asked.

He said, 'Funnily enough, when I gave a draft of my father's story to a friend of mine to read, she commented that one major reason it hadn't been a victory for Hitler was because he didn't manage to remove my father's humanity.'

'It's possible, I think, your father defeated Hitler by refusing to take revenge. You know, when he first came out of the camps and dreamed about vengeance, when he thought about killing Germans indiscriminately in revenge for all those he had seen led to the gas chambers, and the murder of those he had loved and all the terrible things he'd endured himself, he didn't do it in the end. That proves that Hitler's hatred had not infected him. I think it also proves maybe that he could not be infected,' I said. 'I think that to have murdered indiscriminately, the way the Nazis did, a person needs a certain amount of hate and a certain amount of fear. I think he had neither.'

'It's true what you say. But it's true of a lot of people. A lot of survivors didn't take revenge after they got out of the camps.'

'But not all of them felt they had to take their own lives.' I paused for a moment, then added, 'Maybe, Sam, that's why he died in the end, because he was one of those good people at the side of the bell curve. Maybe he was just a good man in a bad world and in the end he couldn't cope with that. Maybe the only person he could kill was himself.'

Sam puffed on his cigarette, 'That's good enough for me,' he said. A moment passed and he added: 'Actually it makes me proud.'

After he hung up, I felt the strangest sensation that Hershl had finally, after all those years, been laid peacefully to rest. I closed my eyes, and words I now remembered from an accompaniment to the Jewish prayer for the dead on the Day of Atonement came flooding back:

Man born of woman, his days are short,
yet he has his fill of sorrow.
Frail man, his days are like the grass,
he blossoms like a flower in the field;
but the breeze passes over it and it is gone
and its place knows it no more.

… So mark the man of integrity, and watch the upright,
for the end of such a man is peace.

PIECING TOGETHER A LIFE

All the people and events depicted in this book are real. The issues that are dealt with are also real and they are very important to me. Hershl's story is another piece of the Holocaust jigsaw, which, if not told, would vanish from twentieth-century history. He was one of the few surviving witnesses to live through so much of the Nazi horror – from the first day of the Polish invasion and the subsequent depravations of Częstochowa ghetto, through to Treblinka, Auschwitz-Birkenau and Dachau. The courage of his escape from Treblinka amid an uprising that razed one of the most horrendous death factories in the history of humanity cannot be overstated. He was one of the very few to have left us authentic testimony. His story is part of the fabric of what really happened all those years ago.

The form this book has ultimately taken has permitted its characters, some of whom remain very dear to me, to tell their version of events and their thoughts in their own way. In essence, I have allowed three people to tell this story: Firstly, Hershl himself; but when Hershl's voice falls silent, his sons Alan and Sam step in. They fill the emptiness with their words and wisdom, which could so easily be the voice of their father.

For a long time, I was concerned that I would be unable to render an accurate enough portrait of Hershl Sperling. In my dreams over the past year, I have often seen Hershl's face staring out at me, his gentle green eyes watching. I know that he ached for the arms of loved ones from a time too short-lived. There is a parallel between Hershl's shattered life and my own hunt for the thousands of shards to piece it back together. I was often disturbed by the knowledge that I would never be able to find all the disparate fragments and therefore could not create a true replica of all that had existed. Then my eleven-year-old son said something that stunned me. 'Dad, when you break a mirror, you can still see your face in every single piece that's broken.' It gradually dawned on me that I did not need to find every lost piece of Hershl's shattered life, because his image was stamped in each of the fragments I already had.

APPENDIX

HERSHL'S TESTIMONY

What follows is an English translation by Heather Valencia of Hershl Sperling's personal testimony relating to his ten months in Treblinka. It is one of only a handful of eyewitness accounts. In the months that followed the revolt, the remnants of the camp were systematically dismantled by the Nazis and removed. A farm was built on the site to disguise what it had been. So thorough was the Nazi cover-up that Holocaust deniers today continue to dispute its very existence. Without Hershl Sperling's written record, and those of other eyewitnesses to the carnage of Treblinka, these denials would have greater power. For this reason alone, Hershl's testimony has incalculable worth. The work was written at the latest, some eighteen months after liberation – probably before that. The events that Hershl describe were fresh in his mind. The tone of writing comes across as matter-of-fact and remarkably balanced, given the subject matter and the dreadfulness of the experience itself. Its focus is the systematic killings and the atrocities carried out by the Nazis and their accomplices, but also the vulnerability of the elderly, of mothers and children. However, below the surface runs another current. There is also pain and the sense that this is a kind of internal conversation, and an act of identification, with those who did not survive. Although it is a translation, the grammar of the work – although at times erratic – has generally been left as published, to retain historical veracity.

TREBLINKA BY HERSHL SPERLING

In September 1942, the deportation of the Jews of Częstochowa began. We had already sensed it coming weeks before. The town was surrounded by SS units. We are all woken from sleep before daybreak by the noise of wild shooting, vehicles, and people screaming and wailing. We look out into the street and see the SS men savagely bursting into people's houses and driving the occupants out into the street with blows from their rifle-butts. We watch them arbitrarily dividing up people after a superficial glance at their work-permits; a very small minority of them is assigned to work, and the rest are transported away en masse. Some kind of premonition tells us that this is the route to death, and we decide to hide in the bunker, which we had already prepared. Some elderly Jews join us and we lie together, hidden in the bunker, cut off from the world, and discuss our dangerous situation. We don't dare to go out in daylight, but at night we creep out into the fields to find something to eat. There are cabbages, turnips and other vegetables. We bring them back and cook them on an electric stove. At night, when it is dark, we enter the houses of the deported Jews and search through the abandoned rooms.

Our bunker is discovered almost at the end of the period of deportations. Whether we were betrayed by someone, or whether it was purely chance, we don't know. The commander of the deportations, Degenhardt makes a personal appearance and commands us all to leave the bunker. We all comply, because we know if we were discovered during a second search, it will be certain death. We are taken to Pszemiszlaver Street, where the last deportees are just being taken away. Of the seven thousand Jews who are rounded up here, three hundred men and ten women are assigned to a work-detail in Częstochowa. The remainder are forced into a large factory yard. They are destined for the furnace in Treblinka. On the day before the deportation one loaf is distributed to each person, for which they have to pay one zloty. This is a carefully worked out plan of the Germans. According to the number of zlotys they will know the number of people and can estimate how many wagons they need, and how many people should be loaded into each wagon.

At four o'clock in the morning the deportation began. Everyone has to assemble. Everyone has to take off their shoes, tie them together and hang them over their shoulders. Then begins, silent and barefoot, the march to annihilation. At the exit to the factory yard a box has been placed. Under threat of punishment by death, everybody has to throw all their valuables into it. Hardly anyone does it. As they marched on, however, their fear grows. They have second thoughts about it, and from all sides valuables, foreign currency, money and so on are dropped by the wayside. The route of the death-march is littered with Jewish possessions.

When we arrive at the train, the SS shove eighty to hundred people into each of the wagons. The disinfectant calcium chloride is scattered liberally into every wagon. Each wagon receives three small loaves of bread and a little water. Then the doors are pushed shut, locked and sealed. Ukrainian and Lithuanian SS stand guard at the steps of each wagon. We are shut in like cattle, tightly crammed together. Only a tiny bit of air comes in through the one small wire-covered window, so that we can hardly breathe. The calcium chloride hardly helps to combat the unbearable smell, which gets worse all the time. Some women faint and others vomit. The natural functions also have to be performed in the wagon, which makes the situation even more terrible, and on top of everything else we are tormented by a dreadful thirst. We become utterly desperate and keep begging the SS guards to bring us some water. They refuse for a long time but eventually they agree to give us some water, but only for money. We manage to collect a few thousand zlotys and give them to the guards. The SS take the money, but no water appears. Thus, in pain and torment, the journey drags on until we reach Warsaw. There our train is shunted into a siding. It's not until the following morning that we travel on to Malkinia, seven kilometres from Treblinka.

Here we see Poles working in the fields and try to communicate with them. We just want to find out what our fate is going to be. They, however, hardly lift their eyes from their work, and when they do, they just shout one word at us: 'Death!' We're seized by terror. We can't believe it. Our minds simply won't take it in. Is there really and truly no escape for us? One of the Polish workers mentions burnings, another, shootings, and a third – gassings. Another tells of inhuman, unbelievable tortures. An unbearable state of tension mounts among us, which in some cases even leads to outbreaks of hysteria.

However, we don't have much time to think about all this. A special locomotive takes away twenty of the sixty wagons which made up our train. After five minutes it comes back and takes another twenty wagons. A woman beside me is wailing and moaning: 'They're murdered already, they're dead, dead, dead … My God, why has this happened to us?' An icy horror comes over me, and I clench my fists helplessly.

And now the last twenty wagons are being moved. I am in one of them. Slowly we roll on. One can clearly see that the forest here has recently been dug up. Full of trepidation, we roll towards a huge gate guarded by a large number of SS with machine-guns.

The train stops and the escort is commanded to get out and wait there. Then the gate opens and the locomotive shunts all the wagons into the camp. It remains outside. The gate closes behind us. The wagons roll slowly towards the big ramp. Round about it stands an SS unit, ready to receive us with hand-grenades, rubber truncheons and loaded guns. Now the doors of the wagons are flung open and, half-fainting, we are driven out onto the ramp. We can hardly stand, and desperately gulp deep breaths of the fresh air. There is terrible wailing, screaming and weeping. Children are searching for their parents. Weak and sick people are begging for help. Desperate women are tearing out their own hair. But straightaway the SS rush at us and force everyone to move on. The stragglers – the old, the sick, the weak and little children without parents – are either lifted onto stretchers by a squad wearing Red Cross armbands, or helped along. They are all brought into a large building, the so-called 'Lazarett' or infirmary. A fire burns in the middle of the room. On one side stands a long bench. The old, the sick and the children have to strip naked, supposedly for a medical examination. Then they are made to sit on the bench, one beside the other, facing the fire. When they ask what the fire is for, it is explained that it is to keep the room warm so that none of the sick people should catch cold. Then a group of men armed with machine-guns appears behind them. A short, muffled burst of machine-gun fire is heard – and, shot through the head, they all fall into the burning fire. Another work-squad comes immediately and lays new branches on the dead bodies, because new victims are already waiting to be annihilated.

While this was going on, the savage SS herded the rest of the men and women down from the ramp with their truncheons and drove them through a gate leading to a large square. This square is surrounded with barbed wire carefully camouflaged with leafy branches. On the right stands a large open barracks, the women's barracks. On the left stands another high, open barracks for the men. A command rings out: women to the right, men to the left! There are indescribable, heart-breaking farewell scenes, but the SS drive the people apart. The terrified children cling to their mothers. At last the people have been divided into two groups. Then comes the order: undress, and tie your clothes up in a bundle, tie your shoes together in pairs. The huge crowd just stands there as if waiting for something, until the savage SS let fly with their rubber truncheons and force the people to undress. Some more slowly, some more quickly, with greater or lesser degrees of embarrassment, the men and women undress and lay their clothes aside. Some still try to exchange a word with the Jews who are working in the squads in order to find out something about what awaits us. We are told the terrible truth: from this camp no one comes out alive, and there can be no question of escaping; we have come to our death. But we simply can't believe it. The human being is too attached to life, even if the truth of these predictions should be confirmed a thousand times.

At last all the men and women are undressed. We are dying of thirst and scream for a drink of water. But we are not given it, even though there is a well in the middle of the yard, as if to spite us. Now the naked women are driven into the barracks. They do their best to cover their breasts with their arms. At the entrance to the barracks a shearing-squad awaits them. With one cut all the women's hair is hacked off and immediately packed into waiting sacks. Then the women are assembled in groups and, with their hands above their heads, they are led through a back door into the death-camp.

Meanwhile the naked men are forced to pack up all the male and female clothing. Everyone has to carry a heavy load and go at a running pace through another gate into a second huge square surrounded by long, single-storey barracks. The clothing is laid down by the barracks. Then everyone has to get into line, their hands above their heads and, at a marching pace, to the rhythm of the beating rubber truncheons, we go back to the main square. There the men are made to run many times round the square until they are completely exhausted. This is so that, when they are marched to their death they will be so tired that they will not be able to offer any resistance in the death-chamber.

Finally everyone is driven into the men's barracks and towards a door, which leads to the death camp. At the very door 30 men are pulled out, of whom I am one. We are divided into five groups with six men in each. A couple of workers are assigned to each group. We have been chosen to form the work-squads in the camp. For the meantime we are safe.

★ ★ ★

Treblinka consisted of two camps: Camp I, which received the transports, dealt with the plundered goods and prepared the victims to be taken to their deaths; then there was Camp II, the so-called 'death camp' in which the swift and systematic annihilation of the people who had arrived on the transports took place. I was in Camp I, where the work was carried out by various squads. There is the 'blue' squad: its members wear blue armbands and have responsibility for the newly arrived transports at the ramp. This squad has to cleanse the newly arrived wagons of their dead bodies, filth and excrement as quickly as possible. The squad works with brooms. Each pair of workers has to clean out one wagon in ten minutes.

Then there is the red squad – men with a red-cross symbol. Their task is to carry the old, the sick and children up to the age of six, or those who have lost their parents, on stretchers or in their arms from the ramp to the 'death-infirmary'. Apart from these there were also special transport-squads, train-squads, sorting-squads, barracks-camouflage squads and also squads of carpenters, tailors, shoemakers and so on. A kapo was assigned to be in charge of each squad. He was responsible to the *Lagerälteste* [senior camp inmate, or elder].

I belonged to the sorting squad, which had to sort the discarded clothing into better and poorer quality and put them into the appropriate sections of the barracks. Every garment was minutely examined to see whether any valuables were sewn into or hidden in it. From each garment the Star of David had to be removed as carefully as possible so that no one could see it had belonged to a Jew.

Each tin of shoe-polish, each pocket-torch or belt is prised or cut open to find anything of value which might be there. Watches and gold are put in separate piles. The following things are also put in separate piles: diamonds, rings, gold roubles, gold dollars and so on. The collection and sorting of pictures is particularly strictly controlled. For the crime of taking a picture to keep, a Jew was punished by death. Mass shootings took place simply because one of the Jews had hidden on his person a picture of his wife or near relatives. When each bundle was tied up, the Jewish sorter had to put a piece of paper with his name on it in the bundle, so that it would immediately be known which individual to punish for the smallest breach of the regulations. I can still see before me the punishment that was meted out to a nineteen-year-old boy who had forgotten to remove the Star of David from one garment. He is shot dead on the *Appellplatz* before the eyes of the assembled work-squads. He is forced to look directly into the gun-barrel. For making a movement of his head when the final command is given, he gets two brutal blows to the face. A few seconds later, he falls to the ground, his head shattered and is quickly removed.

When each order for clothes comes in, the carefully sorted and packed stolen clothes are sent away. Usually a whole transport will depart with one article. There goes, for instance, a transport consisting entirely of suits, another consisting entirely of women's silk dresses, a third of shoes, and so forth. Gold is loaded onto lorries and taken away separately. The SS units become enormously rich. As compensation for the gruesome work in the camp, they are granted four weeks' leave and always travel dressed in civilian clothes. Each time, they take with them about ten suitcases. They take the best and most expensive clothes and the most beautiful gold and diamond jewellery for their families.

Between Camp I and Camp II, three huge excavators work day and night, piling up huge mountains of earth between the two camps. Day and night, the bright glow of the burning bodies rises up to the sky. It is visible for miles. When the wind blows in the direction of our camp, it brings such a terrible smell that we can't manage to do any work. Only when the wind changes direction can we start doing our normal work again. It was strictly forbidden to cross from one camp to the other. In the early period the food carriers used to come to us from Camp II and bring us all the minute details of the cruel deeds that were being perpetrated there. When we heard about them we choked and our heads whirled feverishly. It often took hours before we could start working again. The tears running down our faces did not alleviate our helpless rage and our searing pain.

The food-carriers describe to us how the path to the death camp goes through a garden. Just before you come to the death-shower there is a hut, where everyone is instructed once again to relinquish money and gold. This is always accompanied by the threat of punishment by death. The greed of the Nazis is such that they won't let even the smallest item of any value slip through their hands. At the shower room of death, which is adorned only by a Star of David, the victims are received with bayonets. They are driven into the shower rooms, prodded with these bayonets. Whereas the men go into the showers in a fairly restrained fashion, terrible scenes take place among the women. Showing no mercy, the only way the SS can think of to quieten the women is with their rifle-butts or bayonets. When all the wretched victims have been forced into the showers, the doors are hermetically sealed. After a few seconds, uncanny, horrifying screams are heard through the walls. These screams go up to heaven, demanding revenge. The screaming becomes weaker and weaker, finally dying away. At last everything is completely silent. Then the doors are opened, and the corpses are thrown into huge mass graves, which hold about 60 to 70 thousand people. When there was no room for any new victims in the mass graves, there came a new command to burn the dead bodies. They would dig out a deep trench, and throw in a few old trunks, boxes, wood and things like that. All that is set alight, and a layer of corpses is thrown onto it, then more branches, and more corpses, and so on. Later the order was given to dig out the dead in the mass graves, and burn them too.

When the corpses, which are already decomposing, are dug up, a considerable amount of money and valuables is found in the stomachs and guts of the victims. This proves that even when looking death in the face, the Jews still believed in life. The smell of blood, the dreadful stench of the decomposing and burnt corpses wafts death itself over the workers of the death-brigade. No one can stomach this work for more than a few weeks. Even the SS units are changed every two weeks, and sent on immediate leave; even the murderers themselves cannot bear this diabolical bestiality.

Later on, communication between the work-squads from the two camps was forbidden. Even during the hand-over of shoes or clothes by the squads of Camp II, our people were only allowed to go up to the border between the camps. There the workers from the death camp would hand over the fearfully stinking, blood-soaked clothing.

Once a large-scale typhus epidemic broke out in Death-Camp II. In order to prevent the spread of the epidemic, the sick people were separated from the others, stripped naked and only allowed to wrap themselves in a blanket. They were driven outdoors and chased up the high piled-up mounds of earth by the death-chambers. There the SS opened fire on them, and the bodies rolled down into the fires which were already burning in the ditches below. Shortly after this, barbed wire fences were erected between the two camps. This work was carried out by the work-squads of both camps. Once again we had the opportunity to pour out our woes to each other, and to lament our terrible fate.

New transports arrive at Treblinka all the time. Sometimes there is a break of a few days. But on average ten thousand people per day are murdered in Treblinka. There was one day in fact when the human transport reached the figure of twenty-four thousand! The Polish Jews, who in the early days had been sent only to Treblinka, already sensed in advance what their fate would be. It was as if they understood that Treblinka meant the end for them, and they let themselves be handled like animals for the slaughter. They are beaten while they are being put into the wagons, while they are being driven from the ramp, when they are getting undressed and when they are going to their death. Only once did any of them put up some resistance, when some Jews in a transport from Warsaw managed to smuggle in some revolvers and hand-grenades. They did not, however, achieve any great success. Just a few wounded SS The punishment for the rebels was very severe. *Oberscharführer* Franz deliberately kept them alive in order to beat and torture them until death released them.

Those who managed to commit suicide were mainly doctors and their families; they secretly brought cyanide capsules with them.

The transports of German and Czech Jews were received with all kinds of tricks and pretences which masked the true situation. On the platform, signposts were put up: 'to Bialystok', 'to Wolkowice'. There were also signs saying: 'Platform 1', 'Exit', 'To the Toilets', etc. The people were not beaten on arrival and even the commands were given in a polite and friendly fashion. One woman who has brought a lot of suitcases with her and does not want to go into the 'Lazarett', is given assurances that her luggage will be sent on after her. She, however, won't hear of it; all her life, she says, she has worked for the things she has brought with her and she isn't going to entrust them to anyone else. *Unterscharführer* Sepp finally loses 'patience' with her and cannot resist using his whip. Then she leaves her suitcases and goes off weeping and wailing to the 'Lazarett' with the man from the red brigade. On the way there she tells him that she is hoping to have a good rest here in order to get her strength back.

The SS take even more care over the transports of Bulgarian Jews. They arrive in nicely appointed passenger coaches. Their trains have coaches with wine, bread, fruit and other foods, The SS make a real banquet of these delicacies, and the Bulgarian Jews go with carefree minds to their death. They are given soap and bath-towels. Whistling to themselves and waving their towels they go merrily to the death-camp.

The Gypsies are not brought in wagons but in small groups on horses and carts. They are not sent to the death camp but are brought to the 'Lazarett' where they are shot and burned.

Only once did Jews leave the camp alive. The Front had demanded women. So one hundred and ten of the most beautiful Jewish girls, accompanied by a Jewish doctor, were sent off.

In the camp, which in any case was so full of terrible cruelty, there were individual SS men who were famous for particular 'specialities'. *Unterscharführer* Sepp, for example, had the habit of choosing small children from the newly arrived transports, and skilfully splitting their little heads with a spade. *Untersturmführer* Kurt Franz – the deputy camp commandant – used to pick out people from the work-brigades every day, and under various pretexts (working too slowly, giving hostile glances and so on) he would order them to strip naked and then beat them to death with his riding whip. But the absolute demon in our camp was *Unterscharführer* Mütter. He has to have several victims every day. So he goes and picks someone at random and searches that person's pockets. If he finds something, he beats the victim with extreme brutality until he falls down dead. If he doesn't find anything, he looks at the person for a moment and says: 'You have an evil look about you – you definitely think too much; therefore you are dangerous and must die.' After this explanation Mütter beats his victim until the latter shows no sign of life. *Unterscharführer* Suchomil, the head of the barracks, had a special interest in the 'gold-Jews'. These were Jews who sorted the gold and valuables. Suchomül constantly used to send home huge amounts of gold and other valuable objects, and the gold-Jews who knew about his plundering were naturally not permitted to remain alive for long.

I only once met an SS man in Treblinka who was unwilling to participate in the inhuman deeds. The first day he was there he found everything so incredible that he took a Jew from a work-squad aside and asked him to tell him the absolute truth. 'Impossible, impossible!' he kept on murmuring, shaking his head slowly as he spoke. From that day on he was never seen again.

Our life was a constant round of fear and pain. We often envied those who had it all behind them. Death is constantly before our eyes. The food is never adequate and all the time we have to work out methods of stealing little bits of food such as bread, potatoes and so on from the newly arrived transports. We steal, even though we know that we run the risk of suffering a terrible death. For smoking, you are shot. One man was killed because he was so cold that he lay down on a heap of clothes and covered himself with a torn fur: for that crime he was torn to pieces by the dog Barry which was specially kept for such things. The man's overseer, who had not reported him, was killed on the spot by *Unterscharführer* Franz with one blow to the face.

Our working hours were from six in the morning till six in the evening. We had one hour at midday. In the evening, when we are dead tired, we have to sing various songs to the accompaniment of an orchestra. First the Treblinka March, then a Polish song which tells of a mother who sells her child in order not to die of hunger.

In the early days Jews used to try to escape from Treblinka almost every day, but then the control became very strict. For trying to run away, people were hung up by the feet on a high pole until they breathed their last in terrible agony. Once two Jews were hung up like this. As they hung there, they kept screaming at us: 'Run, run, all of you! In the end death awaits you too. Don't be fooled because you've got enough to eat to-day – tomorrow you'll share our fate!'

Reporting sick is not really a possibility either; you are only admitted to the hospital with a fever of over 40 degrees, and anyone who is ill for more than six days is shot. In general, death by shooting became a daily occurrence. The Jews who had been shot were replaced by new workers from the latest transports.

Our situation becomes more dreadful every day. Day and night we think about ways of avoiding our terrible fate. Then suddenly, a chance happening came to our aid. In the camp there was a Jewish doctor, Chorazycki, who used to treat the SS too. Once *Unterscharführer* Franz comes to be examined by him. He suddenly notices the doctor's bulging wallet. He asks the doctor about the contents of his wallet and the doctor answers him by grabbing a surgical knife and plunging it into *Unterscharführer* Franz's body. The latter runs round the yard, and the doctor pursues him with the knife. Instantly, Ukrainians appear from every side and throw themselves on the doctor. He manages, however, to swallow poison. Straight away all the doctors in the camp are alerted. They do their best to keep Dr. Chorazycki alive by pumping out his stomach. When that doesn't help, Franz takes revenge by taking his riding whip and beating the dying doctor until he is completely dead.

The next day a search is made of the belongings of the Jewish kapo and a sack of gold is found among his things. He is shot dead on the spot. The tension mounts every day. We Jews realise that it is now a question of life or death. A while ago we buried money and valuables, knowing that without financial means we cannot even think about running away. We have also managed to procure a few weapons. Now we have to organise the attempt. Engineer Galewski, the *Lagerälteste*, the new kapo Kurland, and Moniek, the kapo of the 'yard-Jews' (who worked in the yard of the camp) were the leaders of the uprising. A fourteen-year-old Jewish boy steals into the Ukrainian guardroom at night and removes weapons, bullets and several machine-guns. The arms are divided out, and the day on which the revolt will be launched is decided upon. As far as I remember it was a day at the end of the summer, 1943. On that day the terrible *Oberscharführer* Franz and forty Ukrainians are due to leave the camp to bathe. At six in the morning a shot is to be fired as a signal that the uprising has started. There is enormous tension among the Jews.

At four in the morning we find out that our plan is in danger of collapsing. *Oberscharführer* Kittner has arrested twenty Jews whom he found in possession of gold. Finding Jews with gold or valuables was a sign for the SS that people were planning to escape and therefore had to supply themselves with valuables so that they could live illegally. In such a case the SS would instantly carry out a search of the other Jews in the camp.

It is not long before we see the SS taking these twenty Jews off to the 'Lazarett' in order to kill them. After a short discussion we decide to launch the revolt this very minute. A hand grenade is thrown at *Oberscharführer* Franz. The signal to fight is given and the Ukrainian SS open heavy fire on the Jews. But the Jews remain firm, throw hand grenades and position their machine-guns. Some Ukrainians fall, and the thousand or so Jews in the camp break through the fence. On the other side of the fence a path leads into the wood. Heavy fire from the Ukrainians accompanies the escapees. Some are hit, but the great majority reach the woods in safety. A frenzied activity begins. All the telephone lines are cut; the vehicles are disabled, so that they can't be driven; whatever petrol we can obtain is poured out and lit; the death-camp Treblinka begins to burn. Pillars of fire ascend to the sky. The SS shoot back chaotically into the fire.

A mad pursuit begins. The Jews divide themselves into very small groups. I am with three other people. Now there is just one command: forward, forward! We manage to get twelve kilometres away from Treblinka. By day we do not dare to move, for fear of being seen. We hide in inaccessible places. At night fear drives us on. But we are beginning to be tormented by hunger.

We wonder whether we still have any chance of staying alive, or whether it would not be easier to take our own lives. One of us talks of hanging himself. But in the end the will to live is stronger.

Being the best Polish speaker, I creep into the nearby village to get something to eat. Slowly, hesitatingly, indecisively, with a pounding heart, I come out of the wood and approach a peasant house standing on its own. It is about 30 kilometres from Treblinka. Raising my eyes to heaven and praying, I step onto the threshold of the house. One glance at the woman tells me that she realises what I am. 'You must have escaped from Treblinka,' she exclaims. The state I am in, my clothes, and above all the expression of desperation on my face have all given me away. I am prepared for the worst. But the woman reassures me, saying that I mustn't be afraid, that she will help me as much as she can. She can't hide me, however. The SS are snooping around and searching all the villages in the area. She is not prepared to expose herself and all her family to mortal danger. She gives me bread and milk and tells me to come back at eleven o'clock at night.

At the appointed hour, all three of us are in her house. This time her husband and daughter are also there. We discuss the situation and decide that the best thing would be to go to a particular place and jump onto the roof of the moving train. At that particular point the train moves with a speed of ten kilometres per hour at most. We have no other way out and we agree to try this. They give us a substantial supper and bread and eggs for our journey. As an expression of our gratitude we leave them twenty gold dollars.

Under cover of darkness we set out on our way. We come to the agreed place but we decide not to jump onto the roof of the moving train after all, because we might fall through into the train itself. Instead, we carry on on foot until we reach Rembertow. We have decided to go on from there by train, but we haven't any Polish money. We sell a diamond ring worth twenty thousand zlotys to a peasant, getting only five hundred zlotys for it. Quaking with fear we buy our tickets and manage to get to Warsaw safely.

A great number of the escapees were soon killed or captured. The suffering of the others was to be long and terrible. Only a few of the escapees from Treblinka, round about twenty, got to freedom. I later met some of them personally in the American zone of Germany. They were: Shmuel Rajzman from Wegow; Kudlik from Częstochowa; Schneiderman who now lives in Foehrenwald Camp; Turowski, who now lives in Berchtesgaden.

INDEX